Women Redefining the Experience of Food Insecurity

Women Redefining the Experience of Food Insecurity

Life off the Edge of the Table

Edited by

Janet Page-Reeves

LEXINGTON BOOKS
Lanham • Boulder • New York • London

Published by Lexington Books
An imprint of The Rowman & Littlefield Publishing Group, Inc.
4501 Forbes Boulevard, Suite 200, Lanham, Maryland 20706
www.rowman.com

16 Carlisle Street, London W1D 3BT, United Kingdom

British Library Cataloguing in Publication Information Available

Library of Congress Cataloging-in-Publication Data
Library of Congress Cataloging-in-Publication Data Available
ISBN: 978-0-7391-8526-1 (cloth: alk. paper)
ISBN: 978-0-7391-8527-8 (electronic)

♾™ The paper used in this publication meets the minimum requirements of American National Standard for Information Sciences—Permanence of Paper for Printed Library Materials, ANSI/NISO Z39.48-1992.

Printed in the United States of America

This book is dedicated to my husband, Paul, who over the years has provided much-appreciated but rarely sufficiently acknowledged support; to June Nash who has been my primary anthropological sage and mentor; to Art Kaufman who has become my professional champion as I navigate a new career in public health; and to the many women I have worked with in Bolivia and New Mexico who inspire me through their strength and wisdom to strive to make my work relevant and meaningful in a world too often defined by injustice.

Contents

Figures

Tables

FOREWORD

June Nash
Distinguished Professor Emerita
City University of New York
City College and Graduate Center

Issues of food insecurity attract more attention from the general public in the face of the increasing gap in distribution of income and skyrocketing prices. Visible evidence of the problem commands the attention of health workers, welfare providers, and educational professionals who are alerting the public to growing food insecurity in the richest nation in the world. Janet Page-Reeves has brought together research findings of investigators who attend to the structural and internalized dimensions of the problem at all levels in an interactive network that is trying to address the causes and consequences of the failure to maintain food sufficiency for our population and our neighbors.

This collection of essays provides standards for evaluating levels of need and the barriers to reaching the goal of eliminating hunger. In addition, it brings to life the lived expressions of those who experience food insecurity and those who are developing programs to alleviate its effects. The authors, in their demystification of the ideological ploys that have for so long blamed the problem on those who are most victimized by food scarcity in a bountiful world, provide a storehouse of knowledge, strategies, and programs to address ways of transforming the food chain hierarchy put in place by global corporations. Comparative evidence of how neoliberal globalization has intensified the problem is drawn from the U.S., Central America, and Canada, providing a grid to assess the degree to which food scarcity is a growing problem and why some strategies fail where others alleviate the damage.

Anthropologists who have done fieldwork outside the U.S. in past decades have often been impressed with the way in which people with limited mechanical technologies achieved a balanced diet with the sustainable techniques that they controlled. Their knowledge and selection of seed varieties that they developed over hundreds of years enabled them to grow crops without major irrigation systems and chemical additives. Collective modes of sharing food in times of scarcity obviated the shame associated with poverty that cripples such endeavors in industrialized countries today. Small plot farmers with whom I worked in Chiapas, Mexico, a half a century ago, guarded the precious inheritance of seeds their grandparents endowed them with, and even today they draw upon this wealth to ensure their harvests. They grow up learning not to waste food, picking up the kernels from harvested crops that escaped net bags and leaving just an offering to birds and wild animals to justify their use of the land. Their pride in meeting the challenges of their environment exemplified the satisfaction they gained from preserving a way of life that was their own.

I returned to Chiapas after working twenty five years in mining communities of Bolivia and an industrialized city of the United States to find communities that were no longer able to ensure a living at home for succeeding generations. Migration and the disruption caused by wage work in distant cities were the only alternatives available for young men who could not acquire plots in the communal lands that were part of the revolutionary land reform grants of the past century. An increase in population due to better health care was the positive impetus to this change in some cases, but negative effects of chemical fertilizers and pesticides on the soil and in their food had mitigated the benefits of modernity. Although indigenous people are no more able to return to the past than their neighbors to the North, they are seeking alternative resolutions in organic cultivation, crop rotation, and commercializing artisan production of traditional weaving and pottery.

The problems faced by families in Chiapas are part of the same dynamic that creates food insecurity in our own backyard. Global problems related to food insufficiency require global solutions that can address shortfalls in production and unequal access to resources, and overcome the growing disparities in income that cause increasing numbers to live with hunger and malnutrition. This collection takes major steps in providing the information that will enable a reorientation of public policy. In the first place, researchers are defining the magnitude of the problem of food scarcity, calling the attention of governing agencies to the disparities caused by corporate mismanagement of the available food supplies and socio-economic inequality and injustice that increasingly defeat the attempts of people to make a living, and urging policies to promote locally based food production and consumption practices, and more attention to food justice issues. This is accomplished in four major sections: The first section on structural limits to access to food provides insight into the gender and ethnic disparities that heighten food insecurity for some in the midst of plenty. The second section addresses the health issues that emerge with poor food consumption practices that are highly correlated with economic standing. The third section considers women's agency in provisioning food at the point of preparation and consumption and mobilizing for support. The fourth section looks at means of empowerment that have been and could possibly be further advanced as women gain control over food system processes that affect their lives.

The changing gender division of labor inducing women to enter the work force has had a detrimental impact on food provisioning. The general lack of esteem in the reproductive roles assigned to women is in part responsible for a massive disregard of their contribution to the family and community that occurs when they enter the wage work force. The loss of home cooking is resolved in the turn to processed foods that have reduced nutritional value. The home has become the site of contested claims where women's wage work outside the home is often not compensated by male assistance, with the blame for irresponsible nurturing of children focused on the woman. In contrast with European countries where the state has attended to some aspects of the resulting problem by providing after-school programs for children, mothers find themselves criminalized by a state that fails to provide alternatives for working mothers to attend to children. Living in a small community as I do, I see how in times of unpredictable climate change when schools close for storms, women are caught in the double tension of trying to find caretakers for their children or facing the loss of a job for staying at home to fulfill these tasks.

In addition to addressing substantive issues related to managing food security, the book provides us with methodological strategies for research on a topic that is so mundane that it is often ignored. In tackling the multiplex issues involving women in intolerable situations, Teresa Mares attributes her success in the study of immigrant women in Seattle to "feminist ethnography." Empathizing with the many contradictions her collaborators face in their daily lives, she seeks ways of compensating them for their assistance to her in providing them with food vouchers. Her account recalled the affectation of my male colleagues in mid-twentieth century anthropology when they dominated the field, asserting that they would never stoop to pay collaborators for their assistance. This position reached an extreme absurdity when Oscar Lewis was interviewing people for his book on urban settlers living in extreme poverty in Mexico City back in the 1950s. His returns from the published books and film rights netted thousands of dollars which, according to those familiar with the case, were not given to collaborators. Feminist methodology cultivates an intimate awareness of the needs of informants that takes into account the necessity to compensate them for the time and attention. It also promotes a need for sharing the rewards as well as the work of a collaboration.

Megan Carney's use of what she calls "a feminist epistemological framework" also reveals underlying conditions in her study of transnational migration from the Central America to the US. The efforts of one woman to recreate a sense of home in Santa Barbara, California, focused on Salvadoran dishes on which she spent hours "grooming" the dishes she prepared for her family to acquire the same flavors associated with her country of origin. The kind of empathetic collaboration cultivated in feminist ethnography with the respondents also promotes an informed interpretation in assessing government programs. The SNAP program was one of the more enlightened programmatic approaches for addressing the food insecurity of poor women until the Reforms of 1996. As Maggie Dickinson shows in her analysis, by making what had been an entitlement for people in need of food, SNAP funds were made a block grant that was capped, with the recipient forced to work. This in effect created a class of poorly treated people working at wages that would not even cover child care. The current attack on food stamps continues to promote this trend. Clearly the program organizers do not value child care as work in itself by imposing what Maggie Dickinson calls a "disenfranchising" act for poor women and children, and particularly immigrant women who have no alternatives.

Janet Page-Reeves and her collaborators' work with Hispanic women in New Mexico reveals the extremes to which these programs reduce the status of marginalized groups in this new class warfare. The increase in food insecurity since 2009 is, Page-Reeves contends, a sign of the breakdown in governance. Women are responding by expanding their mobilization networks, utilizing safety-net programs when available, and "stretching buying" tactics to include less processed foods. Like Page-Reeves, David Rose signals the importance of personal agency as central to success in their mobilizing strategies.

The structural basis for these inequities in the economic system has also increased throughout Central America and Mexico with trade agreements introduced by the United States in the 1990s. David Himmelgreen's study of global factors in the Monteverte Zone of Costa Rica in response to the North American Free Trade Agreement reveals the impact of the extension of neoliberal capitalism as it invaded neighboring countries. Undermining agricultural practices that had provided a stable diet, the trade agreement introduced new imbalances along with wealth distinctions. The growing importance of tourism as a source of income drew people away from cultivation and increased prices for imported food which substituted for home grown cultivation.

The many stories of food scarcity in the U.S. and Mexico provide us with the lived experience of the figures recording these facts. What is truly impressive in these stories is that the women themselves retain their agency and ability to resist, which is the central focus for the third section of the book. Economic changes can have disrupting changes on deeply rooted gender roles. For example, the immigrant experience disrupts the culturally ascribed gender roles expressed in food preparation, as shown by Sharon Stowers in her study of Salvadoran immigrants in Somerville, Massachusetts. Health problems of obesity, coronary and kidney diseases and tooth decay that are associated with poverty proliferate with the changed diet to processed foods and short cuts in preparation.

Similarly, when Newfoundland was incorporated in the Canadian government, fishing villages were incorporated in ways that had a paradoxical impact on women's work. Women had combined work as subsistence food producers as well as family caretakers in the previous era without much value associated with their contribution to the family food by the community. They perceived their entry into modernity with the incorporation of the economy in the Canadian nation as one in which they rejected the drudgery of food production, becoming consumers of the new commercial imports. The government failed to recognize the importance of locally grown nutritious fresh vegetables and did not subsidize this source of food since women were not as vocal advocates for their activities. As a result, the whole community suffered the loss of what is only now becoming recognized as a superior approach to food sustainability.

Given the set of impossible hurdles they face, women are providing labor and leadership in food system organizing and mobilization to make structural change. Christine Porter and LaDonna Redmond are part of the National Community Food Movement that is attempting to counter the use of pesticides, the exploitation of agricultural laborers, and consumption-related health problems. They see the root cause of these problems to be structurally connected with the undervaluation of women's roles in the food movement. As the authors show, at the national level there are few women leaders, but in the local ranks women are often the initial organizers whose concerns stem from family health problems related to food consumption. They argue that "gendering" the activities and priorities of the movement will create a greater likelihood of success.

Most of the collaborators in this anthology express an awareness of the need for fundamental change in a food system dominated by global corporations that trade on peoples' anxieties. This requires intervention that is explicitly "*off the edge of the table*" in a U.S.-dominated hemisphere. As the chapter by Patricia Williams demonstrates, when women became participants in the research, they gained an understanding of underlying critical dynamics. Unfortunately, it has not yet been possible to extend this critical understanding to programs to alleviate the problems in the food supply. Frustrating as is the task to reorder priorities and put food security at the top of the agenda, the collaborators in the anthology light the path to a new era.

ACKNOWLEGMENTS

This book would not have been possible without the essential support that I have received from others. Amy King, my editor at Lexington Press, sought me out and planted the idea of a book in my head. Along the way, she offered encouragement and technical assistance. Despite an already over-full schedule, Kathy Sullivan reviewed the manuscript and provided helpful editorial comments and suggestions that improved the content and readability of the chapters. Art Kaufman's encouragement has allowed me to reclaim my "anthropological" self, which was a necessary precursor to the conceptualization of this volume. He, Rob Williams, Robert Rhyne and Martha McGrew are my professional cheerleaders in the Department of Family and Community Medicine at the University of New Mexico Health Sciences Center where I am forging a new career in public health research. Without the supportive institutional environment that they consciously and actively create, this book would not exist.

The women and other community members I work with on projects related to food insecurity, diabetes, and youth gardening provided me with the inspiration for thinking about the issues discussed in these chapters. The sweaterknitters I worked with in Bolivia continue to occupy my thoughts and it is fascinating how this collection of works on women's agency reflects insights I developed through their tutelage and by contemplating their experience. And not inconsequentially, the chapter contributors agreed to jump (rather blindly I fear) on board with this book project. They put-up with my learning curve in terms of the technical aspects of book formatting and bureaucratic requirements, and they have produced what I believe to be a really amazing collection. I am hopeful that readers will find this book to be a valuable contribution to an ongoing but now intensifying dialogue about food insecurity, its consequences, and the possibility of creating an alternative, more just reality where people do not have the absurd need to worry about whether or not they will have enough to eat.

PART I

Introduction

INTRODUCTION

Conceptualizing Food Insecurity and Women's Agency: A Synthetic Introduction

Janet Page-Reeves

Food is a basic need, as are shelter, transportation to and from work, care for children and elderly family members, and medical expenses such as prescription drugs and doctor's visits. How much these cost are usually not negotiable. But food is one that can be negotiated on a daily basis, with oneself and/or one's family members—by purchasing cheaper, less nutritious items, by cutting back on portion sizes, or by skipping meals altogether. This is how families in poverty cope: some member, generally the adults, endure spells of hunger. Parents live with the constant stress of food running out, of exhausting their wages and whatever assistance they can secure before the end of the month.
Bread for the World Institute (2014 Hunger Report)

Once we pierce the ideological veils of neoliberalism, then, we can grasp the fact that contemporary economic and social policy owes much more to historical forces that are deeply invested in the enhancement of corporate power, the renewal of patriarchal authority, and the xenophobic and racist oppression of ethnic and racial minorities, rather than to an inexorable unfolding of laissez-faire economic laws.
Anna Marie Smith (2008)

Problematizing Food Insecurity

Food insecurity, the term that has replaced the concept of *hunger* in policy parlance, is defined as "limited or uncertain availability of nutritionally adequate and safe foods or limited or uncertain ability to acquire acceptable foods in socially acceptable ways" (Andersen 1990). Shockingly, nearly 50 million people in over 17 million U.S. households are food insecure (Coleman-Jensen, Nord and Singh 2013). After decades of public myopia regarding the growing number of people who routinely struggle to have enough food to feed their families, the fact that one in five children in the U.S. do not know where they will get their next meal (Gundersen, et al. 2013) has now become part of mainstream media messaging. For over a decade, Kraft Foods has sponsored a nationally televised post-season college *Hunger Bowl* football event; cable TV channels including the Cooking Channel have been involved in a number of high visibility strategies to raise public awareness about hunger; and the next time you "Dine Out," the restaurant you eat at may contribute to the No Kid Hungry campaign sponsored by the national nonprofit Share Our Strength.

Knowing that someone is doing something for the hungry makes us feel good as we enjoy the football game or our favorite cooking show, or as we eat a tasty restaurant dinner, yet how often do we ask *why* there are so many hungry people or how such an enormous problem can seem so remote and invisible? How often do we try to imagine what everyday existence is like for a person in our own community who does not have enough to eat? If 50 million people in America are food insecure, what does it really take *not* to be hungry these days? Recognition that a problem exists is a huge leap forward, but in order to understand the dynamics that sustain and foster inequality in the ability of people to eat, we need to move beyond a superficial portrait of food insecurity based on our own feelings of pity or on the perceived shortcomings of the poor that are naturalized in mainstream discourse and opinion.

This book contributes to literature that has begun to illuminate more nuanced ways of thinking about the food system and about the dinner table. In particular, the authors think about the people who are *not* at the table because they do not have food and the extent to which a meal that ends-up on the dinner table is profoundly influenced by processes, activities and power relationships that perhaps appear only indirectly related to the food itself. These are what I call the people and things that are *off the edge of the table*. Conceptualizing the nature of these dynamics involves thinking differently about food insecurity by investigating local actions, meanings, and relationships related to food and how they find expression in individual lives—and connecting this analysis to broader structures of inequality. The emphasis in these chapters is on the experience of food insecurity as it relates to women's quotidian reality.

Food system issues are currently *en vogue* with great public, academic and media interest in community gardens, local food, corner markets, farmers markets, CSA's (community supported agriculture initiatives), slow food, obesity, diabetes, and GM (genetically modified) food products. Yet we still lack a clear vision of the social, cultural and economic dynamics underpinning the operation and meaning of these components and dimensions of the food system. In this context, insufficient attention has been paid in the literature to understanding and characterizing women's experience with food insecurity, the social and cultural meanings that they attach to food and food practices when food supplies are insufficient and food budgets are stretched, or the supportive social relationships that women rely upon in the context of scarcity and hunger. Food insecurity has been a sub-theme in ethnographic studies (Counihan 2009), a subsidiary focus in research on safety net programs (Himmelgreen, et al. 2000), an issue for understanding global processes of economic development (Pottier 1999), a lens for viewing the institutionalization of emergency food initiatives (Poppendieck 2013), and a platform for analyzing neoliberal dynamics underpinning the relationship between obesity and poverty (Albritton 2013). These important studies highlight the need to develop a more detailed portrait of how food insecurity intersects with everyday experience, and how cultural frameworks and social relationships influence food provisioning and food access, a process that affects entire households.

Connecting these dynamics with the voluminous literature on the feminization of poverty in the context of neoliberal restructuring is key to appreciating gendered, experiential, and structural dimensions of food insecurity, and how they are transformed by and connected with family and community social dynamics that manifest themselves in the shopping cart and the kitchen (e.g., Pearce 1978; Hawkesworth 2001; Smith, Appio and Cho 2011). For example, Sandra Morgen's seminal special edited collection, *The Impoverishment of Women* (2002), speaks to the extent to which current global economic and political dynamics have a disproportionate negative impact on the lives of women and children. She emphasizes how the approach we use to analyze complex issues like poverty or food insecurity influences the way we conceptualize what is happening on the ground, in people's lives. She admonishes us regarding the importance of keeping sight of the fact that "impoverishment is produced by capitalist economic and political policies and practices" (p. 4). Contributors to her collection help to uncover the dynamics of the strategic impoverishment of women occurring under the guise of an ideology of the free market (Kingsolver 2002), the gendered character of poverty in the enactment of welfare policy (Henrici 2002), and the essentiality of grounding our analyses in material specificity and the materiality of social life (Weismantel 2002). The chapters presented here embrace this approach in their exploration of the dimensionality of food insecurity in women's lives while connecting their struggles to broader political, economic and social contexts and structures, challenging what *New York Times* columnist, Paul Krugman (2013), ironically designated as the current drive to protect our "[freedom] to be hungry."

Contributors to this book explore both the structural constraints that limit what and how much people eat, and the myriad ways that women creatively and strategically restructure their own fields of action in relation to food, demonstrating that the nature of food insecurity is multi-dimensional. In the U.S., relationships structured by policy define who is "food insecure" but also the resources available to them. Economic recession creates local economic and political dynamics that impoverish households and whole communities. *Food deserts* and *"food gaps"* (Winne 2008) create challenges for people to have access to sufficient and healthy food, with significant disparities experienced by culturally diverse and low-wealth communities. Immigrants, in particular, face greater barriers to ensuring that their families have enough to eat. Internationally, the decline of agriculturally based economies and changing diets are associated with chronic disease and an increase in food insecurity. The significant role of women in the provisioning and preparation of food also creates unique gender dynamics that are played out in relationships and activities within food insecure households. In all cases, however, the chapters presented here demonstrate how women push boundaries to make it possible to have food in the cupboard and on the table to be able to feed their families. Exploring these themes, this book offers a lens for thinking about the food system that incorporates women as agentive actors and links women's everyday food-related activities with ideas about *food justice* (Alkon and Agyeman 2011; Gottlieb and Joshi 2010), *food sovereignty* (Mares and Alkon 2011; Alkon and Mares 2012; Holt-Giménez 2011), and *food citizenship* (Phillips 2012).

The Concept of Food Insecurity

Most people would probably say that *hunger* is an unproblematic concept, easy to define and understand—epitomized by the image of a starving child with a swollen belly in some distant, famine-ravaged part of the world. Yet there has been a shift away from the public use of the term *hunger* since the 1970s. Various gradations of *food insecurity* (e.g., marginal food security, low food security, and very low food security) are now employed to identify people or households in need, to target the reach of public policy, and to define access to benefit programs. Survey questions (e.g., In the last 12 months, were you ever hungry, but didn't eat because you couldn't afford enough food? or, In the last 12 months, did any of your children ever not eat for a whole day because there wasn't enough money for food?) are used to determine where individuals and households fall in the food security continuum. However, identification of food insecurity is based on responses to questions that require interpretation rather than on a specific quantifiable measure that can be applied in the same way to all households. Moreover, survey questions fail to indicate why people in a household are hungry (e.g., because they were out gambling or spent all their money on cigarettes and beer, because they don't know how to shop economically or cook healthy meals and spent their limited resources on junk food and fast food take-out, or because they live below the poverty level even though they work 40 hours a week in a context where the price of food, rent, transportation and healthcare has risen dramatically) or why they are not (e.g., because of the creative and time/labor-intensive strategies they use to procure and prepare food, because they routinely visit the local food pantry and get "free" food, because they use federal food benefits paid for by taxpayers, because their family helps them out using their own scarce resources, or because they sell their bodies for sex in order to have the money to buy food). None of these things are captured in survey questions or are reflected in official statistics. Official definitions of what constitutes food insecurity and the criteria used to include or exclude people do not necessarily coincide with common perceptions or understanding. Food insecurity is a complex, multi-factoral, and multi-dimensional issue. Conceptually it is flexible; measurements are slippery. Yet policy makers and the public like for things to be simple—simple problems that can be addressed with simple policies that produce simple solutions. Food insecurity is both complex and seemingly intransigent; it resists the desired simplistic approaches. As such, our inability to clearly define and measure food insecurity has implications for the way we understand the issues involved, the nature of the problem, and the policies necessary to bring about change.

The idea of *food security/food insecurity* emerged in the 1970s following a number of high profile international food crises and regional famines that should have been predicted or could have been prevented. The world was horrified by images of widespread starvation and death. The focus of international attention became the need to understand and address food supply problems. *Hunger*, an individually experienced physical sensation, was seen as deficient for conceptualizing these larger forces. A World Food Conference in 1974 sponsored by the U.N. Food and Agriculture Organization (FAO) led to the creation of a number of global and regional institutional arrangements to provide information, establish systems, or develop services to help prevent famine and severe crises from recurring. *Food security* was defined at the conference as "availability at all times of adequate world food supplies of basic foodstuffs to sustain a steady expansion of food consumption and to offset fluctuations in production and prices" (FAO 2003). *Food insecurity* was its antithesis. The dialogue that materialized from this forum contributed to a mounting critique of Green Revolution technologies as having failed to be a panacea for global nutritional needs, and helped to highlight the extent to which famine does not occur in a vacuum. It did not, however, provide a coherent metric to apply to industrialized nations.

Since the 1970s, the concept of food insecurity has continued to evolve, expanding to include growing concern over the role of nutritional value and cultural preference in the food insecurity equation. Increasingly it has been recognized that food insecurity is not only about having *nothing* to eat, but also about the quality and appropriateness of the food that is available. In 1994, a U.N. Development Report attempted to place this broader idea of food insecurity under an umbrella of human rights (UNDP 1994). But the promulgation of a more complex definition incorporating broadened social determinants that play a role in structuring individual access to food ultimately acted to defy this logic. Inclusion of food preferences and social access issues was meant to acknowledge the multi-dimensional nature of people's relationship to food from a social justice perspective. Ultimately, however, the addition of consumption-based criteria diluted the effectiveness of food insecurity as an analytical concept. These issues, while relevant to understanding food insecurity as a phenomenon, led to a weakening of the analytical connection between structural factors that limit access to food and the incidence of hunger—especially in public discourse. The broadened definition led in some cases to a focus on lack of individual knowledge or skills rather than on systems, structures, and policies that chronically deprive people of food. As it came to encompass relative nutritional content and personal preference—what appear to be *lifestyle choices*—as well as the actual physical lack of food, food insecurity as a concept began to loose the evocative emotional power it had following public images of famine that abounded in the 1970s. Although its history reflects an attempt on the part of the world community to develop terminology that would help to illuminate and reveal the systemic nature of global hunger, food insecurity as a concept was emerging in the context of an expanding hegemonic neoliberal paradigm. Emphasis on individuals as independent arbiters of their own reality with personal responsibility as the primary factor defining individual health and well-being was antithetical to a rights-based conceptualization of food insecurity.

This trajectory is apparent in the evolution of the concept of food insecurity in the U.S. (FRAC 2013). Following the global shift away from the use of hunger terminology, the U.S. Department of Agriculture (USDA) began using gradations of *food insecurity*—with *food insecurity with hunger* only used to characterize the worst-case designation. However, in 2006, the USDA sought guidance from an expert panel from the Committee on National Statistics of the National Academies that advised that the word *hunger* can suggest qualitatively different things (as had been recognized in the original U.N. concept of food insecurity). Hunger is a physical sensation that is experienced individually, but that may or may not be related to constrained resources. Following recommendations by the panel, USDA abandoned the word *hunger* entirely and adopted the category of *very low food security* to designate households experiencing significant hunger in a context of lack of resources. Although the panel recommended that USDA adopt consideration of both physiological and psycho-social dimensions of food insecurity, the current USDA annual household food security survey does not gather information required to assess these dimensions, nor have measures been developed to determine the social or economic context in which people and households experience food insecurity.

These semantic and bureaucratic changes enacted as part of USDA policy did not occur merely in response to concern about definitional integrity or commitment to incorporating "expert" input; they must be understood in the context of the political landscape in which they were enacted. The discursive shift from *hunger* to *food security/insecurity* has been criticized as part of a broader ideological narrative designed to move away from an entitlement-based conceptualization of government responsibility—ironic, of course, given that the history of the term reflects the world community's concern for human rights. The shift in focus from *hunger* to *food insecurity with hunger* and then to *very low food security* dovetailed with and helped to demonstrate the neoliberal logic that has defined U.S. public policy since the 1980s. Adoption of food insecurity language in U.S. policy coincided with a decided political shift toward a market-centered paradigm emphasizing individual responsibility as a cornerstone political philosophy and delegitimizing the role of public institutions and policy in protecting or promoting citizen welfare. This change was accomplished while avoiding any discussion of the moral and ethical dimensions of social justice issues that were the logical extension of the historic construction of hunger and integral to the initial formulation of the concept of food insecurity. Part of the critique of the official discursive shift centers on the obfuscatory quality that the language of food insecurity tends to have on public understanding of the issue of hunger—a *collateral damage* lexicon of poverty analysis. It is easy to feel horror if you are told that one in four children in your state is *hungry*. But that gut reaction is less likely if you are told that those children have *very low food security*. Very low food security may not sound very good, but it lacks the visceral impact associated with the word *hunger*. While we can easily envision the face of hunger as a starving child with a distended belly, most people cannot picture what *very low food security* looks like or imagine what if feels like. Frankly, it is difficult to even know what it means, especially when we now understand how the increasing availability of cheap, highly processed, low-nutrient food creates a counter-intuitive, synergistic relationship between food insecurity and obesity (Troy, Olson and Miller 2011; Albritton 2013).

Although the USDA uses "access by all people at all times to enough food for an active, healthy life" [1] as a launching point for defining access to federal food assistance programs, in the shift away from addressing systems issues, concern over individual nutrition and caloric intake has become the focus of much policy. This tendency is highlighted by USDA findings that very low food security is generally episodic in nature—representing occasional disrupted eating patterns that are *not considered chronic* (Coleman-Jensen, Nord, and Singh 2013). This conclusion is only possible using a very narrow view of people's relationship with food. The concept of food security is concerned with making sure that people have access to food *without emergency measures*. But given the chronic, extensive, and growing use of public food programs and emergency food services by the poor, the fact that some people may have access to food only via welfare or charity rather than being able to support themselves and their families using any reasonable standard related to the concept of a healthy life implies deficiencies of a systemic nature that require deeper analysis. This contradiction also raises questions about the meaningfulness of the concept of food security/food insecurity, as currently defined and used, as a measure of the problem. Are we merely concerned with feeding the hungry? Or are we interested in ending hunger? And can we realistically imagine that we can end hunger without dealing with poverty and inequality? Food security is only meaningful when it is understood from a food system framework that includes the sorts of social determinants that create and structure the environment in which an individual might have the ability to make reasonable, healthy choices. Food access is much more complicated than commonly acknowledged.

This complexity is manifest in the policy environment as contradiction. At the same time that there is an ideological failure to really define the systemic nature of individual food insecurity, some USDA analysis *does* reveal structural factors at play:

> States differ in the extent to which their residents are food secure—meaning that they have consistent access to enough food for active, healthy living. The prevalence of food security in a State depends not only on the characteristics of households in the State, such as their income, employment, and household structure, but also on State-level characteristics, such as average wages, cost of housing, levels of participation in food assistance programs, and tax policies. Taken together, an identified set of household-level and State-level factors account for most of the State-to-State differences in food security. Some State-level factors point to specific policies that are likely to improve food security, such as policies that increase the supply of affordable housing, promote the use of Federal food assistance programs, or reduce the total tax burden on low-income households (Bartfeld, et al. 2006).

Similarly, the USDA Community Food Projects Competitive Grant program is explicitly designed to "fund proactive approaches to making communities more self-reliant at maintaining their food systems" [2] and USDA economic and job security programs "help low-income people attain living wage jobs and self-sufficiency" [3]. So, while we use the concept of food insecurity because that has become the normative way of thinking about hunger, until systems dynamics that produce and sustain inequality in the ability of people to eat are acknowledged at the level of public understanding and in the formulation of broader policy measures, the policy environment will continue to be contradictory.

Alternatives to the Concept of Food Insecurity

In the literature on food systems, a number of alternative discourses have been developed. In the U.K., for example, the concept of *food poverty* is used more commonly than food insecurity, and is applied to anti-hunger analyses both at home and abroad. The food poverty concept derives from formulations that calculate food consumption expenditures in relation to officially determined poverty criteria (e.g., the poverty line) in a way that can be measured and traced to financial circumstances of specific households. However, the normative usage of the term in the media and by anti-hunger advocates is similar to the way we use food insecurity. Interestingly, the Food Bank for New York City has adopted food poverty language to describe the focus of their work and the cause of hunger. Specifically, they highlight the fact that food poverty caused by financial stress makes it difficult or impossible for both low- and middle-income people to buy food for themselves or their families, and that lack of access to affordable, nutritious food is environmentally structured into low-income neighborhoods as *food deserts* in a way that nurtures the development of food-related health disparities. Discursively, *food poverty* has more evocative power to link lack of access to food with structural- and social justice-oriented perspectives in a way that the rather soggy milquetoast *food insecurity* rhetoric does not—a point made by Dickinson in this volume (chapter 2).

In a comprehensive review of discourses employed by contemporary social movements centered on food, Mares and Alkon (2011, 80) use both "celebratory and critical scholarship" to "map" other alternative ways of conceptualizing the relationship between people and food. They analyze how the rhetoric of *community food security* embraces the *local food* focus of much current popular food system advocacy reflecting the original emphasis on food supply chains in the development of the 1970s FAO food security concept. But, rather than focusing on individual households as a primary locus of control as is common in local food-oriented strategies, community food security expands the lens to include a community-level perspective. This expansiveness allows for a synthesis of concerns about local food production, sustainability, and hunger that does not tend to be emphasized in local food movement discourse. However, critiques have suggested that both the local food and community food security movements are ultimately constrained by their lack of attention to class and racial differences, and their reliance on market-based individual consumption to reorient rather than transform the "neoliberal rationalities" (72) of the system.

The more recently developed *food justice* framework (Alkon and Agyeman 2012; Gottlieb and Joshi 2010) builds on these approaches but emphasizes social, racial and ethnic equity as key to transformative change in the dynamics of the food system. The concept of food justice engages with rights-based discourse to locate food as a human right and connects with the paradigm of environmental justice by implicating the food environment and food access more centrally as core determinants of health. In addition, "cultivating food justice"

(Alkon and Agyeman 2011) through a movement is seen to be an empowering process, engaging individuals and groups in challenging structural inequality. However, despite food justice's relatively radical critique of existing food system dynamics and politics, Mares and Alkon acknowledge that it too relies primarily on market-driven strategies of individual consumers in individual households and often fails to appreciate the insidious ways that the work of the food movement articulates with the interests of the neoliberal project.

In contrast, Mares and Alkon argue that *food sovereignty* discourse (Mares and Alkon 2011; Alkon and Mares 2012) which emerged from the struggles of agricultural producers in the global south, by focusing on neoliberal trade and agricultural policy, offers a way to frame food-related rights as being more than just about the food itself, but about the structural relationships that define access to land, resources and power. The framework of food sovereignty

> transcends the boundaries of the local to demand consideration of the impacts of industrialization and centralization on local food economies everywhere, forging an interdependent connection between local food systems in the United States to local food systems around the world....[allowing] local activists to locate the sources of the injustices they rally against in the intersection of the corporate food regime, the transnational neoliberal policies that ensure its dominance, and the racist U.S. policies that ensure that the harshest domestic effects are felt by communities of color (80).

At the same time, while food sovereignty may be conceptually more expansive and have the capacity to provide a mobilizing discourse and vision for food movement and academic stakeholders, it is not clear that expansiveness is the most appropriate narrative for theoretically capturing the everyday experience of individual people who, while they are not agricultural producers or members of a movement, struggle to put food on the table.

Illusions of Hunger

A revealing way to understand the structural dynamics of food insecurity is to explore current debates about public food assistance. Although negative discourse (e.g., *welfare mother, welfare queen*) commonly permeates mainstream discussions of poverty and federal safety net support systems, there has been a recent escalation of rhetoric vilifying the poor and Food Stamp recipients in particular. In 2008, to move away from stigma associated with receiving Food Stamp benefits, the Food Stamp program was renamed SNAP—the *Supplemental Nutrition Assistance Program*. However, almost everyone continues to use the name *Food Stamps*, especially in the media and among politicians. People who work with Food Stamp-eligible populations would argue that part of the stigma is that the vast majority of hard working people who find it necessary to rely on Food Stamps feel their own need as personal failure rather than, or often as much as, a reflection of structural dynamics over which they have no control (e.g., Page-Reeves, et al. 2014). However, in August 2013, Fox News ran a piece on *The Great Food Stamp Binge* (Berrier 2013), lamenting a perceived loss of stigma associated with Food Stamp usage and bemoaning that Food Stamp recipients (of which the commentators felt there should be few) do not feel *sufficiently shameful* about the fact that they receive benefits. Food Stamp recipients were portrayed as lazy freeloaders who bilk the system and exploit taxpayer beneficence (Wyatt 2013).

While this framing reflects a well-discussed tenet of American political discourse and is nothing new *per se*, in the context of the current economic recession and the ideologically charged political landscape, the tenor of the lament has become more shrill. Take, for example, Fox News' portrayal of *"Lobster Boy"* in that same segment—the slacker surfer dude who nonchalantly tells us that he has made a *lifestyle choice* to use Food Stamps—a program that is *awesome man* because it allows him to *like* live on a diet of sushi and lobster without having to work (Delaney 2013; Halloran 2013). His unmitigated *slackerism* was presented as a slap in the face to hard working Americans and offered as proof of the dangers of a *nanny state*. Although Lobster Boy is suspiciously similar in his caricatured surfer demeanor to the unscrupulous pretend pimp in the fraudulent videos that resulted in the 2010 defunding of the nonprofit voting rights organization, ACORN, he may really be a surfer—and there would appear to be no one suggesting he is not a slacker. However, you cannot actually get much sushi or lobster for the $2.19 per meal that would be the maximum Food Stamp benefit he would be eligible for in California. So, we would be talking about eating sushi or lobster maybe a few times a week *total,* with no other meals or food in between--meaning that he must get awfully hungry between those tasty California rolls.

The underlying narrative at work here is that people are hungry by fault of their own *choices*, thus absolving systemic or structural dynamics that make it impossible for people to get ahead. In fact, hunger is really nothing more than an *illusion* created by lazy slackers who do not want to work hard like the rest of us. Hungry people *choose* their condition by virtue of their own profligacy. In keeping with the neoliberal ideological principle of individual responsibility, this narrative has conveniently been linked to concern over rising levels of obesity. A pitch-perfect example of the way that this connection is being construed is in an op-ed on the *Forbes* blog (Gregory 2013). Hoover Institute Research Fellow and self-described free-marketer, Paul Roderick Gregory, opines that Food Stamp benefits should be cut because the *"hunger crisis"* is *"hysteria"* that has been *"fabricated"* by what he, in an ironic twist from a *Forbes* editorial contributor, calls the *"powerful 'hunger lobby.'"* Leveraging the slippery quality of food insecurity discourse discussed earlier, Gregory uses USDA food insecurity data reflecting the fact that people *"worry about affording food"* or *"skip meals"* to disdainfully argue that food insecurity is nothing like hunger; the U.S. does not have the type of starving people found in the third world and in fact, the real problem is *obesity*. Never mind the recent study that found that hospitalizations for hypoglycemia (low blood sugar often a proxy for not having eaten) among the poor significantly rise at the end of the month when food budgets run out and cupboards are empty (Seligman, et al. 2014). Instead, he selectively quotes facts and uses out of context analyses from the anti-hunger advocacy organizations Feeding America and the Food Research Action Center regarding the synergistic relationship between food insecurity and obesity to demonstrate that poor people are actually fat, not hungry—victims of nothing more than their own inability to control themselves from overeating a diet based on junk food. In fact, he takes this one step further to argue that Food Stamps and federally funded school meals programs have *caused* the obesity epidemic. The poor are not *hungry*—they have *too much food* because we shamefully give it to them for free, enabling and encouraging their laziness and personal irresponsibility.

The sound byte-ization of this narrative through outrageous quotes from Lobster Boy and blame-the-poor analyses by neoliberal and Tea Party talking heads on political talk shows and in op-ed columns has dovetailed with the realities of the current economic and political context. Outrage by congressional Republicans over the bilking of American taxpayers by freeloading Food Stamp recipients and personally irresponsible low-income fat people—people who do not really *need* assistance—rallied the House to vote to cut Food Stamps by $40 billion. Millions of people are in jeopardy of loosing their benefits—millions of people who depend on food assistance since they do not make enough money to afford to eat. Following on the same logic, in New Mexico where I live and where research was conducted for two of the chapters in this collection, the New Mexico Human Services Department Secretary, Sidonie Squier, who is the head of the state's Food Stamp program and a variety of other food assistance programs, wrote an email to her Department upper management staff in September 2013 (coincidentally, just after the whole Lobster Boy media hype) regarding a draft of a report for the Governor's Hunger Task Force (of which, ironically, Secretary Squier is a member). Her email stated that she feared that the Task Force might be inclined to *"just expand every government food program in existence"* (Monteleone 2013). She suggested that *"since there has never been and is not now any significant evidence of hunger in New Mexico, I would offer that the focus of the report should be on getting proper nutrition to children"* (Monteleone 2013).

In other words, never mind those hospitalization statistics, it is really just about getting the poor to cook and shop properly so they will not be so fat—that is, when they are not busy feasting on sushi and lobster or bilking the government. Given the fact that New Mexico is the state ranked worst in child food insecurity (Feeding America 2013) and eighth for food insecurity in general (Coleman-Jensen, et al. 2011), following release of her email there was public outrage. There were calls for the Secretary's resignation, arguing that her lack of understanding of hunger in New Mexico makes her unqualified to run the state's food safety net programs. Ultimately, however, the Governor provided cover, back-pedaling that "*of course we know there is hunger in New Mexico*" (Monteleone 2013), and the Secretary offered a partial retraction, saying that she regretted that her email had been "*poorly worded*" (Simonich 2013).

The way this played out and was framed in New Mexico must be understood in the context of the larger *there is no hunger in America* narrative. Goode and Maskovsky (2002) describe how under neoliberalism, a "*regime of disappearance*" marginalizes or erases the poor from popular and political consciousness by naturalizing poverty, not as something produced by the dynamics of current economic and political systems, but as something that has always existed that we really just cannot do much about. This is accomplished by ideologically driven constructions of poverty as a "natural" state separate from rather than generated by structural relations that actively promote the concentration of wealth, social benefits, privilege and power. But the current narrative goes further. Insinuated into public discourse in New Mexico, Lobster Boy, the caricature of a chubby kid receiving a meal through the Free and Reduced School Lunch program, and their protractors, provided legitimacy for attempting to eliminate the reality and experience of thousands of New Mexicans who struggle to put food on the table every day or who go to bed hungry. Hungry people are being *erased* because it is being denied that they actually *exist*. They aren't *real*. Or if they do happen to exist, their hunger and food insecurity are what is not real—it is merely a "*lifestyle choice.*"

Public outrage over hungry citizens has been displaced by outrage over parasitic and personally irresponsible citizens. In the current political climate, the former problem seems intractable, while the latter has a simple solution—just cut them off. Seen from this perspective, $40 billion in congressional cuts to the SNAP program appear rational. However, anecdotal evidence of slackerism from Lobster Boy and data regarding growing rates of obesity—*including among the poor*—that may seem intuitive from inside the neoliberal bubble are belied by facts. In New Mexico, for example, the New Mexico Association of Food Banks reports that 40,000 New Mexicans stand in line for food at food pantries and soup kitchens each week at more than 600 emergency food distribution sites across the state (NMAFB 2010), and Roadrunner Foodbank, the state's largest emergency food provider, delivers more than 26 million pounds of food a year (Roadrunner Food Bank n.d.). On a more personal level, a little boy wrote a note to a Food Stamp outreach worker in the context of a Food Stamp outreach project I was working on that had a picture of a happy-faced refrigerator filled with food, thanking her for helping his family because before they had Food Stamps, "*the refrigerator was so empty that even the flies were hungry.*"

In their argument that the hungry are merely moochers or gluttons, delegitimizing the individual people who are victims of a system that creates food insecurity, the voices of power effectively ignore any need to confront these very concrete facts. But that, of course, is the point of counterfactual narratives that focus on the moral failings of the people who are marginalized—they are constructed to avoid a critique of the system and those in power. As a refutation of hegemonic discourse that locates blame for food insecurity, obesity and a variety of social ills on individuals and their choices, the work presented in this book is based not just on simplistic anecdotes, but on multiple person-years of research in different contexts. We find that it is the *strategically constructive personal choices* of women who have few resources and lack political influence that mitigate the worst effects of food insecurity and make it possible for families to eat even as the options they have available to them dwindle because of the *irresponsible, ideologically driven, and self-gratifying professional and political choices* being made by those in power.

The Kitchen as a Domain of Women's Identity Creation and Agency

While analysis of the public conceptualization of food policy is instructive, a lens for thinking more intimately about women's agency in relation to the issue of food insecurity is through the extensive social science literature linking women, food, and cooking. Despite the fact that food and cooking as a domain may seem mundane or even insignificant, Sutton (2001, 3) suggests these very qualities mask an underlying significance because the "obviousness and taken-for-grantedness of food can be deceptive." Food is a keystone cultural symbol (McCracken 1982) and cooking has often been shown to be associated with women's core gender identity in different contexts (Charles and Kerr 1988; Moisio, et al. 2004). Food and cooking are quintessentially associated with "women's work," a gendered domain responsible for reproducing not only the family (DeVault 1991; Moisio, et al. 2004), but even national identity (Bower 1997; Pilcher 1997). Within this paradigm, women are inextricably linked with "*kitchenspace*" (Christie 2008) that is constitutive of self (Avakian 1997; Counihan 2009), family (Charles and Kerr 1988; DeVault 1991; Moisio, et al. 2004), or ethnicity (Beoku-Betts 1995; D'Sylva and Beagan 2011; Rabikowska 2010). This identity production is often achieved through specific food preparation practices (Moisio, et al. 2004) or in sync with poetic rhythms of daily life (Krögel 2011). Within this identity, nurturing construed as peculiarly female (DeVault 1991) is enacted through the cooking pot (Beagan, et al. 2008; James and Curtis 2010; McIntosh, et al. 2010) or in transactions of giving and receiving food outside of the household that generate significant social meanings and relationships (Counihan 2009; Sutton 2001). Even recipes can be understood as embedded in webs of meaning not confined to the kitchen (Bower 1997; Cotter 1997; Pilcher 1997). Although the kitchen can be an arena of female subordination (Beagan, et al. 2008), women's control over food has also been shown to be a source of power (Counihan 1999; Counihan and Kaplan 1998). Inequality in the gendered landscape can be reconfigured by women's ability to determine the disposition of mealtime resources within the family (Weismantel 1998), to withhold men's lunchboxes (Nash 1979), and to mobilize capital through the sale of food (Babb 1998; Gill 1993; Gordon 2011; Sukovic, et al. 2011). Avakian (2005, 2) suggests that "women reproduce, resist and rebel against gender constructions as they are practiced and contested" in the kitchen. In Counihan's (2009) "food-centered life histories," women's narratives demonstrate how they resist being boxed-in to gendered fields of action. Food becomes a vehicle for women's self-expression and agency.

At the same time, the intensely intimate nature of food can also become an impetus for women's politicization, mobilization and empowerment in the context of scarcity, inequality and neoliberal economics (Gvion 2006; Lemke, et al. 2003; Preibisch, et al. 2002; Randall 1997; Tarasuk 2001; Witt 2001). With the encroachment of structural forces "upon the 'female' sphere of nurturing, where women act as keepers of culture, primary agents of children's socialization and defenders of the private reality of family life" (Julier 2005, 168), food procurement and cooking become a domain for understanding broader dimensions of women's experience and agency. Yet, if women's cooking activities can represent a source of power, women's agency is directly undermined by the dynamics of food insecurity that limit a household's access to food. In a provocative paper that she expands upon in her chapter in this book, Carney (2010, 7) discusses how women's ability to manage food resources is "compromised by a lack of sufficient resources." The kitchen can then also be seen as a location for women to resist not only gender inequality, but structural dynamics of poverty and hunger that threaten to undermine positive sources of female identity and power and negatively impact the health of their families. Mullings (2001, 49) describes what she calls women's "transformative work" in their "efforts to sustain continuity under transformed circumstances and efforts to transform circumstances in order to maintain continuity." Women may not have the capacity to structurally transform broader food and social systems or their direct relationship to those systems, but as they struggle to redefine the boundaries of their own fields of action within their own homes, neighborhoods and communities in relation to the food that they serve to their families, they create new sources of power and identity.

Off the Edge of the Table

This book began as a panel I organized for the 2012 American Anthropological Association meeting in San Francisco with the title, *Off the Edge of the Table: Women Redefining the Limits of the Food System and the Experience of Food Insecurity.* The conference theme was "borders and boundaries" and I was interested in pulling together a group to provide a context for presenting research from a project on women and food insecurity that my colleagues and I had been conducting in a historic Hispanic community in Albuquerque, New Mexico (see chapter 3). The panel explored the ways that family meals reflect power dynamics outside of women's kitchens and how the food that does end up on the table is constructed by women through their everyday struggles. A meal is merely an endpoint that can only be understood in relation to dynamics and things that happen *off the edge of the table*. At the same time, the metaphoric idea that something or someone is *off the edge of the table*—not likely to be available to eat or not allowed to sit at the table—is conceptually well-suited to thinking about food insecurity and captures a reality that is missing in more dispassionate and antiseptic considerations of survey data. Panelists included Teresa Mares, Lois Stanford, Megan Carney, Daniel J. Rose, and David Himmelgreen and colleagues. The panel presentations turned out to be very compelling and were well received. I was encouraged to turn the whole thing into a book. Subsequent to conceptualizing the book manuscript in early 2013, I identified a number of other contributors that I thought would round-out and add spice to the discussion (e.g., Dickinson, Stowers, Mary Alice Scott, Phillips, Porter and Redmond, and Williams). Additionally, thinking that her extensive expertise on gender and political economy would offer the perfect backdrop for this collection, I invited June Nash to write the Foreward.

Research with Hispanic/Latina women is presented in seven of the twelve chapters, reflecting the original focus and context of my own work with women in a Hispanic community in New Mexico. Five of those seven chapters discuss research conducted within the U.S., with four of those five involving Mexican or Salvadoran immigrants. Two of the chapters present data gathered in Latin America (Mexico and Costa Rica). One of the chapters involves discussion of an African-American community, one presents an African-American woman's story as an *entre* to discuss the politics of gender in the food movement, one follows the story of an immigrant from Africa, and two explore the experience of women in Canada—one urban and one rural. In addition to population and geographic diversity, the authors who contributed chapters to this book are themselves professionally diverse, representing views from anthropology, sociology, history public health, and the activist community. This expansiveness informs the content of this collection and provides a holistic, synthetic framework for understanding the issues involved in thinking about the food system, food insecurity and women's agency. Reflecting feminist principles and practice, an *applied* focus, a commitment to socially meaningful research, and the use of a participatory methodological design are common themes in many of the chapters.

Taken together, the chapters provide a unique perspective on how we can think broadly about the issue of food insecurity in relation to gender, culture, inequality, poverty, and health disparity. By problematizing the mundane world of how women procure and prepare food in a context of scarcity, this book reveals dynamics, relationships and experiences that would otherwise go unremarked. Normally under the radar, these processes are embedded in power relations that demand analysis, and demonstrate strategic individual action that requires recognition. All of the chapters provide a counter to caricatured notions that the lives of women from low-income, low-wealth communities are predicated on ignorance, impotence and weakness. Yet, the authors do not romanticize women as uniformly resilient or consistently heroic. Instead, they explore the contradictions inherent in the ways that marginalized, seemingly powerless women ignore, resist, embrace and challenge hegemonic, patriarchal systems through their relationship with food.

The Dimensionality of Food Insecurity: Structural Limits and Women's Strategies

The first section of this book explores women's struggles with having enough food to put on the table, and the strategic and innovative methods they devise to ensure that their families have enough to eat. These are not things that are commonly measured in studies of food insecurity. Subtleties of the *dimensionality* of food insecurity in terms of both cause and experience are not revealed through household surveys or statistical analyses of population level food sufficiency. It is one thing to talk about percentages of food insecurity or very low food security, and quite another to envision what that percentage looks like in the shopping cart, what it feels like in the kitchen, how it cooks on the stove, how it tastes at the table, and how it operates and is manifest in what people eat for dinner, or better said, in what people *are not able to eat for dinner*. Moreover, as discussed above, mainstream discourses tend to paint an ideologically derived portrait of hunger that at best fails to capture the real dynamics involved in women's everyday lives, and at worst misrepresents or discounts the reality of their struggles.

While the underlying cause of food insecurity may be poverty, access to food is also influenced by a variety of structural, cultural and personal dynamics. In fact, although many of the authors in this book discuss dimensions of cooking and food preparation, food access takes a more central stage in most of the studies given that the primary struggle in food insecure households is having *enough* food. Knowing how to navigate the food system landscape (e.g., public food programs; private food charities; grocery stores with low prices, periodic sales, higher quality products, or culturally desirable foods) to put together healthy, culturally appealing, satisfying meals is a major challenge. A number of the chapters in this collection describe women's knowledge regarding sites and tactics for food procurement and their skill at combining them effectively as a form of what I call *food access expertise* that is often overlooked in the literature on nutrition in low-income households. The authors explore the multidimensionality of women's food procurement and preparation strategies. To avoid the empty cooking pot, women develop their *food access expertise* through a combination of personal knowledge, skilled social relationship-building, time-consuming food sourcing, and labor-intensive production activity. This expertise allows them to combine use of public and private food resources and programs, mobilization of family and social networks, and clever shopping and cooking techniques to make choices that ensure there is food on the table.

Although women's stories repeatedly demonstrate the use of formal public programs and private assistance charities as facets of a multidimensional household food provisioning strategy, policies enacted in response to negative caricatures of the poor affect women's ability to participate in both public food support programs and private emergency food distribution sites. Definitions of who qualifies and how one qualifies intersect with stereotypical assumptions about women and their families, ideologies regarding the dynamics of the economy, immigration policy, and the pejorative mainstream discourses discussed above, often resulting in punitive, humiliating systems for those who find it necessary to use them. Many of the contributors discuss the nature of these policies and the way that they impact the lives of individual women. In the context of neoliberal restructuring that is narrowing employment options while simultaneously reducing or eliminating safety net services and supports, the strategies women develop to feed their families take on new meaning. The chapters in this book demonstrate how close everyday reality brings them to *the edge of the table* where there is no food, and the precarious nature of having to rely on a multifaceted approach to feeding a family. The contradiction of rights versus needs becomes a central issue in how we conceptualize the struggle to eat, belied by the vagaries of terms like food insecurity or very low food security.

In her chapter, *Another Time of Hunger*, Teresa Mares opens this collection with a discussion of the need to think about disparities in food access as being about more than the food itself. She develops a framework based on rights, choices and cultural practices to understand the everyday lives of Latina immigrant women in Vermont, and to connect with the literature on food justice. She demonstrates how the struggle to eat is a form of structural violence where citizenship status becomes the arbiter of access to both government food benefits and privately funded emergency food resources. Within this context, women develop deliberate food-related strategies to assert their own personhood as part of a strategy to resist oppressive structural forces. They normalize the use of emergency food resources, they rescue wasted food, and they strategically maximize food budgets to obtain specific food items that their families desire. Women go to great lengths to maintain a connection with foodways based on personal and cultural traditions that allow them to nurture cultural memory and a sense of connectedness for themselves and their families. Mares suggests that for women in her study, *dreaming* is a common thread that underlies women's food-related resistance strategies. Women's dreams of a happy life provide meaning for the struggles they experience and their work to feed their families. Despite the fact that immigrant women operate from a position of weakness (e.g., poverty, gender inequality, racial and ethnic disparities), they strive for and value autonomy in practice related to food access (e.g., food access expertise, community gardens) and in policy (e.g., political citizenship). Mares' study illuminates the ways that women creatively enact their own agency through micro-level food-related practices, choices and processes. At the same time, however, the experience she documents among immigrant women in Vermont highlights the constraints that temper and restrict their capacity to influence meaningful systems changes to create equity. For the women she spoke with, food embodies contradiction. The family kitchen pantry conjoins women's active attempts to redefine the right to food as an entitlement in relation to both cultural and legal citizenship status, with power residing beyond the authority of individual women and outside of their households that simultaneously operates to deny these claims. In the process, however, women are reshaping their own identity in relation to the experience of food insecurity.

In chapter 2, *Women, Welfare, and Food Insecurity*, Maggie Dickinson expands our understanding of how the landscape of food insecurity reflects other complex dimensions of public policy. She discusses how the politics of welfare reform intersect with daily food practice to increase food insecurity in households that receive TANF (Temporary Aid for Needy Families) Cash Assistance. Following the experience of Adwa who is a single mother and an immigrant from Gabon living in Brooklyn, New York, we see how access to public food assistance (SNAP/ Food Stamps) is diminished by problematic program operational dynamics and rules that seem designed to stigmatize. Public benefit program office procedures that are unresponsive to the needs of recipients, administrative errors, long wait times, excessive paperwork, and coarse, often disparaging or insulting treatment clerks and caseworkers make the process of obtaining benefits onerous. At the same time, changes in SNAP eligibility for women receiving TANF that were enacted in the 1990s as *reforms* to the system have made it necessary for women to choose between supportive mothering behaviors and low-wage labor. Strict, often excessive work requirements have transformed TANF from what was originally conceptualized as a program to provide support for single mothers in low-income households into a jobs program that forces women into the labor market at below-market wages. Failure to *comply* with work requirements results in dramatic reductions in SNAP benefits. Yet, when she follows the rules, Adwa finds it impossible to be the responsible mother she believes she must be in relation to her son's asthma health and his need for homework supervision. Welfare reform in which the *good mother* is construed as first and foremost a *good worker* devalues the mothering work of women living in poverty while undermining their ability to provide for the well-being of their children and families. In short, *reforms* enacted in public food program policy have resulted in a paradigm shift from publically funded entitlements to assist the poor, to a disenfranchising conditional food aid system that uses the fiction of a market-based ideology to support extra-market exploitation of women's labor. Moreover, funding levels for individual and household SNAP benefits are predicated on a Thrifty Food Plan that makes problematic and unrealistic assumptions about a household's knowledge, skill, food access, food storage and preparation facilities, and eating habits. Dickinson shows how these assumptions are challenged by everyday reality. Even spending extra time shopping for bargains and employing cooking techniques to stretch food ingredients does not make it possible for Adwa's family to eat properly or sufficiently. Adwa is forced to rely on the food pantry as a primary source for groceries. Dickinson discusses how receipt of food as charity increases the stigma and shame associated with food insecurity. Charity is, by definition, an uneven power relationship since it cannot be reciprocated. Adwa tries to mitigate her shame at having to accept charity by volunteering at the pantry. However, lack of control over the food received through charitable services further undermines her autonomy to procure, prepare and serve food that is both healthy and appropriate according to her own standards. Dickinson suggests the term *food poverty* is better than *food insecurity* at capturing the nuance involved in this dynamic. Viewing household level food access as the critical determinant allows us to examine the relationship of households to the broader social, economic and policy context when thinking about women's agency.

In chapter 3, "*I took the lemons and I made lemonade*": Women's Quotidian Strategies and the Re-Contouring of Food Insecurity in a Hispanic Community in New Mexico, my colleagues and I explore women's everyday response to food insecurity. The discussion demonstrates how food insecurity textures daily life for women from a historic urban food desert community in Albuquerque, New Mexico and the ways that women confront the reality of scarcity and the challenge to put food on the table for their families. Although they struggle with food insecurity, women we spoke with emphasized their own resilience in the strategies they develop to buffer the experience of hunger for family and for themselves. For women with strong social networks and significant social capital that is traditionally characteristic of the neighborhood, informal resources and social relationships become sources of support through cultural constructs that prioritize sharing. But not everyone has a network. Social and economic dynamics that have acted to disrupt local social relationships reduce the viability of sharing behaviors as a generalizable strategy. Accessing benefit programs is another key component of women's overall food management strategy and women expressed personal satisfaction in their knowledge of benefit resources and their ability to navigate benefit systems (*food access expertise*). At the same time, like the experience of Adwa discussed by Dickinson in chapter 2, the women we spoke with described experiences that illustrate policy and operational dynamics that make food benefit programs challenging to access. Women in Albuquerque also engage in *stretching* techniques similar to those described by Dickinson. The expertise involved in *making do* with insufficient resources, including tactics learned from mothers and grandmothers, was a source of pride and power for the women in our study. However, women's ability to *stretch* is not infinite and *making do* becomes less viable in the context of neoliberal restructuring. Together, these coping strategies reveal dimensions of women's agency in re-contouring the food landscape to make it more likely that families can satisfy their hunger. Women *make lemonade out of lemons* as they confront the *status quo* and structural boundaries through their mundane, everyday activities and habits. This view expands our definition of what food justice means for women in their kitchens and communities, and operationalizes our understanding of how women actively redefine the experience of food insecurity and challenge the limits of the current inequitable food system.

In her study in an immigrant community on the New Mexico border with Mexico, *Negotiating Food Security along the U.S.-Mexico Border: Social Strategies, Practice and Networks among Mexican Immigrant Women*, Lois Stanford examines food insecurity as a socially constituted state and demonstrates the ways that policies and institutional arrangements misrepresent the nature of food insecurity. She emphasizes the arbitrariness of official measures that are used to define categories of need such as *food insecure* or *poverty* that are then used to determine eligibility for benefit programs. In the chapters by Mares and Dickinson, we saw how legal citizenship status and work compliance have become a part of the algorithm for demonstrating benefit-worthiness. Here, Stanford explores how the USDA model of *food secure/food insecure* is a false dichotomy that fails to apprehend the dynamics of episodic or chronic food insecurity. She explores the extent to which some households are dependent on formalized food support systems or charitable emergency food resources in a way that is disguised by discourses of *supplemental* and *emergency* food, and the structure of both public and private assistance programs. Using what she calls a *desde abajo* (bottom-up) perspective and a community-level rather than a household-level lens, she demonstrates that in a context of poverty and lack of economic opportunity, both *supplemental* and *emergency* food programs are incorporated by women as part of permanent, multidimensional food provisioning strategies within a diversified household economy. Stanford uses a food provisioning framework to describe how women negotiate systems, navigate networks and build social relationships that allow them to overcome obstacles created by problematic immigration status, local food pantry volunteers who operate as gate keepers, and stigmatizing processes. Although, unlike previous chapters where women tended to operate in isolation, the women in her study expressed a shared sense of struggle that helps to construct a common community identity. However, the destructive dynamics of poverty and the politics of immigration ultimately act to undermine women's agency and capacity. As we see in all of the chapters, despite significant effort, women's everyday resistance is not able to change the underlying economic and social conditions that exist in their own households, nor have they succeeded in mounting a meaningful challenge at the level of the community.

Disparities in Access to Healthy Food:
The Social Determinants of Health

The first section of this book focuses on the dynamics of food access. In that context, a number of the authors mention women's concerns about food quality, the unhealthful nature of food stuffs obtained through emergency food sources, and women's inability to afford to serve sufficient, healthy meals for themselves and their families. The second section uses these issues as a framework for exploring the health dimensions of food insecurity. Food insecurity is clearly a health issue in that lack of food can have severe health consequences, especially among children (Olson 1999; Lee and Frongillo Jr 2001; Perry, et al., 2007; Rose-Jacobs et al. 2008; Kirkpatrick, McIntyre and Potestio 2010; Burns, Jones and Frongillo 2010; Ridge 2011; Troy, Olson, and Miller 2011). Yet the type of severe hunger we tend to associate with other, less industrialized countries in the context of war or famine does not exist in the U.S., and apart from those $5 donations we are routinely asked for as we check-out at the grocery store, we rarely think about or are confronted with the nature of hunger in this country. Recently, given growing alarm over increasing rates of obesity, more attention is being paid to the ways that the diet of food insecure households can be undernourishing in that inexpensive food is generally filling but nutrient-deficient while containing a high content of unhealthy, processed ingredients. Although it may come as some surprise to *Forbes* blogger Paul Roderick Gregory whose ideas about obesity and poverty were discussed above, individuals who live in food insecure households are chronically or episodically exposed to a nutritional environment that is damaging to their health—both in terms of lacking essential micronutrients and in being *obesogenic*. However, because of the almost purely medical focus of this literature, elsewhere my colleagues and I have argued that food insecurity is often under-appreciated as a public health issue (Page-Reeves, et. al. n.d.). The tendency in the public health literature is to focus on understanding or addressing *what food insecurity does to people* rather than on understanding or addressing *the factors that lead people to be food insecure*. The medical dimensions of food insecurity are often treated as existing somehow apart from larger political and economic conditions that are not discussed or addressed. We argue that silos of discipline expertise provide an excuse for many to see discussions of root causes as *too political*—potentially socially dangerous (e.g., challenging existing social privilege) or professionally damaging (e.g., may be distasteful to funders).

More recently, however, there has been a shift in the medical paradigm in public health towards the *social determinants of health* (Bambra, et al. 2010; Braveman, Egerter, and Williams 2011). This shift demonstrates greater appreciation of the extent to which individuals are embedded in contexts that can nurture wellness or produce illness. This focus allows us to think differently about food insecurity as a public health issue. One of the foremost proponents of this approach in relation to food insecurity in public health has been Children's Health Watch, an organization founded by pediatricians in Boston that produces medical research to support policy advocacy. For example, their innovative report on *Food Stamps as Medicine: A New Perspective on Children's Health* (Perry, et al. 2007) argued that policy laid out in the reauthorization of the Farm Bill—not an issue normally construed as concern in public health—offers an opportunity to significantly influence the health of children from low-income families by increasing access to Food Stamps. This approach exemplifies a social determinants framework that makes—in addition to poverty—things like corporate subsidies, tax law, immigration policy, the built environment, racialized neighborhood landscapes, tourism, and trade policy, more explicitly into public health issues.

Megan Carney's chapter, *"La Lucha Diaria": Migrant Women in the Fight for Healthy Food*, embraces this approach. She describes the nuanced ways that women encounter and survive food insecurity based on research she conducted in Santa Barbara, California. Like the chapters by Mares and Stanford, Carney focuses on immigrant status as a key determinant of food insecurity. She calls the time and expertise that is required to obtain and prepare meals in low-income households, *women's food work*. Reminiscent of the experience of Adwa in chapter 2, she sees this as incompatible with the long hours required in a low-wage job, and an undervalued dimension of the everyday experience of women living in poverty. Carney argues that in this context, health needs to be considered more expansively to include both women's psychosocial well-being and the diet-related diseases (e.g., food insecurity, obesity, diabetes, heart disease) that affect the health of women in her study and their families. She uses meals as a frame for her portrait of women's lives. Like women in the earlier chapters, immigrant women in Santa Barbara engage in a type of multi-tasking that combines a variety of tactics and activities in order to ensure that families can eat. They use big-box stores for bulk buying, they struggle to overcome transportation challenges, they take advantage of specials, they engage in rigorous price surveillance, they navigate abusive gender relationships that place controls on their activities and behavior, they economize, and they utilize multiple food support programs, including nutrition education classes. Like the women in our study in Albuquerque discussed in chapter 3, they derive happiness, pride and self-worth from knowing how to do these things—from their own cleverness (*food access expertise*). However, Carney pushes us to consider the health consequences, not only of poverty, but of immigration status in structuring women's experience of food and the food environment. She argues that the social isolation experienced by women who live in households with individuals who *lack documents* creates a type of gendered suffering. Immigrant women experience high levels of stress related to fear associated with *illegality,* but also fear of failing to fulfill gendered responsibilities and social expectations of wife and mother. The pervasiveness of fear in the immigrant community (Larchanché

2011; Page-Reeves, et al. 2013a; Page-Reeves, et al. 2013b) and the shame and stigma experienced by women in food insecure households (Hamelin, Habicht and Beaudry 1999; Rock, McIntyre and Rondeau 2009; Page-Reeves, et al. 2014) become part of a complex of chronic stress and depression. Mendenhall (2012) found that immigration stress and depression were components of a *syndemic* that contributed to diabetes risk among the Mexican immigrant women in her study. In Santa Barbara, rather than considering the social and economic struggles that prevent immigrant households from access to healthy, sufficient food resources, public health messages encourage social scrutiny of immigrant women who do not spend all day engaged in food work, blaming them for the poor health of their children. Carney found that similar to dynamics described in chapter 1 by Mares, to counter this dynamic women attempt to make claims to resources. They use *deservingness* as a rationale, demonstrated by their devotion to food work activities. Given the current politics and discourse around immigration, it is clear that the biopolitics of women's food-related struggles are not only under-appreciated, they are generally ignored.

Similarly, Daniel J. Rose uses a social determinants approach to understand the food environment in two urban African-American communities in Detroit. He explores how the framework of personal responsibility in health discourse is played out in the lives of women in his chapter, *Women's Knowledge and Experiences Obtaining Food in Low-Income Detroit Neighborhoods*. Rose engages with the emerging literature on food deserts, arguing that food environments in urban settings may not be complete *deserts* since food is available, but rather are better understood as *out of balance food environments* characterized by *fringe food* that he calls *food jungles*. His study challenges the paradigm that treats individuals and specific neighborhoods as deficient, with poor women seen as lacking in the knowledge or motivation to engage in healthy shopping and cooking behaviors. As discussed above, mainstream discourse tends to treat obesity and diabetes in low-income communities as a reflection of ignorance and lack of personal responsibility. Rose explores what women know about nutrition and what they do in a context of limited resources and food access. He found that women he spoke with in Detroit had rather sophisticated nutritional knowledge and good motivation unrelated to their weight or the general quality of their diet. Instead, neighborhood barriers related to food cost, availability, and quality, in addition to transportation challenges, neighborhood safety, and an unpleasant or unwelcoming physical and social environment in grocery stores, were significant factors influencing the food women buy and prepare. He uses data from his study in Detroit to explore how women enact their own agency in relation to diet in a context of neighborhood and structural constraints. He reminds us that food is a site for complex integration of agency and structure. However, while structural conditions may outweigh agency in our understanding of diet as personal responsibility and choice, we cannot ignore the agentive strategies involved in women's food work. Rose demonstrates the multidimensionality of the food-related survival strategies that women deploy and the elaborate efforts they develop to make a limited food budget suffice. Yet in this context of an interplay between struggles (e.g., lack of resources or access) and strategies (e.g., women's *food access expertise*), taste becomes a key component of women's sense of independence, culture and self-worth, and a significant dimension of women's agency. He argues that the concept of agency provides a mechanism for understanding the way that people are embedded in an environment—a core tenet of social determinants thinking. His analysis counters dichotomous treatments of individuals and context found in the literature on agency and structure, and challenges simplistic treatment of social determinants as a concern with *barriers* and *promoters* that is rife in the public health literature.

In the final chapter in this section dealing with health, *Is the Cup Half Empty or Is It Half Full? Economic Transition and Changing Ideas About Food Insecurity in Rural Costa Rica*, David Himmelgreen and colleagues explore how food security and health are bound together with global economic processes. Research they conducted in the Monteverde Zone of Costa Rica demonstrates how delocalization of food production, increased availability of nonlocal food products, increased food cost, changes in employment opportunities, and increased tourism following the enactment of the North American Free Trade Agreement (NAFTA) have resulted in transformation of diets and health-related lifestyles, both chosen and imposed. Using methods (e.g., a large scale survey) and a quantitative analytical approach (e.g., Pearson's chi-square test and Spearman's correlation coefficient) not as commonly pursued in anthropological research, they examine the downstream effects of globalization among respondents from 215 households, 87 percent of which were women. Like previous authors, they show the nexus of individual and structural factors that affect food-related behaviors, food preferences, and food procurement and coping strategies, and they discuss the impact of this nexus on health through compromised dietary intake and implications for broader well-being in terms of stress and anxiety. Like Rose, they highlight the significance of food preference and taste as an area in which women enact agency in a context of food systems over which they have little control. They also reveal the important social and experiential dimensions of the food procurement process in the socializing that goes on at the farmers' market, in the importance attributed to smells and sounds at the market, and the social significance of the opportunity for women to interact with the food (e.g., touching, squeezing, inspecting). While globalization has wrought changes that are contradictory, some improving individual choice and health, and others reducing choice options and damaging health, disparities are evident in how these processes are played out in individual households. The ability of households to adopt healthier lifestyles in relation to increased availability of new food products and changing food preferences is contingent upon a combination of wealth, resources, and access that are not within reach of all households. The nutrition transition that is occurring in Costa Rica is indicative of the neoliberal *black box* approach that focuses on economic growth with no attention to equity. Understanding food insecurity as a health disparity that reflects social determinants generated by broader structural processes helps us to see the flaws inherent in such black box thinking and foregrounds food inequality as a social justice issue.

Women's Agency and Contested Practices: The Contradictions of Agentive Actors

The third section of this book expands our understanding of women's agency in relation to contradictions associated with women's food work. In earlier chapters, we saw how women's strategic action is played out, for example, in decisions about whether or not to comply with oppressive work requirements in order to maintain SNAP/Food Stamp benefits (chapter 2: Dickinson) or in how to interpret health messaging with respect to personal shopping and eating habits (chapter 6: Rose). In this section, the authors take this theme further to explore contradictions that emerge in relation to women's food work in the context of food insecurity as a gendered domain. As the chapters in this section make clear, women's actions are not unidimensional, but rather, must be understood in relation to a variety of often competing personal, social and cultural frameworks. Women's agency is therefore not uniform, nor is it uniformly heroic. Instead, through these chapters, we come to further appreciate the complexity and multi-dimensionality of women's food-related practice.

Similar to earlier chapters by Mares, Stanford and Carney, in *Salvadoran Immigrant Women and the Culinary Making of Gendered Identities: "Food Grooming" as a Class and Meaning-Making Process*, Sharon Stowers demonstrates how the immigration experience operates to constrain women's lives and disrupt accepted gender, ethnic and class identities within the immigrant community. To counter these negative dynamics, the Salvadoran women she spoke with in Somerville, Massachusetts, embrace an idealized female identity that exaggerates the nurturing role of wife and mother by recreating and reinventing Salvadoran cuisine through *food grooming*. Women assert their agency by increasing self-exploitation in the kitchen to create an illusion that fits with unrealized and illusive dreams of a middle class lifestyle. Women infuse or *supercharge* food through *culinary meaning making*. Despite increasing pressure in terms of time and money, they resist the use of convenience food and insist on maintaining elaborate food preparation techniques seen to be based on Salvadoran cultural heritage. They enact their own culinary identity through *food access expertise* involving extensive shopping and social relationships with vendors. Food preparation necessarily involves an intimate relationship with ingredients established through touch, taste and style that makes the idealized Salvadoran meal an extension of the woman who prepared it and a symbol of desire— culinary, economic and sexual. Women's *food grooming* and culinary nurturing construct new gender boundaries that reinforce and shore-up men's identity as providers and heads of household. By creating *gastronomic nostalgia* through their own excessive culinary labor, women challenge the structural relations outside the home that reduce men's status and economic power through low-wage, unstable employment, and immigration politics. However, through this process, women reported increasing demands and control by men that some women experience as oppressive and that are creating both economic and domestic crises. Stowers suggests that in this context, the identity that women have actively invented through their food work is turning them into *culinary serfs*—something women have now, in turn, begun to resist.

In chapter 9, *The Social Life of Coca-Cola in Southern Veracruz, Mexico: How Women Navigate Public Health Messages and Social Support through Drink*, Mary Alice Scott develops a fascinating argument regarding women's relationship with Coca Cola in the town of Los Cañales in southern Veracruz in rural Mexico based on a self-reflexive experience she had doing field work for a project on cancer. In a context of increasing diabetes, obesity, coronary and kidney disease, and tooth decay, Coca Cola is the quintessential symbol of bad individual dietary choices (Leatherman and Goodman 2005). Yet despite extensive knowledge about the health consequences of soft drink consumption, women in Los Cañales continue to consume and serve Coke. Scott explores this contradiction, critiquing narrow public health messaging that fails to consider the multivalent symbolic nature of Coke and the complex context in which soft drinks are consumed. She argues that the public health model assumes and promotes a type of personal responsibility that is increasingly untenable given neoliberal transformation that has impoverished household economies, reduced funding for support systems, and fractured personal social networks. In this context, women's strategic use of soft drinks takes on new and expanded meaning. The symbolic value of Coca Cola is enacted through everyday visiting behaviors where drink simultaneously physically represents household status, demonstrates respect for visitors, and contributes to the creation of social ties through shared consumption. The priority of class and interpersonal dynamics results in noncompliance with health messaging regarding the consumption of soft drinks. In addition, Scott identifies further contradictions in that Coke may actually be healthier than water given people's experience with bottled water distributors who dispense tainted or untreated water. But it is not just physical health that is implicated in the consumption of Coke. Scott describes the enjoyment quotient of drinking a cool, sweet, refreshing beverage on a hot afternoon and how Coke *"flow[s] through daily life in Los Canales."* She demonstrates that women's noncompliance with health messages, rather than being a reflection of ignorance, is better understood as a conflict between the narrow conceptualization of well-being in the biomedical public health model and a locally embraced, more expansive view that connects physical health with powerful social, emotional and experiential dimensions of everyday life. Women resist health messages regarding soft drinks that conflict with their ability to construct social relation-ships and experiences as they navigate the health and well-being landscape. Scott suggests that we need a new framework to replace the normative binary of good/bad health behavior by contextualizing choices. By accounting for the complexity of meanings associated with consuming food and beverages, Scott believes that women's agency could be leveraged and harnessed to develop more appropriate health messaging and approaches with more likelihood of im-proving the health of the community.

Lynne Phillips, in Chapter 10, *"Women not like they used to be": Food and Modernity in Rural Newfoundland,* presents an analysis of women's identity and power in relation to the food system in the late modern (post-WWII 20th centu-ry) period. She demonstrates the bidirectional influence of ideas of progress on defining the types of food that the modern woman should aspire to prepare with the ways that food helped to define the proper modern woman. She explores how rural women from fishing communities in Newfoundland embraced these ideas and created a gender identity that allowed them to discontinue supplemen-tary small plot agricultural work which although it provided significant food resources for the family table, was experienced by women as drudgery. She ex-plores contradictions and unintended consequences of this transformation in a context where household diets are often insufficient and have now become de-pendent on processed, purchased food, and in relation to current broader food-related discourse that romanticizes "gardening" as utopia. Using historical data, Phillips demonstrates how discourses of modernity defined supplementary household agriculture as unnecessary, inefficient and backward. In fact, despite evidence that women's agricultural labor contributed significant resources to the household subsistence economy in a context where families struggled to have enough food, official technical documents from the time which place a high val-ue on modern production and marketing systems tend to make it seem as if women's supplementary agriculture did not even exist. In a novel use of gov-ernment reports to explore women's agency, Phillips examines historical docu-ments to understand what she calls the *paradox* of why women *departed* from small plot agriculture even though it was an important source of food. Modern-izing discourse framed the proper role for women as mothers and housewives whose job it was to prepare aesthetically pleasing and satisfying meals. This positioned them in the kitchen, not in the fields. As *good food* was redefined as *purchased food,* gardening was increasingly seen as dirty and backward, and it communicated poverty and stigma. Women's proper expertise was construed as deriving from their role as nurturers, while agricultural knowledge required sci-entific expertise. Although women were being disciplined by this new discourse, Phillips demonstrates how new products like cellophane wrapping enhanced women's autonomy in being able to see the food for themselves and make their own purchasing decisions, without having to rely on male butchers or grocers. At the same time, Phillips shows how changes in the state welfare system helped to buffer family economies as women departed from supplemental agricultural activities, while the popularity of baking contexts provided a positive source of identity for women in their kitchens. In this context, she suggests that women developed new metrics by which to measure themselves and their labor that allowed them to actively *refuse* to continue to participate in agricultural labor that was experienced as oppressive and demeaning.

Empowerment and Challenging the System: Possibilities for Transformative Action

The final section of this book explores the ways that women's agency can be seen from beyond the level of the household. The two chapters in this section provide us with a different view of how women have challenged food-related systems of oppression and hierarchy. The chapter by Christine Porter and La-Donna Redmond, *Labor and Leadership: Women in U.S. Community Food Organizing*, analyzes gendered dynamics within the national Community Food Movement. The movement emerged in response to concerns over dangerous food system practices (e.g., pesticide and genetic modification), inappropriate or unacceptable food system practices (e.g., exploitative labor relations in farm production, resource-intensive transportation of food products), and consumption-related health problems (e.g., food insecurity, diabetes, obesity, food allergy). Although much of the rhetoric and activity within the movement has been focused on issues of race and class, Porter and Redmond found that gender has been so underappreciated that it is virtually absent from food movement discourse. Based on an analysis of literature and social media together with data from a survey of 118 individuals involved in the Community Food Movement, they argue that this gap is reflected in the undervaluation of women's role in the movement and a lack of women identified as leaders, despite overrepresentation of women in the membership of the movement, and their day-to-day involvement in creating and sustaining activities and relationships that are the foundational of the movement's vigor and success. Porter and Redmond suggest that women have become involved in the movement as an alternative to the existing food system precisely because women are more personally affected by food insecurity of children and families. They believe that the movement needs women leaders in order to develop realistic, viable solutions that connect food to broader systems of inequality.

In the final chapter, *"I would have never...": A Critical Examination of Women's Agency for Food Security through Participatory Action Research*, Patricia Williams describes how women she worked with in a Participatory Action Research (PAR) "food-costing" project developed agency on both personal and collective levels. Women from low-income households in Nova Scotia, Canada collected data on the cost of food items in different neighborhoods and in relation to the budget capacity of the typical low-income household. Women developed an understanding of their own experience of food-insecurity in relation to structural dynamics of the food system, and of the health implications of associated stress and social isolation experienced by women in food insecure households. By working together, they acquired a sense of community and connection. Through the development of findings which were disseminated as official reports where their contribution was recognized as *expertise*, they developed confidence, improved their own self-valuation, and felt they had a voice. Findings contributed to a shift in the public conceptualization of food insecurity from a focus on what happens within individual households to political economic and structural factors. This shift has had implications for policy. Williams argues that this process promoted equity in material, institutional and discursive power. Critical knowledge helped to undermine women's internalization of hegemonic ideas about individual choices as the cause of food insecurity, and countered mainstream questioning of women's *deservingness*. As women have come to see that they are not alone in their struggles (also see Page-Reeves, et al. 2014), they have begun to question the normalization of poverty and inequality. Williams suggests that this experience demonstrates how "*everyday actions can become political practices.*" At the same time, however, she acknowledges that affecting economic and political change to promote equity and undo disparity has not happened. Women have been personally empowered, but no tangible change has occurred in the material conditions of their lives or in the broader structure of power. In this case, PAR was able to organize women in the struggle against oppression, but was unable to transform the underlying political and economic reality that produces and is responsible for food insecurity.

Challenging Boundaries and Redefining (But Not Erasing) Limits

The chapters in this book provide a unifying look at disparate dimensions of food insecurity as they are manifest in women's everyday lives. A key takeaway for the reader is the extent to which mundane existence is predicated on the need for agentive actors to engage in constant, strategic decision-making executed within a context of structural limitation. Rather than problematic lifestyle choices that nurture personal irresponsibility or poor decisions about the content of meals ignorantly leading to food insecurity and poor health outcomes, the choices made by women in this volume overwhelmingly strategically contribute to *reducing* food insecurity and *improving* household nutrition. Their strategic action buffers families from the harshest effects of living the reality of *problematic, irresponsible and ignorant choices* on the part of policy makers enacting a neoliberal agenda that disregards or purposely erodes the well-being of average people and destroys the fabric of entire communities. Women's hard work and choices, and the food access expertise they cultivate, are *constructive*; they mitigate food insecurity, not cause it. The nature and outcomes of these decisions are often overlooked and are rarely deemed consequential in the literature or taken into account by policy makers. Repeatedly we see how these decisions shape not only women's daily experience but the food security landscape inside of and between households. Women in these chapters respond to the challenges of feeding families through different forms of agency. Without their relentless efforts to obtain and prepare food despite often interminable challenges, the cooking pot would be empty, and women and their families would go hungry. Yet while in the process women push the boundaries of different systems of oppression at different levels, they cannot erase them (Page-Reeves 1999). Women's agency may alter the everyday limitations in which their lives are contained, but boundaries remain nevertheless. At the same time, food is a domain in which it is easy to see how women's agency in this process is not always heroic, and how inequality in terms of economic capacity, gender hierarchy, political position, and food access translate into health disparities and identity conflicts. Women's priorities and agentive action can also have unintended consequences.

In order to develop a deeper understanding of these dynamics, Passidomo (2013) in her article entitled *Beyond Food* exhorts those of us interested in food studies to move beyond a focus on food itself to critical analyses of the food system and structures of inequality. Food, then, becomes merely a fulcrum for understanding certain domains of disparity. When thinking about these issues in relation to food insecurity, the growing literature on *food justice* (Alkon and Agyeman 2011; Gottlieb and Joshi 2010) and *food sovereignty* (Mares and Alkon 2011; Alkon and Mares 2012; Holt-Giménez 2011) taps into underlying critical dynamics that produce food access inequality and nutritional disparity in households across America and throughout the world. However, for the women who inhabit this book, these concepts are little more than abstractions. The rights- and equity-based framework of the food justice paradigm offers hope of overcoming the everyday food struggles that are a quotidian dimension of their lives. But without critical knowledge, political mobilization, or a vehicle for group empowerment, demanding justice from an inherently unjust system does not conceptually connect with the reality of their experience. The expansive focus of the food sovereignty framework on structural relations of production and consumption offers a way to connect individual struggles with political and corporate systems of power, yet again, the majority of the women in these chapters are not affiliated with a movement that can consolidate their individual experiences into a coherent strategy or vision. Despite the individual agentive action repeatedly demonstrated in the studies presented here, we have seen that systems transformation remains elusive. Moreover, and likely more crucial, the women in these chapters would not necessarily embrace the agricultural producer identity at the core of food sovereignty as a framework for action (as exemplified in Phillips' analysis in chapter 10).

Like Mares and Alkon (2011), in her piece on *Eating Cars*, Phillips (2012) explores the class-based contradictions inherent in the dynamics a food movement focused on local agricultural production or middle-class consumption utopias. Similar to the concepts of social and cultural citizenship discussed by Mares in chapter 1, she suggests that the idea of *food citizenship* captures the fault lines and conflicting visions that exist in and between communities, and between producers and consumers in relation to food. Of course, anything with the word *citizenship* attached to it automatically conjures the politics of immigration policy which would not *per se* be particularly helpful in developing a broad theoretical construction for understanding the dynamics of food insecurity. However, *food citizenship* implies a framework of rights and responsibilities that is less clearly articulated in other ways of talking about the food system. While *food justice* and *food sovereignty* offer approaches for thinking about what *could be*, perhaps *food citizenship* provides theoretical language and a vision for conceptualizing *what is*—for integrating disparate constructions of the dialectic between the structural limits of food insecurity and women's agency as an on-the-ground process.

The chapters in this collection contribute to critical analysis of the food system by highlighting the multi-faceted nature of women's relationship to and experience with food insecurity. Underlying this discussion are issues of rights and entitlements that are touched on directly or indirectly by all of the authors. Yet as we see in the earlier section of this introduction that discussed *The Illusion of Hunger*, in the current ideologically charged arena of public debate, rights have been "dislocated from a sense of responsibility in others" in what Smith (2002, 46) referred to in 2002 as the "sequestration of experience." This is an ironic prescience given the impact of the 2013 federal budgetary *sequester* on the state's ability to respond to and support the basic needs of citizens. While women in these chapters may or may not engage in demanding or even envision specific policy or structural changes that would improve their lives, their inherent capacity to do so is constrained by their lack of social, political and economic *citizenship*. As we see repeatedly in the chapters in this volume, this more broadly construed sense of citizenship embedded in the concept of *civil society* is defined as much by social and cultural dimensions of people's lives as by legal documentation.

Porter and Redmond, and Williams, in their chapters in the final section of this book, come closest to describing processes for activating women's food citizenship beyond the boundaries of their own kitchens through their respective work with the community food movement and "food costing." Elsewhere my colleagues and I have described a similar process of community engagement that we refer to as developing women's *critical food literacy* (Page-Reeves, et al. 2013). These processes "link the everyday reality and understanding of women from food insecure households to broader concepts and struggles in a way that gives meaning to their own experience and creates the potential for empowerment and action" (Page-Reeves, et al. 2014). Critical literacy of the systematic impoverishment being enacted upon households and communities disrupts the expanding hegemony of the neoliberal project and provides answers to the questions posed at the beginning of this introduction—*why* are there so many people hungry? How can such an enormous problem seem so remote and invisible? What is existence like for someone who does not have enough to eat? And, what does it really take *not* to be hungry these days? Yet, critical literacy is only the beginning. Linking critically literate knowledge to political mobilization is key to any transformation of the grueling, mundane reality of hunger and poverty that embalms people's lives and dismantles their hopes. As McIntyre (2003, 51) so aptly phrased it,

> food insecurity is more than a social determinant of health…[it] is perhaps the most precious of all determinants…If we make the necessary investments, we can reap a food security dividend that enriches all of society with payoffs in health, social capital, sustainability of our physical and social environments, justice, and cost savings and wealth creation.

The food citizenship concept offers a way to think about women's agency in their kitchens and how it operates within structural parameters to keep family meals from falling *off the edge of the table*. Community engagement and the development of women's critical food literacy as empowered denizens of the food system provide possible mechanisms for connecting that citizenship with the more remote promises of food justice and food sovereignty by creating a blueprint for individual involvement in advocacy and collective action.

Notes

1.*http://www.ers.usda.gov/topics/food-nutrition-assistance/food-security-in-the-us.aspx#.Ur4SmPZ9uVl*

2. *http://www.nifa.usda.gov/nea/food/sri/hunger_sri_awards.html*

3 .*http://www.nifa.usda.gov/nea/food/in_focus/hunger_if_economic.html*

Bibliography

Albritton, R. 2013. "Between Obesity and Hunger: The Capitalist Food Industry." In *Food and Culture: A Reader*, edited by C. Counihan and P. Van Esterick, 342-354. New York: Routledge.

Alkon, A., and T. Mares. 2012. "Food Sovereignty in U.S. Food Movements: Radical Visions and Neoliberal Constraints." *Agriculture and Human Values* 29, no. 3: 347-359.

————, and J. Agyeman, editors. 2011. *Cultivating Food Justice: Race, Class, and Sustainability.* Boston: The MIT Press.

Andersen, E. 1990. "Core Indicators of Nutritional State for Difficult to Sample Populations." *The Journal of Nutrition* 120: 1557S-1600S.

Avakian, A.V. 1997. *Through the Kitchen Window: Women Writers Explore the Intimate Meanings of Food and Cooking.* Boston: Beacon Press.

————— 2005. "Feminist Food Studies: A Brief History." In *From Betty Crocker to Feminist Food Studies: Critical Perspectives on Women and Food*, edited by A.V. Avakian and B. Haber, 1-28. Amhurst: University of Massachusetts Press.

Babb, F. 1998. *Between Field and Cooking Pot: The Political Economy of Marketwomen in Peru.* Austin: University of Texas Press.

Bambra, C., M. Gibson, A. Sowden, K. Wright, M. Whitehead, and M. Petticrew. 2010. "Tackling the Wider Social Determinants of Health and Health Inequalities: Evidence from Systematic Reviews." *Journal of Epidemiology and Community Health* 64, no. 4: 284-291.

Bartfeld, J., R. Dunifon, M. Nord and S. Carlson. 2006. *What Factors Account for State-to-State Differences in Food Security.* Economic Research Service. Economic Information Bulletin #20. USDA.

Beoku-Betts, J. 1995. "We Got our Way of Cooking Things." *Gender and Society* 9, no. 5: 535-555.

Berrier, J. 2013. "Fox Ramps Up Food Stamp Stigmatizing Ahead of Special." *Media Matters* August 9, 2013. http://mediamatters.org/blog/2013/08/09/fox-ramps-up-food-stamp-stigmatizing-ahead-of-s/195327 (accessed January 8, 2014).

Bower, A., editor. 1997. *Recipes for Reading: Community Cookbooks, Stories, Histories.* Amherst: University of Massachusetts Press.

Braveman, P., S. Egerter, and D.R. Williams. 2011. "The Social Determinants of Health: Coming of Age." *Annual Review of Public Health* 32: 381-398.

Bread for the World Institute. 2013. *Ending Hunger in America: 2014 Hunger Report.* Washington, DC.

Carney, M. 2010. *Women and the Human Right to Food: Examining Rights-based Approaches to the Gendered Cost of Food in the U.S.* UCLA Center for the Study of Women, Thinking Gender Papers Series.

Charles, N., and M. Kerr. 1988. *Women, Food, and Families.* Manchester: Manchester University Press ND.

Christie, M. 2008. *Kitchenspace: Women, Fiestas, and Everyday Life in Central Mexico.* Austin: University of Texas Press.

Coleman-Jensen, A, M. Nord, M. Andrews, and S. Carlson. 2011. *Household Food Security in the United States in 2011.* Economic Research Service Report #141. Washington, D.C.: U.S. Department of Agriculture; 2011 [Last accessed August 12, 2013]; Available from:
http://www.ers.usda.gov/media/884525/err141.pdf (accessed January 8, 2014).

————, A., M. Nord, and A. Singh. 2012. *Household Food Security in the United States in 2012.* Economic Research Service Report #141. Washington, D.C.: U.S. Department of Agriculture. http://www.ers.usda.gov/media/1183208/err-155.pdf (accessed January 8, 2014).

Cotter, C. 1997. "Claiming a Piece of the Pie: How the Language of Recipes Defines Communities." In *Recipes for Reading: Community Cookbooks, Stories, Histories*, edited by A. Bower, 51-71. Amhurst: University of Massuchesetts Press.

Counihan, C. 1999. "Food, Power, and Female Identity in Contemporary Florence." In *The Anthropology of Food and Body: Gender, Meaning, and Power*, edited by C. Counihan. New York: Routledge.

————, 2009. *A Tortilla is Like Life: Food and Culture in the San Luis Valley of Colorado*. Austin: University of Texas Press.

————, and S. Kaplan, editors. 1998. *Food and Gender: Identity and Power*. Newark: Gordon and Breach.

D'Sylva, A., and B.L. Beagan. 2011. "Food is Culture, But It's Also Power: The Role of Food in Ethnic and Gender Identity Construction Among Goan Canadian Women." *Journal of Gender Studies* 20, no. 3: 279-289.Gill 1993

Delaney, A. 2013. "Food Stamp Work Requirements Not just for Surfer Dudes in New Bill." *The Huffington Post*, September 19, 2013. http://www.huffingtonpost.com/2013/09/19/food-stamp-work-requirements_n_3949716.html (accessed January 8, 2014).

DeVault, M. 1991. *Feeding the Family: The Social Organization of Caring as Gendered Work*. Chicago: University of Chicago Press.

FAO (Food and Agriculture Organization of the United Nations). 2003. *Trade Reforms and Food Security: Conceptualizing the Linkages*. Commodity Policy and Projections Service. Commodities and Trade Division.

Feeding America. 2013. *Map the Meal Gap: Highlight of Findings for Overall and Child Food Insecurity: A Report on county and Congressional District Level Food Insecurity and Food Cost in the United States in 2011*. http://feedingamerica.org/hunger-in-america/hunger-studies/map-the-meal-gap/~/media/Files/a-map-2011/2011-mmg-exec-summary.ashx (accessed January 8, 2014).

FRAC (Food Research Action Center). 2013. *A History of the Food Insecurity Measure*. http://frac.org/reports-and-resources/hunger-and-poverty/a-history-of-the-food-insecurity-measure/ (accessed January 8, 2014).

Goode, J., and J. Maskovsky, editors. 2001. *The New Poverty Studies: The Ethnography of Power, Politics, and Impoverished People in the United States*. New York: New York University Press.

Gordon, K.E. 2011. ""*What is Important to Me Is My Business, Nothing More*": Neoliberalism, Ideology and the Work of Selling in Highland Bolivia." *Anthropology of Work Review* 32, no. 1: 30-39.

Gottlieb, R., and A. Joshi, eds. 2010. *Food Justice*. Boston: The MIT Press.

Gregory, P.R. 2013. "The Problem is Obesity Not Hunger (Thoughts on the Food Stamps Debate)." *Forbes Blog* September 23, 2013. http://www.forbes.com/sites/paulroderickgregory/2013/09/23/the-problem-is-obesity-not-hunger-thoughts-on-the-food-stamps-debate/ (accessed January 8, 2014).

Gundersen, C., E. Waxman, E. Engelhard, A. Satoh, and N. Chawla. 2013. *Map the Meal Gap 2013*. Feeding America. http://feedingamerica.org/press-room/press-releases/map-the-meal-gap-2013.aspx (accessed January 8, 2014).

Gvion, L. 2006. "Cuisines of Poverty as Means of Empowerment: Arab Food in Israel." *Agriculture and Human Values* 23, no. 3: 299-312.

Halloran, L. 2013. "Lobster Boy Looms Large in Food Stamp Debate." National Public Radio. September 19, 2013.
http://www.npr.org/blogs/itsallpolitics/2013/09/19/223796325/lobster-boy-looms-large-in-food-stamp-debate (accessed January 8, 2014).

Hamelin A.M., J. Habicht, and M. Beaudry. 1999. "Food Insecurity: Consequences for the Household and Broader Social Implications." *Journal of Nutrition* 129, no. 2S: 525S-528S.

Hawkesworth, M. E. 2001. "Democratization: Reflections on Gendered Dislocations in the Public Sphere." In, *Gender, Globalization, and Democratization*, edited by Rita Mae Kelly, 223-236. New York: Rowman and Littlefield.

Henrici, J. 2002. U.S. "Women and Poverty." In *The Impoverishment of Women. Special Edition*, edited by S. Morgan, 27-31. *Voices: A Publication of the Association for Feminist Anthropology.*

Himmelgreen, D.A., R. Perez-Escamilla, S. Segura-Millan, Y. Peng, A. Gonzalez, M. Singer, and A. Ferris. 2000. "Food Insecurity Among Low-Income Hispanics in Hartford, Connecticut: Implications for Public Health Policy." *Human Organization* 59, no. 3: 334-342.

Holt-Giménez E. 2011. "Food Security, Food Justice, or Food Sovereignty." In, *Cultivating Food Justice: Race, Class, and Sustainability,* edited by A. Alkon and J. Agyeman, 309-330. Boston: The MIT Press.

James, A., and P. Curtis. 2010. "Family Displays and Personal Lives." *Sociology* 44, no. 6: 1163-1180.

Julier, A. 2005. "Hiding Gender and Race in the Discourse of Commercial Food Consuption." In *Betty Crocker to Feminist Food Studies: Critical Perspectives on Women and Food*, edited by A.V. Avakian and B. Haber, 163-184. Amherst: University of Massachusetts Press.

Kingsolver, A. 2002. "Poverty on Purpose: Life with the Free Marketeers." In *The Impoverishment of Women. Special Edition*, edited by S. Morgan, 23-26. *Voices: A Publication of the Association for Feminist Anthropology.*

Kirkpatrick, S.I., L. McIntyre, and M.L. Potestio. 2010. "Child Hunger and Long-Term Adverse Consequences for Health. *Archives of Pediatrics and Adolescent Medicine* 164, no.8: 754.

Krögel, A. 2011. *Food, Power, and Resistance in the Andes: Exploring Quechua Verbal and Visual Narratives.* Lanham: Lexington Books.

Krugman, P. 2013. "Free to be Hungry." *New York Times* September 22, 2013.
http://www.nytimes.com/2013/09/23/opinion/krugman-free-to-be-hungry.html?_r=0 (accessed January 8, 2014).

Larchanché, S. 2012. "Intangible Obstacles: Health Implications of Stigmatization, Structural Violence, and Fear Among Undocumented Immigrants in France." *Social Science and Medicine* 74, no. 6: 858-863.

Leatherman, T., and A. Goodman 2005 "Coca-Colonization of Diets in the Yucatan." *Social Science and Medicine* 61: 833-846.

Lee, J.S., and E.A. Frongillo Jr. 2001. "Nutritional and health consequences are associated with food insecurity among U.S. elderly persons." *The Journal of Nutrition* 131, no. 5: 1503-1509.

Lemke, S., H.H. Vorster, N.S. van Rensburg, and J. Ziche. 2003. "Empowered Women, Social Networks and the Contribution of Qualitative Research: Broadening Our

Understanding of Underlying Causes for Food and Nutrition Insecurity." *Public Health Nutrition* 6, no. 8: 759-764.

Mares, T., and A. Alkon. 2011. "Mapping the Food Movement: Addressing Inequality and Neoliberalism." *Environment and Society: Advances in Research* 2, no. 1: 68-86.

McCracken, R.D. 1982. "Cultural Differences in Food Preferences and Meanings." *Human Organization* 41, no. 2: 161-167.

McIntosh, W.A., K.S. Kubena, G. Tolle, W.R. Dean, J.S. Jan, and J. Anding. 2010. "Mothers and Meals: The Effects of Mothers' Meal Planning and Shopping Motivations on Children's Participation in Family Meals." *Appetite* 55, no. 3: 623-628.

McIntyre L. 2003. "Food Security: More Than a Determinant of Health. *Policy Options.* http://www.chumirethicsfoundation.ca/files/pdf/FoodSecurity-MorethanDeterminantofHealth.pdf. (accessed January 8, 2014).

Mendenhall, E. 2012. *Syndemic Suffering: Social Distress, Depression, and Diabetes among Mexican Immigrant Women.* Walnut Creek, CA: Left Coast Press.

Moisio, R., E.J. Arnould, and L.L. Price. 2004. "Between Mothers and Markets: Constructing Family Identity Through Homemade Food." *Journal of Consumer Culture* 4, no. 3: 361-384.

Monteleone, J. 2013. "NM Human Services Secretary Under Fire for 'No Hunger' Claim." *The Albuquerque Journal* September 26, 2013. http://www.abqjournal.com/269393/news/official-rethinks-no-hunger-view-2.html (accessed January 8, 2014).

Morgen, S., editor. 2002. "The Impoverishment of Women: Special Edition." *Voices: A Publication of the Association for Feminist Anthropology.*

Mullings, L. 2001. "Households Headed by Women: The Politics of Class, Race and Gender." In *The New Poverty Studies: The Ethnography of Power, Politics and Impoverished People in the United States,* edited by J. Goode and J. Maskovsky, 37-56. New York: New York University Press.

Nash, J.C. 1979. *We Eat the Mines and the Mines Eat Us: Dependency and Exploitation in Bolivian Tin Mines.* New York: Columbia University Press.

NMAFB (New Mexico Association of Food Banks). 2010. *Hungry People in NM Hunger Study Fact Sheet.* http://www.nmfoodbanks.org/hungry-people-in-new-mexico/fact-sheets/ (accessed January 8, 2014).

Olson, C.M. 1999. "Nutrition and Health Outcomes Associated with Food Insecurity and Hunger." *The Journal of Nutrition* 129, no. 2S Suppl: 521S.

Page-Reeves, J. 1999. Challenging the Boundaries, Redefining the Limits: The Experience of Bolivian Handknitters in the Global Market. Doctoral Dissertation in Cultural Anthropology. The City University of New York (CUNY).

Page-Reeves, J., A. Scott, V. Apodaca, V. Apodaca and M. Moffett. 2014 "'*It is always that sense of wanting...never really being satisfied*': Women's Quotidian Struggles with Food Insecurity in a Hispanic Community in New Mexico." *Journal of Hunger and Environmental Nutrition.* 9(2): In press.

————, M. Moffett, A. Scott, and M. Bleecker. 2013. "Supper Clubs and Social Ties: Women Confront Hunger in Albuquerque, New Mexico." Paper presented at a panel on "Food Insecurity from the Ground-Up: Anthropological Perspectives on Food Accessibility" at the annual meeting of the American Anthropological Association, Chicago.

————, J. Niforatos, S. Mishra, L. Regino, A. Gingrich, and R. Bulten. 2013a. "Health Disparity and Structural Violence: How Fear Undermines Health Among Immigrants at Risk for Diabetes." *Health Disparities Research and Practice* 6, no. 2: 30-48.

————, S. Mishra, J. Niforatos, L. Regino, A. Gingrich, and R. Bulten. 2013b. "An Integrated Approach to Diabetes Prevention: Anthropology, Public Health and Community Engagement." *The Qualitative Report* 18, no. 98: 1-22.

Passidomo, C. 2013. "Going 'Beyond Food': Confronting Structures of Injustice in Food Systems Research and Praxis." *Journal of Agriculture, Food Systems, and Community Development. http://dx. doi. org/10.5304/jafscd* 9. (accessed January 8, 2014).

Pearce, D. 1978. "The Feminization of Poverty: Women, Work, and Welfare." *Urban and Social Change Review* 11: 28–36.

Perry, A., S. Ettinger de Cuba, J. Cook, and D.A. Frank. 2007. "Food Stamps as Medicine: A New Perspective on Children's Health." Boston, MA: Children's Sentinel Nutrition Assessment Program.

Phillips, L. 2012. "Eating Cars: Food Citizenship in a 'Community in Crisis.'" *Environnement urbain/Urban Environment* 6: 64-73.

Pilcher, J. 1997. "Recipes for Patria: Cuisine, Gender and Nature in 19th Century Mexico." In *Recipes for Reading Community Cookbooks, Stories, Histories*, edited by A. Bower, 26-38. Amhurst: University of Massachuesetts Press.

Poppendieck, J. 2013. "Want Amid Plenty: From Hunger to Inequality." In *Food and Culture: A Reader*, edited by C. Counihan and P. Van Esterick, 563-571. New York: Routledge.

Pottier, J. 1999. *Anthropology of Food: The Social Dynamics of Food Security.* Cambridge, UK: Polity Press.

Preibisch, K.L., G.R. Herrejón, and S.L. Wiggins. 2002. "Defending Food Security in a Free-Market Economy: The Gendered Dimensions of Restructuring in Rural Mexico." *Human Organization* 61, no. 1: 68-79.

Rabikowska, M. 2010. "The Ritualisation of Food, Home and National Identity Among Polish Migrants in London." *Social Identities* 16, no. 3: 377-398.

Randall, M. 1997. *Hunger's Table: Women, Food and Politics*. Watsonville, CA: Papier-Mache Press.

Ridge, T. 2011. "The Everyday Costs of Poverty in Childhood: A Review of Qualitative Research Exploring the Lives and Experiences of Low-Income Children in the U.K." *Children and Society* 25, no. 1: 73-84.

Roadrunner Food Bank. n.d. "Fact Sheet: Helping Nearly 40,000 Hungry People Weekly." http://www.rrfb.org/wp-content/upload/RRFB-General-Fact-Sheet.pdf (accessed January 8, 2014).

Rock, M., L. McIntyre, and K. Rondeau. 2009. "Discomforting Comfort Foods: Stirring the Pot on Kraft Dinner® and Social Inequality in Canada." *Agriculture and Human Values* 26, no. 3: 167-176.

Rose-Jacobs, R., M.M. Black, P.H. Casey, J.T. Cook, D.B. Cutts, M. Chilton, T. Heeren, S.M. Levenson, A.F. Meyers, and D.A. Frank. 2008. "Household Food Insecurity: Associations with At-Risk Infant and Toddler Development." *Pediatrics* 121, no. 1: 65-72.

Seligman, H., A. Aolger, D. Guzman, A. Lopez, and K. Bibbins-Domingo. 2014. "Exhaustion of Food Budgets at Month's End and Hospital Admissions for Hypoglycemia." *HealthAffairs* 33, no. 1: 116-123.

Simonich, M. 2013. "NM Cabinet Secretary Does Turnabout, Says Hunger is a Problem in New Mexico: Department Head Retreats from Earlier Email Remark." *The Las Cruces Sun-News.* 9/27/13. http://www.lcsun-news.com/las_cruces-news/ci_24192361/nm-cabinet-secretary-does-turnabout-says-hunger-is (accessed January 8, 2014).

Smith, A.M. 2008. "Neoliberalism, Welfare Policy, and Feminist Theories of Social Justice: Feminist Theory." Special Issue: Feminist Theory and Welfare. *Feminist Theory* 9, no. 2: 131-144

Smith, C. 2002. "The Sequestration of Experience: Rights Talk and Moral Thinking in 'Late Modernity.'" *Sociology* 36, no. 1: 43-66.

Smith, L., L.M. Appio, and R. Cho. 2011. "The Feminization of Poverty." *Women and Mental Disorders* 99.

Sukovic, M., B. Sharf, J. Sharkey, and J. St. John. 2011. "Seasoning for the Soul: Empowerment Through Food Preparation Among Mexican Women in the Texas Colonias." *Food and Foodways* 19, no. 3: 228-247.

Sutton, D.E. 2001. *Remembrance of Repasts: An Anthropology of Food and Memory.* New York: Berg Publishers.

Tarasuk, V.S. 2001. "Household Food Insecurity with Hunger is Associated with Women's Food Intakes, Health and Household Circumstances." *The Journal of Nutrition* 131, no. 10: 2670-2676.

Troy, L.M., S. Olson, and E.A. Miller. 2011. *Hunger and Obesity: Understanding a Food Insecurity Paradigm: Workshop Summary.* Washington, DC: National Academy Press.

UNDP (United Nations Development Program). 1994. *Human Development Report 1994.* New York: Oxford University Press.

Weismantel, M.J. 1998. *Food, Gender, and Poverty in the Ecuadorian Andes:* California: Waveland Press.

————— 2002. "After Butler: Materializing and Historicizing the Anthropology of Gender." In "The Impoverishment of Women. Special Edition," edited by S. Morgen. *Voices: A Publication of the Association for Feminist Anthropology.*

Winne, M. 2008. *Closing the Food Gap: Resetting the Table in the Land of Plenty.* Boston: Beacon Press.

Witt, D. 2008. "Global Feminisms and Food: A Review Essay." *Meridians* 1, no. 2: 73-93.

Wyatt, S. 2013. "Fox's Shameless Misrepresentation of SNAP Recipients." *Media Matters.* 8/9/13. http://mediamatters.org/blog/2013/08/09/foxs-shameless-misrepresentation-of-snap-recipi/195338 (accessed January 8, 2014).

PART II

The Dimensionality of
Food Insecurity

CHAPTER 1

Another Time of Hunger

Teresa Mares

Introduction

Year after year, statistics reveal the startling disparities in food access that persist in the United States. In the wake of the economic crash, these disparities have deepened as growing numbers of people encounter inadequate and irregular food access on an even more regular basis. The most recent figures collected by researchers at the U.S. Department of Agriculture (USDA) show that nearly 15 percent of people in the United States experienced food insecurity at some point in 2011, with nearly 6 percent experiencing "very low food security." For "Hispanic" households, the rate of food insecurity in this same year was more than 26 percent, with nearly 18 percent experiencing very low food security (Coleman-Jensen et al. 2012). These numbers are deeply troubling for a nation of supposed plenty and expose the multiple fractures within our current food system that parallel other inequities along lines of race, ethnicity, class, and gender.

Meanwhile, we are in a moment where national concerns around immigration are intensifying, despite the fact that net migration from Mexico has stalled, and is said by some experts to be at zero (Passel et. al. 2012). It is commonly thought that this decline stems from the very same economic conditions that have exacerbated inequalities in food access as migrating to the United States becomes a less promising strategy to improve one's economic standing. As the pieces of comprehensive immigration reform fall into place amidst the backdrop of a newly militarized border and supposed pathways to citizenship, the material realities of Latino/a immigrants merit deeper consideration. Examining food access, particularly from the perspective of women, provides one vantage point into these realities and the gendered obligations that come with feeding one's family.

Immigrant women are often portrayed as lacking agency, resources, and knowledge—a portrayal that fuels a continual disavowal of their central role in sustaining the well-being of their families, cultural traditions, and a workforce upon which many of us depend. This chapter follows an alternative path to raise two central questions: First, how do immigrant women inhabiting the margins of U.S. society exercise their agency through developing survival strategies to protect their own well-being and that of their families? Second, how is this agency reshaped and constrained by social and political institutions and policies? In raising these questions, I argue that food security is about much more than just the access to food, but rather is best understood as a broader set of rights, choices, and cultural practices. Given the centrality of food security to questions of entitlements and social, cultural, and biological reproduction, this line of thought pushes our understanding of citizenship into a more embodied realm and illuminates a wide range of choices and responses to the structural violence embedded in our food and immigration systems.

This chapter begins with an overview of relevant literature, tracing the conceptual tools that I connect and mobilize throughout my analysis of ethnographic data. In particular, notions of marginality, structural violence, and the dimensionality of citizenship are central to the theoretical foundation of this chapter. Next, I turn to a description of my methodological approach and the specific research tools that I employed in the broader study that this chapter draws upon, highlighting how feminist approaches were central to designing and carrying out field research. In turning to the ethnographic narratives of Latina immigrants living and working in the Seattle area, I then describe the different ways that Latinas navigate the processes of migrating and settling into new environments as they seek to provide for their families and maintain foodways that are both meaningful and familiar. The concluding discussion weaves together the theoretical foundations with the ethnographic data shared, making the case for further applied ethnographic endeavors into the topic of food security.

Theoretical Framework

The concept of marginality has been theorized by social scientists since Robert Park (1928) first wrote of the inventiveness of the "marginal man." While much of this research has only served to silence, speak for, or further objectify those on the margins, some ethnographers have instead followed Park's original line of thought in order to document and analyze how marginal peoples engage, resist, and subvert dominant structures in creative ways (Lamphere 1992, Lomnitz 1977, Peña 1997, Perlman 1976, Tsing 1993 and 1994). This rearticulation of marginality is well expressed by anthropologist Anna Tsing:

Margins here are not a geographical, descriptive location. Nor do I refer to margins as the sites of deviance from social norms. Instead, I use the term to indicate an analytic placement that makes evident both the constraining, oppressive quality of cultural exclusion and the creative potential of rearticulating, enlivening, and rearranging the very social categories that peripheralize a group's existence [Tsing 1994, 279].

Studies that theorize marginality through exploring the disjunctures and linkages between the local and the global, and everyday experiences and social structure, serve as models for the analysis offered in this chapter.

Conducting ethnographic research within marginal spaces and amongst marginalized individuals has informed my analysis and critique of structural violence. Anthropologists including Paul Farmer (2005) and Nancy Scheper-Hughes (1992) have both employed ethnographic methods in their efforts to demystify the social inequalities that pervade everyday life and decrease the life chances of the poor and other socially marginalized groups. Paul Farmer describes structural violence as a

broad rubric that includes a host of offenses against human dignity: extreme and relative poverty, social inequalities ranging from racism to gender inequality, and the more spectacular forms of violence that are uncontestedly human rights abuses, some of them punishment for efforts to escape structural violence [2005, 8].

In Farmer's view, human suffering is structured by historic and economic factors that conspire to constrain agency. In this study, I consider how structural violence is a factor that both leads women to migrate and shapes their lived realities in the United States. The experiences of hunger that I describe in this chapter are undoubtedly different from the "madness of hunger" that Scheper-Hughes witnessed in the Brazilian shantytown of Alto do Cruzeiro, in which she describes heartbreaking cases of adults competing with their own children for food. Rather, I consider the madness of the persistence of hunger in a nation of supposed plenty.

Scholars of migration and citizenship have long utilized ethnographic methods to study cultural identity and community membership (Alvarez 1987; Bourgois 1996; Chavez 1991 and 1994; Flores and Benmayor 1997; Hondagneu-Sotelo 1994; Lewis 1966; Mahler 1995; Massey 1987 and 1997; Pessar 1999; Rosaldo and Flores 1997; Rouse 1991 and 1992; Sharff 1998). Of these scholars, Renato Rosaldo, Rina Benmayor, William Flores, and their colleagues in the Latino/a Cultural Studies Working Group have made the greatest contributions to the framework of cultural citizenship within Latino/a studies. In their formulation of cultural citizenship, the realities and brutalities of legal citizenship are indeed significant, but the concept of citizenship extends further to encompass a broader spectrum of social and cultural practices.

These authors argue that the contributions of Latinos/as enrich the cultural fabric of the United States, thereby viewing difference as a resource, not a threat, to U.S. society. In this formulation of cultural citizenship, the citizen is understood as a political agent, and agency is defined as taking an active role in claiming rights, entitlements, and membership. This pushes the idea of a citizen beyond the sum of laws defined by one's belonging to a nation-state, to instead consider one's broader engagement in cultural practices and claims-making. More recently, social scientists have begun to develop the connections between cultural citizenship and food studies. Drawing heavily upon the work of Flores and Benmayor, Carole Counihan (2009) grounds this theoretical framework in her study of *Mexicanas* in the San Luis Valley of Colorado. As one of the only scholars to specifically consider the connections between food and cultural citizenship, Counihan offers an ethnographic portrait of how women in the small town of Antonito exercise agency and maintain community cohesion through cooking and other food practices.

Although the understanding of cultural citizenship offered by Rosaldo, Benmayor and Counihan is compelling in its focus on agency and claims-making, it pays less attention to the other side—how these claims are denied and reshaped through the disciplinary structures of the state, the market, and civil society. For this perspective, the work of Aiwha Ong proves essential. As a key figure in the anthropology of transnationalism and citizenship, Ong (1996) considers citizenship "a cultural process of 'subject-ification,'" and draws heavily upon a Foucauldian analysis of power and the production of consent through "schemes of surveillance, discipline, control and administration" (1996, 737). She defines cultural citizenship more specifically as the cultural practices that arise out of negotiations between the migrant, the state, and civil society, negotiations that she terms "self-making" and "being-made" (1996, 738). Combined, these formulations of cultural citizenship provide a more robust conceptual tool to explore how food access strategies are a site of both claiming and denying rights and entitlements within and against social, economic, and political institutions.

This integrated understanding of cultural citizenship has advanced through the work of Adelaida Del Castillo (2007) among Mexican women living in southern Illinois. Grounding her analysis in a "postnational approach," Del Castillo argues for a framework of "social citizenship," defined as the expression of social rights, or the "minimum expectation of standards, goods, and services to be anticipated from the welfare state," in addition to assuming the duty to work and generate the necessary tax revenues for the provisioning of these social rights (2007, 95). Del Castillo traces how Tarascan women from the state of Michoacan—women who are excluded from U.S. political citizenship—reproduce cultural and social citizenship through deploying survival strategies and garnering resources for their families, including those afforded by established norms and institutions, but also by informal networks of social services and resources like networks of mutual aid. This chapter picks up this line of in-quiry as it connects food access strategies of Latinas in the Seattle area with an analysis of the multiple ways that agency becomes constrained by broader social, political, and economic forces.

Methods

As a set of practices grounded in everyday life, ethnographic methods are uniquely capable of allowing researchers to hold in constant tension intimate and embodied practices and broad political-economic processes and structures. This chapter draws upon data collected during a four-year period of ethnograph-ic fieldwork in the Seattle area from 2005 through 2009. In addition to integrat-ing elements of participatory and applied methodologies into my work, I have been guided by the insights and approaches of feminist ethnographers. In recog-nizing that what gets counted as "feminist" has been not only a point of contes-tation, but has also been critiqued as a hegemonic move to make certain femi-nisms invisible—particular those developed by third-world and first-world women of color—I argue that broader definitions are actually more productive. Sharlene Hesse-Biber and her colleagues offer a useful framework for this broader definition, asserting "(s)cholars create a feminist methodology by argu-ing against the mainstream ways research has proceeded and how theory has been applied to research questions and to data. In other words, feminists explic-itly link theory with methods" (2004, 15).

Linking theory with methods is clearly not a uniquely feminist quality how-ever, as indigenous scholars and participatory researchers also center this link-age in their research practices. Therefore, to take Hesse-Biber's definition one step further, I also draw upon Virginia Olesen (2005) who argues "(f)eminist research, in its many variants, whether or not self-consciously defined as femi-nist, centers and makes problematic women's diverse situations as well as the institutions that frame those situations" (2005, 216). While my broader study focused equally on the experiences of men and women, in this chapter I draw attention to the myriad ways that gender shapes women's experiences in access-ing, preparing, and sharing food and how power inequities unfold within and through women's relationships with food.

In addition to archival research and participant observation, field methods included two sets of semi-structured interviews. In the first set, I interviewed representatives from thirteen agencies around the Seattle area, including emer-gency food providers, organizations working in urban agriculture, and institu-tions doing food systems work from a standpoint of political advocacy. From this first set of interviews, I aimed to better understand the various programs and services related to food that were available in the Seattle area, if and how these organizations sought to provide services and programs to Latino immigrant pop-ulations, and what kinds of decision-making processes were involved in designing and running these programs. In the second set, I interviewed 46 first-generation immigrants who have moved to the U.S. from various regions of Latin America, with an equal sampling of men and women. This second set of interviews aimed to better understand immigrant's relationships to food both in the United States and in their home countries, perspectives on healthy eating, and participants' experiences with the various food-related programs and services in the Seattle area. In this chapter, I draw primarily upon this second set of interviews and use pseudonyms when quoting interviewees.

To recruit this group of interviewees, I leveraged my connections to local organizations and the rapport that I had built through prior fieldwork and research on Latino/a involvement in Seattle's urban agriculture programs. I distributed recruitment flyers to several community organizations and also recruited interviewees at two large meetings run for and by members of the Latino/a community—one at a day labor center and one at a weekly family support group for Latina mothers. These two organizations proved to be productive sites to connect with interviewees as both offered the use of their office space for interviewing. Working at these sites also allowed me to interact with a community of participants that utilized a wide array of programs and services across the Seattle area. I conducted all interviews in Spanish and with their oral consent, recorded, transcribed, and translated each interview. All interviewees were compensated for their time with a gift card to a grocery store of their choosing. At both organizations, staff members commented to me that offering this compensation proved to them that I was valuing the time of their members and that they wished more researchers would do the same.

Of the 46 Latino/a interviewees, 35 were from Mexico, three were from Peru, two were from Honduras, two were from El Salvador, and one participant each came from Guatemala, Cuba, Nicaragua, and Ecuador. A significant number of questions focused specifically on food access and utilization of emergency food programs. Given the sensitivities around documentation status and Human Subjects restrictions, I did not include questions about citizenship status; but in analyzing the narrative data in which individuals voluntary spoke about their immigration status, I estimate that at least 90 percent of the interviewees were living in the U.S. without official documentation. As I will discuss, these citizenship factors have a significant impact on experiences with food insecurity.

Through my examination of the narratives below, I illuminate stories of plenty and scarcity shared by study participants. Although the terms hunger and food (in)security both appear throughout this chapter, it is necessary to emphasize the contested nature of both terms that stems in large part from of a government-led shift in terminology that has mainly served to further abstract the lived experiences of food injustices. In late 2006, the USDA replaced their category of hunger and replaced it with "very low food security," a shift that has provoked a strong response from both hunger advocates and the press, most notably prominent agri-food scholar Patricia Allen (2007). Spurred by what she calls "a methodological decision," Allen argues that the USDA's act of dropping the category of hunger has dangerous and violent material implications, but is equally disturbed by how this change undermines progressive work done under the banner of Community Food Security. For the time being, I keep both terms on the table but note that the framing of my interview questions around the term "hunger" surely impacted how interview participants narrated their lives. However, in each interview, I asked, "what does hunger mean to you?" This question revealed a multitude of answers that pointed to the biophysical, social, and emotional meanings of hunger, and in no case did a participant refer to the idea of "food security."

Interview Findings

Throughout conducting and analyzing my fieldwork, I have been continually struck by how Latino/a women and men experienced Seattle's food system in such different ways. In previously published work, I have described how interviewees utilize emergency food programs for very different purposes, and how men and women differentially negotiate the gendered responsibilities that accompany the efforts to feed one's family in new and often unfamiliar environments (Mares 2012 and 2013). In the analysis below, I seek to illuminate the narratives of five women whose migration and settlement experiences in particular reveal the often hidden dynamics connected to food security that immigrant women encounter both prior to and after moving to the United States. These stories, while certainly not generalizable to all immigrant women, are significant in the patterns they reveal about structural violence and the challenges and resilience that women living in society's margins often exhibit.

Cristina, a 39 year-old woman who moved to Seattle from Mexico seven years before our interview, described in detail her own profound experiences with hunger and how the severity of these experiences was worsened because of her gender and her relationships with men. Because of the complexity of her own analysis of her lived experiences, I quote her at length:

> *I have experienced a lot of hunger here. And when I was a child in Mexico my dad earned very little and had six children, but fortunately we had to eat a lot of rice and eggs, but we hardly ever had meat, we only ate it once in a while. And so, I got angry, I rebelled because I thought I should eat everything with tortillas, and so in my house, it was so small and I was so mad, so mad. And so I sometimes went to eat with a friend who invited me, and I saw that they ate differently, and in my house, because of the lack of food we were very small, and my dad got angry with me because I was the smallest, and didn't weigh anything, and he gave me cereal, we almost never had cereal, but for me, it's a way to gain weight very quickly. And so, what happened, I experienced hunger when I was in preparatory, when I was 15 and 16, I was hungry a lot. And I would be out on the streets, and asking for cookies, and I would get cookies. This is one time that I was hungry.*

Cristina's childhood experiences with food scarcity not only made her angry, but also angered her father who had to purchase cereal for her to gain weight. Here, she makes an important connection between the physical experience of hunger and the emotional dimension. As difficult as these experiences were, her struggles with food scarcity only got more severe when she was living in the United States and attempting to care for her own children while being abused by her husband:

And another time of hunger happened, which was much more serious, was here. It was when I was pregnant, because unfortunately, my first husband is a very awful person, and he would abuse me, not caring that I had children inside me, and when I couldn't deal with it any longer, I didn't want to be in the house with him. And then, a time that I was very very hungry, we had to go to him for help. And he is a person that has a lot of food in his home, his fridge is full, but he wouldn't give me money. And he would tell me, if you want eat, you should work, and this was when I had my baby and I didn't have papers, this was very abusive. We had to go to the shelters, and unfortunately, in the shelters we didn't have money and I couldn't get work, and I had to take the things that they gave me, and I lived in the shelter with my children, my older child and I was pregnant, and it's ugly because there is a lot of canned food, it tastes horrible, the cans, and one time, the food came out black, because it didn't have an expiration date.

And so, I realized that when one is pregnant, you have to worry about eating fresh food, vegetables and a lot of fruit and meat for protein, but I didn't have these resources and so, this is what I had to do, and I went to the food banks, and on the same side, they had pasta, grains, and it wasn't good, I ate it and I didn't feel good, but I was pregnant with my second child, the little one. And also, he was hungry, and they had bread, or things like that, sometimes fruit, but they didn't have protein and he stopped moving. And so, I had about fifty dollars worth of stamps, I was studying and didn't have any other resources, and the father didn't give me anything. So, this is when I experienced hunger.

Thanks to God, when I had my daughter, we had more stamps and we weren't hungry. But, I go to food banks because there is one here in Seattle that gives out fruit and vegetables, and they give us frozen foods and a lot of this is expensive. They give us a lot of canned things too. They give us a lot of canned food, and the eggs and all of this, and we go when we don't have anything else. But before this, I never used the food banks because I lived in Kent, and they hardly give out anything, just a little bit and it's horrible. So, we were hungry. I know how to work to buy food, but when my child arrived, because we were from Mexico, we didn't qualify for anything. I only could earn eight dollars an hour, the minimum wage, but I worked in housekeeping and they didn't give me enough hours and in 2002, after 9-11, it was very hard to find work, and I didn't have papers at that time. So, when I found work and stayed there, my friends envied me, my Mexican friends, but I had to clean a lot of rooms in a short amount of time, so that they could keep their costs down, and so, this was a very difficult situation. It was a time that we had little food, my child was only about two. And my son wanted meat, but we didn't have money because I didn't have stamps.

And what happened is very sad, because we were very hungry, and in Mexico, I was as hungry because unfortunately I married to a really horrible person, a very cruel man, and he didn't care about his children or the fact that I was pregnant...But the fact is, women shouldn't go hungry when they are pregnant, because it harms the children, my children all were harmed because I couldn't find enough food, and what affects me affects the child. And so, I think that women suffer more from physical effects or more weaknesses, because they aren't eating enough. So, since I came here from Mexico, which is a country that lives in crisis, always, and one learns how to spend money, how to buy food intelligently and eat as healthy as possible. But people from here, people are accustomed to living in opulence, they are very rich and have a lot of everything. I see that a lot people that are buying on sale, or eating lots of cookies that don't do anything. So, the best thing is to eat more healthfully. So, I think that it gives me a lot to come from a country that is poor or developing, where there is poverty, and I teach this to my children. There is value to being here, but you have to be careful with what is there and use your head because in the future, at whatever moment, you can have poverty and difficulties, because this country is so much more expensive than in Mexico.

Throughout Cristina's life, her own health and her ability to provide for her children's health have been dictated by her relationship with men, first by her father when she was a child in Mexico and next, by her husband while living in the United States. While she was living in the shelter, she found herself unable to exercise agency over what her family was eating, instead being forced to consume canned foods past their expiration date because of her limited options. The patterns of structural violence and intimate partner violence experienced over the course of her life leads Cristina to identify the source of this oppression as a dominating force rooted in patriarchy. Because Cristina was prevented from accessing programs and services because she didn't "have papers," the violence that is inflicted by her husband is compounded by the structural violence that is enacted against her and her children. At the same time, her struggle with scarcity makes her acutely aware of what it means to not take plenty for granted, as seen in her critique of people *"living in opulence"* in the United States. Despite the structural and domestic conditions that brutalized Cristina, she still holds tight a normative understanding of an ideal citizen—one who is grateful for what one has while continually looking to improve her lot through paid work and study. However, as this narrative makes clear, her experiences and cultural values that were shaped in Mexico provide her with a worldview from which she can critique the contradictions and the level of waste in the United States while simultaneously finding value in her own cultural identity.

While she was significantly older than Cristina, Marisol too shared a concern for her children's well-being and the continuation of foodways that rooted her to her Mexican upbringing. At the time of our interview Marisol was 62 years old, and had migrated from Mexico 32 years before, becoming a US citizen along the way. Our interview was conducted in a mix of Spanish and English as this was the most comfortable form of communication for her after living in the U.S. for so long. Having raised her children exclusively in the United States, Marisol had balanced her role as a working mother with the obligations of passing along cultural traditions connected to food to her children. Despite (of perhaps due to) having lived in the U.S. for more than thirty years, she explained with delight her luck in finding ingredients like *verdolagas* (goosefoot), *tejocote* (Mexican hawthorn) and guava that allowed her to prepare traditional Mexican dishes and pass down the recipes and traditions to her children, all of whom were living in separate households as adults. With the recent opening of a farmers market near her home, she also told me about finding other foods that she had long missed and introducing them to her family for the first time. These foods were all grown by a Mexican farmer from the state of Puebla:

> *I bought squash flowers and huauzontles [goosefoot]. It was so many years since I've had those, here I don't eat them because I can't find them. This year I made huauzontles for my whole family, and there's twenty of us! And they were all fascinated with them, they were like, how do you eat these? And yes, I prepared them, all day I was cooking and then we ate them.*

Marisol's deliberate attempts to find, prepare, and share culturally meaningful foods with her family, even after thirty years away from Mexico, reveals a strong desire to enact agency over her children's foodways and their collective experience of the dinner table. In this way, she carves out a space to express her cultural identity as a woman born and raised in Mexico and restores her family's deep sense of culinary and cultural tradition.

Like Cristina, Marisol also reflected upon the scarcity in her country of origin and how her lived experiences with this scarcity taught her cultural values that allowed her to critique the amount of excess in the United States.[1] Specifically, she told me about her experiences working at the Seattle Convention Center and her observations of the quality and quantity of food that was wasted:

> *Right now, for six months, I've been disabled. But usually I work at the Convention Center of Seattle, in the kitchen, but I had a problem with my eye. But in the Convention Center there is so much food that is thrown in the trash! They wouldn't let us take it out. Many times, our boss, the head chef saw that we would take food out of the trash to take home, and he told us, if you do this, I didn't see it! But I would take meat, because they throw the clean dishes into the trash! And so, I would take a bag of meat, the best food! I would take salmon, meat, whatever it was and I would share with my neighbors, I would come with my bag and share it…And those of us that were working, all the food that*

we made each day! We were cooking and we would send out the food, and then it would return and the plates weren't touched, still hot! And the cleaning people would take the plates and throw out all the food, it was such a shame! And bread! All the bread! When I worked there I never bought bread. I always brought bread home. I always gave it to my neighbors, bread, cookies, pie, it was very good food!

Through turning a blind eye to the efforts of Marisol and her coworkers to rescue this high quality food, her boss also turns a blind eye to the contradictions of throwing away food while people go hungry. However, her persistence in resisting this contradiction by taking food home and sharing it with her neighbors reveals not only a sense of righteous indignation, but also her role in sustaining networks of mutual aid where people look out for the well-being of one another. In many ways, these sharing practices reveal an ethics of *convide*, or what Estevan Arellano (2010) defines as "sharing food among neighbors.[2]" However, these practices of resistance—despite upholding relationships of *convide* - unfold within a broader set of social hierarchies where Marisol, by virtue of her position in the service economy, is not only forced to resist in silence, but also endure the wages and working conditions that make rescuing wasted food a viable option. While Marisol and her coworkers survive on the excesses of a nation of plenty, they enact cultural and material practices that both critique U.S. society and uphold the culture of immigration that forces people to strategize how to stay alive and help each other along the way, much like the women that Del Castillo describes in her work on social citizenship. These forms of individualized and spontaneous resistance, while indeed significant, are less likely to create transformational change than if they were to be channeled through more collective and public organizational forms. Over the course of my fieldwork, I witnessed the movements for immigrant and worker rights develop in the Seattle area, but rarely were these movements connected with other efforts for food justice and food security.

Unlike Marisol, Valentina, a 35-year old mother from Mexico who had lived in the United States for thirteen years, was still struggling with the challenges of raising a family whose members did not all have access to U.S. citizenship. She told me of the impacts of the arrest and detention of her husband on her use of emergency food programs, explaining:

When my husband was picked up by immigration two years ago, I was alone for five months, and in this time, I quickly got help from the emergency stamps, maybe for three months. I don't know how long, but they gave me the stamps because the food bank wasn't sufficient, because I don't work. My husband is the only one that works and so we didn't have food, and I usually had rice, and things like that, but when he wasn't there, we were left without milk, my children always asked me for milk, and I felt so bad but then the stamps helped me a lot. They let me buy all the things I needed to eat, so yes, they helped me a lot.

In Valentina's account, it becomes clear how patterns of structural violence against the working poor take a different toll on undocumented workers amidst practices of surveillance and detention. For her, having a husband working full time meant that she did not need to depend upon state-provided food stamps for her U.S.-born children. However, she was forced to file for "emergency stamps" when he was detained at the detention center in Tacoma, Washington. Upon his release five months later, these benefits were cut off. She described her coping strategies: *"(w)hen my husband got out, they cut off the service of the stamps, because once again, life was normal. But, I kept going to the food bank for help."* The wages lost during these five months continued to impact the family even after his release, making the food bank a viable, and increasingly normalized, option for obtaining the "help" they needed. In previous work, I have argued that the emergency food system, particularly private sector and faith-based providers, fill in a crucial gap in the absence of state provisioning, as many of these providers do not make citizenship status a condition of receiving food (Mares 2013). Valentina's use of the food bank both during and after her husband's detention illustrates this point clearly.

Even amidst these challenging conditions, Valentina strove to provide her children with healthy food, though she admitted giving in to certain foods more common in the U.S.:

> We like pizza a lot, and we do eat it, but not a lot. We try to not eat the kinds with pepperoni, I look at it, and I'm like, no! Just look at the fat, so for me, since I always think this is entering into my body, this fat, so if you eat these fatty things, they don't go away. So, when I look at this, I think no! And when I see it's very fatty I tell my children that they shouldn't eat it, because it has a lot of fat. I always look to see if it has fat or not.

Although she admitted that her family ate fast food *"on the street"* more than she would have liked, the fact that her husband had recently developed an ulcer encouraged them to eat at home more often. Given his condition, she was especially keen on learning new recipes and preparation styles for traditional Mexican meals. Over her time living in Seattle, she had seen significant changes in the foods that were available and familiar, stating:

> I can find pretty much anything. A few years ago, I didn't find everything, it was pretty difficult, like 13 years ago. But now, it's easier to find things, because now that I've lived in the same place for so many years, now I know which stores are there, For example, in the big markets, I find everything, I don't have to run to the Mexican stores or go to Chinatown, as a Latina, I can find everything, and I know where it is. In general, I find everything.

As Seattle's Latino/a community has steadily grown over the past two decades, this demographic shift has had a significant impact on the varieties of foods that are available. Several of the big box grocery stores began to stock an aisle of Mexican ingredients that rivaled any specialty tienda, and often sold them at lower prices. However, as seen in this vignette, many interview participants, including Valentina, commonly shopped at the Asian markets in Chinatown because they sold many of the same foods they had grown accustomed to in Mexico, particularly varieties of fruits and vegetables. These kinds of deliberate efforts to find and prepare foods that reminded Valentina of home illustrate her attempts to integrate the navigation of her new environment with maintaining some semblance of her Mexican foodways.

Despite these successes in navigating her culinary landscape, Valentina still dreamed of returning home and gaining more autonomy over what and how she eats. She told me about her efforts to grow small amounts of culturally significant ingredients, remembering her own mother's garden fondly:

I live in a building of apartments, and there is a little square, where I can plant just a bit of mint, and yerba Buena [variety of mint], in the garden, I planted it because it's very expensive! When I buy it, when I need it for meatballs or whatever dish, just a little bit costs $5 or more! And so, I planted it and I just cut off a few fresh leaves and I add them to my food. But I would love to have a bigger space to plant, this is my dream, when I think of the future, my dream is to eat fresh food, make a chicken broth and use my own green beans, my own tomatoes, I would love this. My mother had a big patio, and she had corn and yerba Buena [variety of mint], she had chilies, she had a few things, they were very good. And my dream is, that if I return to Mexico, when I am a little old lady, to have some space and have my piece of land so that I can grow my own things.

As part of the applied nature of my research, I always brought with me information about Seattle's municipal community gardening program and the contact information for a staff member who speaks Spanish in case participants expressed interest. After discussing with Valentina the idea of getting involved in a community garden near her home, she became very excited about the possibility of not having to wait to return to Mexico to have a space to grow her own food and about getting her children involved.

Rebeca, who had moved to the United States from Nicaragua only one year earlier at the age of 30, also shared an appreciation of her family's agricultural background. Trained as an economist, she had spent more years in formal schooling than most women I interviewed, yet was having significant difficulty in finding relevant work in the United States because of language barriers. In light of this, she expressed her fond memories of growing up in an agricultural area that provided an abundance of locally sourced foods:

In Nicaragua, there are only white corn tortillas, yellow corn doesn't exist. And if there is yellow corn, it's used to cook another type of food, which is similar to tortillas, but we call it Güirila [white corn tortilla]. I'm from the central part of

Nicaragua, and if you look at a map, it's right in the belly button of America. I was born in the center of Nicaragua and the food is pretty basic. Everything is grown there, and food is mainly based on corn, but since it's in the northern part, there is also a lot of dairy. And Latinos, we eat a lot of dairy. At least in Nicaragua, we never go without cream or cheese. And it's all based on beans, corn, and rice.

In raising her young daughter in the United States, she explained her efforts to replicate the recipes of her grandmother and mother despite not having access to the same kinds of cooking technologies:

Generally, all recipes are only written down if they aren't from your family, the grandmother usually tells them to the mother, the mother teaches it to their children, and there you go. And yes, my mom cooked perfectly, I have yet to, but to cook with the limitations that one has here, it's a significant thing. The food in Nicaragua is usually cooked over a wood fire. I don't know about other parts, but that's how it is in my country.

With her diverse experiences with both agrarian livelihoods and in white-collar work, Rebeca saw hunger as a complex combination of economic, social, and cultural factors. Defining hunger as simply "not having anything to eat," she told me: *"You can have land, but not have anything to cultivate it, so it turns into an economic problem. Or you could have the opportunity to grow, but not have the means to do it. So, it's a social problem. It's a combination of everything."* When I asked her whether she saw hunger as a bigger issue in the U.S. or in Nicaragua, she also examined the cultural factors that cause farmers to go hungry in her home country:

The thing that happens sometimes, is that a lot of people are hungry because of a cultural issue. I will tell you why... here, they teach you a little bit about how to eat differently, in my country, there are a lot of farmers and they don't even see any rice, or corn, or beans. There isn't food for them.

Here, Rebeca reveals a deep understanding of the contradictions related to farmers in her country going hungry as they are stripped of their ability to feed themselves. While she does not directly mention the reasons behind this, it could very likely stem from the pressures confronting farmers in the Global South to grow for export rather than for their own self-sufficiency.

Having grown up in Michoacan, Mexico Juana presented a slightly different view of the plight of the Latin American farmer. At age 41, Juana had lived in the United States for 15 years, a period of time that prompted a deep reflection on growing up within a family of subsistence farmers. Despite preferring a more *"convenient"* lifestyle in the United States, she also had mixed feelings about the relationship between the control over the means of agricultural production and social understandings of wealth. When asked if she believed if there was more hunger in Mexico, she responded:

> *This question is very hard to answer, because here, here people have for exam-*
> *ple, medical from the government, stamps, food banks, there are a lot of eco-*
> *nomic things, and work, and well, a lot of people from there come here suppos-*
> *edly to make money here. All of the people that come over the border, they*
> *come here because supposedly there is wealth. But also, there people also don't*
> *die from hunger, there, like I said, there we have everything. And it's good to*
> *have your own animals and your own land to grow, there people are not dying*
> *from hunger.*

In describing the ownership of land and animals as "*everything*," she finds it difficult to make equivalent the abundance of the countryside with the economic benefits of wage work and the U.S. welfare system. However, her emphasis on the *supposed* wealth and money in the U.S. reveals that her own expectations perhaps did not match up to the realities of life in the United States.

However, unlike Valentina, who dreamed of returning to Mexico and grow-ing her own food, Juana asserted that she had no desire to return an agrarian-based livelihood and the hard work that it entailed:

> *Well, I am now accustomed to being here because here you just throw the*
> *clothing in the washer and you buy the tortillas in the store, and there, no.*
> *There, you have to make them on a comal [griddle], and grow the corn. And*
> *then, you have to grind it, and I lived in a little town! Yes, here it's easier, eve-*
> *rything. Because of this, when I think of a farm, I think, "Oh god, no! I want to*
> *go, but for vacation!"*

During her time living in the United States, Juana had grown accustomed to more processed foods and mechanized household appliances, appreciating the minimal time it took to prepare foods and maintain her household. She reiterated that she would only like to return to Mexico for vacation when asked if she would like to return:

> *Like I said, for vacation. Nothing more than that because although there it's*
> *healthy and the food is better it's a lot more work there than here because here*
> *you just go the store and get tortillas and some steaks, and a lot of prepared*
> *food, and there, no. There, you have to get the wood and make a fire in an*
> *earthen oven to make food. All of the food. Everything that you need to cook.*
> *And here for example, if a person has work, you can buy a stove and a washing*
> *machine, everything that we have here. So I like it better here than there.*

By choosing to remain in the United States and become accustomed to what she sees as a more convenient and leisurely lifestyle, Juana is exercising agency in a manner unlike the other women whose narratives I shared earlier. While she strives to prepare Mexican foods in her household, she is selective about the time she will devote to cooking and the kinds of ingredients she will use. Like U.S.-born women adopting the microwave and the washing machine years before, Juana is simultaneously choosing her own place in mainstream U.S. culture and becoming accustomed to her role as a wage laborer who buys packages of tortillas rather than growing and grinding the corn and preparing them by hand.

Conclusion: Migrating for Food?

The stories and perspectives that Cristina, Marisol, Valentina, Rebeca, and Juana offer us underscore the point that food security entails so much more than just accessing food. It is about navigating unfamiliar grocery stores, surviving and escaping domestic abuse, delighting in the availability of specific produce at the neighborhood farmers market, and dreaming of replicating a mother's garden when the time and living conditions permit. It is about normalizing the usage of food banks, rescuing wasted food under the watchful eye of a supervisor, and reveling in the time freed up by store-bought tortillas. These kinds of experiences are not captured in the statistics on food security churned out each year by the USDA, but I firmly believe that hearing and recognizing these experiences, and the individual women that share them, is essential in building more fair and equitable food and immigration systems and policies. In this way, food security is more than just disembodied statistics, it is a broader set of rights, choices, and cultural practices.

Nevertheless, for the majority of these women, and the other 51 participants in this study, demanding more relevant policies and institutions is tempered by the lack of access to political citizenship. Even in exercising their social and cultural citizenship, these individuals remain constrained by situations where only half of the household is eligible for food assistance programs or where the only refuge from violence is a shelter filled with expired foods. The conditions of social marginality, exacerbated by the structural violence that is inflicted upon immigrants and others struggling with poverty and discrimination, have definitive impacts on the kinds of food that are available, the amount of money one has to spend, and the ability of a mother to raise her children in a household filled with meaningful and healthy foods. Despite these conditions, these women still strive to provide for their families in a manner that is both inventive and resilient.

While the narratives of these five women reveal a tremendous amount about the daily realities that Latina immigrants encounter in the United States, it is also essential to acknowledge that for most (if not all) of the women (and men) who participated in this project, migration itself was understood as a strategy to provide for one's family. Various immigration theories attempt to unpack the macro-level motivations and conditions behind why people migrate, considering the "push" and "pull" factors and the "rational choice" that immigrants make when seeking a better life north of the border. The narratives offered here help to humanize the women involved in these flows northward as they shed light on the micro-level practices, choices, and processes that they engage on the ground and in their kitchens. In these stories of hunger and plenty, we can observe how these individuals seek access to the nation through making claims to food-based rights and entitlements, how these claims are swiftly constrained and denied, and the practices of negotiation and making-do that follow these denials.

Collectively, these narratives also reveal a crucial need to fundamentally rethink the motivations and results of efforts to address issues of food insecurity and hunger, and to critically engage the ways that inequitable access to food disparately impacts the lives of Latino/a immigrants. As these women demonstrate, struggles with food insecurity are not limited to their lives and experiences in the United States, but rather follow from longer histories of displacement, underemployment, the absence of a living wage, and a scarcity of resources in their countries of origin. Although there are impressive efforts in the Seattle area to address food insecurity, these measures are not sufficient to fully address the poverty from which food insecurity stems or the transnational inequalities that impel people to migrate in the first place.

My goal throughout this chapter has been to highlight stories that reveal the complex ways that structural violence unfolds and is resisted in everyday life. In this chapter, I have also followed Renato Rosaldo's call for social scientists to resist reproducing dominant ideologies by anchoring "...their studies in the aspirations and perceptions of people who occupy subordinate social positions" (1997, 38). Through discussing the agency that these women exhibit over what and how their families eat, I have drawn attention to manifestations of individual and collective resistance that have the potential to transform the current food system and how people are fed. At the same time, through exposing the ways that agency and resistance are constrained, I have rendered visible the contradictions inherent to the market, the state, and civil society as mechanisms of regulation and control that dramatically impact the lives of Latino/a immigrants. My efforts underscore the relevance and need for applied ethnographic methodologies that draw upon stories, narratives, practices, and discourses to elucidate the inequalities and brutalities that follow immigrants to multiple points throughout the United States and the creative ways that these inequalities and brutalities are reworked, resisted, and reshaped.

Notes

1. These critiques and sustainable practices echo what Larissa Lomnitz found through her work on the ecologically sound livelihoods and footprints of Mexican shantytown dwellers. See Lomnitz 1977.

2. In a 2010 blog entry on the Environmental and Food Justice Blog, Arellano describes the shared practices of *convide, repartimiento* (water sharing), and cooperative labor that strengthen bonds among his fellow *acequia* farmers in New Mexico. Arellano describes how through an ethics of *convide, acequia* farming families historically rarely

went hungry. He notes that this practice has been embraced within Slow Food's use of the related term, *convivium*. The use of *convide* also parallels Ivan Illich's thoughts in his 1973 book *Tools for Conviviality*.

Bibliography

Alvarez, Robert R. 1987. "The Foundations and Genesis of a Mexican-American Community: A Sociohistorical Perspective." In *Cities of the United States: Studies in Urban Anthropology*, edited by Leith Mullings, 176-197. New York: Columbia University Press.

Bourgois, Philippe. 1996. *In Search of Respect: Selling Crack in El Barrio*. Cambridge: Cambridge University Press.

Chavez, Leo R. 1991. *Shadowed Lives: Undocumented Immigrants in American Society*. New York: Harcourt Brace Jovanovich.

———. 1994. "The Power of the Imagined Community: The Settlement of Undocumented Mexicans and Central Americans in the United States." *American Anthropologist* 96, no. 1: 52-73.

Coleman-Jensen, Alisha, Mark Nord, Margaret Andrews, and Steven Carlson. 2012. *Household Food Security in the United States in 2011*. U.S. Department of Agriculture: Economic Research Service.

Counihan, Carole. 2009. *A Tortilla is Like Life: Food and Culture in the San Luis Valley of Colorado*. Austin: University of Texas Press.

Del Castillo, and R. Adelaida. 2007. "Illegal Status and Social Citizenship: Thoughts on Mexican Immigrants in a Postnational World." In *Women and Migration in the U.S. Mexico Borderlands*, edited by Denise A. Segura and Patricia Zavella, 93-105. Durham: Duke University Press.

Farmer, Paul. 2005. *Pathologies of Power: Health, Human Rights, and the New War on the Poor*. Berkeley: University of California Press.

Flores, William V., and Rina Benmayor. 1997. "Constructing Cultural Citizenship." In *Latino Cultural Citizenship: Claiming Identity, Space, and Rights*, edited by William V. Flores and Rina Benmayor, 1-23. Boston: Beacon Press.

Hesse-Biber, Sharlene Nagy, Patricia Leavy, and Michelle L. Yaiser. 2004. "Feminist Approaches to Research as a Process: Reconceptualizing Epistemology, Methodology, and Method." In *Feminist Perspectives on Social Research*, edited by Sharlene Nagy Hesse-Biber and Michelle L. Yaiser, 3-26. New York: Oxford University Press.

Hondagneu-Sotelo, Pierrette. 1994. *Gendered Transitions: Mexican Experiences of Immigration*. Berkeley: University of California Press.

Lamphere, Louise. 1992. "Introduction: The Shaping of Diversity." In *Structuring Diversity: Ethnographic Perspectives on the New Immigration*, edited by Louise Lamphere, 1-34. Chicago: University of Chicago Press.

Lewis, Oscar. 1966. *La Vida: A Puerto Rican Family in the Culture of Poverty, San Juan and New York*. New York: Random House.

Lomnitz, Larissa Adler. 1977. *Networks and Marginality: Life in a Mexican Shantytown*. Translated by Cinna Lomnitz. New York: Academic Press.

Mahler, Sarah J. 1995. *American Dreaming: Immigrant Life on the Margins*. Princeton: Princeton University Press.

Mares, Teresa. 2012. "Tracing Immigrant Identity Through the Plate and the Palate." *Latino Studies* 10, no. 3: 334-354.

————. 2013. "'Here We Have the Food Bank': Latino/a Immigration and the Contradictions of Emergency Food." *Food and Foodways* 21, no. 1: 1-21.

Massey, Douglas S., Rafael Alarcón, Jorge Durand, and Humberto González. 1987. *Return to Aztlan: The Social Process of International Migration from Western Mexico.* Berkeley: University of California Press.

————, and Kristin E. Espinosa. 1997. "What's Driving Mexico-U.S. Migration? A Theoretical, Empirical, and Policy Analysis." *The American Journal of Sociology* 102, no. 4: 939-999.

Olesen, Virginia. 2005. "Feminisms and Qualitative Research at and into the Millennium." In *Handbook of Qualitative Research,* edited by Norman Denzin and Yvonna Lincoln, 215-253. Thousand Oaks, CA: Sage.

Ong, Aiwha. 1996. "Cultural Citizenship as Subject-Making: Immigrants Negotiate Racial and Cultural Boundaries in the United States." *Current Anthropology* 37, no. 5: 737-762.

Park, Robert. 1928. "Human Migration and the Marginal Man." *American Journal of Sociology* 33, no. 6: 881-893.

Passel, Jeffrey, D'Vera Cohn, and Ana Gonzalez-Barrera. 2012. "Net Migration from Mexico Falls to Zero—and Perhaps Less." Pew Research Hispanic Center. http://www.pewhispanic.org/2012/04/23/net-migration-from-mexico-falls-to-zero-and-perhaps-less (Accessed July 1, 2013).

Peña, Devon G. 1997. *The Terror of the Machine: Technology, Work, Gender and Ecology on the U.S.- Mexico Border.* Austin: Center for Mexican American Studies.

Perlman, Janice E. 1976. *The Myth of Marginality: Urban Poverty and Politics in Rio de Janeiro.* Berkeley: University of California Press.

Pessar, Patricia R. 1999. "The Role of Gender, Households, and Social Networks in the Migration Process: A Review and Appraisal." In *Handbook of International Migration: The American Experience,* edited by C. Hirschman, P. Kasinitiz and J. DeWind, 53-70. New York: Russell Sage Foundation.

Rosaldo, Renato. 1997. "Cultural Citizenship, Inequality, and Multiculturalism." In *Latino Cultural Citizenship: Claiming Identity, Space, and Rights,* edited by William V. Flores and Rina Benmayor, 27-38. Boston: Beacon Press.

————, and William V. Flores. 1997. "Identity, Conflict, and Evolving Latino Communities: Cultural Citizenship in San Jose, California." In *Latino Cultural Citizenship: Claiming Identity, Space, and Rights,* edited by William V. Flores and Rina Benmayor, 57-96. Boston: Beacon Press.

Rouse, Roger. 1991. "Mexican Migration and the Social Space of Postmodernism." *Diaspora* 1, no. 1: 8-23.

————. 1992. "Making Sense of Settlement: Class Transformation, Cultural Struggle, and Transnationalism among Mexican Migrants in the United States." In *Towards a Transnational Perspective on Migration: Race, Class, Ethnicity and Nationalism Reconsidered,* edited by Nina Glick Schiller, Linda Basch and Cristina Blanc-Szanton, 24-52. New York: New York Academy of Sciences.

Scheper-Hughes, Nancy. 1992. *Death Without Weeping: The Violence of Everyday Life in Brazil.* Berkeley: University of California Press.

Sharff, Jagna Wojcicka. 1998. *King Kong on 4th Street: Families and the Violence of Poverty on the Lower East Side.* Boulder: Westview Press.

Tsing, Anna Lowenhaupt. 1993. *In the Realm of the Diamond Queen: Marginality in an Out-of-the-Way Place*. Princeton: Princeton University Press.
————. 1994. "From the Margins." *Cultural Anthropology* 9, no. 3: 279-297.

CHAPTER 2

Women, Welfare, and Food Insecurity

Maggie Dickinson

Introduction

During the 2012 presidential campaign when Republican Candidate Mitt Romney commented that he is not worried about the very poor because there is a safety net to take care of them, he was giving voice to a widely held belief. The growth in the Food Stamp rolls, with one in seven Americans now receiving SNAP benefits, has created a sense that, at least in terms of hunger, we are doing a good job, even in the face of a severe economic downturn.[1] Popular media accounts portray either a Food Stamp program that is working as it should or one that is working too well, providing too much comfort to those down on their luck. What neither of these accounts pay much attention to are the ways in which changes to the Food Stamp program as part of the welfare reforms enacted in 1996 exacerbate food insecurity for some Americans, creating significant inequalities in who is able to access benefits. Drawing on 18 months of field research in Brooklyn, this chapter looks at the ways in which welfare reform has shaped the experience of food insecurity for women in need of cash assistance whose access to Food Stamp benefits has been severely disrupted by welfare reform policies.

Adwa and her sons were regular fixtures at the soup kitchen where I volunteered for a year and a half. She was a slight, black woman who had immigrated to the U.S. from Gabon fifteen years earlier. She had a bright smile and her sons, who were ages 7 and 9, were always quiet and well behaved. We had exchanged brief hellos as I dished out whatever was on the menu, but we never really interacted until she came to see me one Monday afternoon. I had set up regular hours for Food Stamp outreach, where people could come by and fill out applications or get help with their Food Stamp cases. It was a rainy afternoon and Adwa took her time taking off her wet coat and shaking the water off her bag before extracting a sheaf of papers from the welfare office neatly held together with a rubber band. The most recent notification informed Adwa that her case was being moved from the welfare office near her house in Brooklyn to one far out in Queens, to a neighborhood she had never been to before and was unfamiliar with. She hoped I could intervene and find out why they were moving her case and if it could be moved back.

I was part of a program that allowed people in community-based organizations to email directly with Food Stamp offices about issues that came up with clients' cases. The goal was to resolve these issues over email so that clients would not go to the Food Stamp offices, which were severely overcrowded. New York City's welfare administration (HRA) had been criticized in the press and by City Council for over-crowding issues and keeping clients out of the centers had become a top priority. I had sent a dozen or so of these emails for various problems with Food Stamp cases and had resolved a host of small issues for food pantry clients. However, when I emailed about Adwa's case, I got a stony reply that boiled down to, *"There's nothing we can do because this is a cash assistance case."*

A simple administrative error had moved her case to the wrong center, but moving it back was no simple task. Like many of the cash assistance cases I saw, a mix of administrative errors and oversights, strict work requirements and an unresponsive welfare office meant that women like Adwa, who had applied for cash assistance were continually at risk of losing their benefits—including their Food Stamp benefits. While significant efforts have been made to make applying for and receiving Food Stamp benefits easier, both in New York City and nationally, these efforts do not extend to women who are also applying for or receiving cash assistance. These women are under the constant threat of being cut off from Food Stamp benefits for any number of errors or infractions, with serious implications for their families' food security.

A Legal History of
Food Stamps and Welfare Reform

Prior to 1996, cash assistance (AFDC and later TANF) and the Food Stamp program (now called SNAP) had fairly distinct policy histories, with the AFDC program being codified into a national entitlement program during the New Deal, and Food Stamps only becoming a federal entitlement program in the early 1970's. These programs were often lumped together as "welfare programs" both in common parlance and in mainstream discourse, but this was largely due to the fact that they were both administered out of the same welfare offices by personnel trained to enroll people in both programs simultaneously.

In the political battle over welfare reform in the mid-1990s there were concerted efforts to overhaul Food Stamps along with the AFDC program, by making it a block grant program, something the Clinton administration opposed. Clinton vetoed the final bill several times over this provision. In the final version of PRWORA, Food Stamps retained the status of a federal entitlement, meaning there would be no cap on the funding for this program and that it would continue to be available to all qualifying citizens. This entitlement structure is what has enabled the Food Stamp program to expand so rapidly to meet rising need since the onset of the economic crisis in 2007, though the program had grown substantially even before the crisis hit. AFDC, which had been structured as a federal entitlement prior to 1996 was restructured as a block grant, capping the funds available for this program and limiting the number of eligible families that could be served. Families that did apply for and receive cash assistance would be required to search for paid employment and to perform "workfare" assignments in exchange for these benefits.

Even after the passage of PRWORA, there was considerable political wrangling over how to actually implement the new law. Provisions requiring single mothers to perform workfare assignments as a condition of receiving cash assistance raised a host of questions about these women's labor rights. How would they be paid? Would they be covered by minimum wage laws? Could they unionize? What would happen if they were hurt on the job?

In an attempt to clarify workfare rules, the Clinton administration's labor department issued a ruling that workfare assignments were subject to wage and hour laws, meaning women had to be paid minimum wage for the hours they were required to work. This was far more radical than it might appear on the surface. Paying poor women minimum wage for their workfare assignments would create parity between these workfare jobs and jobs in the private sector. This had the potential to radically alter the relationship between welfare and the labor market, which has long been organized around the principle of less eligibility, meaning welfare benefits are set low enough to make "any job at any wage a preferable alternative" (Piven and Cloward 1993, xix).

In effect, paying women minimum wage would undermine the dramaturgical function of the welfare system in which welfare creates a class of people who are poorly treated and can act as a warning to everyone else about what would befall them if they refuse to work. Paying women minimum wage for their workfare assignments would put these work assignments on par with jobs in the private sector. As such, this labor department ruling had the potential to transform the TANF program from a stigmatized cash assistance program into a federal jobs program, providing minimum wage employment to unemployed families with children.

The Food Stamp program was the key to undermining the radical potential of Clinton's labor department ruling. It was not clear in 1996 that the push to "end welfare as we know it" would end with the passage of PRWORA. Republicans and fiscal conservatives have long had their eye on a whole host of federal welfare programs, including Food Stamps, Social Security, Medicaid and Medicare. Food Stamps, which had narrowly escaped a major overhaul, appeared to be the low hanging fruit for on-going welfare retrenchment efforts. In a defensive move, the USDA approved Simplified Food Stamp Programs shortly after the passage of welfare reform in order to bring Food Stamps in line with "work first welfare" (Super 2004). Simplified Food Stamp programs allowed Food Stamp benefits to be counted as wages for workfare assignments. They also gave states significant discretion in how to apply many of the rules for TANF work requirements to Food Stamp benefits for families who applied for cash assistance.

Allowing states to count Food Stamps as wages provided a loophole to the rule that women had to be paid minimum wage by allowing them to be paid the equivalent of minimum wage largely in in-kind benefits. Using Food Stamp benefits as wages preserved the principle of less eligibility for cash assistance. But this ruling also had another important impact on poor women and their children. By tying Food Stamp eligibility to TANF work rules, poor women's access to Food Stamp benefits became increasingly tenuous and conditional. As we will see, Adwa's struggles to maintain her Food Stamp benefits are the direct result of the new relationship between Food Stamps and cash assistance forged by the welfare reforms in 1996.

Feeding a Family and Failure to Comply

Adwa's struggle to keep her Food Stamp benefits started long before she came to see me that rainy Monday. She had applied for assistance two years before for herself and her two sons. Her husband had been in a car accident and was arrested for drunk driving and reckless endangerment. At the hospital, a social worker had recommended that they apply for public assistance, because her husband had been the family breadwinner and his incarceration would leave Adwa and her sons with no income. At first she was unsure, but the social worker explained the program and Adwa thought, *"okay that will help"*. But once she had enrolled, she quickly discovered that the policy and the practice were two different things. As she described it, *"Sometimes lies sound good. Lies are pretty. You take it. You don't know that they're lying to you."*

One of the primary innovations of welfare reform was the implementation of sanctions for failure to comply with new work rules. These sanction policies apply not only to cash assistance, but also to a client's Food Stamp benefits, since Food Stamps are considered part of the compensation for a client's required workfare assignment. These sanction policies have largely been determined by the states and the severity of these policies appears to be intricately tied to the racial composition of the population in each state. Scholar's have shown that state's with larger African American populations have consistently enacted more punitive welfare policies (Soss, Fording, and Schram 2011). States can also determine how to apply their sanction policies to the Food Stamp benefits of adults who fail to comply. Twelve states currently employ full-family sanctions, meaning all family members lose Food Stamp benefits if the adult on the case fails to comply with work rules or any other requirements. In New York State, partial sanctions are applied to the Food Stamp benefits, cutting off only the adult's portion of Food Stamp benefits. However, sanctions are longer in New York State than the minimum sanctions required by the USDA, cutting families off from part of their Food Stamp benefits for up to six months at a time.

In order to understand the impact of welfare reforms on poor women's food security, we have to unpack what "failure to comply" means. On the surface, it appears to mean following the rules. Women who apply for cash assistance and play by the rules won't have their benefits cut. But in reality, proving one's willingness to comply with work first welfare is easier said than done. Women who apply for cash assistance face an uphill battle to obtain and maintain benefits, particularly in New York City where diversionary tactics have long been the norm (Davis 2002).

After the passage of welfare reform, success was judged not on the number of children kept out of poverty (a number that has steadily worsened since 1996), but the number of people who were removed from the rolls. State-level welfare administrators competed with one another to remove as many families as possible. In New York City, where the welfare rolls had been quite high, the drop in eligible participants receiving welfare benefits has been dramatic. In March of 1995, cash assistance rolls in NYC hit their peak, at 1,160,593. By June 2010 they had fallen to 346,321. This massive reduction in the rolls was achieved through diversionary tactics, which kept people from applying in the first place and the implementation of one of the toughest workfare programs in the country, the Work Experience Program (WEP). WEP requires welfare recipients to work in one of three capacities in city agencies – sanitation, clerical or maintenance work. Clients are often required to participate in a job search program and work assignment for 45 days before they can receive any benefits. WEP workers are required to report for up to 35 hours of work in addition to a whole range of appointments and, often, an investigation in their home by welfare officials. This myriad of appointments and work assignments all carry the threat of sanctions for failure to comply.

Missing one appointment can result in being cut off or never receiving benefits in the first place. As Vickie Lens has found, sanctions, which are supposed to be imposed when a case worker determines that a client is no longer willing to comply with the work rules, has become a clerical function in New York City. The computer system used by case workers is set to automatically mark clients as having missed their scheduled appointments unless the case worker goes in and manually marks that the client attended. Case workers are under an incredible amount of pressure and errors and oversights are rampant (FPWA 2012). Sanctions are often applied in error and clients have to engage in long bureaucratic battles to have them lifted and to continue receiving benefits (McNeil 2011).

Being cut off from one's benefits for failure to comply creates significant food hardship for women and their children. Adwa had already been sanctioned off her welfare case when I met her. She had what was called a child only case. She had been assigned to a workfare assignment when she first applied for cash assistance. She had been receiving $353 in cash, $526 in Food Stamps and $400 in housing assistance each month. She was required to work 35 hours per week in a WEP assignment, meaning she was being paid $2.30 an hour in cash, with the rest of her compensation coming in in-kind benefits. If her rent allowance is counted in that hourly wage, then she was being paid $4.88 an hour. The rent allowance did not come close to covering her $1,200 a month rent, so she began sleeping in her sons' room and rented their second bedroom in order to make up the difference.

She was assigned to the parks department as well as to job search through the Back to Work Program. She found it impossible to balance taking care of her children and the demands of the welfare office.

They ask me to work for certain hours, certain days. You have to work on Sunday. You have to work on Saturday. And if you don't work on Saturday, they fire you. And then they create a situation where you, the recipient, will have a problem with ACS (child protective services) because you will get the children late from an afterschool program or, you know, day care. And this is very ugly. They create situations, ugly situations against you, the recipient, but for their benefit. They say oh, okay you're not doing what you're supposed to do. It's like they force you to do certain things that you don't want.

Welfare recipients in New York are offered very little choice about what kind of work assignment they are given. Though Adwa wanted to go to school and get an associate's degree, she was not offered any opportunity to count education for part of her work requirements. This is standard practice in New York State, where fewer than 14 percent of welfare recipients are allowed to count school towards their work participation, despite the fact that federal law allows for up to 30 percent of the case load to be engaged in educational activities (Dunlea 2009). Though Adwa was sanctioned off the case, she still had to regularly report to the welfare office to provide documentation of her situation to keep her son's benefits. She described her interactions with caseworkers as disorienting. "*Where is your pay tab? Where's your this? What are you doing with the time? What are you? What is this? What is this? You don't... They make you lost. They have you in their face-to-face hearing or in the office. They trap you with all kinds of questions. Sometimes I can't even respond properly.*"

Adwa's experience was common. Welfare rules are difficult to understand and caseworkers are under a tremendous amount of pressure to move people through the system as quickly as possible. I regularly accompanied people to the welfare office over the course of my fieldwork where we would sit in the waiting room for four or five hours before seeing a worker. The waiting rooms were always crowded and sometimes there would even be a line outside the building just to get in. As one front line worker who certifies cash assistance cases reported, *"we're doing quantity, not quality."* The interactions I observed in these offices were terse and difficult to follow. Workers rarely explained the situation in plain language, instead relying on codes and technical administrative language that was difficult to decipher. Welfare workers are focused on doing their job, which, according to one worker, means, *"You're pushing them through. You just get enough information to process and then keep them moving."*

The incredibly low benefits also contribute to a pervasive atmosphere of suspicion. Benefit levels are far lower than anyone could reasonably survive on in New York without additional help from family and friends, off the books employment, or living in the shelter system or on the street (Lein and Edin 1997). Women like Adwa, who still lived in her own apartment, are subject to intense scrutiny by welfare workers who are trying to ascertain how they make ends meet and if they can "move them to self-sufficiency," which in practice means cutting them off from benefits. As one front line employee told me, *"It's sad to say, the majority of them are lying. I know they are lying, but its not because they want to."* Clients are required to supply extensive documentation of their expenses, their income, reasons for their lack of income, work and housing history. Missing documents or insufficient documentation are reasons for denying aid. Additionally, clients are required to attend numerous appointments in addition to their work assignments. Missing even one of these can result in cases being sanctioned or cut off.

Eventually Adwa was sanctioned for failing to attend a mandatory job search appointment, which she was required to attend in addition to her WEP assignment, and her portion of the household benefits were cut. At the time I met her, her children were getting $153 in cash assistance, $325 in Food Stamps, and $141 in rent assistance each month. Adwa was attending school on her own and working cleaning homes off the books when she could find work.

Sanctions are intended to be the "sticks" that get welfare recipients to comply with work rules. Cutting the adult portion of the benefits was meant to motivate women like Adwa either to comply with her workfare assignment or to find a job. Cutting Food Stamp benefits in order to force compliance or labor market participation is a particularly cruel punishment for women with children. Adwa was one of the thriftiest and most inventive cooks I met over the course of my fieldwork. She was incredibly economical, preparing cheap, nutritious meals for herself and her two boys. But she had struggled to keep them fed when they had a full Food Stamp budget for a family of three. Once she was sanctioned and their Food Stamp budget dropped from $526 a month to $325, feeding them all became even more difficult.

Adwa attempted to make up the difference in a range of ways. One of them was to intensify her labor. This is a common response to food insecurity, though the particular strategies Adwa employed are specific to the urban U.S. context (Shipton 1990). Adwa, like many of the low and no-income New Yorkers I met over the course of my fieldwork, spent a considerable amount of time and energy on shopping and preparing food in order to make a tiny budget stretch. She travelled from Brooklyn to Harlem, an hour each way on the subway, to buy groceries.

> When I go to Harlem the food is less expensive. I don't know why they do that. But when I do go to Key Food or Associated (local grocery stores), the food is expensive. And I compare the same food with Harlem, I say oh they have three dollars more here. And over there it's affordable and the pack of rice or potatoes is affordable. I sacrificed the energy and the strength to go to Harlem and shop. I take my backpack and put food in my bag and bring it here. 325 I spent for Food Stamps. And when you shop here the money goes quickly and it's... Most people may think I'm using money for what? I'm buying expensive things. It's not true. It's the same chicken they eat. The same vegetables, the same rice, the same potatoes. And they say what happened? That cost you $1.99, $2.99. In Harlem, sometimes its $1.09. Or I go to Pathmark in downtown Brooklyn. I go shopping there too. It's, it's ugly. Because you have to travel so you will still have something in the food budget to reach the end of the month.

One of the difficulties of conducting research on hunger and food insecurity, particularly with women who have children, is determining the degree of food hardship they experience. I asked Adwa if she ever ran out of Food Stamps and cash at the end of the month and she laughed and replied "*of course!*" I asked her what they do when that happens and she told me that, "*If we don't have cash, we conserve food.*" But asking if this meant that they sometimes ate less than she felt they should or if they ever went hungry made her visibly uncomfortable. This was a common response, as other researchers studying hunger in the urban U.S. have confirmed. "Caregivers are often reluctant to admit that their children may not be getting enough food due to shame or due to the fear that their children might be removed from the home by authorities" (Chilton and Rabinowich 2012, 2). Tina Lee's research on the child welfare system in New York City confirms that this is a legitimate, and widely held, concern among low-income parents (Lee 2010).

Adwa may or may not have been able to cobble together sufficient food for herself and her two sons. What is clear, however, was that in order to do so she had to work incredibly hard, travelling to distant grocery stores, budgeting carefully, cooking large meals that could last two or three days in order to stretch the food she made, and eating at the food pantry—something she felt shame about, but about which she had little choice. We will return to the significance of being forced to rely on food pantries and soup kitchens below.

Adwa was a resourceful cook. The thrifty food plan on which Food Stamp allotments are based, presumes a level of knowledge and skill in shopping, food preparation and storage that is rare. These were skills Adwa had and her descriptions of the meals she cooked—lentils, rice, small amounts of meat and no processed foods—are identical to the kinds of foods one must prepare in order for a family's Food Stamp budget to meet all (or even nearly all) of their food needs. Growing up in West Africa, she was accustomed to cooking and eating this way and this cultural knowledge certainly aided her in her efforts to feed her family on a small budget. Her cultural background was most likely also an asset because, as Janet Fitchen points out, the poor in the U.S. follow many of the dominant American cultural practices, which may actually exacerbate malnourishment, specifically through the desire to eat like everyone else (Fitchen 1988). Adwa is, in many ways, a best-case scenario in terms of eating habits and food knowledge. Even so, her food knowledge and cooking skill would not be enough to make a small Food Stamp budget for a family of two stretch to feed a family of three.

In addition to travelling to cheaper grocery stores, budgeting and preparing food carefully, Adwa also pursued paid employment. She had gotten a job as a cashier, making the minimum wage of $7.25 an hour, but they would only give her twenty hours a week. The schedule did not work for her and the pay did not even come close to covering her expenses. Instead she looked for work cleaning houses, which might pay slightly more than the minimum and give her a bit more control over her schedule.

There is a growing emphasis, heavily influenced by social scientists studying the various outcomes of welfare reforms, on the importance of mothers working in the labor force to improve outcomes for their children (Chase-Lansdale et al. 2003). Mothering has long been stratified in the U.S., with some women being valued as mothers and others prevented from caring for their children as they would like (Mullings 1997; Colen 1995). African-American mothers in particular have long struggled for the right to care for their own children. The emphasis on work-first welfare redefines good mothering as working for wages to provide monetarily for children and, in so doing, providing them with a "good role model."

Adwa rejected this definition of good mothering. She saw her role as supervisor and caretaker as crucial responsibilities that neither the low wage jobs that were available to her or the welfare office were willing to accommodate. *"Those jobs, for example, I told you about – the cashier job – is a bad schedule. The manager doesn't care if you have children, if you go to school. They don't care. What they need is, what they care about is that you provide the service they want from you."*

The week before, Adwa's older son had had an asthma attack and spent three days in the hospital. He needed to take medication every four hours for several days after coming home. This was a chronic problem for Adwa.

This week was a bad week. David was ill. I had to put work aside and school aside. And I have to be in the hospital encouraging him because I think encouraging lifts him up. So my presence counts for a lot when he is ill and in hospital. So I have to be there. That's this week. And today I started to come back slowly by doing one of my school projects, working on this and giving David encouragement that despite being ill I want you to study. And he has his medication, because the doctor said I needed to still supervise him, because if he neglects it he's going to get sick and go back to the hospital. Every four hours. I have to count the hours I don't want him to miss. They don't care if your child is sick. If I was employed when he was three days in the hospital, they will fire me.

Her role as a mother, with all the duties that entailed, came into direct conflict with the demands of welfare and low-wage work.

They need to accommodate their schedule as well as, they need to know that, ok, we need you. And you need us. We need to work on the schedule. They need to be flexible to both of them. Because cashier job, they don't care. You have to work on Sunday. You have to work on Saturday. They don't care if you supervise—look, I'm supervising them (points to the children). If I am at work, and leave them they will not do what they are doing.

She gestures to the two boys who were sitting at a small kitchen table, working on homework. "*So you see? That is because, I have to work. The manager will not care that I need to supervise the children. They don't care.*"

Food aid is used by the welfare agencies to coerce women like Adwa into accepting this role as a "good mother" who models good behavior for her sons by going to work, earning wages, and submitting to the needs of her employer. The goal of welfare after the passage of welfare reform is to move women like Adwa into the labor force—to take any job at all at any wages. Sanctioning women who resist this idea of the "good mother" and cutting off their Food Stamp benefits purposefully creates hardship for these families to induce them into adopting the "correct" behavior. It is reflected in the inordinate pressures put on women who enroll in cash welfare programs to become 'job ready' at the same time that jobs in the U.S. are far from being "mother ready." Jobs at the low end of the wage spectrum are far less likely to provide regular hours and scheduling that can help parents to arrange schedules and childcare. The use of food aid to push women into the workplace is especially troubling in the broader context of a deeply depressed labor market, where one in four jobs is now considered low-wage (NELP 2012).

Given the rigid schedules imposed on women by both the welfare office and low-wage employers, Adwa looked to the informal labor market as an alternative to bring in some cash and make up the difference between the aid she received for her sons and the needs of the household. She had been working for a man, cleaning his Manhattan home and office for 15 dollars an hour.

> You have to clean somebody toilet bowl. It's not funny. But the guy says oh no ay ay ay it's too much money. And I say, oh God. You have a company. It's producing. I'm here you're maid, cleaning all your mess. And you feel bad about that. You don't want to clean it so you have some body to clean. And you say oh you are paying me too much! And then he lopped down my salary, my days. Maybe he hires a Spanish (maid), paying her maybe nine dollars or ten dollars for all of this mess. That's not fair to me.

Though this off the books work was better paid with more flexible hours, it was highly unstable and unreliable.

At the same time, the imperative for women to give birth—to engage in social reproduction—was also deeply felt.

> If you don't give birth they say oh what happened? You are young, you are healthy why don't you give birth? What happened? Go to fertilization. Have children. And when you have them, they cause you problems. Oh why do you have children? You want to depend on PA (public assistance). You want to depend on this service, you want to depend... You say to me that I'm healthy. I'm able to give birth. And if you don't have this you go to in vitro or, I don't know. We need a population, so why are you blaming me when I have them.

At an intuitive level, what Adwa is describing is the tension between demands on women to reproduce a population that can continue to work and consume, a necessity for future profit making, and the demands that they sell their labor on the market today, in order to contribute to profit making right now. Her desire to invest in her children, in their education and their health, is minimized in the contemporary urban political economy. Welfare, as a secondary institution that operates to regulate the labor force, is designed to move poor women as quickly as possible into paid labor and food aid is used as both a punishment and an incentive to induce them to prioritize the needs of current employers over the immediate or long-term needs of their children. The contradictions that Adwa found herself grappling with are part of the broader restructuring of the U.S. economy in which, "reproductive activities have been reorganized as value-producing services that workers must purchase and pay for. In this way, the value that reproductive activities produce is immediately realized, rather than being made conditional on the performance of the workers that they reproduce" (Federici 2012). The stark contradictions that poor women and women of color have long felt, between their role as mothers who are responsible for taking care of their children and their role as workers have been intensified by welfare reforms that prioritize immediate labor force attachment and further devalue non-commodified forms of care-taking. These welfare reforms have impacted the Food Stamp program so that food aid has become a novel policy tool being used to enforce these new norms around work, motherhood and caring labor.

It is important to note that Food Stamps operate very differently for women who do engage in low-wage labor, operating as a supplement to wages—not as wages for workfare assignments. Food aid is frequently withheld as a punishment for unemployed women who turn to cash assistance and an incentive for those who engage in low-wage labor. This is the legacy of welfare reforms and their impact on the Food Stamp program, which has been significantly restructured away from its original purpose – preventing hunger and malnutrition in the U.S. Today the Food Stamp program fully embodies neoliberal urban poverty governance, by acting as both a punishment and an incentive with the ultimate goal of creating "compliant and competent worker-citizens" (Soss, Fording, and Schram 2011, 9). Women, like Adwa, who resist the idea that good mothering means being a good worker, are punished with a reduction in food aid and are forced to make up the difference through intensifying their labor or turning to charity.

From Entitlement to Charity

Despite her best efforts, Adwa could not feed her family with the Food Stamps she received for her children and the money she earned cleaning homes. She could not reconcile her sense of self as a mother and the needs of her children with the demands of the welfare office on the one hand and the low wage labor market on the other. Her punishment, being sanctioned off Food Stamps, pushed her into regular reliance on soup kitchens and food pantries to meet her family's needs for food. This was a common experience among women I met who either did not have access to Food Stamp benefits because they had been sanctioned or because they were immigrants who did not qualify for benefits in the first place. Sanctions that were designed to punish women for resisting work rules and ideas about what constitutes a good mother typically forced these women into increased reliance on emergency food providers. Heavy reliance on emergency food further undercut these women's abilities to mother as they saw fit.

In her classic article on women and the right to food, Penny Van Esterik makes a distinction between the right to food and the right to be fed. Like many anthropologists, she insists that our understanding of hunger must encompass both the metabolic need for food and the social and cultural roles food and eating play in our everyday lives. This is particularly important for women, given that, "in many parts of the world, women's sense of self is based on her ability and her right to feed her family" (Van Esterik 1999, 228). The right to feed one's family goes beyond the right to provide them with enough calories and encompasses ideas of what is culturally appropriate and acceptable.

Emergency food providers, like food pantries and soup kitchens, operate on a food security approach, providing needed food to hungry Americans, but in ways that undercut basic ideas of cultural appropriateness. One of the primary ways emergency food providers do this is to undercut women's control over what they feed their families. The other is to provide food in a way that is socially stigmatized—as charity.

In the urban U.S., food is primarily purchased on the market, either with cash or with Food Stamps. Food Stamps have become far less stigmatized now that they are disbursed on electronic benefit cards that are virtually indistinguishable from credit and debit cards. Buying food in the grocery store allows women to buy the foods they and their families prefer, as well as what they think is healthy and appropriate.

Emergency food providers receive food either as surplus from the USDA or from food processors when a product fails to find a market or is damaged or unsalable for some reason. I volunteered in a pantry regularly for eighteen months. The foods we gave out were often a strange mix and complaints about the food were frequent and persistent. There were weeks when we had a decent mix of rice or pasta, chicken, some fresh or canned vegetables, peanut butter and bread. But these weeks were rare. Other times we would have old Easter candy, cans of fruit, some juice and crackers or some other awkward selection of random foods.

Katherine, a regular volunteer at the pantry described her dissatisfaction with the food we would hand out.

I think we should make the bags more nourishing. Give them something that they can make. I want to take all that candy and dump it in the garbage. It's nothing but sugar. I mean we had like 30 boxes of candy. We could have had tuna, peanut butter and jelly. That's nourishing. They need nourishing foods. Like the fresh carrots, string beans, a piece of meat. Just one balanced diet.

Pantry directors also complained about the lack of choice and, often, the lack of any food at all. There were several weeks in the summer of 2011 where the only thing the Food Bank had to order was canned corn. We handed out bags with nothing but corn in them and closed early when that ran out. Much of the food that emergency food providers hand out comes from TEFAP, which is the federal funding that is used to buy surplus commodities that are then distributed to emergency food providers through the regional food banks. A large portion of TEFAP funding is used to support farmers by buying up surplus commodities when they over-produce. These price supports primarily benefit large, industrial farms that produce one or two commodities. That year, however, commodity prices were high and so the USDA did not purchase additional food. Many of the families who come to the North Brooklyn Food Pantry, like Adwa's, rely on this food to make ends meet. When these resources are spotty, scarce or non-existent as they were that summer, families with very little to begin with are left with even less.

Even when there is food to be had, clients have very little choice over what they get. People like Adwa take the food because they need it, but it is often food that they would not choose and which does not contribute to the long-term health and well-being of families. The more reliant mothers are on emergency food, the less control they are able to exercise over what their families can eat. In cutting Adwa's Food Stamp benefits, the welfare office was cutting her ability to feed her children in ways she felt were appropriate.

However, the lack of choice is perhaps secondary to the social stigma of accepting charity. This was something Adwa felt particularly uncomfortable with. *"For me it's a shame, asking somebody to give you food."* Though Adwa felt that applying for public assistance was humiliating, going to the grocery store to buy food once she had benefits was fine. Getting food from food pantries and soup kitchens, on the other hand, means *"asking somebody to give you food every time you go to eat or to shop."*

Emergency food providers are premised on the idea of the gift. Food is given to help the needy with the presumption that this gift cannot or should not be reciprocated. As anthropologists have long been aware, reciprocity plays a crucial role in structuring social relations. Accepting help in the form of food that cannot be repaid is unsettling. Adwa used several strategies to deal with this uneven, stigmatized power relationship. She made efforts to involve herself in the pantry, befriending the pastor and several of the volunteers. She also received help from another pantry at the church she attended every Sunday. She explained that this was not charity, but part of the reciprocal relationship grounded in a religious community. For her, building these personal relationships helped minimize the stigma of relying on charitable food. She emphasized her personal relationships as the primary reason for going to these churches and described the food as secondary.

As the Food Stamp program has become more conditional and contingent on women's participation in the labor market, the emergency food system has come to fill in the gaps in people's food needs. But emergency food providers further undercut women's citizenship rights. Instead of being able to exercise control and make decisions about how and what to feed their families, they increasingly are forced to rely on emergency food providers that operate on the right to be fed—the right to have one's bodily needs met, but not the right to exert agency over how that is accomplished.

This is largely because the food that comes to these institutions is surplus food—whether it is commodity food purchased as a price support by the USDA, donations from manufacturers who fail to find a market for their product, or individual's who donate what they do not need or want from their own kitchens. The haphazard selection of foods at many food pantries is the direct result of where this food comes from. The food given out by emergency food providers, as Janet Fitchen says, "are not exactly scraps from the tables of the affluent, but they are clearly the left overs from the food production industry" (Fitchen 1988, 398).

Reliance on these sources of food are structured by welfare policy. Families and individuals who receive Food Stamps and public assistance regularly supplement these benefits with food from pantries and soup kitchens. Families whose Food Stamps run out at the end of the month will come to get a bag of food to make up the difference. But sanctioned families, like Adwa's, or families who have difficulties in opening a public assistance case at all depend much more heavily on these resources. Instead of making up for a shortfall at the end of the month, Adwa relied on emergency food to make up for a full third of her families food budget. She never missed a week at the soup kitchen. It was often possible to guess the status of people's Food Stamp cases by whether or not I saw them at the pantry or the soup kitchen each week, and Adwa was no exception. Several months after our last interview, she won a settlement with her landlord from a dispute that had been going on for several years. She was awarded $60,000 dollars and immediately stopped coming to the soup kitchen and food pantry.

If we take the right to food seriously as a substantive right of citizenship, then the restructuring of the Food Stamp program in the wake of welfare reform must be seen as a form of disenfranchisement for poor women and their children. The shift from food aid as an entitlement to a conditional food aid system that relegates those who cannot meet these conditions to rely on charity, erodes poor women's citizenship rights—their right to feed and to be fed (Van Esterik 1999).

Conclusion

Anthropologists have argued that hunger is a metabolic phenomenon with absolute dimensions, but one that is shaped by social and cultural norms and expectations (Mintz 1996; Fitchen 1988; Scheper-Hughes 1992; Shack 1997). Hunger, and the response to hunger, is never simply an issue of adequate food because food and food practices are so deeply rooted in transactional relationships between individuals. Food is inherently social and it both constitutes and shapes social relationships.

The Food Stamp program in the U.S. was institutionalized as a national entitlement in the early 1970s in response to the "discovery" of hunger in America. This discovery shocked Americans and the political response was surprisingly swift and dramatic. At the time, the Food Stamp program was considered a response to hunger, which, as Senator George McGovern articulated at the time, "profoundly disturbs the American conscience" (Poppendieck 1998, 11). Evidence of clinical malnutrition was key in prompting swift political action to do something about the hunger problem and the actions taken proved effective. But, as Harvey Levenstein demonstrates, the hunger problem faded from national prominence almost as quickly as it had become a national issue (Levenstein 1993).

Since the mid-1970s, both the Food Stamp program and cash assistance for mothers and their children have been subject to criticisms that they are too generous. The over-riding political concerns have been dependency, fraud and abuse. At the same time, economic restructuring in the U.S., with the loss of a manufacturing base, the rise of finance capitalism and the growth of the low-wage service sector, have increased the ranks of the American poor and their hardships. In this context, hunger became a prominent national concern again in the early 1980's, but the response was far different than it had been in a decade earlier (Dehavenon 1985; Nestle and Guttmacher 1992). Instead of expanding federal entitlements, policy makers passed legislation establishing the Temporary Emergency Food Assistance Program (TEFAP), laying the groundwork for a massive expansion of the charitable emergency food system in the U.S. (Poppendieck 1998).

Though Food Stamps have enjoyed something of a renaissance since the passage of welfare reform in 1996, with steadily increasing rolls and widespread political support, this program does not benefit all families in need evenly. As we have seen, mothers who apply for cash assistance are disproportionately impacted by changes to the Food Stamp program that allow these benefits to be counted as wages for workfare assignments. These changes put the very poorest families at the greatest risk of hunger and food insecurity. Reliance on emergency food providers, whose ability to distribute food is still tied to farm price supports and corporate largesse, is an unstable, unreliable method for addressing hunger and food insecurity.

It is hard for people to imagine hunger in the U.S. precisely because there is no shortage of food here. We produce far more than we can consume and waste a considerable amount of food as well. Understanding hunger in the U.S. requires a more nuanced view of the problem, one that can account for differential access to food. Though food is abundant in the U.S., individual households still experience food shortages because they lack the financial resources to purchase food. Anthropological approaches that examine every day eating practices help us to distinguish between hunger caused by regional food shortages and food poverty – which means a food shortage at the household level. Food poverty is a much more useful term for understanding hunger in the U.S. and, as we have seen in Adwa's case, welfare reforms directly contribute to food poverty at the household level.

Understanding how Food Stamp and welfare policy work together in the U.S. to create situations of food poverty for some households—primarily households of women and children who apply for cash assistance—helps clarify a policy agenda for more effectively addressing hunger in the U.S. It is clear from this discussion that separating Food Stamp policy from TANF work rules should be a priority for both welfare rights activists and anti-hunger activists.

There is a vast network of anti-hunger advocates in the U.S. who work tirelessly on issues of hunger and food insecurity. The growth of emergency food providers has in some ways given this anti-hunger network shape and form as well as a broad popular base of citizens who are engaged in anti-hunger work and can be (and quite frequently are) mobilized to oppose spending cuts to SNAP and cuts to funding for emergency food providers. This network has been successful in preventing any serious cuts to food aid programs in the U.S. Even so, preserving the current programs has done little to actually decrease the number of people in the U.S. who struggle with hunger and food insecurity.

At the same time, anti-hunger advocates almost never raise issues related to TANF or work rules, even though these issues contribute directly to food poverty at the household level and put enormous pressure on emergency food providers who are left to make up the difference when a family is sanctioned and loses part of their Food Stamp benefits. Advocates who work on hunger are wary of raising work requirements as an issue. As one advocate told me, "we don't do very well on the work thing."

Taking up the issue of using SNAP benefits as compensation for workfare assignments has enormous potential for improving food security outcomes for poor women and their families. Food Stamps have become, through a twist of political fate, the key to maintaining TANF as a highly stigmatized welfare program by keeping the compensation for workfare work well below the minimum wage. Minimum wage workers are eligible for Food Stamp benefits that supplement their low wages, while women who apply for cash assistance and are forced to perform workfare work are made to labor for these same benefits.

Anti-hunger activists are not likely to take up this issue, but doing so could be a powerful way to address household food poverty that is caused by work-first welfare reforms. Most proposals for expanding the SNAP program have come in the form of increased benefit levels across the board. But addressing the historical legacy of welfare reform on the Food Stamp program has the potential for much more far reaching effects.

Reversing the legacy of welfare reform on the Food Stamp program has the potential to reformulate TANF as a jobs program. Historically, AFDC and TANF have been programs that isolate poor single mothers politically, making them easy targets for welfare retrenchment (Gordon 1994). Programs serving broad, politically enfranchised groups, like social security, have been able to withstand calls for austerity, retrenchment and privatization much more effectively. Paying workfare workers a real minimum wage would unite the concerns of the so-called working poor and the unemployed, undermining the fairly arbitrary distinctions between them. It changes the terrain of struggle, so that fighting for an increase in the minimum wage becomes a fight that low-wage workers and welfare workers can fight together.

Though anti-hunger advocates are wary of challenging the dominant political narrative around the "success" of work-first welfare reform, women like Adwa, who are attempting to feed families in the face of falling wages, restricted welfare benefits and punitive work-first welfare policies, are not. Grassroots, membership-based community organizations, like Community Voices Heard and Neighbors Together, made up of current and former welfare recipients and food pantry clients, actively organize around demands to end workfare and WEP in New York City. These demands and tactics resonate with women like Adwa. When I asked her what she thought might make the welfare office and low wage employers more responsive to the needs of mothers like herself, she quickly replied, "*We need protest.*"

Notes

1. The federal Food Stamp program was re-named the Supplemental Nutrition Assistance Program (SNAP) in 2008. At the time of this research, New York State still referred to the program as Food Stamps. I primarily use the term Food Stamps because my research takes place in New York and that is how all of my informants referred to the program, but the names are interchangeable.

Bibliography

Chase-Lansdale, P., Robert A. Moffitt, Brenda Lohman, Andrew Cherlin, Rebekah Levine Coley, Laura Pittman, Jennifer Roff, and Elizabeth Votruba-Drzal. 2003. "Mothers' Transitions from Welfare to Work and the Well-Being of Preschoolers and Adolescents." *Science* no. 299 (March 7, 2003): 1548-1552.
Chilton, Mariana, and Jenny Rabinowich. 2012. "Toxic Stress and Child Hunger Over the Life Course: Three Case Studies." *Journal of Applied Research on Children: Informing Policy for Children at Risk* no. 3 (1).
Colen, Shellee. 1995. "Like a Mother to Them: Stratified Reproduction and West Indian Childcare Workers and Employers in New York." In *Conceiving the New World Order: The Global Politics of Reproduction*, edited by Faye D Ginsburg and Rayna Rapp. Berkeley: University of California Press.
Davis, Dana Ain et. al. 2002. "The Impact of Welfare Reform on Two Communities in New York City." In *The Devolution Initiative*, edited by Scholar Practitioner Program: W. K. Kellogg Foundation.
Dehavenon, Anna Lou. 1985. *The Tyranny of Indifference and Reinstitutionalization of Hunger, Homelessness and the Poor*: Unknown Binding.
Dunlea, Mark. 2009. Evaluating a Decade of Welfare Reform in New York State. New York: Hunger Action Network.
Federici, Sylvia. 2012. "The Reproduction of Labor Power in the Global Economy and the Unfinished Feminist Revolution." In *Revolution at Point Zero: Housework, Reproduction and Feminist Struggle*, edited by Sylvia Federici. Brooklyn, NY: Common Notions.

Fitchen, J.M. 1988. "Hunger, Malnutrition and Poverty in the Contemporary United States: Some Observations on their Social and Cultural Context." *Food and Foodways* no. 2: 309-333.

FPWA. 2012. Guilty Until Proven Innocent: Sanctions, Agency Error, and Financial Punishment within New York State's Welfare System. New York, NY: Federation of Protestant Welfare Agencies.

Gordon, Linda. 1994. *Pitied but not Entitled: Single Mothers and the History of Welfare.* New York: Free Press.

Lee, Tina. 2010. *Stratified Reproduction and Definitions of Child Neglect: State Practices and Parents' Responses.* Anthropology, CUNY, New York.

Lein, Laura, and Kathryn Edin. 1997. *Making Ends Meet: How Single Mothers Survive Welfare and Low-Wage Work.* New York: Russell Sage Foundation.

Levenstein, Harvey. 1993. *Paradox of Plenty: A Social History of Eating in Modern America.* New York: Oxford University Press.

McNeil, Lori. 2011. Case Closed: An Examination of Exclusion in New York City's Public Assistance Programs. New York, NY: Homelessness Outreach and Prevention Project at Urban Justice Center.

Mintz, Sidney Wilfred. 1996. *Tasting Food, Tasting Freedom: Excursions into Eating, Culture, and the Past.* Boston: Beacon Press.

Mullings, Leith. 1997. "Uneven Development: Class, Race and Gender in the United States Before 1900." In *On Our Own Terms: Race, Class and Gender in the Lives of African American Women,* edited by Leith Mullings. New York: Routledge.

NELP. 2012. The Low-Wage Recovery and Growing Inequality. edited by National Employment Law Project. New York: National Employment Law Project.

Nestle, Marion, and Sally Guttmacher. 1992. "Hunger in the United States: Rationale, Methods and Policy Implications of State Hunger Surveys." *Journal of Nutrition Education* no. 24 (1).

Piven, Frances Fox, and Richard Cloward. 1993. *Regulating the Poor: The Functions of Public Welfare.* Updated ed. New York: Vintage Books.

Poppendieck, Janet. 1998. *Sweet Charity: Emergency Food and the End of Entitlement.* New York: Viking Press.

Scheper-Hughes, Nancy. 1992. *Death Without Weeping: The Violence of Everyday Life in Brazil.* Los Angeles, CA: University of California Press.

Shack, Willilam. 1997. "Hunger, Anxiety and Ritual: Deprivation and Spirit Possession Among the Gurage of Ethiopia." In *Food and Culture,* edited by Carole Counihan and Penny Van Esterik. New York: Routledge.

Shipton, P. 1990. "African Famines and Food Security: Anthropological Perspectives." *Annual Review of Anthropology* no. 19: 353-94.

Soss, Joe, Richard Fording, and Sanford Schram. 2011. *Disciplining the Poor: Neoliberal Paternalism and the Persistent Power of Race.* Chicago and London: University of Chicago Press.

Super, David A. 2004. "The Quiet 'Welfare' Revolution: Resurrecting the Food Stamp Program in the Wake of the 1996 Welfare Law." *New York University Law Review* no. 79 (October).

Van Esterik, Penny. 1999. "Right to Food; Right to Feed; Right to be Fed: The Intersection of Women's Rights and the Right to Food." *Agriculture and Human Values* no. 16: 225-232.

CHAPTER 3

"I took the lemons and I made lemonade": Women's Quotidian Strategies and the Re-Contouring of Food Insecurity in a Hispanic Community in New Mexico

Janet Page-Reeves
Amy Anixter Scott
Maurice Moffett
Veronica Apodaca
Vanessa Apodaca

Food practices and their representations, interwoven as they are into the dailiness of life, can reveal the particularities of time, place and culture, providing an excellent vehicle to contextualize women's lives.

Avakian (2005, 7)

Her study demonstrates a point I made long ago, that cooking is a powerful— and powerfully gendered—nexus that connects the household to the larger world in all its material and symbolic dimensions.

Weismantel (2008, XII)

Introduction

In 2011, close to 15 percent of U.S. households were food insecure, affecting 17.9 million families, 33.5 million adults and 16.7 million children (Coleman-Jensen, et al. 2012). Hispanic households are disproportionately affected, with one fourth (26.2 percent) experiencing food insecurity, including more than one third of Hispanic children (Coleman-Jensen, et al. 2012). Hispanic households also have a high rate of accessing emergency food resources (Malbi, et al. 2010). Feeding America, the largest national emergency food provider, reports a 66 percent increase in the number of Hispanic clients between 2005 and 2009 (Malbi, et al. 2010). Over the past decade, New Mexico has battled with a handful of other impoverished states for last place (2008) or near last place for food security. Today, New Mexico is ranked as the state with the highest rate of child food insecurity (Feeding America 2013) and is the eighth most food insecure state in the nation (Food Research Action Center 2011). Local emergency food providers report overwhelming increases in demand that cannot be met by current food pantry and soup kitchen resources,[1] and local medical providers report concerns about malnutrition and hunger among the populations they serve, especially among children.[2]

Contextualizing Food Insecurity in New Mexico

New Mexico's chronically poor (and apparently deteriorating) food security status is a reflection of the state's broader social and economic context. New Mexico is statistically tied with Mississippi as the poorest state in the nation, and is third for the percentage of women living in poverty (20 percent of women versus 10.6 percent of men), including disproportionate burden among Hispanic women (25.7 percent) (U.S. Census Bureau 2012). Nationally, one quarter of Hispanic women are poor, but compared to all women, Hispanic women as a group experienced greater increases in poverty since 2009 (U.S. Census Bureau 2011). New Mexico, as the state with the highest percentage of Hispanics (U.S. Census Bureau 2011), is significantly influenced by this fact. Moreover, because 12 percent of Hispanic households in New Mexico (as compared to 4 percent among non-Hispanic whites) are female-headed households with children, the impact of poverty is particularly acute. Concomitantly, New Mexico was also ranked worst among the states for the percentage of *working* families that are low-income—44 percent of families in New Mexico are the *working poor* (Working Poor Families Project 2013). Although New Mexico increased the state minimum wage to $7.50 an hour in 2009, more than 6 percent of the value of that increase has been lost to inflation, which has reduced the buying power of minimum wage workers by more than $1,000 a year (Bradley 2012a). The hourly wage needed by a family of three to rise above the federal poverty level is now over $9.25. Given that in Albuquerque, minimum wage workers are 52 percent female and 57 percent Hispanic, the fact that Hispanic women are overrepresented in poverty statistics is no aberration.

From 2003 to 2008, New Mexico mirrored national trends in economic expansion, and like the rest of the nation, beginning in 2008, was beset by economic crisis. However, specific local economic and political dynamics have influenced the demographic impact and pace of economic changes. Although not a panacea for New Mexico's entrenched inequality and underdevelopment, prosperity in the early part of the decade brought expanded employment and an increase in household income, with Hispanics making significant gains (Bradley 2012b). State tax revenues increased 45 percent (NM Voices 2010) with the housing boom creating artificially large construction industry-related state tax revenues at the same time that high prices for crude oil and natural gas (two important industries in New Mexico) further inflated state coffers. Increased state revenue provided for some public spending increases but spending was significantly offset by large personal income tax cuts reflecting national neoliberal trends (NM Voices 2010). With the economic downturn between 2008 and 2010, New Mexico lost more than 50,000 jobs—6 percent of total state employment (NM Voices 2010). The collapse of the housing market had a dramatic impact on the construction sector, which has a large Hispanic workforce, many from low-income households. Construction jobs shrank by nearly 30 percent (NM Voices 2010). The number of Hispanics working in construction fell 25 percent from 49,000 to 37,000 (Bradley 2012b). The overall disproportionate impact of job losses on the Hispanic community is demonstrated by the tripling of the unemployment rate among Hispanics during that same period, rising to 11.3 percent, compared with 7.2 percent among non-Hispanic whites (Bradley 2012b).

In the first years of the recession, New Mexico ironically fared well relative to many other parts of the country. Lack of broad-based economic development has meant that New Mexico has an overdeveloped public sector—one of the most government-job-dependent states (Thompson 2012). The public sector tended to bleed fewer jobs when the recession was first taking hold. Similarly, chronically high poverty rates have made New Mexico the recipient of large levels of federal funding through "transfer payments" such as Social Security, Medicaid, Medicare, Disability, and SNAP (the Supplemental Nutrition Assistance Program previously known as "Food Stamps") (NM Voices 2010). Initially, federal funds compensated for declining economic activity and "stabilized" or offset the recession in New Mexico, yet high levels of unemployment and decreased energy prices have now reduced state revenues in a context where there is no political will to rescind tax cuts implemented during the boom. Fewer state funds are currently available for social support services even as demand is rising, and cuts have been made to safety net resources including a 15 percent reduction in TANF (Temporary Aid for Needy Families) cash assistance which is only available to women with children who live in extreme poverty (Rodriguez 2010). Moreover, it is estimated that "*sequestration*" which took effect in 2013 will mean a $41 million further reduction in federal funds to state programs in addition to significant decreases in New Mexico's large defense industry sector (Wallin 2012). And in-step with the ongoing national neoliberal ideological shift, in the closing minutes of the 2013 legislative session, the New Mexico legislature passed an omnibus tax bill with provisions for corporate tax incentives that will ostensibly make the state more competitive in jobs and attractive to corporate industry, but subsequent analyses have demonstrated that in reality these measures will act to decrease corporate tax load and shift the burden of tax responsibility further to consumers with a disproportionate impact on the poor (Bradley 2013). Given these statistics, it is not surprising that New Mexico was recently identified as the worst state for income equality, *with the wealthiest fifth having ten times the income as the poorest fifth* (Center on Budget and Policy Priorities 2012).

Food insecurity, then, is part of broader social and economic dynamics in New Mexico. Yet food insecurity is of particular concern for women (Ivers and Cullen 2011) because of their often primary role in food procurement, production and preparation, their role in nurturing families, and the disproportionate likelihood that they will be sole providers (single-parent households) and living in poverty. The significant role of women in the provisioning and preparation of food creates unique gender dynamics that are played out in relationships and activities within food insecure households.

Methods

Project Design

This chapter was developed from interview data gathered as part of a larger, community-engaged, mixed method research study sponsored through the NM CARES Health Disparities Research Center at the University of New Mexico with funding from the National Institutes of Health and the National Institute of Minority Health and Health Disparities (NIMHD). Investigators from the Office for Community Health at the University of New Mexico are partnering with the Santa Barbara/Martineztown (SB/MT) Community Learning Center in a historic, urban, primarily Hispanic neighborhood in Albuquerque, New Mexico on "*Fiestas: Improving Food Security in an Urban Hispanic Community.*" This two-year, multi-dimensional study from September 2011 to September 2013 investigated the issue of food insecurity in SB/MT with a focus on women's perspectives, experiences, and relationships related to food and how they find expression in individual lives. A separate research component also explored an innovative social network strategy to promote the development of positive social relationships among women as a way to reduce the incidence of food insecurity. Approval to conduct the research was obtained in November 2011 through a Full Committee Review by the Human Research Protections Office at UNM. Although the study qualified for expedited review in terms of research methods and approach, Full Committee approval was required by NIMHD for projects under this award mechanism. All participants provided signed informed consent and chose pseudonyms for us to use in referring to their input.[3]

The SB/MT Community Learning Center, our community partner for this research, is a community-run organization housed in a city-owned building that was once a school in the historic Santa Barbara/Martineztown neighborhood in downtown Albuquerque (described below). The Learning Center operates after-school and summer youth programs to promote literacy with an emphasis on culture and community-building. The Learning Center Director (Veronica Apodaca) served as the Study Community Coordinator for this research and recruited three community members to serve, together with herself and the project Graduate Research Assistant (Vanessa Apodaca—who is also a SB/MT community resident) on a Project Community Board (CB):

> *#1. Jeannie is from northern New Mexico. She moved to the community three decades ago with her husband who had been born in the community. Jeannie has adult children who attended the Learning Center in the 1990s. She currently operates a day care center in her home where she lives with her adult son.*

> *#2. Carol is a life-long resident of the community whose adult daughter attended the Learning Center. She has training as a doula and in body/joint manipulation, and is actively job hunting. Carol currently serves as Neighborhood Association President. Her husband is a well-known local musician.*

> *#3. Brenda is in her 20's and is a nursing student at a local college. She moved to the community from another Albuquerque neighborhood when she was a young child. As a child, she attended the Learning Center and until recently, she worked as one of the Learning Center's after-school and summer youth counselors. Brenda lives with her mother.*

We used a "structured dialogue" approach similar to that described by Williams and colleagues (Williams, chapter 12; Williams, et al. 2012; Labonte and Feather 2006) but developed independently, to engage CB members in understanding the issue of food insecurity and women's experience in SB/MT. CB members met with the researchers twice a month at the residence of Jeannie (CB member #1 above) between December 2011 and May 2013, and once a month from May 2013 to December 2013 to identify and discuss community issues related to food and health (including Food Stamps/SNAP, diabetes, women's household strategies, community dynamics, senior social isolation, food access, community health, neighborhood crime, etc.), to discuss and decide upon interview questions, to discuss and interpret findings, and to plan and implement social network building strategies with women in the community. This approach allowed the CB to provide input and guidance for the design and direction of this study. CB members received a monthly stipend to remunerate them for the time they spent contributing to the research.

Research Site: Santa Barbara/Martineztown (SB/MT)

The SB/MT neighborhood, an urban food desert in downtown Albuquerque, was identified for participation in this study as a result of an existing relationship between the investigators and the Learning Center, and through community conversations. Food insecurity, hunger and food system issues have been identified by members of the community as priority concerns. SB/MT is one of the oldest neighborhoods in Albuquerque, home to over 2,287 residents, is considered an "old Hispanic" population with strong ancestral roots in the community; 67.8 percent of residents are Hispanic or Latino but only 17 percent identify as immigrants and even fewer (16 percent) are monolingual Spanish speakers (American Community Survey 2010). SB/MT was founded in the mid 19th century on a segment of the *Camino Real* on the periphery of the original Albuquerque "Old Town" city center. The area founded as SB/MT had access to water resources and was established as an agricultural community with distinct Protestant and Catholic contingents. In the late 19th century, construction of the railroad on land through and adjacent to the community encouraged extensive land speculation and industrial land use (e.g., warehouses for loading and off loading goods) that significantly impacted the existing agricultural lifestyle in SB/MT (Sanchez 2008). In the early 20th century, the area was further transformed by urban development as downtown Albuquerque expanded to encapsulate SB/MT from the west and south, and by mid-century construction of Interstate 25 that passes along the Eastern border of the community (Wheeler and Patterson 2007). Despite these changes, SB/MT has been able to maintain a notable physical and geographic cohesion, and a certain cultural continuity as a Hispanic community with deep historic roots. At the same time, however, demographic statistics attest to the barriers and limits to access to food that residents confront. Local-level food insecurity data do not currently exist, but the neighborhood has high risk for food insecurity given that median annual income is $16,161, which is only 35 percent of the city's median household income of $46,662 (American Community Survey 2010). Moreover, 31 percent of households with children in SB/MT fall below the Federal Poverty Level, but only 13 percent of households use SNAP (American Community Survey 2010). As a result, residents of SB/MT often rely on emergency food services.[4] The largest emergency food provider in Albuquerque reports that 1350 households including 1,542 children were served in 2011 by two mobile pantry food distribution sites in SB/MT.[5]

Data Collection and Analysis

Information collected in 16 in-depth interviews with women from SB/MT conducted in January and February 2012 is used to frame the discussion presented here. Interviewee selection was "purposive" and "dynamic" (Ellingson 2011).

Participants were mothers of children who currently attend or formerly attended the Learning Center after-school program or are members of the SB/MT Neighborhood Association, and many were known to the Learning Center staff or to the CB as being interested in health and community issues. Individuals were invited to participate in the research because they are from households that were identified by the Study Community Coordinator as experiencing or being knowledgeable about food insecurity. Five of the interviewees have lived in the neighborhood their entire lives, and eight have lived in the neighborhood for more than ten years. Four are married or widowed, seven are single mothers of young children or had been single mothers when they were raising their children who are now adults, and two are single with no children. Fifteen of the sixteen women we interviewed identify in some way as Hispanic or Latina. One is part Native American. One interviewee who moved to New Mexico from another state was jokingly described by herself and others as "*a white woman*" in contrast to other women in the community. Ten women interviewed are from families that would be considered "old New Mexico" families, and six have at least one parent who is an immigrant from Mexico, but none of the women interviewed are themselves immigrants.

Interviews were held at locations of convenience to participants, including the Learning Center, participants' homes, or in one case, a local Starbucks café. Interviews lasted one to two hours and followed a semi-structured format that allowed for interviewees to drive the flow of conversation. A conscious decision was made to privilege voices of women who are not well represented in the mainstream literature or taken into account by policy makers. Interview tools were collaboratively developed by researchers and the CB. Questions were broadly framed and open-ended to allow participants to develop answers in relation to issues and ideas that they consider to be the most relevant and important. Questioning was designed to obtain perspectives on social and cultural dimensions of food and the experience of food insecurity. Participants received a $20 merchandise card (VISA card) to compensate them for their time.

A rigorous, disciplined, empirical analysis of the data, using Hammersley's (2008) criteria based on plausibility, credibility, and relevance focused on understanding meanings and perceptions expressed by interviewees. The data was analyzed inductively using modified grounded theory (Charmaz 2011; Glaser and Strauss 1967) to identify conceptual categories and patterns. Text from interviews was read consecutive times and themes were identified and coded. Coded data was analyzed for coherence and interpreted for patterns within each theme. Interconnections between theme categories were explored through constant comparison (Parry 2003) in order to provide holistic interpretation of the data. Interpretations were presented to the CB for discussion and their input informed development of this article and further iterative interview questions. We also invited all interviewees to an evening dinner event at the Learning Center in

September 2012 where we presented findings from the interviews and gave interviewees an opportunity for further input or interpretation. Interviewees interested in more in-depth understanding of our findings were provided with copies
of academic manuscripts (Page-Reeves, et al. 2012; Page-Reeves, et al. 2014),
including this one, for them to review and comment on.

Women's Quotidian Strategies
for Coping with Food Insecurity

Although women we spoke with were candid about their struggles with food
insecurity (see Page-Reeves, et al. 2014), they also emphasized their own resilience. Women actively confront these struggles with ingenuity, hard work and
love to ensure the well-being of their families. For example, despite the daily
challenges she faces, Janelle proudly described her ability to make a comfortable
home for her family, announcing, "*I took the lemons and made lemonade.*" The
narratives of Janelle and other women in this study help us to understand the
strategies women develop to achieve this transmogrification in SB/MT.

Sharing "*Platos*" and Leveraging Women's Social Wealth

One of the first strategies for coping with food insecurity that we discovered in
our research in SB/MT was that women rely on the mobilization of social capital
to make sure they have food. This is in-line with literature describing how wom-
en mobilize "informal" resources (Swanson, et al. 2008). Social relationships
have been identified in the literature as a key factor influencing levels of food
insecurity. Dhokarh and colleagues (2010) found that individuals and families
with low levels of cultural integration, a lack of social networks, and poor skills
to access safety net programs were more likely to have insufficient food resources. Conversely, Martin and colleagues (2004) found that households with
significant '*social capital*' (significant positive social ties) have a decreased risk
of hunger. Lemke and colleagues (2003) demonstrate that food insecurity can be
lessened through fostering of social ties to create an environment that can be
especially empowering to women. Women play a central role in managing family resources, including the disposition of food, serving as critical gate keepers
for what food is purchased, as well as how often and who eats within a household (Seefeldt 2010; Tarasuk 2001). Supportive social networks are seen to give
women the capacity to take more control over their lives with positive outcomes
for themselves and their families. Although an integrated social fabric has been
shown to provide a system of support that can keep individuals and families
from going without food, many disadvantaged communities lack a social environment that is conducive to supportive social relationships.

In SB/MT, women discussed these dynamics with us. There are families
that have lived in SB/MT for generations (Macias 2007). As mentioned above,
five of the 15 interviewees for this project are from such families, but eight of

those not born in the neighborhood have lived in SB/MT for more than ten years—many for more than 20. As a result, a number of the women we spoke with have deep social ties in the neighborhood that include family, neighbors and friends who may even live on the same block or directly next door to each other. Sandra explained,

> I think this neighborhood is very close and it goes back four or five genera-
> tions. Our grandmothers knew each other... I know this block for sure is like
> that. There are some "outsiders" moving in but for the most part it is pretty
> historic. I think it is a good thing. It is always nice to know your neighbors and
> to be able to count on them when you need them.

Marie described how she and her neighbors stick together and look out for each other with the example of a neighbor who

> didn't have food and was kind of stressed out about getting groceries and asked
> if we had a sack of beans and a couple potatoes and so we gave them to her. It
> was hard for her, it isn't easy to ask someone for help, but a lot of the neigh-
> borhood if we need anything like a glass of milk we could go and ask the
> neighbor...and it wouldn't be embarrassing.

Among these neighbors, the fact that sharing is a neighborhood "value" makes the act of asking for help less shameful. Micaela explained that in traditional New Mexico Hispanic communities that trace their roots to a historic relation-ship with Mexico, there is a tradition of "*platos*" (plates of food), saying it is "*common to ask to take a plate home...That is what my grandma would do. In Mexican tradition, you make way more than enough so that people can take stuff home. That is how I grew up...you don't feel shy about asking for seconds or a plate.*" Valerie described how this is played out in her family, telling us how her sister

> would come over to eat... and I would tell her to just come over. I knew that she
> was having trouble so I invited her. It makes a difference...if I have to ask, I am
> admitting that I can't do it and I feel like a failure...you feel like by asking,
> maybe people can tell that you are scared and you don't want to show your
> weak side and being in need relates in your mind to being weak, and it's more
> like since you are inviting me it is OK, but if you ask me it is like admitting...so
> that is why it is better.

The expectation that family members will help each other, together with the priority in Hispanic culture placed on serving others food (Page-Reeves, et al. 2013) helps to reduce the shame involved in accepting food. By anticipating her sister's needs, Valerie makes it unnecessary for her sister to have to ask for help.

Framing the provision of food as a *"plato"* or an *"invitation"* rather than as *"help"* effectively makes it almost impossible for the person in need to refuse without transgressing cultural boundaries and causing offence.

Counihan (Counihan 2009) examines the issue of hunger with women in Antonito in the San Luis Valley of Colorado. Similar to women in SB/MT, they described sharing food as a priority. In Antonito it is understood locally that you have to *"give because it multiplies"* (181). In other words, one's own fortune is seen to depend on generosity shown to others. Women she spoke with were in agreement that *"nobody who has food will deny somebody who's hungry who asks for food"* (181). Counihan suggests that this "idyllic picture of...people taking care of each other" (182) may or may not be a reality for everyone in the community. However, the tradition of sharing food is a form of "community beneficence [that has helped] people to survive poverty before there were formal institutions to help them."

Although women's strategies to mobilize social wealth in the context of food insecurity in SB/MT can be effective at reducing shame and stigma while providing access to food resources, there are limits to these strategies. In SB/MT, despite the depth of some family histories and networks in the neighborhood, not everyone shares, or knows people who will share with them. While some of the women we spoke with feel that the neighborhood is close-knit, others feel that it is closed to them. Only people connected through social relations have the support that comes from sharing *platos*. Not everyone feels they can approach a neighbor or has family close by. Victoria, who does not have a strong or extensive social network in the neighborhood lamented this fact, saying,

> We try to help each other out but you have to know each other. Like myself, I'm not very sociable and not good about asking for help. A lot of people won't ask for help. If they know each other they will...people mind their own business. There is a lot of new people moving in here that we don't know. Some people are sociable. I'm not. I don't really have a network around here.

Others felt that even for those with deep roots and a large network in the community, times are changing. Ruth, who has lived in the neighborhood for many years, believes that

> what has changed now-a-days is that I just wave at my neighbor and that is it, it isn't any longer like I can borrow a cup of sugar, or maybe I'm not that intimate with my neighbors...I don't know, now-a-days the whole community has changed. We aren't that close any more, depending on who your neighbors are.

Kwong (2001, 57) discusses how "current social science literature is full of articles lauding the value of family as a powerful institution that can deflect individuals from sliding into poverty" but demonstrates how external structural factors often weaken the ability of the family to play this role in the contemporary context. In SB/MT, the historic character of the neighborhood not with-standing, most people's local social and family networks are not as substantial or as strong as the neighborhood's reputation in Albuquerque (and incidentally, in SB/MT itself) would suggest. Seventy-four percent of the households in SB/MT are renter-occupied compared to 40 percent for the city of Albuquerque (American Community Survey 2010). Moreover, according to a housing afford-ability analysis conducted by the City of Albuquerque (City of Albuquerque, n.d.), because of the low median income of residents in SB/MT, substantial af-fordability gaps exist for both renters and homeowners. Sixty-three percent of SB/MT renter households spend in excess of 30 percent of the household's monthly gross income on rent and are considered "cost-burdened," and home purchase prices are $100,000 to $125,000 over what a low-income family can afford. Neighborhoods with high rates of renter-occupied housing units and sub-stantial housing affordability gaps are associated with significant neighborhood transience that disrupts neighborhood social and family networks (Warr 2005; Keene, Bader and Ailshire 2013). For the women in our study, what this means is that the likelihood that they have or can maintain meaningful local social con-nections is being eroded by economic and housing market dynamics that influ-ence the configuration of the neighborhood. As a result, many women increas-ingly lack a network of support that can be mobilized to improve their own household food security. For those who do have a network, the expanding need for food sharing as a product of economic recession can become a burden for family or social network members who are struggling to put food on their own tables. In describing her neighbor, Ernestine said, *"she would share her last bowl of beans with me if I needed it."* But when sharing becomes an ongoing necessity in a context of diminishing resources, social networks and relation-ships can become strained. These dynamics have been discussed as "weather-ing" (Gould, Mijanovich and Dillman 2001; Geronimus 1992)—the accumulat-ed stress in a disadvantaged, low-income neighborhood that lowers the environmental quality of already limited resources and relationships, and makes people even more vulnerable.

Utilizing Safety Net Programs

Women in SB/MT routinely expand their food budgets through the use of public safety net programs. Women we spoke with rely on free and reduced cost break-fast and lunch programs offered to children at school. Despite extensive criti-cism of school food both nationally (Tucker 2012) and locally,[6] interviewees expressed a positive view of the programs in terms of providing healthy food for children and supporting their household food budgets. Melia said, *"It is good ...I think it helps families. I really notice when the kids aren't at school... we go through more food with them being home."* Many of those interviewed have a similar view of the free summer lunch program that is offered at the local park and are thankful to have it as a resource. In addition, many of the women in this study use SNAP (Food Stamps). Although problems with the functioning and policy of the SNAP program in New Mexico have been identified (Page-Reeves 2008), most of interviewees' perspectives on the program were positive, especially in terms of allowing the purchase of healthier food. Victoria shared that because she uses SNAP, *"We have more access to healthier foods now...I am able to afford it because of the Food Stamps so I can make the choices so that instead of fried potatoes, I can make the choice to buy fish or vegetables, whereas before the only time we had fish was when my uncle went fishing and brought us some."*

Although Anna also spoke very positively about how the SNAP program supports her food budget and initially had little negative to say about the process of applying or the program itself, as the discussion unfolded, she recounted how she has had to overcome barriers that could prevent some women from applying.

> *I would go to SNAP. The first time I went they were really fast efficient and then I got a letter saying that there was something missing and I had to do a phone interview and that person was so rude! I felt like I was a burden to that person, like they had something better to do and I felt like maybe I will call you back when a time is better for you... I really needed her help but she did not want to help me and just the questions and no talk. It was just business and I understand that this is your job but I am a person and I'm not an automated system. I need your help. I don't want to be in the system, but I need it. It was a very bad conversation. I had to go back and she closed my case. So I had to go back. They don't assign you a caseworker [anymore]. I talked with a man who was really nice and he reopened my case. He gave me his extension so he will help me even though that is not what he is supposed to be doing, but he takes that initiative. I can't go down to the office because I work. They aren't open when I go in and they are closed when I get off. He has been a blessing.*

Obviated in this account are the weaknesses that plague the New Mexico SNAP program in terms of policy (*e.g.*, not being open during hours to serve individuals who work) and operation (*e.g.*, unprofessional behavior of the caseworker on the call and inappropriate closure of Anna's case). At the same time, women's narratives from SB/MT clearly identify program supports and individual champions within the program as assets. Interestingly, Anna's experience can be seen in light of the dynamics identified by Lamphere and colleagues (2005) in the operation of the Medicaid Program in New Mexico. In the context of neoliberal reductions in benefits and infrastructure for benefit programs, staff compensate for institutional and structural deficits in order to buffer the client from negative impact. The caseworker who provided Anna with his phone number is inadvertently operating to make the system appear more rational and equitable than it really is. People's "invisible" actions to resist external forces in order to support one another ironically collude at some level to maintain processes that generate inequality.

Stretching Food

One of the key strategies that women engage in to confront the reality of food insecurity is "*stretching*" food. Women we spoke with were extremely proud of their stretching skills. They said things like, "*when the kids stay home there is less and we have to buy more and there is really nothing you can do...but you have to minimize and stretch it and make more out of less*" (Janelle), and " *I have to stretch it for my children...that is my way of affording it. I stretch it and I get Food Stamps*" (Valerie). Stretching is how women make their ends meet and how they have enough to feed their families. Soo explained, "*I think that homemakers do what they have done for millennia. They make things stretch, putting fillers in. That is usually starchy...noodles, rice, beans.*" Many of the women we interviewed have specific strategies for stretching. Other women we spoke with want to know more about how to stretch their food or how to make their money go farther at the store, but still be healthy. Some women have stretching strategies that originate with shopping. Valerie described stretching as being a frugal shopper: "*I won't buy too much of instant stuff. The food that you have to make from scratch is more lasting and more nutritious and that is how I do it.*" Melia framed it as making her SNAP benefits last: "*I know I have a certain amount of EBT [SNAP Electronic Benefits Transfer card] but we have to stretch it at the end of the month and I really have to watch it or I would be in trouble.*" Anna described stretching as something she does in the kitchen:

> *We call it pasta goulash. I gather up all the leftover odds and ends ...things going bad or old pasta sauce. They sell big jars. I put half in the fridge and I will save that spaghetti sauce for the pasta goulash. I try not to be wasteful and use what I can. I use stale crackers for my meatloaf. I will dry out stale bread.*

A number of women identified times when children are out of school as more challenging because when they are at home, they do not receive school meals. Since food budgets do not expand just because children are home and need to eat, women described some of the strategies they use to keep their children fed. Janelle says that she has

> *noticed when the kids stay home there is less and we have to buy more and there is really nothing you can do. I buy a couple of things of oatmeal. That is breakfast. Sometimes they don't like it, but it is breakfast. For lunch I will go home and make grilled cheese, and then I make dinner, but you have to minimize and stretch it and make more out of less—throw some cinnamon on the oatmeal.*

Similarly, Valerie explained,

In the summer the days are longer you have to pay more attention to it because they will be hungry and you can't just make one thing. They have to eat and take it seriously because you don't want them to not feel like they haven't eaten and they will be up til like 9:00 because the days are longer. You have to think about it, maybe like make more of like the potatoes, more of like rice and beans, have plenty of that, eggs, rice, beans, potatoes, plenty of tortillas, bread, milk, and maybe once a week buy a frozen pizza for them.

Recognizing that friends and family are facing the same economic struggles that participants in this study experience, there was a sense among many of the participants that *"knowing how to stretch"* was a particular skill that women could cultivate that is not entirely dependent on economic circumstances. Those who know how to stretch theorized about some of the reasons other women they know have a hard time making their food or their money suffice. Valerie suggested it is a combination of lifestyle and knowledge, saying,

many times because they spent on fast food for the convenience and with what you spent on fast food you can buy a bag of potatoes that will last you for a week. They aren't keeping track of what they are spending on fast food. They don't realize because it was little by little. If they were to be more conscious, they could make a budget...They are like where did all my money go? Buying the $1 muffin everyday, that is $30 at the end of the month, so they don't realize... Now that the economy has gone down I think people are becoming more aware, more conscious about how to save money. People don't think about it...everything is prepared and they don't learn to make something like that. You just learn to order and pay and go. It is the fast life and people just getting used to it. It is like normal, you know.

Others identified tricks or techniques that they learned from mothers and grandmothers as key. Ruth explained that, *"I don't like to serve. The Hispanic custom is to serve you and sometimes they over-serve you. The only time I will serve someone food is if I am limited in quantity. I see that now, we grew up with people serving us."* Ernestine said that the thing that has gotten her by is a value she learned from her grandmother: *"tiene que rendir—you have to make it last."*

The type of skill and resourcefulness with respect to food resources that was described by women in SB/MT has been well-documented in the literature, challenging stereotypes of low-income mothers as lacking in knowledge or motivation to engage in economical, healthful food preparation behaviors (Williams, et al. 2012). Yet, in McLaughlin, Tarasuk and Kreiger's (2003) study of food preparation activity among low-income food-insecure women, they did not find an association between food security and the reported use of "careful" shopping or economical preparation techniques. The implication is that food skills alone are unlikely to address the food security needs of low-income women and families. However, participants in our study were convinced of the value and efficacy of their own actions to stretch meals. In SB/MT, food insecurity exists and is expanding in a context of rising prices for food in general (Andreyeva, et al. 2010) and healthy foods in particular (Monsivais, Aggarwal, and Drewnowski 2012), the existence of food desert environments where geographic access to food is limited (Lane, et al. 2008), high housing cost burden (City of Albuquerque n.d.), low wages (Bradley 2012a), decreasing availability of a wide range of safety net resources (Rodriguez 2010), and an economic climate that limits employment opportunities (Bradley 2012b). Empirical data to identify whether women's food stretching provides a buffer from hunger for some families will require further research, but what was clear from our study is that women's quotidian strategies to put food on the table in a context of scarcity are key to the way that women view themselves and their contribution to the nutritional health of their families. At the same time, Harrison (2013) cautions that while it is important to counter hegemonic narratives of women's weakness and vulnerability, focusing on women's resilience can overemphasize the capacity of poor women to continually overcome challenges. Women's coping strategies that make it possible for families to weather adversity are not a resource that can be continually replenished without cost. After a certain point, women cannot just keep *stretching*.

Food Insecurity and Women's Agency

The discussion presented here explores how food insecurity textures daily life for women from a historic Hispanic urban food desert community in Albuquerque, New Mexico, and the ways that women confront the reality of scarcity to be able to put food on the table for their families. We paint a portrait of how food insecurity generated by economic forces outside of SB/MT intersects with everyday experience for women in their homes and kitchens, and how cultural frameworks and social relationships influence access to food and food provisioning. This research contributes to conceptualizing the relationship between food, gender and power. At the same time, this study provides information to help refine current conceptualizations of food justice.

Although women struggle with the experience of food insecurity in a variety of physically and emotionally challenging ways (Page-Reeves, et al. 2014), they nurture and activate social networks for support and food sharing, avail themselves of safety net resources, and creatively stretch food budgets and supplies. These dynamics provide insight into the nature of food insecurity in SB/MT and how women "*make lemonade out of lemons.*" Women's narratives help us understand the role of women's agency in recontouring the food landscape to make it more likely that families can satisfy their hunger. The women who participated in this study act strategically, even if their actions might appear *unconscious* and *inconsequential. Too often we fail to account for the underlying agency involved in everyday life.* We believe that women's strategies can be seen not just as *resilience*, but as a form of *resistance* to structural relations that create poverty and health disparities. Christie (2008, 260) suggests that

> Women's adaptive strategies are essential in kitchenspace, where *la cocinera* [the cook] is always adjusting her menus and recipes based on availability of ingredients, cookware and fuel, not to mention changes in her own life cycle and schedule and in the demands of people around her...[so] to conclude that the *cocinera* has no power is to ignore the dialectic that exists between supply and demand and women's protagonism in the ongoing process of negotiation, adaptation, and innovation in kitchenspace.

Thinking about women's kitchen strategies, Weismantel (2008) argues that resistance must be understood as more than opposition or reaction to domination—it can be creative and transforming. As such, women's reconstitution of kitchenspace activities to confront the realities of food insecurity provides an opportunity to explore the dynamics of agency and structure at the interface of women's individual experiences, and how women navigate the structural realities of food system dynamics that generate health disparity in their lives and community.

The *seeming inconsequence* of women's coping strategies and food procurement and preparation practices disguises the underlying conceptual significance of what women do in their homes and communities as social actors everyday and at every meal, and what is potentially at stake. Examining processes involved contributes to our understanding of the ways that women can mobilize social and cultural assets at their disposal in novel ways to expand their own fields of action. In the context of the emerging food justice literature (Alkon and Agyeman 2011) that has tended to focus on alternative systems of food production, their activity is of interest because it helps us to reconsider the extent to which individuals and communities in marginal urban environments and urban food deserts can resuscitate or reinvent their own foodways to challenge the "corporate food regime" (Alkon and Mares 2012) in ways other than prosaic food movement requisites of local, organic or *slow*. What women do with their food budgets and the strategies they employ in their kitchens reveal the reality involved in challenging a system defined by social and economic inequity. Taking this perspective on women's efforts to feed their families in a context of food insecurity in this country, we can more fully appreciate the ways that food procurement and preparation are part of an embedded, multidimensional process, where social actors create agendas to challenge the *status quo* and structural boundaries. This approach operationalizes our understanding of how women actively redefine the experience of food insecurity and challenge the limits of the current inequitable food system.

Acknowledgments

Research reported in this chapter was supported by the National Institute on Minority Health and Health Disparities of the National Institutes of Health under Award Number P20MD004811. The content of this article is solely the responsibility of the authors and does not necessarily represent the official views of the National Institutes of Health. We are especially grateful to the women who participated in interviews for this research and to Jeannie Romero, Carol Carrillo-Pimental, and Brenda Garcia for their role as members of a Community Board for this project.

Notes

1. Personal communication, Lee Maynard, Director, The Storehouse, February 2012.
2. Personal communication, Dr. Javier Aceves, Medical Director, UNM Young Children's Health Center, 2008.
3. References to individuals from our research use pseudonyms that were chosen by the individual participants. We were inspired to have interviewees choose their own pseudonyms following Counihan's (2010) work with women in Antonito.
4. Personal Communication with Art Fine, Operations Director, RoadRunner *Food Bank*, 2011
5. Personal Communication with Alissa Wolfe, *RoadRunner Food Bank*, 1/13/12
6. Rethinking School Lunch NM, http://www.ecoliteracy.org/essays/dispatch-new-mexico-rethinking-school-lunch

Bibliography

Alkon, A.H., and J. Agyeman. 2011. *Cultivating Food Justice: Race, Class, and Sustainability*. Boston, MA: MIT Press.

———— and T.M. Mares. 2012. "Food Sovereignty in U.S. Food Movements: Radical Visions and Neoliberal Constraints." *Agriculture and Human Values* 29, no. 3: 347-359.

American Community Survey. 2010. "American Community Survey 2006-2010 5-yr File." U.S. Census 2010: United States Census Bereau, U.S. Department of Commerce.

Andreyeva, T., M. Long, and K. Brownell. 2010. "The Impact of Food Prices on Consumption: A Systematic Review of Research on the Price Elasticity of Demand for Food." *American Journal of Public Health* 100, no. 2: 216-222.

Avakian, A.V. 2005. "Feminist Food Studies: A Brief History." In *From Betty Crocker to Feminist Food Studies: Critical Perspectives on Women and Food*, edited by A. V. Avakian and B. Haber, 1-28. Amhurst: University of Massachusetts Press,.

Bradley, G. 2012a. "Raising Albuquerque's Minimum Wage: Good for Workers, Good for the Economy." New Mexico Voices for Children. Fiscal Policy Project Policy Brief. Albuquerque, NM.

―――. 2012b. "Mind the Gap: Unemployment, Income and Earnings for Hispanics and Non-Hispanic Whites In and Before the Great Recession." New Mexico Voices for Children. Fiscal Policy Project Policy Brief. Albuquerque, NM.

―――. 2013. "HB-641: Bad Bill, Flawed Process, Empty Promises." New Mexico Voices for Children. Fiscal Policy Project Policy Brief. Albuquerque, NM.

Center on Budget and Policy Priorities. 2012. "Pulling Apart: A State-by-State Analysis of Income Trends." Washington, D.C.

Charmaz, K. 2011. "Grounded Theory Methods in Social Science." In *The SAGE Handbook of Qualitative Research*. 4th edition, edited by N.K. Denzin and Y.S. Lincoln, 359-380. Thousand Oaks, CA: Sage Publications.

Chilton, M., J. Rabinowich, C. Council, and J. Breaux. 2009. "Witnesses to Hunger: Participation Through Photovoice to Ensure the Right to Food." *Health and Human Rights* 11(1): 73-85.

Christie, M.E. 2008. *Kitchenspace: Women, Fiestas, and Everyday Life in Central Mexico*. Austin: University of Texas Press.

City of Albuquerque. n.d. "Housing Inventory for Santa Barbara/Martineztown Including Occupancy, Tenure, Need, Value, Cost, Affordability and Forclosure Activity." Unpublished report produced by the Department of City Planning.

Coleman-Jensen, A., M. Nord, M. Andrews, and S. Carlson. 2012. *Household Food Security in the United States in 2011*. USDA Research Economic Service; Economic Research Report #141.

Counihan, C. 2012. *A Tortilla is Like Life: Food and Culture in the San Luis Valley of Colorado*. Austin: University of Texas Press.

―――. 2008. "'Mexicanas' Food Voice and Differential Consciousness in the San Luis Valley of Colorado." In *Food and culture: a Reader*, edited by C. Counihan and P. Van Esterick, 354-368. New York: Routledge.

Dhokarh, R., D. Himmelgreen, Y. K. Peng, S. Segura-Pérez, A. Hromi-Fiedler, and R. Pérez-Escamilla. 2011. "Food Insecurity is Associated with Acculturation and Social Networks in Puerto Rican Households." *Journal of Nutrition Education and Behavior* 43(4): 288-294.

Ellingson, L.L. 2011. "Analysis and Representation Across the Continuum." In *The Sage Handbook of Qualitative Research*, 4th edition, N.K. Denzin and Y.S. Lincoln, editors, 595-610. Thousand Oaks, CA: Sage Publications.

Feeding America. 2013. "Map the Meal: Highlights of Findings for Overall and Child Food Insecurity."

Food Research Action Center. 2011. *A Half-Empty Plate: Fruit and Vegetable Affordability and Access Challenges in America*.

Geronimus, A.T. 1992. "The Weathering Hypothesis and the Health of African-American Women and Infants: Evidence and Specuations." *Ethnicity and Disease* 2: 207-221.

Glaser, B.G., and A.L. Strauss. 1967. *The Discovery of Grounded Theory: Strategies for Qualitative Research*. Chicago: Aldine de Gruyter.

Gould, I., T. Mijanovich, and K. Dillman. 2001. "Neighborhood Effects on Health: Exploring the Links and Assessing the Evidence." *Journal of Urban Affairs* 23(3-4): 391-408.

Hammersley, M. 2008. *Questioning Qualitative Inquiry: Critical Essays*. London: Sage Publications Ltd.

Harrison, E. 2013. "Bouncing Back? Recession, Resilience and Everyday Lives." *Critical Social Policy* 33(1): 97-113.

Ivers, L and K. Cullen. 2011. "Food Insecurity: Special Considerations for Women." *American Journal of Clinical Nutrition* 94(Suppl): 1740S-1744S.

Keene, D., M. Bader, and J. Ailshire. 2013. "Length of Residence and Social Integration: The Contingent Effects of Neighborhood Poverty." *Health and Place* 21: 171-178.

Kwong, P. 2001. "Poverty Despite Family Ties." In *The New Poverty Studies: The Ethnography of Power, Politics and Impoverished People in the United States*, J. Goode and J. Maskovsky, editors, 57-78. New York: New York University Press.

Labonte, R. and J. Feather. 2006. *Handbook on Using Stories in Health Promotion Practice*. Ottawa, Canada; Health Canada.

Lamphere, L. 2005. "Providers and Staff Respond to Medicaid Managed Care: The Unintended Consequences of Reform in New Mexico." *Medical Anthropology Quarterly* 19(1): 3-25.

Lane, S., R. Keefe, R. Rubinstein, B. Lavandowski, N. Webster, D. Cibula, A. Boahene, O. Dele-Michael, D. Carter, T. Jones, M. Wojtowycz, and J. Brill. 2008. "Structural Violence, Urban Retail Food Markets, and Low Birth Weight." *Health and Place* 14: 415-423.

Macias, V. 2007. "'*En unidad, hay poder*': Community Activism and Ethnicity in South Martineztown, 1930-1974." *New Mexico Historical Review* 82(1): 71-96.

Malbi, J., R. Cohen, F. Potter, and Z. Zhao. 2010. *Hunger in America 2010*. Feeding America.

Martin, K, B. Rogers, J. Cook and H. Joseph. 2004. "Social Capital is Associated with Decreased Risk of Hunger." *Social Science and Medicine* 58(12): 2645-2654.

McLaughlin, C, V. Tarasuk, and N. Kreiger. 2003. "An Examination of At-Home Food Preparation Activity Among Low-Income, Food-Insecure Women." *Journal of the American Dietetic Association* 103(11): 1506-1512.

Moffett, M., J. Page-Reeves, A. Anixter Scott, V. Apodaca, and V. Apodaca. n.d. "Results of a Food Security Survey in Santa Barbara /Martineztown in Albuquerque, NM." Unpublished manuscript submitted for peer review.

Monsivais, P., A. Aggarwal, and A. Drewnowski. 2012. "Are Socio-Economic Disparities in Diet Quality Explained by Diet Cost?" *Journal of Epidemiology and Community Health* 66(6): 530-535.

NM Voices. 2010. "New Mexico Revenues and Expenditures: A Mid-Recession Snapshot." New Mexico Voices for Children. Fiscal Policy Project Policy Brief. Albuquerque, NM.

Page-Reeves, J. 2008. "Increasing Food Stamp Participation in New Mexico: Strategies for Success in 2008-2009 Advocacy Tool." Community Report. New Mexico Food Stamp Working Group.

———. A. Anixter Scott, M. Moffett, V. Apodaca, and V. Apodaca. 2012. "'*It is always that sense of wanting...never really being satisfied*': How Sharing '*Platos*', Meal-Stretching, and Women's Social Wealth Re-Contour the Experience of Food Insecurity in an Urban Food Desert Community." Paper presented at the annual meeting of the American Anthropological Association, San Francisco.

———. S. Mishra, J. Niforatos, L. Regino, R. Bulten, and A. Gingerich. 2013. "An Integrated Approach to Diabetes Prevention: Anthropology, Public Health and Community Engagement." *The Qualitative Report* 18, no. 98: 1-22.

————. A. Anixter Scott, M. Moffett, V. Apodaca, and V. Apodaca. 2014. "*It is always that sense of wanting...never really being satisfied*': Women's Quotidian Struggles with Food Insecurity in a Hispanic Community in New Mexico." *Hunger and Environmental Nutrition.* In press.

Parry, K. 2003. "Constant Comparison." In *The SAGE Encyclopedia of Social Science Research Methods*, M. Lewis-Beck, A. Bryman, and T. Futing, editors. Thousand Oaks, CA: Sage Publications.

Rodriguez, J.C. 2010. "Squeezed Tighter: Public Assistance Benefits Face Reductions as State Battles Budget Woes, Leaving Struggling Families to do Without Necessities." *Albuquerque Journal*, December 27, 2010.

Sanchez, J. 2008. *Martineztown, 1823–1950: Hispanics, Italians, Jesuits and Land Investors in New Town Albuquerque.* Albuquerque, NM: Rio Grande Books.

Seefeldt, K.S. 2010. "Low-Income Women's Experiences with Food Programs, Food Spending, and Food-Related Hardships: Evidence from Qualitative Data." Report #57. Washington, DC: U.S. Department of Agriculture; Economic Research Service.

Sukovic, M., B. Sharf, J. Sharkey, and Julie St. John. 2011. "Seasoning for the Soul: Empowerment through Food Preparation among Mexican Women in the Texas *Colonias.*" *Food and Foodways* 19(3): 228-247.

Swanson, J., C. Olson, E. Miller, and F. Lawrence. 2008. "Rural Mothers' Use of Formal Programs and Informal Social Supports to Meet Family Food Needs: A Mixed Methods Study." *Journal of Family Economic Issues* 29: 674-690.

Thompson, J. 2012. "What's the Matter with New Mexico." *High Country News.*

Tucker, C. 2012. "Food Variety, Quality Affect Some Students' School Lunch decisions." *The Nation's Health* 41(10): 14-14.

U.S. Census Bureau. 2011. *Income, Poverty, and Health Insurance Coverage in the United States 2010.*

————. 2012. *Currrent population survey annual social and economic supplement.*

Wallin, A. 2012. "Facing the Fiscal Cliff: How Nondefense Sequestration Cuts Will Impact New Mexico." New Mexico Voices for Children. Fiscal Policy Project Policy Brief. Albuquerque, NM.

Warr, D. 2005. "Social Networks in a 'Discredited' Neighborhood." *Journal of Sociology* 41(3): 285-308.

Weismantel, M.J. 2008. "Forward." In *Kitchenspace: Women, Fiestas and Everyday Life in Central Mexico* by M.E. Christie. Austin, TX: University of Texas Press.

Wheeler, S. and W. Patterson. 2007. "The Rise of the Regional City: Spatial Development of the Albuquerque Metropolitan Area." *New Mexico Historical Review* 82(1): 1-36.

Williams, P., R. MacAulay, B. Anderson, K. Barro, D. Gillis, C. Johnson, L. Langille, S. Moran and D. Reimer. 2012. "'*I Would Have Never Thought That I Would Be in Such a Predicament*': Voices From Women Experiencing Food Insecurity in Nova Scotia, Canada." *Journal of Hunger and Environmental Nutrition* 7(2-3): 253-270.

Working Poor Families Project. 2013. "Low-Income Working Families: The Growing Economic Gap." The Brookings Institute. Washington, DC.

CHAPTER 4

Negotiating Food Security along the U.S.-Mexico Border: Social Strategies, Practice, and Networks among Mexican Immigrant Women

Lois Stanford

Introduction: Constructing Food Security

Food security continues to be a challenge for poorer households around the world, reflecting complex political, social, and economic factors. In general, food security is recognized as a household's ability to access enough food to meet family members' needs and to lead a healthy life, but varying definitions and measurements of household food security across different nations and government agencies shape the way that societies perceive food insecurity and those households needing assistance (Lappé, et al. 2013, 1). Yet, these definitions and policies may misrepresent the very nature of food insecurity and what it means to those households most affected. Understanding how poorer households address food insecurity requires looking more closely at how food insecurity is constructed and the strategies adopted by these households to ameliorate it.

In the United States, the Great Depression first defined the public's experience and understanding of food insecurity, but, in the following decades, there was little public discussion or recognition of hunger. In the 1960s, Congressional visits to the Mississippi Delta and the CBS television documentary, "Hunger in America," brought public attention to the persistence of poverty and hunger in certain regions of the United States (Wilde 2013, 173). By the late 1980s and early 1990s, the U.S. government moved to assess household food security and hunger, constructing social categories that would then serve as the underlying basis for federal programs of food assistance. As well, defining the term "hunger" and categorizing those households that were "hungry" became caught up in political debates within federal agencies, such that the USDA has dropped the term in favor of the less controversial "very low food insecurity." Thus understanding exactly what constitutes "food insecurity," "households with hunger," and/or "under-nutrition" is critical because federal agencies apply these concepts to delineate different categories of those at risk (Bickel, et al. 2000; and Lappé, et al. 2013, 2-3).

The U.S. Department of Agriculture defines food security as when all people at all times have access to sufficient, safe, and nutritious food for an active and healthy life. Based on this definition, USDA then categorizes food insecurity as a "household-level economic and social condition of limited access to food, while hunger is an individual-level physiological condition that may result from food insecurity." Reflecting this conceptualization of "categories," the USDA has constructed a range of food security, a continuum that moves from high food security, to marginal food security, to low food security, and finally to very low food security. Determining the regions, cities, and/or neighborhoods that are characterized by food hardship emerges as an important focus of USDA studies of food security and, thus, of efforts to address food insecurity.

Based on the USDA's classificatory systems discussed above, the prevalence of food insecurity has fluctuated over time in the United States. In 1995, the U.S. government initially established a national goal to reduce household food insecurity from 12 percent to 6 percent by 2010 (Wilde 2013, 177). By 2006, USDA estimates were that 10.9 percent of households were food insecure, and that this food insecurity was recurrent, i.e., occasional or episodic, rather than chronic (Nord, et al. 2007: 9). While the report's tone is somewhat optimistic, given the national level declines in food insecurity, the analysis of food insecurity across different kinds of households indicated that certain households (i.e., female-headed, households of color, households in the South and Southwest, and low-income households) displayed higher rates of food insecurity than national averages. By 2008, the crisis in the U.S. national economy undermined earlier gains in reducing household food insecurity, and the 2008 and 2010 studies report incremental increases in household food insecurity (Nord 2009; Coleman-Jensen, et al. 2001). The most recent 2012 report now identifies an estimated 14.5 percent of U.S. households as food insecure, including 5.7 percent with very low food security (Coleman-Jensen, et al. 2013, 5). The 2012 study indicates that previously identified vulnerable households, discussed above, continued to exhibit even higher rates of food insecurity than the national average. Furthermore, those households identified with very low food security, an estimated 5.7 percent of the U.S. population, reported practices such as cutting the size of adult household meals, having adult members go without eating for entire days, etc., practices that suggested patterns of reduced food intake. Further-more, 89 percent of these households reporting adults skipping meals for 3 or more months out of the year, suggesting more chronic conditions of food insecu-rity than reported in earlier years (Coleman-Jensen, et al. 2013, 5).

These statistics paint a picture in which federal food assistance becomes critical in alleviating local food insecurity and providing a safety net. The most important food program is the Supplemental Nutritional Assistance Program (SNAP) that provides supplementary funds for food to low-income households with gross income of less than 130 percent of the federal poverty standard. Other eligibility criteria are important; that is, households must have limited financial assets, legal immigrants are eligible, and undocumented immigrants are ineligi-ble for the program. Research indicates that SNAP participation can vary from year to year, reflecting in the percentages of eligible unemployed people, but in the past few years, the percentage of eligible employed people seeking SNAP benefits has increased. By 2011, an estimated 14 percent of the entire U.S. popu-lation, that is, 44.7 million people, obtained SNAP benefits (Wilde 2013, 183).

Despite the increased levels of food insecurity, the growing number of citi-zens in the SNAP program, and chronic persistent nature of many households' dependence on SNAP, the USDA model of food security/insecurity constructs a false categorization of household types, distinguishing between those house-holds that are food secure, on the one hand, and those that are not, on the other. This framework overlooks the complexity and dynamics of these food insecure households. As well, this framework, constructed for the purpose of "measur-ing" food insecurity, labels certain households, placing them in a social and eco-nomic situation of dependency. While well meaning in its intent, these political structures affect the manner in which agency officials and representatives inter-act with emergency food assistance recipients.

Food Security *Desde Abajo* (From Below)

Recent research on food security at the household level in Third World countries has documented the complexity of assessing household food security, identify-ing hunger experience, dietary diversity and coping strategies as important vary-ing indicators of households' capacities to address food insecurity. In rural South Africa, households actively adopt coping strategies, such as collecting wild foods, migrating for work, or selling livestock (Kirkland, et. al. 2013, 69-70). Other studies, focusing on food accessibility in Cuba, have demonstrated that individuals' memories and perceptions shape how they use and relate to state food rationing and food provisioning through the black market (Garth 2009, 32). In all cases, these studies provide a more complete understanding of food security by situating individuals' strategies and practices within the context of a broader food provisioning framework.

In the United States, viewed from "below," poorer, food insecure households engage in a series of practices that reinforce their own household security, moving shared food through community and kin networks, and insuring long-term survival. SNAP assistance shifts from being a form of emergency food assistance to one of a myriad of food provisioning strategies by which poor households redistribute food through their own networks, share food with neighbors and friends, and secure some semblance of household and community food security. The reality of this perspective is reinforced by food provisioning studies of Latino households that report the use of convenience stores, mobile food vendors, and neighbors as important sources of food for households (Sharkey, Dean and Johnson 2012, 705-710; Sharkey, Dean, Nalty, and Xu 2013, 1-18). Examining food security through the lens of family and community food provisioning strategies provides a more appropriate framework for understanding how poorer families negotiate their economic challenges, the severity of constraints faced, the role of food assistance in household survival, and the important role of social relations and kin networks in economic survival.[1]

The Setting: The U.S.-Mexico Border

The U.S.-Mexico Border has been subjected to a long history of migration, contested boundaries, and international disputes. Neglected by both the United States and Mexico, this vast desert region remained isolated until improved infrastructure and capital investment led to increased population growth in the late 19th century. In the early 20th century, the nature of the region's economic development, dependent on agriculture and mining, relied heavily on an abundance of cheap, unregulated immigrant labor (Esparza and Donelson 2008, 28-35). In the 1960s, agricultural declines and urban growth encouraged the transition to government employment and a service economy. The growth of the *maquildaora* industry in the 1970s and 1980s attracted Mexican migrants to the northern Mexican border and border communities, an industrial growth that was later devastated by the passage of the North American Free Trade Agreement (NAFTA) in 1994 (Martinez 2010, 22-23). This pattern of economic development fostered the growth of a differentiated labor force, a small highly educated professional sector supported by a vast reserve of lesser skilled, minority workforce, heavily dominated by Mexican immigrants.

Within this restricted economy, Mexican immigrant households established homes, often in trailers or makeshift shelters, in less expensive, unincorporated rural settlements situated near the urban and agricultural centers that offered them temporary employment. These communities, known as *colonias*, grew in an unorganized fashion without the support of services, public transportation, and government support. Yet, within this category, the *colonias* themselves exhibit a wide range of infrastructure, access to interstates, and level of economic development (Czerniak and Hohstadt 2010, 48-50). The U.S. Department of Housing and Urban Development (HUD) and the federal government define a *colonia* as a community that is in the state of Arizona, California, New Mexico or Texas; within 150 miles of the U.S.-Mexico border, and lacks adequate sewage systems and safe housing. While these communities range in infrastructural development, many lack adequate housing, potable water, sewer systems, and/or drainage systems.

The state of New Mexico now contains 55 federally designated *colonias*, of which 37 of these unincorporated rural settlements are clustered in Doña Ana County, in close proximity to the U.S.-Mexico border. The combination of poverty and rural isolation weigh heavily, and this region along the U.S.-Mexico border has been designated as an area with persistently high poverty rates for decades. The New Mexico Environment Department estimates that 97 percent of *colonias* residents are Hispanic (at the same time that 85 percent are U.S. citizens). Communities that satisfy conditions to be recognized as colonias qualify for federal and state aid in projects to improve infrastructure, housing, and public health conditions.

The second largest county in New Mexico, Doña Ana County encompasses 3,807 square miles, with only few incorporated municipalities. Las Cruces, the only metropolitan area in the county, accounts for about 50 percent of the total population of 209,000 people. Of that population, an estimated 65.7 percent are county residents of Hispanic or Latino origin, with an estimated 51.8 percent speaking a language other than English at home, usually Spanish. The median household income between 2006 and 2010 is $36,657, compared to the U.S. national average of $50,053. Doña Ana County faces extreme challenges of economic poverty, high levels of unemployment, rural isolation, and an established population of undocumented Mexican immigrants.

Characterized by low incomes, persistent poverty, high ethnic diversity, lack of educational opportunities, and rural isolation, this region now exhibits deteriorating food security throughout the region and pockets of permanent food insecurity in certain sectors (Page-Reeves 2012, 33). Based on the USDA calculations, New Mexico has a food insecurity rate of 17.1 percent with an estimated 336,430 people food insecure. Among New Mexican children, the rate is even higher with an estimated 27.3 percent of children (i.e., 137,720 individuals) who are food insecure. Understanding the nature of food insecurity in these communities requires closer examination of how households in these communities negotiate their food security through different provisioning strategies.

Recent estimates suggest that 25 percent of the population lives below the federal poverty guidelines and 20 percent of the population receives food stamps. Doña Ana County has a food insecurity rate of 18.4 percent for adults and an estimated 31.8 percent child food insecurity rate. Within this county, *colonia* residents face even greater challenges. These underdeveloped rural communities have been primarily settled by Mexican descent residents, many of them undocumented immigrants. The communities are marked by low income, low levels of education, high levels of poverty, and high levels of food insecurity.

The *Colonia* of *Vado/Del Cerro*

Situated in the southern part of the county, the area now designated as a *colonia* is actually comprised of a group of small nested communities, each with its own history and nested social network. Vado, the oldest community, was settled in the late 1800s by African-American farmers, descendents from slaves, who migrated into southern New Mexico to establish small farms. In the early 1970s, Bill Stahmann, owner of large commercial pecan orchards in the Mesilla Valley, founded Del Cerro as a housing development for his retired employees, as the pecan industry mechanized. In establishing this neighborhood, Del Cerro was laid out in a grid pattern, recreating the street names and church of the earlier community at Stahmann Farms. By the 1980s, farm workers, attracted by agricultural work in chile and cotton, employment in the dairy industry, and opportunities in a local cement plant, began to acquire individual lots, purchased from investors converting agricultural land into unimproved rural subdivisions. These lots locally expanded in tracts on dirt roads off rural valley roads in the valley, expanding to an estimated three square miles of clustered small homes and mobile trailers. As one resident recalled, "*In Del Cerro, it was not unusual for families to string up an 800 foot extension from one house to another to provide electricity.*"

As the population grew, Doña Ana County officials became worried about living conditions in the isolated rural settlements. In the early 1990s, in response to concerns about substandard housing conditions, county officials targeted the Del Cerro/Vado *colonia* to address problems and turn the community into a "model *colonia*." In 1995, the Colonia Task Force for the Development of Rural and Urban policy proposed a plan to improve conditions in Del Cerro/Vado and other *colonias*. In 1996, with the support of the Catholic Church, community residents formed the *Centro Fuerza y Unidad*, an association of *colonia* residents who successfully lobbied for the construction of a community resource center in Del Cerro. HUD has recognized development efforts in Del Cerro/Vado as a "success story" for model *colonias*. These political efforts provided support for infrastructural improvements during the 1990s, including new flood control, road paving, some subsidized housing, drainage, and a new elementary school, but community residents became disenchanted with the contradiction between political promises and subsequent lack of delivery of these promised services.

Despite the lack of services, the population continued to grow. Over time, the *colonias* grew from an estimated 1,396 in 1990 to 3,003 people in 2000, although locals estimate the population to be much higher. The population is also young, with an estimated 35.3 percent of the residents under 18 years of age. In 2000 Vado/Del Cerro received its legal designation as a *colonia*, but the political delineation does not constitute a community. Residents refer to themselves as residents of either Vado or Del Cerro, and county officials acknowledge the challenge of fostering a single community identity.

Economic conditions and opportunities have not improved significantly in the past twenty years. Historically residents worked in seasonal employment in agriculture, including chile or cotton, neighboring dairies, or one local cement plant. In 1999, a HUD report estimated an unemployment rate of 33 percent in the area. The HUD report also estimated that 33 percent of the families in the Del Cerro/Vado area lived below the poverty level, and 77 percent of the population over 25 had not completed high school. Low incomes increase household food insecurity, to the extent that an estimated 97 percent of all students in the local school district are eligible for free breakfast programs in the schools.

From 2000–2010, the economic crisis, declines in the local agricultural economy, and continued population increases undermined the achievements of the 1990s. The declines in local commercial agriculture combined with declines in the dairy industry reduced local household incomes. At the same time, more people moved into the area. Fleeing the uncertainty, violence, and economic decline in Ciudad Juarez, Mexican residents have sought refuge and housing with family in El Paso and southern New Mexico. In Arizona, new state laws and a hostile political climate have led many Mexican immigrant families to leave Arizona, seeking residence with families in other states. Southern New Mexico draws poorer Mexican immigrants fleeing difficult situations in other regions, yet it also represents an uncertain haven, since most of Doña Ana County is situated south of the main internal U.S. border checkpoint along the north-south interstate. Undocumented immigrants who have managed to cross the U.S.-Mexico border may be asked to produce documentation of legal status at the interstate checkpoint, and they risk incarceration and deportation if they are questioned by the border patrol while going through the checkpoint. The wide distribution of homes and the isolation afford undocumented residents the opportunity to maintain a low profile and avoid deportation. Population increases are not necessarily new, distinct households moving into the area but rather extended family and kin moving into existing households, thus increasing the family size within the existing household.

Despite this rapid growth, the community remains rural and isolated. There are no major grocery stores within the area. One small family-owned grocery store sells meat, packaged foods, and some fresh fruits and vegetables, while residents also purchase small food items at two local "dollar" stores. These small food stores accept SNAP benefits, but no longer allow residents to purchase food on credit. There is also food available at the truck stops located at the nearest freeway exit. For the most part, residents must drive to either Las Cruces or El Paso, an estimated twenty minutes either way, to purchase groceries. The general economic decline combined with the increased pressure of more family and relatives in the same households have increased community dependence on what federal and state agencies categorize as emergency food assistance. Some agency officials believe that it is the food bank and other emergency food assistance programs that allow rural residents, such as those in Del Cerro/Vado, to remain in the rural areas. They contend that, if it were not for this food distribution, residents would have left to move into more urban areas. Yet, community center volunteers note that at the same time that local demand for emergency food assistance has increased, the volume of food delivered has declined. Some months the center has cancelled food distribution because there was not food to distribute.

Food Assistance Programs in the *Colonias*

In Del Cerro/Vado, many households depend on food assistance to increase household food security. The programs available to community residents include the Supplemental Nutritional Assistance Program (SNAP), Women, Infants, and Children (WIC) Program, the USDA Commodity Supplemental Food Programs (CSFP), the National School Lunch Program (NSLP), and emergency food assistance from local charity organizations, in particular *Casa de Peregrinos*. Applicants to the SNAP program must meet federal qualifications of U.S. residency, family size, and household income below federal poverty income guidelines. The WIC program provides supplemental commodities to pregnant women and children up to the age of four, requiring similar qualifications as the SNAP program. For residents of Del Cerro/Vado, the two major limitations to both of these programs are the residency requirements and transportation. Undocumented colonias residents are not eligible for the SNAP program. As well, applicants must commute to the Income Support Office, located in Las Cruces twenty miles to the north. For residents with a car or in households with only one vehicle, applying to the program may be difficult.

The USDA/CSFP program distributes food to resident seniors through the Senior Food Program. An estimated 275 senior citizens are registered for this program. The Senior Food Program uses pre-packaged food boxes that volunteers distribute to senior registrants who must come to the center to pick up their food allotment in boxes. For seniors, food boxes include primarily pasta, canned fruit, canned vegetables, juice, canned beans, cheese, cereal and dried milk. When available, fresh milk and eggs may also be provided. The boxes weigh approximate 40-50 lbs. each and are intended to provide supplemental food for two months. Senior residents will often request a registered proxy to pick up the boxes for them, if they cannot carry or transport the box itself. As well, those senior citizens who have diabetes, an estimated 60 percent of the participants, are not supposed to be consuming much of the food that they receive. They may opt to share this food with other recipients at the center distribution or to take it home, in turn distributing it to other family members.

Administered by the USDA, the National School Lunch Program provides free breakfasts and lunches Monday through Friday in the local Gadsden School District. Statistics indicate that almost all children in the southern Doña Ana County region qualify for these lunch programs. During the summers, the Del Cerro Community Center participates in the Summer Food Service Program (SFSP), through which sack lunches are distributed to community children every week day throughout the summer vacation.

For many community residents, monthly emergency food distribution provided by a local non-profit organization, *Casa de Peregrinos*, provides the most important supplemental food source. Founded in 1979, *Casa de Peregrinos* historically provided services to the homeless population, but since 1982, the non-profit organization shifted to concentrate on providing emergency food services to Las Cruces city residents. In 2011, *Casa de Peregrinos* obtained funding through Roadrunner Food Bank of New Mexico, the state-based agency under the national umbrella organization, Feeding America. Under the Rural Initiative Program, *Casa de Peregrinos* employed a system of mobile food pantries to distribute food on a monthly basis to 1,900 families in isolated rural areas throughout Doña Ana County, expanding to 4,239 families by the first half of 2012. Out of the ten designated rural *colonias*, five have community resource centers that serve as food distribution sites. In January 2013, the non-profit began to deliver nonperishable foods to the community resource centers, allowing the centers to store food staples and distribute food locally in emergency situations.

Households must register in order to qualify to receive food. Applicants must provide identification and some bill addressed to their residence in order to demonstrate that they reside in the *colonia*. Those who are undocumented cannot obtain an identification card without a social security card and thus cannot register for the program. Rumors persist that some applicants may use false identification and bills to apply for food assistance, but in these cases, they would risk being identified, something that would call attention to their situation. Spanish-speaking applicants may experience problems applying for food assistance, as well as any other assistance. In these cases, community center volunteers often help applicants in completing the required forms. Language limitations can frustrate applicants who often don't fully understand the options, such as the designation of proxies to pick up commodities for the applicant. In the words of one elderly gentleman, *"They just tell you to put your name and address, but they don't explain it, and the papers are in English, so we can't read it. I just sign where they tell me."*

Households must register in advance to receive food on the monthly distribution days. At distribution, registered households receive food before households who have not previously registered. In the *colonia* of Del Cerro/Vado, in the past two years, about 175 families are registered monthly to receive food, but an estimated 200-275 families will show up to obtain food on distribution day. In addition, families from other *colonias* now regularly show up in the hopes of receiving food. The community center regularly runs out of food before all households are served.

Negotiating Food Security: Food Provisioning Strategies

From the perspective of community residents, the food assistance programs (discussed above) comprise a range of food sources from which households avail themselves in order to supplement food purchased from household income. Thus food assistance not only supplements food purchases; it also can allow the diversion of money for food towards other necessary household purchases. In all, acquiring and using food assistance becomes an important economic component in a household's diversified economy. This different perspective on accessing food is reflected in a range of different practices that reflect people's attitudes and agency as they negotiate the food assistance "system." Looking at food provisioning from the perspective of community residents also highlights the complexity and dynamics of food assistance, characteristics that are often overlooked in survey research. Here the analysis of the critical components of the food provisioning framework move from general household economic strategies to specific practices within the food assistance system, but, in all cases, these practices are oriented towards insuring household food security.

As well, it is the women in the households, mothers and grandmothers, who assume primary responsibility for negotiating networks, building social relations, and provisioning their households. This responsibility mirrors other studies that detail the gendered division of labor in Latino households and the critical role that women play in both providing food for their families and preserving culinary food traditions (Greder 2012, 154-156). The identification of the critical themes discussed in this section is based on fifteen interviews conducted in Spanish with women residents of the *colonia* as part of an NMSU service learning class conducted in spring 2013.[1] This applied research project was exploratory in nature; further study is needed to elaborate on these strategies, determine the extent of practices, and identify broader barriers to alleviating food insecurity in this community.

Transporting Family and Neighbors

Any discussion about food security in this community begins with transportation. The *colonia* is situated between two major cities, Las Cruces and El Paso, yet approximately twenty miles in either direction from these centers, where major supermarkets and food stores are located. Accessing food in this rural area requires a private vehicle, since there is no public transportation available. Households often possess a single vehicle, and working household members take the vehicle with them to work during the day. In other cases, elderly women in particular may not know how to drive, since their husbands have always driven them. Women express concern about burdening working spouses with requests for rides after their husbands have returned home from work. As women age or lose elderly husbands, they become even more dependent on others for transportation.

Addressing the challenge of transportation requires carpooling and ridesharing. Households will often pool resources, i.e., purchasing gas together, in order to coordinate shopping trips among two to three households, or they may rotate schedules in order to coordinate trips. In the words of one woman, *"We help one another. There are times I take them, and there are times when I can't... But that's when they take me. This is how we help each other."* Individuals who do not have a vehicle often contribute up to $20 to cover the costs of gasoline to someone who has a vehicle. In cases where individuals may lack money to cover gas costs, they may offer food, such as from the monthly food distribution or from their SNAP allotment, as a way of compensating the driver. As well, for those who drive, offering rides provides the driver with a sense of community and recognition of her role in helping others. *"I drive my neighbors everywhere. On Friday, I took a neighbor to her eye appointment, and I drive everywhere. I even take them to appointments in El Paso."*

Pooling Family Income and Resources

In Del Cerro and Vado, households may consist of a husband, wife, and children, but in many cases, households include multiple generations (grandparents, parents, and children) and/or extended families (including cousins, aunts, and uncles). Multiple generations and extended households are more common with the immigration of new residents, often family members. In these cases, households often pool income, and family members contribute what they can to ensuring household economic security. Historically, residents worked in seasonal agricultural labor or nearby dairies, but economic declines in both agricultural industries have reduced labor opportunities. For most youth and young adults, finding employment requires traveling to nearby Anthony, Las Cruces, or El Paso, which in all cases requires transportation. Youth are expected to contribute economically, to help with the rent or family needs, and these demands often discourage youth from continuing their education. For household members who do work, their lack of education, work papers, language skills, and job skills often trap them in part-time, temporary positions that do not provide steady employment. Even for those who work full-time, they work long hours for low wages, usually without health benefits. Household members continue to work into their elderly years. Men who have worked for their adult life in the dairies often continue to look for side jobs, anything that they can find that will help the household's survival.

As well, from the household perspective, food assistance through any program is considered as part of the household's economic resources. Elderly grandparents may no longer contribute income to the household, but if they receive commodities through the Senior Program, they contribute food resources to the household. As one elderly woman explained, *"We need to help our kids because they have kids and they struggle, and we need to help them, too."* Household members do not comply with the eligibility categories assigned by external food assistance programs. Instead, they view food assistance as one component of the household economy, a resource that is distributed throughout the household, insuring the food security of the group.

Expanding Households

In this area of southern New Mexico, all residents, citizens or not, reside in a kind of frontier zone. To leave this region, be it north, west, or east, on all major interstates requires travelers to pass through interior US Border Patrol checkpoints. Undocumented Mexicans who successfully past the U.S.-Mexico border may find it safer to stay in the ambiguity of the U.S. border region, rather than risking deportation by trying to pass interior checkpoints. The pressure of surveillance in the neighboring state of Arizona and the increased violence in Ciudad Juárez has resulted in increased numbers of undocumented Mexicans moving to southern New Mexico for security reasons. People tend to go where they have family, so Del Cerro/Vado residents describe how the community population has grown significantly, yet they cannot give precise numbers. Population does not grow by new households; rather existing households, or trailers, expand, absorbing extended family members fleeing Arizona or violence in northern Mexico.

These new residents must work in seasonal labor or temporary jobs where employers do not require legal work permits. Family members and neighbors assume the responsibility of sharing food with these relatives or neighbors because there is no other way for undocumented residents to obtain food assistance. Furthermore, reflecting their precarious situation, these new "residents" live in fear of being caught by the Border Patrol and deported back into northern Mexico. Not only do they not show up to request emergency food assistance; they may also fear even leaving the trailers, walking down the street to the local convenience store, or being anywhere in public. More established residents talked about this hidden population, noting that they often shared food that they had received through food assistance to those identified as even more needy and desperate. As one woman recounted,

My neighbor across the street is illegal. I know that she cannot go to the food programs because she is scared. When I pick up my food, I always take her something. The same when I go to the store. If something is on sale, I buy a little extra to give her some.

Use of Proxies: Protecting Neighbors

In the monthly food distribution, residents are expected to preregister, as discussed above, and they must show up consistently. If registered residents miss more than two months, they are dropped from the list and must register again before having access to food distribution. Residents who cannot show up personally are allowed to designate another resident as a proxy. Foodbank representatives understand that some residents, such as elderly community residents, may have health issues that prevent them from coming to distribution.

At the same time, as noted above, many community residents are not U.S. citizens. Furthermore, U.S. Border Patrol vehicles often appear *magically* in the community center parking lot on distribution days. Undocumented residents who fear deportation may send designated family members or neighbors to pick up food for them. In cases where Border Patrol trucks are identified in the area or near the community center, residents pass along the word through a "phone tree" to other neighbors who may then send proxies. On those days when the Border Patrol is around, hardly anyone will show up; once they have left, people begin to immediately appear at the center.

The Politics of Volunteering

The non-profit agency delivers the boxes and the food pallets, but community center volunteers must unload the pallets, sort the food packages, and handle distribution. Volunteers sort through the food as well, selecting out food that is rotten, at time almost half the volume of food to be distributed. The volunteers occupy a delicate position of intermediary between non-profit agency employees who regulate access and community residents who must take only the amount allotted. The volunteers themselves are *colonia* residents who qualify to receive food boxes through the food distribution, but they must be discrete and careful about collecting their boxes afterwards because many residents assume that they themselves are county employees. They are sometimes criticized by those residents who think that the volunteers don't deserve food assistance or have taken too much food. The volunteers also respond to the needs of elderly clients, who often cannot wait in long lines for hours in order to obtain food.

Timing on Food Distribution Day

Residents often show up early on the day of the food distribution, waiting in long lines in the community center parking lot while volunteers unload and sort the delivered food. For those who cannot work, their dependence on the food assistance means that many recipients show up hours in advance, waiting in lines to receive food. Missing the distribution can result in losing out on the food needed for subsequent weeks. One interviewee recalled the time she went without food for a month when she was late from a doctor's appointment and did not arrive at the center before the food was gone. "*If you can't come at the time the food is distributed, you don't eat.*"

The food distribution process usually takes three to four hours, during which time people visit and talk among themselves. Those who arrive early are the first ones to pass through the distribution often receive the best selection if fresh fruit and vegetables are of limited quantity. "*The ones who pass first get the good food, and the others don't.*" Participating in the food distribution and taking advantage of the food offered requires showing up hours before distribution and waiting for hours in line.

Negotiating Food Selection

The primary food items distributed include potatoes, canned goods, dried goods, and breads. Foods available will also include frozen foods, eggs, whole grain pasta, and sometimes meat. At times, there may also be fresh fruits and vegetables, but these are often spoiled. Food distribution participants commented on the declining quality of food distributed, recognizing general shifts from fresh fruits and vegetables towards more processed foods and food staples. Residents repeatedly commented on the poor quality of the food, citing the mold on bread, rotten vegetables, post-dated meats, among other problems. Contradicting public assumptions about the docility of food assistance recipients, these residents may comment on food quality as they slowly move through the line, requesting different items or selecting among those they are offered. As one recipient commented, "*Who wants to take home rotten food that they can't eat?*"

As well, residents may sort through food, taking what their families will eat and leaving other items, such as packaged Tuna Helper with no accompanying tuna cans, for which they have little use. Other items, such as whole wheat pasta, are unfamiliar to Mexican immigrants. Preparation instructions on packaged foods usually come in English, and recipients may leave behind food items that are culturally inappropriate or that they do not know how to prepare.

Some residents may leave foods such as juice or bread, if several family members have Type II diabetes and have been advised to avoid certain foods. Residents may also consider cooking time in selecting food items. Given that many residences, i.e., homes or trailers, are not part of the county gas distribution systems, these families cook with propane gas, either on a kitchen stove or outdoor grill. Some residents estimated that they spend $250-300/month on gas to cook and heat water. In these cases, quick food preparation, i.e., canned goods or processed foods, are more economical to prepare, in contrast with other foods, such as dried beans, that require much longer cooking times.

Others, recognizing the inherent value of food items that they themselves may not eat, simply collect everything distributed. In particular, residents commented on the large quantities of canned corn, green beans, and olives. As one woman commented,

> They give us so many canned foods. I cannot feed my children canned vegetables. But, I don't deny the food. I simply take it and pass it on to those who do like it or need it.

Sharing Food With Family and Neighbors

From the household perspective, "emergency food distribution" comprises one component of the range of household food provisioning strategies. For those households with three generations (i.e., grandparents, parents, and grandchildren), each generation is engaged in providing for the family. As noted above, the grandparents may obtain food through the Senior Food Program or Rural Initiatives, while the adult children work full-time. In turn, the grandparents assume responsibility for childcare in the afternoons and summers. The children, if they leave early in the morning, may be able to eat breakfast at school and, during the summers, participate in the summer lunch program at the community center. Elementary age children can spend less than 30 minutes on the school bus to arrive at school, while middle school and high school students require an estimated 1½ hours one way on the bus in the mornings to arrive at school. Multi-generational families exhibit the greatest food security, drawing on the support and practices of all family members, while small households, particularly elderly living alone, remain the most vulnerable.

At the same time, the "households," those families residing within a residence, are embedded in broader kin networks through which food is often shared and redistributed. Food is often shared between families and distributed to families that are most in need. Those who work in agriculture or on farms often bring fresh produce that is in turn distributed among neighbors. In turn, kin networks can also create stress and undermine household food security, since one cannot deny family members food. Elderly residents describe situations where their adult children will send their grandchildren for a "*visit*," at times, hoping that the grandparents may be able to provide for the children at times when their own parents cannot. All respondents indicated that the food received through distribution covered at most two weeks, and they commented on strategies for stretching out the food and rationing it over the course of the month. At the end of the month, elderly residents who live alone may subsist on beans and canned goods, held back from earlier distributions to cover the gap.

In more recent years, health issues have emerged as a concern in people's strategies towards food and food preferences. Middle-aged and elderly residents deal with the development of Type II diabetes as a much more common chronic illness, although statistics are unreliable. Some local residents and agency officials estimated that upwards of 60 percent of the adult population is diabetic, but many adults have not been tested and do not actually know whether or not they have diabetes. Recognizing the gravity of increased obesity and Type II diabetes among younger household members, residents state preferences for less-processed foods, fresh fruits and vegetables, less sugar drinks etc., but financial challenges and dependence on emergency food services limit their capacity to seek alternative foods. As well, according to interviewees, the public health prescriptive for diabetics tends towards the "banned" list approach, in which some of the most commonly consumed foods, i.e., tortillas, enchiladas, gorditas, beans, etc., are forbidden. Diabetic residents must balance their health needs on the one hand with family preferences and the preferred *sazon*, or flavor, that they and their families prefer. Given that historically and culturally, the *sazon* is how one measures food quality, these new demands place burdens on households, in particular on those household members responsible for preparing food.

Swallowing Pride

Finally, community residents recognize the position of dependency that they assume in requesting food assistance. They are fully conscious of the political structure, public attitudes about food assistance, and the humility that they must assume in order to request food. Yet, this process often creates a situation in which subtle differences and resentments are played out. Food recipients often feel humiliated that they must ask for food assistance, and they are often suspicious of the role and practices of community volunteers. Community volunteers, themselves food assistance recipients, feel that recipients question their motives and practices, as if they were part of the system instead of the community. Agency representatives sometimes act as police agents, monitoring the selection of food items and limiting the number of items. At this point, the conflict of attitudes reflects the contradictions between the system of food delivery services imposed by measuring food security and the system of food provisioning in which the community operates.

At the same time, they fully recognize the critical role of food assistance in achieving the food security of their household.

I know that if it wasn't for the center and this food, many families would go hunger. Something is something, and we come because we need it. If we didn't, we wouldn't go.

Equally important in reconciling this sense of dependency is the women's sense that they share these challenges with their neighbors throughout the community. Women attempt to comfort and reassure each other. As one woman relates, "*I tell my neighbor not to worry about it, to remember that her family needs the food.*"

Conclusion: Reconceptualizing Food Security

"We are neighbors; we have to help each other."

The interviews were exploratory, and identification of critical themes preliminary in nature. At the same time, interviews and fieldwork clearly emphasize the active engagement by community residents in seeking to access food and maintain food security. In the interviews, conversations moved back and forth, between discussions about the challenges of applying for food assistance to those of traveling to nearby urban centers for shopping. Seen from these women's perspectives, providing for their families requires a wide range of different kinds of coping strategies, determined in large part by household composition, legal status of household members, and age of different household members. One individual's ability to access certain food programs assisted the entire household in its quest for food security. As well, women planned out coping strategies over the long run. Distributed food can be saved for times when less food is available, or food may be shared with neighbors with the implicit understanding that they in turn may help out at some time of future need.

When the sharing and food redistribution extends beyond family and includes the newer, most vulnerable residents, the food provisioning practices move into the realm of constructing a sense of community. Irrespective of immigration status, as one resident noted, "*Everyone here needs something. We can't just turn our heads the other way.*" The *colonias* along the U.S.-Mexico border are constructed communities, often where residents come together out of economic necessity, but in sharing food and addressing neighbor's needs, these women begin to construct and reinforce the social bonds that can maintain a community.

Finally, the focus on food distribution overlooks the underlying cause, poverty. Inadequate education, inadequate training, lack of employment opportunities, and low wages, among other factors all comprise structural conditions that undermine the capacity of rural households to adequately provide for their family's food security. These women often devote great quantities of time as volunteers, sharing rides with neighbor, completing paperwork to access food support services, and other time-consuming activities to secure food, and yet, in this investment of time and effort, they never really alter the economic conditions of their household. The time that they devote to these practices and strategies enables their families to provide food until the end of the month, but their efforts do not fundamentally alter the precarious nature of their household's existence.

Notes

1. Interviews for this project were conducted with Mexican immigrant residents of a *colonia* along the U.S.-Mexico border. Interviews were conducted in Spanish, and participants were granted complete anonymity. Interviews were conducted by the author and participating anthropology students, including Marisol Díaz, Roxanne Grajeda, Valerie Martinez, and Lisa Peña. Appreciation is expressed to all for their participation and hard work; the author assumes responsibility for the English language translation. The service learning project was approved under IRB Application Number 2012-08, by the NMSU Institutional Review Board.

Bibliography

Bickel, Gary, Mark Nord, Cristofer Price, William Hamilton, and John Cook. 2000. *Guide to Measuring Household Food Security: Measuring Food Security in the United States.* Washington, DC: United State Department of Agriculture/Food and Nutrition Service/Office of Analysis, Nutrition, and Evaluation.

Campbell, Cathy and Ellen Desjardins. 1989. "A Model and Research Approach for Studying the Management of Limited Food Resources by Low Income Families." *Society for Nutrition Education* 21, no. 4: 162-171.

Coates, Jennifer. 2004. *Experience and Expression of Food Insecurity Across Cultures: Practical Implications for Valid Measurement.* Washington, DC: USAID/Food and Nutritional Technical Assistance.

Coleman-Jensen, Alisha, Mark Nord, Margaret Andrews, Steven Carlson. 2011. *Household Food Security in the United States, 2010: Measuring Food Security in the United States.* Economic Research Report Number 49. Washington, DC: United States Department of Agriculture/Economic Research Service.

Coleman-Jensen, Alisha, Mark Nord, and Anita Singh. 2013. *Household Food Security in the United States, 2012: Measuring Food Security in the United States.* Economic Research Report Number 49. Washington, DC: United States Department of Agriculture/Economic Research Service.

Czerniak, Robert, and David Hohstadt. 2010. "Economic Development in New Mexico's Colonias." In *The Colonias Reader: Economy, Housing and Public Health in U.S.-Mexico Border Colonias,* edited by Angela Donelson and Adrian Esparza, 44-55. Tucson: University of Arizona Press.

Dean, Wesley, Joseph Sharkey, Cassandra Johnson, and Julie St. John. 2012. "Cultural Repertoires and Food-related Household Technology within *Colonia* Households Under Conditions of Material Hardship." *International Journal for Equity in Health* 11: 1-13.

Esparza, Adrian, and Angela Donelson. 2008. *Colonias in Arizona and New Mexico: Border Poverty and Community Development Solutions.* Tucson: University of Arizona Press.

Garth, Hanna. 2009. "Things Become Scarce: Food Availability and Accessibility in Santiago de Cuba." *NAPA Bulletin* 32: 178-192.

Greder, Kimberly, Flor Romero de Slowing and Kimberly Doudna. 2012. "Latin Immigrant Mothers: Negotiating New Food Environments to Preserve Cultural Food Practices and Healthy Child Eating. *Family and Consumer Sciences Research Journal* 41, no. 2: 145-160.

Hadley, Craig, Sandra Galea, Vijay Nandi, Arijit Nandi, Gerald Lopez, Stacey Strongarone, and Danielle Ompad. 2007. "Hunger and Health among Undocumented Mexican Migrants in a U.S. Urban Area." *Public Health Nutrition* 11, no. 2: 151-158.

Kirkland, Tracy, Robert Kemp, Lori Hunter, and Wayne Twine. 2013. "Toward Improved Understanding of Food Security: a Methodological Examination Based in Rural South Africa." *Food, Culture, and Society* 16. no. 1: 65-83.

Koszewski, Wanda, Donnia Behrends, Megan Nichols, Natalie Sehi, and Georgia Jones. 2011. "Patterns of Family Meals and Food and Nutrition Intake in Limited Resource Families." *Family and Consumer Sciences Research Journal* 39, no. 4: 431-441.

Lappé, Frances Moore, Jennifer Clapp, Molly Anderson, Robin Broad, Ellen Messer, Thomas Page, and Timothy Wise. 2013. "How We Count Hunger Matters." *Ethics and International Affairs*: 1-9.

Martinez, Oscar. 2010. "The U.S.-Mexico Border Economy." In *The Colonias Reader: Economy, Housing and Public Health in U.S.-Mexico Border Colonias*, edited by Angela Donelson and Adrian Esparza, 15-29. Tucson: University of Arizona Press.

Nabhan, Gary, Maribel Alvarez, Jeffrey Benister, and Regina Fitzsimmons. 2012. "Introduction" In *Hungry for Change: Borderlands Food and Water in the Balance*, 1-3. Tucson: The Southwest Center's Kellogg Program in Sustainable Food Systems.

Nord, Mark, Margaret Andrews, Steven Carlson. 2007. *Household Food Security in the United States, 2006: Measuring Food Security in the United States.* Economic Research Report Number 49. Washington, DC: United States Department of Agriculture/Economic Research Service.

Nord, Mark, Margaret Andrews, Steven Carlson. 2009. *Household Food Security in the United States, 2008: Measuring Food Security in the United States.* Economic Research Report Number 49. Washington, DC: U.S. Department of Agriculture/Economic Research Service.

Page-Reeves, Janet. 2012. "Commentary: The Nexus of Poverty, Hunger, and Homelessness in New Mexico." *Social Justice* 38, no. 3: 33-41.

Sharkey, Joseph, Wesley Dean, and Cassandra Johnson. 2012. "Use of *Vendedores* (Mobile Food Vendors), *Pulgas* (Flea Markets), and *Vecinos o Amigos* (Neighbors or Friends) as Alternative Sources of Food for Purchase among Mexican-Origin Households in Texas Border *Colonias.*" *Journal of the Academy of Nutrition and Dietetics* 112, no. 5: 705-710.

Sharkey, Joseph, Wesley Dean, Courtney Nalty, and Jin Xu. 2013. "Convenience Stores are the Key Food Environment Influence on Nutrients Available from Household Food Supplies in Texas Border *Colonias.*" BMC Public Health 13, no. 45: 1-18.

Weigel, M. Margaret, Rodrigo Armijos, Yolanda Posanda Hall, Yolanda Ramirez, and Rubi Orozco. 2007. "The Household Food Insecurity and Health Outcomes of U.S.-

Mexico Border Migrant and Seasonal Farmworkers." *Journal of Immigrant Minority Health* 9: 157-169.
Wilde, Parke. *Food Policy in the United States: an Introduction.* New York: Routledge, 2013.

PART III

Disparities in Access to Healthy Food

CHAPTER 5

"La Lucha Diaria": Migrant Women in the Fight for Healthy Food

Megan Carney

Introduction

"It is a daily struggle" (Es una lucha diaria). I heard this phrase on countless occasions throughout my fieldwork with migrant women from Mexico and Central America living in southern California as they described and reflected on the everyday challenges to ensuring a steady supply of food in the household. In recent years, people in the United States have become increasingly familiar with the term "food insecurity" amidst a steady increase in the number of food insecure households. As of May 2013, one in six U.S. households were receiving food stamps (Food Research and Action Center 2013). The national network of food banks, Feeding America, claims that millions more U.S. households are experiencing food insecurity but are not income-eligible for food stamps or other forms of government support (Feeding America 2011). Social stigma and fear of legal consequences also prevent income-eligible individuals from applying for government assistance (Carney forthcoming; Fitchen 2000; Poppendieck 1997). Undocumented parents with U.S.-born children, for instance, may elect to withhold from enrollment for fear of detention or deportation (Fitzgerald 2010). In short, there is a high prevalence of food insecurity in the U.S. yet the experiential aspects of food insecurity vary extensively both across and within different social groups.

This chapter attempts to address the nuanced ways in which people in the U.S. experience food insecurity. I present interview and participant-observer data collected through ethnographic fieldwork to render a "day-in-the-life" portrait of one of the most structurally marginalized groups in the U.S. whose present living circumstances have been significantly shaped by global capitalism and a proliferation of neoliberal economic policies. Specifically, I focus on the unique, quotidian experiences of low-income, predominantly undocumented Mexican and Central American migrant women. In rendering this portrait, I align with feminist epistemological frameworks that interpret the underlying conditions of transnational migration from the global South to North and the structural disparities that exist within U.S. society as both products and instruments of neocolonialism that enable the accumulation of capital while also undermining human dignity, rights, and desires for autonomy (Agustín 2003; Boris 2010; Chang 2000; Rosas 2012; Zavella 2007).

In the past decade or so, social scientists have devoted much attention to the influx of women entering transnational labor markets (see for example Agustín 2003; Bank Muñoz 2008; Boris 2010; Otis 2011; Parreñas 2011). These scholars call our attention to a "feminization of migration" in narrating shifts in the global division of labor that have spurred demand for migrant women's labor, specifically in the service economy which includes child care and eldercare, domestic services (such as cleaning), and sex work (Pyle 2006; Yeates 2009; Zimmerman 2006). Much of this literature has focused on how the deployment of gender and race ideologies operates to devalue and exploit migrant women in these work settings. For instance, some allude to the emotional dimensions of administering care for others and how prevailing assumptions about women being "natural" nurturers undermine and often preclude adequate monetary compensation (Browner 2011; Chavkin 2010; Ehrenreich 2003; England 2005; Glenn 2012). Feminists also discuss the "double-duty" workday of women who are employed in wage-labor and who shoulder the bulk of domestic chores and childcare needs (Allen 2007; Beagan 2008). While a substantial body of literature explores the experiences of migrant women as *paid* laborers in formal and informal markets, interestingly there has been less emphasis on the *unpaid* labors of migrant women essential to social reproduction and imbricated in their intimate relations with others as mothers, spouses, daughters, sisters, etc. Foodwork, *i.e.*, the procurement, management, and allocation of food, comprises a significant portion of this unpaid labor (Beagan 2008). Indeed, I found in my research that the amount of foodwork required for avoiding a situation of food insecurity in migrant women's households did not allow for women to invest much time in wage-earning opportunities. Moreover, even as earning a wage helped to improve one's material means, migrant women still reported food insecurity, citing the lack of time they had for foodwork.

In the following pages, I describe what it means to be a migrant woman in the U.S. living with the everyday challenges of food insecurity. I demonstrate how managing household nutritional sources comprises a full-time job for some women and how foodwork is especially difficult for women who do not have as much flexibility in devoting substantial time to food preparation and procurement. I begin by outlining the activities that women identify in narrating a typical day to demonstrate how for food insecure households, concerns about disturbances to the food supply or lack of time to prepare healthy food inform women's labors and punctuate everyday struggles for sufficient resources. The culmination of these activities reveals the ingenuity of limited resource households to deploy multiple coping strategies for alleviating food insecurity in the immediate term and also the need for policy changes to reduce structural disparities in the long-term. I follow this discussion with an exploration of the ways that migrant women's experiences of this *lucha diaria* impinge on their psychosocial well-being.

Methodology

The data presented in this chapter are derived from 20 months of ethnographic fieldwork conducted between 2008 and 2011 with Mexican and Central American migrant women (N=25) and private food assistance programs operating in Santa Barbara County, California. I selected Santa Barbara County as the primary site of my fieldwork for several reasons. The county has one of the highest rates of food insecurity (39 percent of low-income households) in the state of California (California Health Interview Survey 2009). In 2011, the leading local hunger-relief organization reported that more than one-quarter of the county's population sought emergency food assistance. Although food insecurity is a complex problem, much of the problem in Santa Barbara County relates to a high cost of living and relatively low incomes. Poverty in the region has been gradually increasing in recent years; as of 2010, one in five households and one in four children lived at or below the federal poverty level (US Census 2011).

My fieldwork focused on the lived experiences of migrant women and strategies of intervention to food insecurity and "diet-related diseases" being administered by NGOs and public health practitioners. For reasons that undocumented migrants represent a "hard-to-reach" research population, I chose to conduct outreach through established community organizations in Santa Barbara County that had already developed rapport with local migrant communities (Himmelgreen 2007; Pérez-Escamilla 2010). Sites of recruitment included private food assistance distributions and parent meetings at Head Start preschools. Women of age 18 or older who had migrated from Mexico or Central America and had previous experience utilizing some form of food assistance while in the U.S. were eligible to participate in this research. Participants ranged in age from 24 to 60 years (mean age of 38) and originated from Mexico, Honduras, and Guatemala, although the majority of women came from common sending states in Mexico such as Guerrero, Michoacán, and Oaxaca. Five of the women had obtained legal status in the U.S., including a Guatemalan woman who had been granted asylum, but most (20 out of 25) were "*sin papeles*" (*i.e.*, undocumented). Women's length of residency in the U.S. spanned from as short as three months to as long as 30 years. All of the women had children, except for one who was in the process of adopting through familial networks in Mexico. The number of reported children averaged two per household. Of the 25 women, 11 had full- or part-time employment, while the remaining 14 were underemployed ($n=9$), supported by a spouse ($n=4$), or on disability ($n=1$). Two of the women reported obtaining post-secondary training at a university or vocational school while the other women had attended only primary school in their countries of origin. In terms of marital status, 16 of the women were married or living with a spouse, four had never been married, and five were divorced.

Semi-structured and life history interviews, dietary surveys, participant observation, and focus groups served as the primary instruments of data collection. The women and I determined interview times and locations over the phone and we frequently met in their homes or at parks, schools and community centers. As a participant-observer, I documented interactions between staff and volunteers of NGOs with migrant women and I accompanied women in some of their daily activities such as grocery shopping, informal work, picking up kids from school, and preparing meals. Toward the end of fieldwork, I organized three focus groups according to women's area of residence. Focus groups met a total of three times each and were facilitated by an experienced moderator. All interview and focus group interactions were conducted in Spanish. I recorded these interactions with the women's verbal consent and transcribed the recordings with the help of hired research assistants who were also native Spanish speakers. The portion of the transcriptions that appear in this chapter I have translated from Spanish into English.

Day-in-the-Life Portrait of the *Lucha Diaria*

Morning: *El Desayuno* (Breakfast)

Olivia[1] wakes up before 6 AM everyday to prepare breakfast for her husband before he leaves for his job at the carwash, and for her children before they go to school. She insists on feeding her children a substantial meal in the morning in case they do not like the school meal served at lunch, as all of her school-aged children are enrolled in the free- and reduced-price school meal program. In many respects, Olivia's day literally revolves around feeding the family: she wakes up early to feed her family breakfast, she escorts her children to school, she prepares lunch for her husband who comes home for a midday break, she retrieves her children from school, and she prepares dinner.

On the morning that I visit Olivia at home, I find her in the midst of preparing *sopes* in anticipation of her husband returning home at lunchtime. In addition to watching after her own child and the child of another family living under the same roof as her own, she is also babysitting the neighbor's nine-month old twin baby girls. All of the children are busy playing on the floor in front of the television as Olivia cleans up from breakfast and begins to prepare lunch. Leftover on the table from breakfast is a plate of chicken nuggets with ketchup, and a bowl of cereal with milk. She explains that her daughter prefers cereal and her son, chicken nuggets, for breakfast. She then begins to show me step-by-step how she goes about making *sopes*: she mixes the *maseca* (corn flour) with purified water from the tap to make the *masa* and kneads the dough with her hands for two to three minutes. I notice that the flour, like almost all of the products in Olivia's home, is Kirkland brand (*i.e.*, from Costco). She places a griddle over the stovetop and allows it to heat up. She then rolls the *masa* into small balls of dough, flattens the *masa* with a tortilla press, and arranges the uncooked *sopes* on the griddle, lightly toasting them on each side for a few minutes. She says that one knows the *sopes* are "*están cocidos*" (cooked) when they have a "*café*" (coffee) color, emphasizing that undercooked *sopes* will result in poor digestion. Meanwhile, she adds whole green tomatoes to a pot of water and brings it to a boil on the stove. She grills chilies on the same tray as the *sopes* which she combines with tomatoes, cilantro, onion, garlic, and salt in a blender to make a salsa. When the *sopes* are cooked, she pinches the edges to shape into *sopes*. She adds olive oil, beans, and cheese to the *sopes* and allows the ingredients to melt together on the griddle. The beans were prepared the night before. From start to finish, the preparation of this meal today requires about an hour of Olivia's time.

Once Olivia is done preparing lunch, she joins me at her kitchen table and savors her leftover toast with butter and coffee from breakfast. She pages through a coupon mailer to see what discounted items she may be able to purchase today at one of the local grocery stores, even though she does most of her grocery shopping at Costco once every two weeks (the time that her husband and others in the household receive their paychecks). The three families with whom Olivia resides prefer to shop from Costco because they pool their earnings to purchase items in bulk which they believe saves them money. Olivia doesn't mind the bimonthly trip to the large retail outlet except for the fact that she must drive herself the 40 miles round-trip without a valid driver's license. Like any of the other adults in her household, Olivia's undocumented status precludes her from qualifying for this form of identification and authorization to drive on the road.[2] Nonetheless, Olivia sees no excuse for her not to make these sacrifices for the sake of her children's well-being. In her opinion:

> "The problem that children eat junk food is the problem of [a mother]...We have to find options to buy better food or to make food at home. Because here, in this country, as [many] mothers work, it is easier to buy prepared food or to take your kids to McDonald's. But it depends on how you, as a mother, provide them with healthy food."[3]

Mid-morning: *Buscando Las Especiales* (Bargain Hunting)

Juliana likes to plan her meals spontaneously around the best deals she finds. Everyday, after dropping her children off at school, she begins her walk around town to survey prices at the stores within closest proximity to her home. She is always looking to *"aprovechar las especiales"* (take advantage of specials). Shopping lists are useless to her; indeed, she strives to buy every item on sale. Sometimes prior to her mid-morning walkabout, she will leaf through coupon books that arrive in the mail. Knowing about the specials in advance may save her some time, as without access to a car or someone to drive her, the journey between stores to compare prices can be very time-consuming.

Only a handful of the women in my research were able to engage in this type of price surveillance, as others were usually putting in the hours at wage-based sites of work. In the case of Juliana, a hip injury that she incurred while giving birth to one of her three children prevents her from applying to most forms of employment. Thus, Juliana's husband is the primary breadwinner, yet she regrets that they do not have a very civil relationship. She complains of his drinking and overall abusive demeanor toward her. Although she would like to leave him, he threatens to withhold any support from her if she decides to leave: *"es mi dinero"* (it's my money), he says. She reminds him that it is actually *"el dinero de sus hijos"* (your children's money), insinuating that his fiscal responsibility is to them.

During one of my visits to Juliana's home, she is preparing chicken with rice, a smile beaming on her face from having found chicken legs on sale that morning. Displayed on the table are some tomatoes, a package of asparagus, onions, and avocadoes, all of it bounty from today's shopping excursion. She alludes to the package of asparagus on the table noting that she plans to serve it later tonight. Her children love asparagus, she pronounces with obvious pride. She always insists that her children try something even if they think that they will not like it. The day before, for instance, she prepared eggs with green beans for her son who initially eyed her invention with suspicion only to later gloat about how much he liked it. In needing to *"economizar"* (a verb translating as "to balance" or "to economize") and make the most of her purchases, Juliana finds many opportunities to introduce unfamiliar foods to her family, claiming that this practice has encouraged her children to develop a broad palate. Rather than representing herself as limited by the foods that she must procure on sale, Juliana highlights her own cleverness in overseeing her family's diet. She compares herself to working mothers, whom she views as compromised in overseeing matters of personal and family health: *"Women don't have time [to cook], for the reason that they work. So they go buying something quick, because they are working. Eating this way, in large part, is what does them harm, makes them fat."*[4]

Midday: *El Banco de Alimentos* (The Food Bank)

Field notes from October 21, 2010: I arrive to the mobile food pantry minutes before the site supervisor authorizes clients to collect provisions. The site supervisor greets me and explains that the volunteers — who are also clients—have first pick of the provisions. Volunteers are sourced from the community and all of them speak Spanish as a first language. This particular mobile food pantry site has been in operation since 1997. Previously, they administered a number system for attendees but now distributions operate on a first come, first serve basis. The supervisor explains that they get people "from all walks of life" including the disabled, elderly, students, families with children, and working adults, although the majority of clients are undocumented women who stand in line with their children. "Everyone gets the same amount," the site supervisor assures me. He records data from clients as they move forward in the line, including details on household size, number of children, age, sex, ethnicity, and whether or not they are first-time participants. He tells me that this information is used for internal purposes only, and that his organization neither collects any information on, nor discriminates against, employment or immigration status.

The volunteers are wearing latex gloves as they stack boxes of produce onto the tables and place items into clients' bags. Three clients at a time are allowed to approach the tables to collect provisions. Mothers walk through with baby strollers, boxes and bags, picking up lettuce, cabbage, oranges, apples, potatoes, melon, sweet potatoes, onions, strawberries, blueberries, and tomatoes. I observe mothers stuffing bags of produce into the lower reaches of their strollers as older kids help with carrying the load. Some of the mothers struggle to squeeze everything into the bags they brought with them. Volunteers have to recalibrate rations for each participant depending on the number of people still in line. Some clients wait patiently to go through the line again, as the event proceeds until clients have exhausted the inventory. The site supervisor shows me the total day's count of clients on his clipboard: 67. He suspects that the rainy weather today deterred additional people from coming.

As I learned through my interviews with migrant women, securing in-kind resources through private food assistance programs such as the one described above was a particularly important strategy for households and families of mixed immigration status. Women favored these programs over government-administered (public) programs for not inquiring into this aspect of their identity, thereby permitting them a degree of invisibility from the state. Sites distributed what Celeste described as *"that which we lack at home... so one is eating more."*[5] Women often utilized multiple program sites, combining items from different distributions to meet their culinary preferences and household needs. Although women reported *"[using] all that [they] were given, never throwing anything away,"*[6] they still encountered unwanted items. Canned, frozen, or expired foods ranked among the least desirable provisions. During a conversation at one of our focus groups, women expressed disdain for the practice of distributing expired items including bread, cheese, yogurt, and milk: *"This Tuesday, the last day that I went, they were giving out bread that had passed its date. They were also giving out boxes of croutons that had already been expired for a month."*[7] Women also avoided taking canned or frozen foods because they knew others in their household did not like these items or because they lacked certain kitchen appliances such as a microwave to prepare these foods.

In addition to connecting migrant women to *"comida saludable"* (healthy food) such as fresh produce, programs offered clients lessons in nutrition education. These lessons featured information and resources for preventing or managing certain health problems. Paloma appreciated learning at these sites about how to *"try to eat healthy"* (*"tratamos de comer saludable"*) for herself and her husband, both of whom had been diagnosed with diabetes.

Although many program sites distributed food regardless of one's personal circumstances and required minimal information in screening clients, the rules of some programs seemed unnecessarily rigorous and unfair by women's standards. Catholic Charities in particular, with various sites located throughout the county, was one such program, requiring that clients show pay stubs to prove employment status. Catholic Charities did not distribute to the unemployed, ostensibly a mandate imposed by the programs' funders. Women critiqued this mandate for seeming illogical:

> When I went [to Catholic Charities], I told them that neither my husband nor I were working. So they told me that I couldn't receive anything. This seems wrong to me because if one goes, it's because they need help. If we are working, we're not going to go because we have money to buy food, but not when we're not working.[8]

Several women expressed similar sentiments in noting the personal and relational sacrifices that they endured in coming to programs. One woman explained how she had gone without her husband's permission to only then be refused by staff:

> I also went to Catholic Charities when my husband wasn't working and I don't like it there. One assumes that what they give is for people who don't have [anything]. I came here, without permission from my husband because he doesn't like this, because I see the need that I don't have anything to eat, that I can't get ahead. I pay rent or buy food. They say "no, the help here is for people who are working."[9]

Celeste noted how *"sometimes one goes with shame,"* (*"a veces va uno con pena"*) and that being turned away only added insult to injury. Women regretted the behavior of program staff who they perceived as lacking sympathy toward clients, and argued that staff should be more sensitive to the discomfort experienced by those asking for help.

Afternoon: *Hace Las Compras* (Grocery Shopping)

On an afternoon in March, I join Celeste and her two young children on a shopping trip to a discount grocery store, Smart and Final. Upon our entrance, Celeste immediately notes the items on sale and compares them to prices at other stores. She motions to a display that is advertising olive oil at half the price she saw it listed for at another grocery store earlier today. In the refrigerated meats section, she picks up a package of chorizo noting that butcher shops (*carnicerías*) in the neighborhood charge three times as much for the equivalent weight.

Celeste collects two bags of Gala apples; her husband likes these packed in his lunch. She also picks out some bananas after showing me the $6 voucher she received from WIC (Women, Infants and Children Supplemental Nutrition Program) the day before. *"The little one"* (*"el chiquito"*), referring to her younger son, she explains, really likes the bananas. I politely request to see the voucher; it says that the $6 may go toward the purchase of fresh, canned, or frozen fruits and vegetables. Celeste pulls out her phone to calculate exactly how much she can buy with her $6. She weighs the bananas and adds two more to the scale. Earlier she had asked her son if he would like grapes, but at last she determines the WIC voucher will only cover the apples and bananas.

When Celeste goes to pay for her groceries, the cashier, speaking in Spanish, asks her to sign the WIC voucher for the total amount. On top of the WIC purchases, she spends $6.18 of her own cash. She retains the receipt with her packet of WIC information noting that she is supposed to submit these receipts at a later date.

Celeste and her husband have been living in the U.S. for two years. Of their two children (ages four and one), only the youngest is a U.S. citizen and thus eligible for public assistance. Subsequently, private forms of food assistance such as food pantries are very important to Celeste's household. Celeste's husband works as a gardener. The family of four rents a room in a house occupied by two other families. Celeste and her husband decided to leave their home state of Guerrero in Mexico to be closer to her husband's family and to provide their children with a better life. Although she had studied to become a nurse, there were no nursing jobs available in her hometown. Unable to afford school in the U.S., she has had to abandon her aspirations of becoming a nurse, even though a second source of income would provide great benefit to her family. She explains that she likes Santa Barbara except for the high cost of food and housing. Alternatively, she finds that there are many people and services that help to meet the needs of her family. She is emphatic in her conviction that it is the responsibility of *"la mama"* to ensure a balanced and healthy diet.

Late Afternoon: *La Comida* (The Meal)

When I arrive to Dolores' family apartment, she has recently returned from a parent teacher conference at her child's school. On the way home, she had stopped by Santa Cruz Market (a Mexican-style *tienda*) for ingredients for tonight's dinner, *pechuga de pollo con arroz* (chicken breast with rice): chicken, bell peppers, Campbell's Cream of Mushroom soup (two cans), onions, and cilantro. She makes this dish with some regularity, *"cada quince días"* (every two weeks), as it is a favorite among her children. She is also preparing *ensalada* (salad) with lettuce, carrots, cucumbers, and ranch dressing. *"Casi diario comemos la ensalada"* (we eat salad almost everyday), she says. She finds the produce from Santa Cruz Market to be the best price. She chops the onions, bell peppers, cilantro, and garlic as I sit across from her at the kitchen table.

Dolores is one of 12 children. Her mother died during childbirth when Dolores was only two years old. Although her father remarried shortly thereafter, she did not get along with her stepmother and gravitated more toward her grandmother. She learned to cook from her *abuela* around eight or nine years of age, recalling this as the age that most daughters in Mexico are expected to begin cooking. Dolores does not expect her own 11-year-old daughter to learn how to cook yet because in the U.S., she finds that cooking requires *"menos trabajo"* (less labor). For example, rather than shucking and processing corn in the mill for the purpose of making tortillas, Dolores saves times by simply purchasing pre-made tortillas.

Dolores migrated to the U.S. from Guerrero in her teens, when as she remembers, work was much easier to find. In the past fifteen years, Dolores has worked as a hotel housekeeper, a restaurant employee, and a private housecleaner (*limpia de casas*). Currently she is employed part-time as a *limpia de casas*, but she hopes to advance to full-time. She has known several people in the last couple of years who have returned to Guerrero because they could not find enough work to pay the bills. For instance, her three cousins—ages 40, 32, and 27—returned to Mexico last year because they could not find work and their main purpose in being here had been to earn money in support of their families back home. Dolores receives WIC and food stamps for supporting her five children. She also utilizes local food pantries in helping to obtain items that she is unable to buy from the *tiendas*.

Evening:
El Alimentarse (Feeding) and Attempts at Commensality

Carolina prepares meals for everyone in her household, which includes her husband, daughter, two sons, and grandson. She also has a daughter who is married and lives nearby with her husband. During mealtimes, Carolina asserts the role of overseeing how much food each person gets with his or her meal. For instance, when Carolina prepares chicken, she will count the number of pieces and the number of people eating to determine how many to ration to each person.

Carolina reports eating fewer daily meals living in the U.S. because she explains that there is less time to prepare meals and to socialize around food with the family. She describes these changes as contributing to the devaluing importance of the "*comida*." In Mexico and much of Central America, the *comida* is the main meal of the day, consumed in the afternoon and usually over a long duration with others. Thus, it is a time marked for both nourishing oneself and socializing with others. As Carolina is unable to invest much time into preparing meals at home, and her children and husband are less available to share in consuming these meals together, she finds fewer opportunities to sustain the tradition of the *comida* and also discovers herself feeling more socially isolated. She talks of how her children, and youth in the U.S. in general do not spend enough time with their parents or older generations. She claims that intergenerational socializing is a very important and accepted part of life in Mexico and she is upset by the lack of respect youth here extend to elders by preferring to hang out with friends outside of the home. She notes her disappointment at the fact that her second oldest daughter plans to move out of the house as soon as she turns 18. In Mexico, she explains, youth continue to live with their families for much longer.

The irregularity with which Carolina's immediate family gathers around meals is particularly painful for Carolina as she reflects on her estrangement from the rest of her family. While she is one of nine children, she has zero contact with her siblings. She attributes the disintegration of ties within her family to the death of her mother who died giving birth, which happened when Carolina was 15 years old. Since that ill-fated event "*No nos acercábamos como antes,*" (We were not close like before). Her mother had been the one to enforce "*disciplina y orden*" (order and discipline) including sociality around meals; Carolina remembers "*Teníamos hora de comer*" (we had a set meal time). She is saddened by not knowing the present whereabouts of her siblings, as she recalls how once "*éramos una familia unida*" (we were a tight-knit family).

Gendered Suffering

In the preceding pages, I have depicted a day in the life of a migrant woman—a composite portrait—who is striving to obtain healthy food amidst the specter of food insecurity. As I learned through my fieldwork, women were obstructed in their efforts to provide healthy food for their families on a daily basis. In accepting responsibility for the bulk of this labor, women experienced high levels of stress in attempting to overcome obstacles to healthy food and in fearing failure to meet social expectations. Importantly, this source of stress punctuated women's everyday experiences and represented a particularly gendered form of suffering.

For women who lacked legal status, conditions of "illegality"—"the erasure of legal personhood...a space of forced invisibility, exclusion, subjugation, and repression" (De Genova 2002)—hindered women from contesting the circumstances that obstructed their ability to provide healthy food. Women conveyed frustration in feeling unable to communicate with authorities on this issue, as one woman expressed, "*no tenemos facilidad*" (*we don't have this privilege*). Persistent concerns and uncertainty about one's future, exacerbated by the possibility of deportation, prevented many women from planning for the long-term. Reports of record deportations and rumors about ICE (U.S. Immigration and Customs Enforcement) informants living among them in their communities, contributed to migrant women's fear of surveillance by the state. Migrant women frequently avoided social services even if they or their children were eligible because of ambiguity around terms of enrollment and the potential uses of client information. Women articulated a desire for outreach programs specifically tailored to the needs of undocumented migrant communities that would delineate the range of social services available to them in "*nuestra idioma y nos orientaría*" (*in our language and that would orient us*).

Women also articulated discomfort with the social stigma attached to their undocumented status that seemed to underlie various forms of discrimination. Women lamented feeling discriminated against in settings ranging from the most mundane, such as the checkout line at the grocery store, to the exceptional, such as a visit to the emergency room. For instance, Dolores (described in the section "*La Comida*") painfully recalled being humiliated by hospital staff in front of her son when she brought him to the emergency room with a broken arm. They had ridiculed her for ostensibly coming to the U.S. to exploit public programs such as MediCal when indeed she was paying for her son's health insurance. Such experiences of discrimination contributed to feelings of shame (*vergüenza*) among women and deterred them from seeking help.

Women's experiences of "illegality" also interacted with and exacerbated extant constraints on financial resources, isolation from social networks and families, and abusive relationships with spouses to heighten levels of stress sometimes then yielding to general malaise or in more severe cases, depression. In reflecting on high levels of stress, women in my research reported common symptoms of depression such as chronic exhaustion, feelings of helplessness, loss of appetite or its opposite, a tendency toward binge eating. In addition, almost all of the women in my research conveyed that they were struggling to maintain an overall positive attitude toward life. The following reflection from

Linda illustrates how the stress from working, managing a household, being undocumented, and dealing with her husband's alcoholism translated to her own physical suffering and self-deprecating thoughts such as thinking that she is overweight:

> I'm a bit overweight because my husband is fat. He keeps gaining and gaining [weight]. But he drinks and I think this makes him fat and he likes to drink a lot—a lot—everyday. I've gained eight pounds and I think it's because I'm not eating well, because I'm not keeping to a schedule... I think that now my weight is really affecting me, because I have back pain. I'm stressed because my back hurts me so much—three months ago I was at a normal weight...I feel bad, I need to lose weight. I think stress makes one gain weight? Because I'm really stressed. I stress all the time and I think that is what this is. I get nervous but in the form of hunger. Anything I put into my mouth, bread, a cookie, makes me gain weight when I'm stressed. The stress also comes from driving without a license all the way to my job. It comes from needing to pick up my kids quickly, to get home to make the meals. Now my husband is getting home from work very late, like at eight o'clock at night, so every responsibility falls on me: go to work, leave kids at school, return, get them from school, make dinner, do the laundry, everything is for me to do, for this reason I feel so much stress. But I can't stop working because when I do, I feel stressed again because there is no money to pay the rent, the bills, for things we need. If it is not one thing, it is another.[10]

Chronic stress is a strong predictor for many of the diseases disproportionately afflicting Latino communities in the U.S., such as diabetes and hypertension (Quesada 2011; Vélez-Ibáñez 1996). Depression may develop or worsen with diagnosis of disease (Mendenhall, 2012). For instance, several of the women in my research had been diagnosed with diabetes and linked their knowledge of the diagnosis with the process of entering a depression. Women also expressed frustration with health providers who they perceived as being insensitive to and dismissive of their suffering. For instance, Carolina complained that when she visited the doctor about a source of pain, he or she would tell her that this pain was due to stress and would not prescribe any course of treatment for what she was actually feeling.

Conclusion

Undocumented migrant households in the U.S. straddle the precarious boundary between what the USDA has defined as "food security" and the emotionally taxing, health threatening, and socially humiliating realm of food insecurity. I suggested at the beginning of this chapter that overseeing management of food, and furthermore healthy food, could arguably comprise a full-time job for low-income migrant women. Alternatively, women who could not devote their entire day to this activity for the reason of needing to work, were inadvertently blamed for negative health outcomes, as represented by Juliana's statement (described in the section *"Buscando Las Especiales"*): *"Women don't have time, for the reason that they work. So they go buying something quick...in large part, [this] is what does them harm."*[11] As women believed that working outside of the household detracted from a woman's ability to perform foodwork, women who were employed faced social scrutiny around their competence for motherhood. Olivia's assertion that junk food was "the problem of a mother" (featured in the section *"El Desayuno"*), suggested that working mothers were too relaxed about their children's diets. I do not invoke the statements of these women here to surmise about the ways that they are reproducing essentialist or culturally-specific ideas with regards to nourishing through feeding. Rather I do so to allude to the negative forms of social capital that have operated historically to devalue and demoralize certain social groups, particularly low-income women.

In facing myriad constraints such as limited economic resources and social networks, low-income migrant women, particularly single mothers, resist their own further marginalization into a class of those considered by society as "always already"—in the Agamben sense (1998)—less deserving. In pursuing a range of strategies for obtaining and allocating nutritional resources within households, women in my research strived to stake claims on deservingness. They also actively bestowed others in their households with a feeling of deservingness by often emphasizing a practice of cooking *"con amor"* (*with love*), and also pushing others to socialize around mealtimes. Women reflected on the empowering aspects of these activities, specifying the need to identify pathways toward survival.

A critical perspective of food insecurity views contemporary biopolitics, rather than individual failings (Page-Reeves et al. 2014) as responsible for colossal unevenness in access to vital resources (Nally 2011). These biopolitics are visible in markets that stratify labor and produce "disposable" bodies preceding the conditions of food insecurity, as they are also evident in the violence of state interpellations to "food security" (Glenn 1992; Mares 2013). It is a biopolitics dictated by racist, misogynist, and classist thinking. Needs-based entitlement programs intensify disparities between the "haves" and the "have-nots," thereby contributing to the valorization of those who are able to resist any assistance from the state, and to the vilification of a "helpless" and "dependent" Other. Unless public opinion shifts to recognizing structural inequality as morally abject, the multiple strategies of the underprivileged to avoid food insecurity, however "ingenious" or "entrepreneurial," will remain inconsequential.

Acknowledgments

This doctoral research was supported with a grant from the University of California Institute for Mexico and the United States. I would like to thank all of the collaborators and participants in this research, as well as my advisors Drs. Susan

Stonich, Casey Walsh, Melissa Caldwell, Teresa Figueroa, and Leila Rupp. In addition, I would like to thank Dr. Matthew Garcia and the Comparative Border Studies Institute at the School of Transborder Studies at Arizona State University for providing postdoctoral research funding. Finally, I would like to thank Dr. Janet Page-Reeves for organizing this volume.

Notes

1. The actual names of my research participants have been replaced with pseudonyms for the purposes of this chapter.

2. California did not permit undocumented individuals to obtain driver's licenses at the time of this research.

3. El problema que los niños coman comida chatarra es problema de uno. Si nosotros se lo permitimos, pero en cambio, nosotros tenemos ah...como buscar opciones de comprar la mejor comida o este cocinar en casa. Porque aquí en este país, como las madres trabajan, se le hace mas fácil comprar comida ya preparada o no más llevarlos a McDonald's, comer comida. Pero o sea eso ya depende de uno como madre en proporcionarles una comida saludable.

4. Las muchachas, pero no tienen tiempo por el trabajo quieren un pan, pues van comprando algo más rápido, tal vez por el tiempo del trabajo... porque muchas veces comen eh y a la largo eso les hacen daño, se ponen gordos.

5. Nos dan la comida que hace falta... hay cosas que sí, nos hace falta en la casa, por decir la cebolla, las verduras y hay veces como los tercer martes de cada mes nos dan arroz y casi en ese día uno está comiendo más.

6. Yo acabo lo que me dan. Nunca yo ando tirando.

7. Porque también el día martes, el último día que fui, estaban dando el pan pero el pan también ya estaba vencido. Estaban dando unas cajas de crutones, no se cómo le dicen, y ya estaban vencidos también, ya tenían más de un mes de andar venidos.

8. Cuando fuí me le dije que yo no trabajaba y mi esposo tampoco. Pues me dijeron que no, que no podía recibir. Por esa parte está mal porque si uno va es porque tiene la necesidad de que le den ayuda. Como dice Paloma si estamos trabajando claro que no vamos a ir, porque tenemos con que comprar, pero cuando no pues no. Allí si cambiaría eso.

9. Yo fuí [a las Caridades Católicas] cuando también mi esposo dejo de trabajar y no me gustó allí. Se supone que lo que dan allí, se supone que eso es para las personas que no tienen. Yo vengo aquí, incluso, sin el permiso de mi esposo porque el no le gusta eso, porque yo veo la necesidad que yo no tengo que comer, no me alcanzaba. Pago la renta o compro la comida. Dice no la ayuda aquí es para las personas que están trabajando

10. Un poco pasado de peso porque mi esposo está muy gordo. Entre más él, está subiendo y subiendo. Pero él le gusta tomar y yo pienso que eso le engorda el le gusta tomar mucho, mucho, diario...He subido ocho libras y pienso que es por la mala alimentación porque no como en mis horas... Yo pienso que ahorita lo que nos está afectando, porque a mí me afecta mucho en la espalda... Me estreso porque le digo que yo me siento muy mal de la espalda cuando - yo antes estaba hace como tres meses - estaba en un peso normal...Me siento mal, necesito bajar...Piensa que también el estrés sube de peso? Porque me han estresado. Me estreso muchas veces y pienso que eso es. Me da como nervios pero de hambre. Cualquier cosa me hecho a la boca si hay pan, si hay una galleta, lo que

sea pero me sube de peso cuando estoy estresada pienso...El estrés es porque uno no tiene licencia y va manejando hasta allá [Ventura]. El estrés de venida por recoger los niños rápido, por llegar hacer la comida por... Ahorita mi esposo está saliendo muy tarde del trabajo como a las ocho, entonces toda la responsabilidad es para mi. Ir a trabajo, los dejo a la escuela, regreso, los recojo, hago la comida, los meto a bañar, es todo para mi, por eso siento que es más estrés...Cuando dejo de trabajar me estreso porque no hay dinero porque no va alcanzar para la renta, para los viles, para cosas que necesiten, es el estrés de tal manera. De una o otra

11. Las muchachas, pero no tienen tiempo por el trabajo quieren un pan, pues van comprando algo más rápido, tal vez por el tiempo del trabajo... porque muchas veces comen eh y a la largo eso les hacen daño se ponen gordos.

Bibliography

Agamben, G. 1998. *Homo Sacer: Sovereign Power and Bare Life*. Stanford: Stanford University Press.

Agustin, L.M. 2003. "A Migrant World of Services," *Social Politics: International Studies in Gender, State and Society* 10, no. 3: 377-396.

Allen, P., and C. Sachs. 2007. "Women and Food Chains: The Gendered Politics of Food." *International Journal of Sociol. Agric. Food* 15, no. 1: 1-23.

Bank Muñoz, C. 2008. *Transnational Tortillas: Race, Gender, and Shop-Floor Politics in Mexico and the United States*. Ithaca: ILR Press.

Beagan, B. 2008. "'It's Just Easier for Me to Do It': Rationalizing the Family Division of Foodwork." *Sociology* 42, no. 4: 653-671.

Boris, E., and R. Salazar Parreñas. 2010. *Intimate Labors: Cultures, Technologies, and the Politics of Care*. Stanford: Stanford Social Sciences.

Browner, C.H., and C.F. Sargent, editors. 2011. *Reproduction, Globalization, and the State: New Theoretical and Ethnographic Perspectives*. Durham: Duke University Press.

California Health Interview Survey. 2009. "California Health Interview Survey." http://www.chis.ucla.edu. (accessed March 1, 2010).

Carney, M. Forthcoming. "Eating and Feeding at the Margins of the State: Barriers to Healthcare for Undocumented Migrant Women and the 'Clinical' Aspects of Food Assistance."

Carney, M., and L.A. Minkoff-Zern. Forthcoming. "Critical Perspectives on the Neoliberal Underpinnings of Dietary Interventions: Experiences of Latino Im/Migrants with Food Assistance Programs in the U.S."

Chang, G. 2000. *Disposable Domestics*. Cambridge, MA: South End Press.

Chavkin, W., and J. Maher, editors. 2010. *The Globalization of Motherhood: Deconstructions and Reconstructions of Biology and Care*. New York: Routledge.

De Genova, N. 2002. "'Migrant Illegality' and Deportability in Everyday Life." *Annual Review of Anthropology* 31: 419-447.

Ehrenreich, B., and A. Hochschild. 2003. *Global Woman: Nannies, Maids, and Sex Workers in the New Economy*. New York: Metropolitan Books.

England, P. 2005. "Emerging Theories of Care Work." *Annual Review of Sociology* 31: 381-399.

Feeding America. 2011. "Map the Meal Gap." http://feedingamerica.org/hunger-in america /hunger studies/ map-the-meal-gap.aspx. (accessed June 15, 2013)

Fitchen, J.M.. 2000. "Hunger, Malnutrition, and Poverty in the Contemporary United States: Some Observations on Their Social and Cultural Context." In *Nutritional Anthropology: Biocultural Perspectives on Food and Nutrition*, edited by. A.H. Goodman, D.L. Dufour and G.H. Pelto, 309-333. Mountain View: Mayfield Publishing Company.

Fitzgerald, N. 2010. "Acculturation, Socioeconomic Status, and Health among Hispanics." *NAPA Bulletin* 34: 28-46.

Food Research and Action Center. 2013. "SNAP/Food Stamp Monthly Participation Data." http://frac.org/reports-and-resources/snapfood-stamp-monthly participation-data/ - mar. (accessed September 10, 2013).

Glenn, E.N. 2012. *Forced to Care: Coercion and Caregiving in America*. Cambridge: Harvard University Press.

Himmelgreen, D., N. R. Daza, E. Cooper, and D. Martinez. 2007. ""I Don't Make the Soups Anymore": Pre- to Post-Migration Dietary and Lifestyle Changes among Latinos Living in West Central Florida." *Ecology of Food and Nutrition* 46, no. 5-6: 427-444.

Mares, T. 2013. ""Here We Have the Food Bank": Latino/a Immigration and the Contradictions of Emergency Food." *Food and Foodways* 21, no. 1 : 1-21.

Mendenhall, E. 2012. *Syndemic Suffering: Social Distress, Depression, and Diabetes among Mexican Immigrant Women*. Walnut Creek: Left Coast Press.

Nally, D. 2011. "The Biopolitics of Food Provisioning." *Trans Inst Br Geogr* 36: 37-53.

Otis, E. 2011. *Markets and Bodies: Women, Service Work, and the Making of Inequality in China*. Palo Alto: Stanford University Press.

Page-Reeves, J., A. Anixter Scott, M. Moffett, V. Apodaca, and V. Apodaca. 2014. "*It is always that sense of wanting...never really being satisfied*': Women's Quotidian Struggles with Food Insecurity in a Hispanic Community in New Mexico." *Hunger and Environmental Nutrition*. In press.

Parreñas, R.S. 2011. *Illicit Flirtations: Labor, Migration, and Sex Trafficking in Tokyo*. Palo Alto: Stanford University Press.

Pérez-Escamilla, R., J. Garcia, and D. Song. 2010. "Health Care Access among Hispanic Immigrants: Alguien Está Escuchando? (Is Anybody Listening?)." *NAPA Bulletin* 34: 47-67.

Poppendieck, J. 1997. "The USA: Hunger in the Land of Plenty." In *First World Hunger*, edited by. G. Riches, 134-64. New York: St. Martin's Press.

Pyle, J. 2006. "Globalization, Transnational Migration, and Gendered Care Work: Introduction." *Globalizations* 3, no. 3: 283-295.

Quesada, J., L.K. Hart, and P. Bourgois. 2011. "Structural Vulnerability and Health: Latino Migrant Laborers in the United States." *Medical Anthropology* 30, no. 4: 339-62.

Rosas, G. 2012. *Barrio Libre: Criminalizing States and Delinquent Refusals of the New Frontier*. Duke University Press.

US Census. 2010. "Income, Poverty and Health Insurance Coverage in the United States, 2010." http://www.census.gov/newsroom/releases/archives/income_wealth/cb11-157.html.

Vélez-Ibáñez, C.G. 1996. *Border Visions: Mexican Cultures of the Southwest United States*. Tucson: University of Arizona Press.

Yeates, N. 2009. *Globalizing Care Economies and Migrant Workers: Explorations in Global Care Chains.* London: Palgrave, MacMillan.

Zavella, P., and D.A. Segura, editors. 2007. *Women and Migration in the U.S.-Mexico Borderlands: A Reader.* Durham: Duke University Press.

Zimmerman, M.K., J.S. Litt, and C.E. Bose. 2006. *Global Dimensions of Gender and Carework.* Stanford: Stanford University Press.

CHAPTER 6

Women's Knowledge and Experiences Obtaining Food in Low-Income Detroit Neighborhoods

Daniel J. Rose

Introduction

Within most of Detroit's 144 square miles, access to fresh, nutritious food is limited. More than half of Detroiters live in *"out-of-balance"* food environments—areas where they must travel at least twice as far to reach the closest supermarket as they do to reach the closest *"fringe food"* location, such as a fast food restaurant or convenience store (Gallagher 2007). A sample of African Americans living in Detroit's Eastside and Southwest neighborhoods found that 13.5 percent have type II diabetes (Kieffer et al. 2006), compared to an estimated 8.3 percent nationwide (NIH 2011).

Some have called recent increases in the average weights of Americans an obesity epidemic (Olshansky et al. 2005; Wyatt, Winters, and Dubbert 2006). Others refer to it as a moral panic (Campos, Saguy, Ernsberger, Oliver, and Gaesser 2005; Saguy and Riley 2005). It has resulted in increased public concern over eating habits and the effects of obesity. In everyday interactions and popular culture, obesity is highly stigmatized, with personal responsibility viewed as the key to "overcoming" it[1]. Among some policymakers and scholars, lack of nutritional knowledge is seen as a major cause of obesity, with education seen as a key remedy (Nestle and Jacobson 2000). Public health initiatives to promote nutritional knowledge in low-income neighborhoods are widespread (Stolley and Fitzgibbon 1997; Correa et al. 2010; Hasson et al. 2012). This education is often targeted toward women, given social norms about cooking, shopping, caregiving, etc. However, Acheampong and Haldeman (2013) found "good" nutritional knowledge among a sample of low-income African-American women and no significant relationship between their knowledge and weight status or diet quality.

Prior research has shown that food sources in neighborhood environments condition and constrain eating habits. Difficulty obtaining nutritious foods in urban neighborhoods has been cited as a cause of issues such as unhealthy diet (Cheadle et al., 1991) and diabetes (Auchincloss et al. 2009). Detroit residents average 1.1 mile more of distance to their nearest supermarket compared to suburban Detroiters (Zenk et al. 2005). Although many neighborhoods in Detroit do not fall under the USDA's geographic definition of a *"food desert"* (USDA 2013), they might be better described as *"food jungles."* Problems cited in the available supermarkets include higher prices, lower quality, less selection, poor customer service and sanitation (Rose 2011).

Researchers have examined macro- and community-level factors in the health of Detroit residents such as segregation (Schulz et al. 2002), neighborhood environments (Tellez et al. 2006), and the quality of food sources (Zenk et al., 2009). However, less is known about what people actually *know* about nutrition and foodways, and what they *do* when faced with these constraints. In their ethnography of the ways in which Detroit neighborhoods affect the health of their female residents, Schulz and Lempert (2004) argue: "Understanding the nature of inequalities and the *strategies residents devise to address them* are likely to be central to our understanding of, and societal efforts to eliminate, racial disparities in health." (my emphasis).

This chapter will explore the nutritional knowledge and agency of women living in low-income Detroit neighborhoods. In doing so, it addresses broader concerns such as the influence of neighborhood context, relationships between culture, knowledge, agency, and eating habits, and ways that policymakers can learn from women's strategies and lived experiences. Better understandings of the food access and nutritional knowledge of inner-city residents are critical. To the degree that researchers and policymakers view social structures, cultures, neighborhoods, or individuals themselves as deficient, these views will inform their attempts to change health practices. Better orienting health promotion interventions to account for the knowledge, experiences and social environments of Detroit women will increase their relevance and effectiveness.

I understand agency as a powerful force in responding to and changing structures pertaining to food acquisition, but also partially constituted by its location *vis-à-vis* social structures and neighborhood contexts. Agency is neither a constant nor an independent force, but rather a variable that depends partially on structural conditions and neighborhood contexts[2]. In other words, agency's role and potential is conditioned by neighborhood and broader, macro-level social structures. This approach to eating habits avoids the determinism of overly-structural explanations, as well as the victim-blaming and romanticism engendered by an over-emphasis on the agency of individuals with limited access to healthy foods. It is critical that we account for what women know about food, how they acquire it, and what sorts of barriers they face regarding healthy eating.

Neighborhood Barriers

In addition to availability, cost is a significant barrier to healthy food acquisition. Monsivais and Drewnowski (2007) demonstrated that high-energy-density (high-calorie) foods were more affordable and more resistant to inflation than low-energy-density foods. Moreover, Drewnowski and Darmon (2005) found that "added sugars and added fats are far more affordable than are the recommended 'healthful' diets based on lean meats, whole grains, and fresh vegetables and fruit." Economic factors have significant ramifications for the food choices of Detroiters, especially considering that it's the nation's poorest city of over 250,000 residents (American Community Survey 2010).

Beyond cost and availability, Barnes (2005) found more discrete barriers to obtaining food in poor neighborhoods in Gary, Indiana. Through the use of in-depth interviews, residents illuminated issues with food quality, transportation, and the emotional toll of unpleasant Gary markets (e.g., the presence of security guards and bars to keep shopping carts inside the stores). She found that Gary residents spent nearly 50 dollars more per month on the same groceries compared to their counterparts outside the city. They also faced discriminatory encounters when traveling to suburban markets.

Responses to Barriers

Bourdieu's (1984) concept of habitus details the ways in which external structures are internalized along class lines, leading to the reproduction of thought and behavioral processes. Bourdieu sees resources playing a major role in the reproduction of these dispositions and environments. In his discussion of "health lifestyles", Cockerham (2005) argues that health behaviors in practice feedback into the habitus, and that normative social contexts reinforce their approval or rejection. He argues that structure, at minimum, outweighs the potential of agency and, in the extreme, overwhelms it. The work of structural thinkers is important, because it points out serious flaws in understandings of health decisions that focus on "personal responsibility". But that does not mean that we should ignore the agentic strategies of individuals. By studying these actions, we might better understand how health behaviors are influenced by and can influence neighborhood contexts. Food acquisition results in large part from the interaction of residents' agency and neighborhood structures. Social actors have the capacity to pursue numerous responses to their neighborhood environments. Of course, agency, in the Kantian sense of transcendental free will, is never completely independent of the influence of structure and context (Emirbayer and Mische 1998). And as Giddens (1979) pointed out in his theory of "duality", structure and agency are not opposing forces, but rather mutually constituted.

Nutritional Knowledge

Biomedical approaches view obesity as a disease. This model emphasizes the need to change eating and other obesity-related behaviors by sharing knowledge about healthy diets with individuals who are assumed to be uninformed (Labonte and Robertson 1996). In recent years, the emphasis of health promotion has shifted from community-based approaches to the more individualistic biomedical model (Raphael and Bryant 2006). Policy makers may also misidentify lack of education as the source of nutritional deficiencies. Some have argued that unhealthy nutritional practices are often misclassified as nutritional ignorance when they result from lack of access to healthy foods (McEntree 2009; Kirkup et al. 2004). Travers (1996) found that low-income women were aware of and attempted to implement nutritional recommendations to limit salt, fat and caffeine intakes and consume foods rich in essential nutrients, such as vitamins and iron. Bazata and colleagues (2008) found that most individuals with a high risk for diabetes (including those with low incomes and low education) knew that improving their diet would have a positive effect on their health, but had trouble translating that knowledge into practice.

Even if low-income individuals do have lower-levels of nutrition knowledge, its association with food choices may also be overemphasized. Tepper and colleagues (1997) found that nutritional knowledge played only a modest role in food choices. More immediate considerations, such as hunger and stress, have been shown to be stronger predictors of food choices than nutritional knowledge (Mancino and Kinsey 2008). In short, policy makers have overestimated the effects of knowledge or education on health behaviors.

Hoisington and colleagues (2002) found that when low-income women assessed nutritional interventions, they requested information about stretching food dollars more than any other type of education. Similarly, Travers (1996) found that nutritional education was often irrelevant, impractical, and even detrimental to the lives of many low-income women and their families:

> As long as professional practice continues to place primary emphasis on changing individuals without consideration of the context within which they work, the potential remains high for victim blaming on the part of professionals, and guilt on the part of the individual who is unable to live up to expectations. Dogmatic nutrition messages do not assist the disadvantaged in making reasonable and moderate choices among available alternatives, but foster a sense of inadequacy and guilt for failing to live up to the standard set by them.

To improve understandings of food access and nutritional knowledge, community contexts must be thoroughly understood. Parker and colleagues (1998) advocated paying close attention to the context and history of Detroit communities and partnering with residents when designing health interventions. In short, a more grounded approach might actually help policy makers understand how to improve both access to food *and* eating habits.

Methods

To explore barriers to healthy eating, personal knowledge about nutrition, and strategies for everyday food procurement, I conducted 25 semistructured, in-depth interviews with women in two Detroit neighborhoods. I combined interview data with ethnographic fieldnotes, maps, and photographs. Interviews were recorded and transcribed verbatim. I supplemented interview transcripts with fieldnotes taken during and after interviews and informal observations. I analyzed data using a grounded theory approach (Glaser and Strauss 1967; Corbin and Strauss 1990). Using NVivo 7 data analysis software, I coded all of the interview transcripts and fieldnotes to discern relevant themes and then developed themes into memos. I continuously refined theoretical ideas using retroduction, moving from interview data analysis to conceptual reframing (Emerson 2004; Katz 1983). As theoretical concerns and conceptual categories emerged, I sought new forms of relevant data.

Participants came from two distinct neighborhoods each comprised of multiple census tracts (details below). For the sake of anonymity, I changed the names of participants, stores, and streets to pseudonyms. I conducted the interviews in late 2008 and the summer of 2009 as part of my dissertation research (which included men, along with the topic of physical activity barriers, knowledge, and strategies). All of the women identified as African-American, while three women also identified as another race.

I contacted potential participants in a variety of ways. I often rode a bicycle through the neighborhoods, greeting and approaching people sitting on their porches, waiting at bus stops, and otherwise living their lives. Eight participants introduced me to other women who subsequently participated in the study. Hence, the recruitment was a combination of non-random and snowball approaches. Interviewees ranged in age from 18 to 55 years. I offered $15 in compensation for participating. Early in the data collection process, it became apparent that lower-income neighborhood residents were more likely to agree to participate. In order to include some of the neighborhood's higher-income residents, I began to focus recruitment at the neighborhood post office branches.[3]

As a white male academic, I attempted to remain mindful of my social privilege throughout the research process. I was often made acutely conscious of my status as an outsider. On a summer day toward the end of my research, riding down the street on my bicycle after an interview, I was asked by someone as I passed, *"What the fuck are you smiling about?"* I became aware of my inexplicable grin at that point, and it seemed like a fair question. Neighborhood residents occasionally eyed me with suspicion or ignored me altogether. However, as a Detroit native living there at the time of the research, I felt comfortable discussing their neighborhood food options and other community issues. I attempted to develop and maintain rapport with residents throughout our relationships. Many took me up on offers of a ride to the grocery store of their choosing.

Settings: Near-Northwest

The near-northwest neighborhood is comprised of five contiguous census tracts, all with similar levels of income and educational attainment among their residents. The side streets are a mix of duplexes, apartments, and single-family homes. Two major thoroughfares bisect the neighborhood. One is a mainly commercial thoroughfare running roughly east and west through the heart of the neighborhood. The other is a mix of residential and commercial uses and runs roughly north and south. Near the intersection of these two thoroughfares lies the neighborhoods only grocery store. Three other major thoroughfares border the five census tracts. On the western edge of the neighborhood, an interstate highway forms a very difficult to traverse physical barrier. Before its construction, 15 streets at the western edge of the neighborhood went from the neighborhood into communities to the west. Today, 13 of those streets now end at the interstate. Only two streets and two pedestrian bridges are traversable along the 1.96 mile stretch, making it very difficult to access neighborhoods to the west.

The 2005-2009 American Community Survey estimated 11,872 residents living in the five near-northwest tracts. The poverty rate in these tracts is estimated to be 38.5 percent and the high school graduation rate for adults over 25 is estimated at 75.7 percent (American Community Survey 2010). Decennial Census data also show the neighborhood's population slowly declining through decades of deindustrialization, white flight and other social changes. Between 2000 and 2010, the population declined by 2,414 people (16.9 percent). Although the population has declined, the neighborhood remains a significant part of Detroit. Many blocks are still filled with sturdy homes and occupied by economically diverse residents (more than 60 percent of the neighborhood's residents are above the poverty line). Most residents identify as African American.

The neighborhood was initially developed in the 1910s and 1920s. It was first inhabited by skilled laborers and their families. The streets were lined with modest, well-built homes and apartment buildings, attracting a mix of classes (but explicitly hostile to African-Americans and, at first, Jews). Many of the buildings from this period remain in the community today. After World War II, middle-class African-Americans began to purchase and rent homes in the neighborhood. For a brief moment in the early 1950s, the neighborhood had a mixed African-American and White (mostly Jewish) population (Sugrue 2005). As the 1950s progressed, white flight reintroduced racial segregation, and blockbusting (realtors using racial anxieties to buy low from fleeing whites and sell high to African Americans), the development of interstate highways, and cheaper housing in suburbs further destabilized the neighborhood.[4]

Grocery chains fled the near-northwest neighborhood (and Detroit in general) starting in the late 1950s. At that time, at least three supermarkets and several smaller grocers were operating within those five census tracts. The only remaining supermarket, which I will refer to as "Miser's Foods," opened in 1954. But when the supermarket across the street closed in 1973, Miser's became the only remaining full-service market in the five census tracts. Today, Miser's Foods does not compete with any other grocers in the surrounding neighborhood and does most of its business with local residents who have low-levels of access to transportation (although some still drive to the store). Gas stations and convenience stores are closer to the homes of many neighborhood residents and have become important, albeit unhealthy, sources of food.

The near-northwest neighborhood is perhaps most known for being the starting point of a community uprising that began on July 24, 1967, and spread throughout the city. The afterhours club where police raided and tried to arrest approximately 90 patrons celebrating the return of four Vietnam veterans is now gone, replaced by a small park with a monument. Despite perceptions that entire neighborhoods were destroyed during the uprising, hardly any residential buildings went up in flames. Most of the damage was done to white-owned commercial businesses (Widick and Sheffield 1989). Today, many solidly constructed homes remain in the neighborhood, while other neglected, burned, and otherwise uninhabitable structures dot the landscape. Where houses and businesses have been demolished and cleared, urban prairies of tall grass, weeds, wildflowers and trees often grow unchecked. Other deteriorating vacant buildings, particularly commercial properties, await renovation or demolition. The neighborhood, while still thriving residentially, is vastly underserved in terms of grocers, health care providers, and other essential services.

Settings: Lower-East

The lower-east neighborhood is comprised of three contiguous Census tracts and has a population of 6,439 residents. This figure is down 11.8 percent compared to the 2000 Census. Today, the majority of the neighborhood's population identifies as African American. The newer apartments, townhouses, condominiums and parks in lower-east distinguish it from the near-northwest neighborhood. There are virtually no boarded up buildings and no "urban prairies" amid the carefully landscaped, planned communities. Two modest thoroughfares bisect the community. A cemetery forms the northeast border of the neighborhood. A large high school sits at the community's southeast corner. Commerce is limited to one shopping center at the intersection of the major crossroads, but does include a grocery store ("The Food Fare"). The remainder of the neighborhood is dedicated exclusively to residential and park purposes. Lower-east residents can take advantage of numerous resources in nearby parts of Detroit. Its proximity to Downtown, the city's recently redeveloped riverfront parks, and Eastern Market (a farmer's and wholesaler's market), seem to place it among one of Detroit's more desirable locations, but gentrification has not occurred.

Despite having newer buildings and better maintained parks and infrastructure, the lower-east community has slightly higher estimated poverty rates (43.6 percent), compared to the near-northwest (American Community Survey 2010). Two large public housing developments further concentrate poverty within these census tracts. A large soup kitchen just east of the community serves many local residents. Despite the fact that some of Detroit's earliest settlements were located near the lower-east, almost every building currently in the neighborhood was built in the past half century. This is because of some of the most aggressive urban renewal projects in the United States took place in and around the community in the 1940s, 50s and 60s. Before then, most residents lived in ramshackle homes built by European immigrants in the mid-late nineteenth century (Sugrue 2005).

Although Food Fare is the only grocery store within these three census tracts, there are additional grocery stores, as well as a farmer's market, within one mile of the neighborhood.

Comparing and Contrasting the Two Neighborhoods

The choice of these two neighborhoods provides me with ample opportunity to compare the impacts of distinct physical environments on food choices among residents with similar rates of poverty and education. Major differences in the physical environments include the younger age of community infrastructure (e.g.. sidewalks, traffic signals, parks, bus shelters) in the lower-east, the proximity of nearby resources (the near-northwest is surrounded mostly by other high-poverty areas), and the higher levels of abandonment and urban prairie in the near-northwest. The lower-east also has an older population, with a higher proportion of residents aged 65 and above and lower proportion of children under five compared to the near-northwest.

Variation within the communities

Regardless of neighborhood similarities regarding access to food, responses to these contexts vary tremendously—not only in conjunction with factors like access to transportation, class, and age, but also according to things much more difficult to measure, such as creativity, innovation, emotions, and culture. Critics have pointed out that this diversity of experiences and behavior often goes unreported in studies of urban communities (Kelley 1998; Gwantley 1975). The variety of responses possible for individuals in similar circumstances must be considered. Regarding food, DeVault (1991) found that while feeding work is situated in structural contexts, it is carried out with multifarious innovations and practices.

Results

Many women identified "survival strategies" to respond to the challenges of getting food in their neighborhoods. These efforts included sharing transportation to get to grocery stores, carefully inspecting foods before purchasing (especially meat and produce), using multiple food sources to meet different dietary needs, and alerting people in their networks to sales, coupons, and food banks available. Although residents employed similar strategies to obtain food in each of the two communities, the feasibility of these strategies varied according to neighborhood contexts. Key features in each neighborhood, such as resources (e.g. networks, food banks), walkability, and safety concerns encouraged or constrained women's agency. In addition to strategies to access food, women deployed budgetary and health knowledge to maximize the efficiency and utility of their food consumption.

Barriers

Participants discussed a number of challenges to obtaining food. Twenty-four out of 25 expressed some form of dissatisfaction with at least one of their local grocery stores. They felt dissatisfaction regarding prices (22 of 25), food quality (18 of 25), selection (16 of 25), cleanliness (7 of 25), and service (6 of 25). These results were all similar to the concerns expressed to me by men, with the exception of service (10 of 22 men brought that up as an issue with grocery stores). Lack of transportation was a formidable barrier to getting better, cheaper food for many of the people I spoke to. Eighteen of 25 participants did not have their own automobile. Of those without personal transportation, only two lived with someone who had an automobile, meaning sixteen of the 25 women were living in households without access to transportation. The American Community Survey (2009) indicates that approximately 31 percent of households in the near-northwest and 38 percent of those in lower-east live do not have vehicles available. Still, most participants traveled outside of their neighborhoods to get to grocers, restaurants and other food sources. Only three of the 25 interviewees said they rarely or never left their neighborhood to acquire food. Three of the 25 interviewees said they *only* get food from sources outside of their neighborhoods. (two of the three had their own automobiles). Although transportation was a key factor in being able to shop outside the neighborhood, some respondents *with* their own automobiles *did not* shop outside of their neighborhoods, while other respondents *without* their own automobiles *did* shop outside of their neighborhoods. Nine of 25 participants preferred to shop exclusively outside of the neighborhood whenever possible, but did not have access to their own automobiles.

Kiara, a 27-year old woman living in the near-northwest without personal transportation, was one of many respondents who did not see the neighborhood store as a satisfactory option: "*Oh, I don't shop at the Miser. I would not shop there. Their meat is green, their cans are beat.*" She typically walked to a grocery store nearly two miles away. Miser's Foods was less than half a mile away from her home. Although she walked much farther to get to the "Grocery Barn" (a store approximately one mile east of the neighborhood), Kiara was not entirely satisfied with her shopping experience there either. I drove her there after our interview for a small shopping trip. On the way back, she said of it: "*It's just a normal grocery store... And they're pretty high [priced], but, you know, considering the neighborhood.*"

Many, such as Kiara, did not see public transportation (buses) as a viable way to get home with groceries. When I asked her to explain why she didn't use the buses to get to stores beyond her neighborhood, she explored some of these shortcomings:

> *Nothing's really stopping me from taking the bus [to the grocery store] if I had to. But I can get the same thing from a closer store, possibly, maybe a couple cents higher. You know, it's the convenience of how fast you can get there and get back. You know, it would be—yes, it would explain some type of hardship because you'd have to wait on the bus with those products and then, you know, get them home. So, yeah, that would be kind of inconvenient, because the bus won't be there as soon as you're done, so you'll be standing there with your ice cream melting.*

Her feelings about using public transportation for food acquisition were complex and reflected an internalization of blame ("*Nothing's really stopping me*") for shortcomings in the city's bus system. The bus system was not particularly useful for participants needing to purchase large amounts of food. Because each of the grocery stores in the two neighborhoods featured exits designed to prevent shopping cart theft by trapping them just outside the store, shoppers have to carry all of their groceries from the store exits. Combined with shortcomings of stores within the neighborhood, public transportation is not ameliorating the dearth of perceived acceptable options within the community. Gail (2013) describes the difficulties navigating Detroit's bus system, which include routing, overcrowding, and on-time performance.

Food Acquisition Strategies

Lucille, a 40-year old medical professional living in the near-northwest with her own automobile, shopped for food exclusively outside of the neighborhood. Her reasons for employing this strategy related primarily to cost and selection: "*They price gouge you. . . . The fruits and vegetable selections are very limited. So typically, we drive out to Meijer's or Walmart or Trader Joes for our food.*"

Tina, a 43-year old woman living in the lower-east, regularly teamed up with her boyfriend or other friends with automobiles to travel outside of the neighborhood for grocery shopping. She described an ongoing process of collecting sales papers and visiting several stores in a single outing:

> *A bunch of us will go. The sales papers come from way out—Six, Seven Mile, or Livernois. . . . They either come in the mail or, for some reason, they send them out here . . . in the mail or some people have people walking, throwing fliers. And either way we get 'em. And we wait 'til—because [they come] at different times of the month—like, some of them might get there on the first of the month to, maybe, the 10th or even maybe as late as the 16th. If I get mine, I'll hold 'em. Then maybe five or six of us will go at that one time . . . [and] get the best sales at the two or three stores that we're gonna go to. . . . And then we'll wait maybe a couple of weeks and we'll go back to the stores again and get what we couldn't get before from the other stores. It's kind of hectic, but it works out, you know? 'Cus by the time the end of the month rolls around, we'll still have enough to make it through to the next month. But we have to catch the sales.*

Tina must continuously undertake these elaborate efforts to make her limited food budget last for the entire month.

Others used informal cab services (jitneys) to get to or from food outlets. Often, methods were used in combination, such as walking or taking the bus to a store and hiring a jitney to get home with groceries. Wanda, a resident of near-northwest in her mid-50s with severe arthritis, discussed how she got to her local store:

> Wanda: *I will walk up to the Miser and catch a jitney back.*
>
> Dan: *Mmm-hmm. Or you said you might call somebody for a ride back?*
>
> Wanda: *Yeah. Mmm-hmm.*

Wanda endured additional food procurement costs in hiring a cab to take her home. Her ongoing health problems compounded the transportation difficulties, as walking home with groceries from the nearest store (nearly a mile away) was impossible.

When shopping at local stores, residents devised strategies to mitigate the food safety challenges they perceived. Larissa, a 40-year old woman living in near-northwest, described several experiences of purchasing food that was spoiled or otherwise unfit for consumption. After several bad experiences with outdated meat, her husband Jimmy began to poke holes in the plastic packaging of meat to smell its freshness. Despite Larissa's reluctance to pursue this strategy, both she and Jimmy viewed his strategy for checking meat before purchase as necessary because of experiences purchasing spoiled products in the past. Larissa acknowledged that she found it necessary in response to the barriers of stores stocking outdated products. She also discussed the difficulty she had getting her money back from Miser's Foods when she did discover spoiled food after purchasing it. I obtained numerous health inspection reports from the

Michigan Department of Agriculture and found that the store had been cited several times from 2007–2009 for changing expiration dates and otherwise mishandling the meat and other products that they sell. While many researchers and policy makers fixate on the health behaviors and choices of community residents, management of Miser's Foods has faced only minor penalties for their own unhealthy practices.

Women's selective shopping strategies included not only ways to avoid spoiled foods, but also using multiple sources to get the best quality, price, and selection for each type of food they wanted. Jessica, a 26-year-old college student living in the lower east, described having to make separate trips and purchases for multiple types of foods:

> Mustaza's is just good for fruits and vegetables. . . Fresh Food Center, they're good for vegetables and meat and they have frozen products. You know, just the basic things that the market offers. . . . I was getting canned goods from, like, food missions, so I haven't bought any in a while because I still have canned goods.

For each type of food Jessica sought (fruit, vegetables, meat, canned goods), she had a different source that met her dietary, taste, or economic needs. Although she walked for most of her food acquisition, the distance to Mustaza's required her to go with her mother, who owns a vehicle. By combining sources and strategies, Jessica felt generally satisfied with her ability to get the foods she wanted.

Food banks were used by others as a strategy to mitigate cost. Wanda, a near-northwest resident in her 50s, stated that she hadn't bought canned goods in about three years because she could get them from food banks. She felt this strategy enabled her to afford fresh produce, dairy, and meat. Many other residents in the near-northwest took advantage of food bank sources. Numerous churches and food banks serving the poor stood out as one of the near-northwest's only features that enabled food acquisition better than the lower-east. Chantel, a near-northwest resident in her early thirties, discussed the available nearby food bank sources: "Churches and stuff give out free food. . . . You just gotta know which ones to go to." Many residents in near-northwest, like Chantel and Wanda, knew of several food bank sources. In our informal conversation after Chantel's interview, she and some friends shared information about weekly food bank sources in the neighborhood that covered nearly every day of the week.

Traveling outside of the neighborhood to procure food was not an equally viable strategy for residents of the two neighborhoods in this study. June, a 40-year-old resident of the lower-east, was able to get to Eastern Market by walking: "I walk through the apartments and take my little shortcut and I end up over there at the Eastern Market. . . . I get a better deal." Although June did not have an automobile, she was still able to pursue a strategy wherein she could obtain cheaper and healthier foods by walking to an adjacent section of the city. This is because of the lower-east neighborhood's proximity to Eastern Market. Kiara refused to shop at the store nearest to her because of quality concerns. She walked farther to shop at another store. However, she was still unsatisfied with the high prices at her alternative choice. Unlike June in the lower-east, Kiara's extra walking could only reasonably get her to a store that she was still somewhat dissatisfied with.

Seventeen of the 25 women expressed that concerns about crime often prevent them from conducting their everyday routines. Residents who were concerned about crime were more reluctant to walk longer distances to stores they perceived as better than options closer to home. Concerns about crime limited the ability of respondents to shop at stores outside of their immediate communities. Michelle, an 18-year-old woman living in the near-northwest, told how she was robbed during the daytime while walking about one mile from her home: *"It's certain places I won't go in the daytime. . . . Like, the General Market . . . that's where I got robbed at. And it was in daylight, you know? Wasn't nobody helping me."*

This experience made Michelle reluctant to take longer walks to get to stores she perceived as preferable. As a result, she tended to rely on less-desirable food sources closer to her home. Herein lies a key barrier to food access that is experienced more acutely by women. Certain neighborhood barriers, such as fear of crime and street harassment were more prevalent among female respondents. Incidents of sexual assault, rape, and abduction continue to be an epidemic victimizing mostly women and perpetrated almost exclusively by men in Detroit and nationwide (Bureau of Justice Statistics 2010). Lack of adequate street lighting and police presence exacerbated these concerns. Public harassment of women was not an interview topic at the beginning of this study, but several cited it as a barrier to getting food and physical activity. As Gardner (1995) points out, the discomfort created by these interactions often renders women powerless to navigate certain public spaces. Concerns about being outside at night were also more common among women, although the majority of men I spoke to expressed similar reservations. Jessica described the following encounter in her lower-east side apartment complex:

The other night I was walking through the courtyard and some guys were sitting. And a young man walked up and he was looking [straight at me]. I guess he couldn't see what was directly in front of him. So, he's looking, and they asked him what he's looking at. I didn't stick around to see the end results of that.

Jessica told me about this encounter in response to questioning about when she takes trips to the stores. She described how the early sunsets in winter make it especially difficult, because of her reluctance to go out after dark in light of experiences such as the one described above.

Nutritional Knowledge

Most of the women I spoke with detailed nutritional knowledge and food acquisition strategies much more sophisticated than many public health elites might imagine. All 25 women articulated some explicit knowledge about healthy eating habits that resonated with messaging by medical and nutritional experts. Food and beverages that were mentioned as beneficial because of their nutritional value included vegetables, fruits, lean meats, whole grains and water. Fresh foods were mentioned as healthy by the majority of participants. Cooking at home was also described as healthier than eating in restaurants by several participants. Nutritional practices that were mentioned in a negative light included foods or eating habits to avoid, including *"fried"* or *"greasy"* foods, large portions and infrequent meals. Three interviewees had received some formal education in nutrition (two through professional training and one from a health promotion program).

Kimberly, a 24-year-old, unemployed, sole-supporting mother of three children living in the near-northwest, articulated a number of nutritional recommendations:

> *A lot of water—like, some people can't have like eight cups of water. Everybody's intake is different when it comes to food. Like for me, probably about at least four cups of water a day, exercise at least 30 minutes to an hour. Um, as far as eating, I'm think three fruits and maybe two vegetables and some protein—maybe some fish or chicken or turkey. I'm a little worried about, like, the pork and all the beef and all of that. I'm starting to worry a little bit about all of that. Those type of things, eating a salad—that's mainly a healthy diet for me. And juice is okay if it has vitamin C in it—maybe not like taking a lot of it. And I think everybody at my age should be taking vitamins, too.*

Kimberly's views of good nutrition emphasized numerous options and flexibility. She listed three lean meat alternatives to pork and beef. She argued that the recommendation of eight glasses of water per day should not apply to everyone. So she not only could recite professional recommendations but also could criticize them. Additionally, she saw complexity in the benefits and drawbacks of juice—with the sugar content being more acceptable if it's offset by vitamin C.

Chantel described her success in changing her habits of eating before bed:

> *I make sure after I eat I stay awake two hours before I go to sleep. I used to just eat, smoke weed, and go straight to sleep. So all that food would sit on my stomach and I'd wake up with all that body. . . . But now I just take my time and eat, drink water with my food. That keeps my stomach down.*

Chantel's strategies of staying up two hours before going to sleep and drinking water with meals also resonated with the advice of nutritionists.

Because of its wide availability and popularity in both neighborhoods, concerns about fried food were brought up by a number of interviewees. June, a lower-east resident in her late 40s said: *"I try not to eat a lot of greasy food. I try to eat a lot of baked foods, broiled. I'm trying to get away from fried food because of high blood pressure."* The majority participants mentioned that a healthy diet involved avoiding food that was *"greasy"* or *"fried"*. Hence, the consumption of fried food might not reflect a lack of knowledge about its consequences, but rather a lack of otherwise viable and desirable alternatives.

Freshness appeared to be of concern to participants for varying reasons. Some expressed a preference for fresh meat and produced as opposed to canned, packaged, or frozen products. Others were worried about the quality and safety of meats and produce that had sat on the shelves for too long. Many participants were keenly aware of recent national food safety advisories about dangers in the food supplies. Spinach, tomato, and meat were three items in the news around the time of our interviews. The possession of this knowledge came from both media and social networks. June indicated that her daughter had reminded her of a recent tomato recall as they shopped together in a grocery store. Betty, a 38-year-old living in the near-northwest, described how she applied knowledge of threats in the food supply gleaned from news reports to her own food preparation practices:

> *There was a factory and they were talking about. Well, somebody got sick. I think somebody died. Because the canned goods—see what they weren't doing was cleaning 'em. And see, sometimes a rat can get it. What they do when they get on top of things—they pee on 'em! So, here I come and I buy a can of green beans and guess what went into that. So, see, that means a lot to me. Because if I gotta buy something from you, then I gotta come home and scrub it down.*

Again, residents responded to this issue by closely inspecting foods, cleaning, and otherwise dealing with problems they encountered in their local food system and through their personal food procurement strategies.

For others, getting any food at all was more important than the healthfulness of it. Still, others devised strategies to not only stretch limited food budgets, but also to address their nutritional concerns. June discussed balancing her budgetary and health concerns:

> *Since the food has went up [in price], I've been eating a lot of, say, uh, pots, like beans or greens or stews, you know, chili, spaghetti, pasta salad . . . something that's healthy and you can eat on more than one day.*

June's primary concern in her decision-making process was price. With a limited budget, she mentioned *"getting full"* as her foremost concern. But she also found ways to incorporate options she felt were nutritious.

Discussion

Structural explanations point out important barriers to health that the biomedical approach fails to consider. However, they cannot illustrate the processes through which low-income, urban neighborhoods encourage some forms of dietary behaviors and discourage others. The findings demonstrate the value of bringing agency back into discussions of health inequalities. Structural approaches cannot account for the uniqueness and variation of perspectives and actions I found among the 25 interviewees. They also cannot capture the processes involved in the formation of motivations and strategies under sometimes difficult circumstances. Approaches that study eating behaviors from an exclusively structural approach will miss out on these important considerations and lead to an overly deterministic outlook on diverse populations. They also tend to ignore the presence of nutrition-savvy residents who are capable of developing strategies to pursue nutritious foods.

Still, the best approaches to understanding these health behaviors will consider the knowledge and potential of residents alongside the contextual barriers they face. Structural constraints remain important (if not overwhelming) obstacles to food and nutrition. These barriers operated within and beyond the neighborhoods in this study. From municipal factors such as lack of adequate sidewalks, streets, and bus routes, to neighborhood factors such as crime and economic flight, to personal factors such as limited budgets for food, structural barriers had persistent influence in the lives of all participants.

Although some researchers have treated low-income neighborhood residents as a uniform population (and labeled them as the underclass, urban poor, etc.), health behaviors in this study varied tremendously according to the knowledge, emotions and creativity of participants. The findings here demonstrate the role of culture in shaping dispositions and decisions (both within and among geographically defined populations). These dynamics must be explored along with agency.

In contrast to mainstream views of the capacity of low-income people, nutritional knowledge among interviewees was widespread. Knowledge covered an array of nutritional topics such as the healthfulness of foods, the best times to eat, how much to eat, and threats in the food system. However, many participants had difficulty putting this knowledge into practice due to lack of access to food and the prohibitive cost of healthy foods. These findings suggest that health education efforts might be misguided. More appropriate, perhaps, would be interventions to address the lack of available community resources. These findings also call into question the validity of the biomedical model's emphasis on nutritional education to address obesity. Educational programs designed to educate individuals about what they should eat misjudge the levels of nutritional knowledge low-income populations already have. Nor are they as heavily-funded as countervailing messages from fast food advertisements. This research highlights how nutritional knowledge is not sufficient if it cannot be put to use in the community, cultural, and economic contexts of informed individuals.

Neighborhood Effects

Rather than being a constant, the agency of participants in this study varied according to intervening factors. Most notably in this research, the relationship between agency and structure was conditioned by neighborhood environments. Certain neighborhood features augmented the potential for agency while others diminished it. The possibilities for agency were greater in the lower-east, a community with more resources and fewer barriers than the near-northwest. By comparing the unique social environments within and around two Detroit neighborhoods, this research demonstrated that neighborhood resources and barriers exerted differential influence on agency.

The murky and traversable borders of neighborhoods typically delineated by researchers further complicate understandings of agency, structure and community contexts. Although some borders were more difficult to cross (such as the interstate highway at the western edge of the near-northwest), it is important to see neighborhood structures as embedded in wider contexts, potentially located near health resources or characterized by further constraints. Nearby areas reshaped the potential for agency in this study in significant ways. For example, areas adjacent to near-northwest residents contained food sources that most residents saw as only marginally better than the ones closest to home. Conversely, areas adjacent to the lower-east contained numerous well-maintained parks, a farmer's and a retailer's market with fresh produce and a variety of specialty food stores.

Whether the beliefs and practices I have documented are attributable to individual or community characteristics remains an open question. However, I find the dichotomy of compositional (individual) and contextual (neighborhood) effects to be an oversimplification of the social relationships at hand. It is obviously impossible, within the scope of a single qualitative study, to disaggregate individual from neighborhood effects. However, ethnographers do need to examine both variation within neighborhoods and between them.

Implications for Social Policy

A number of policies could improve food and physical activity options for residents in these and other low-income neighborhoods. However, the strategies outlined in this chapter are unlikely to be amenable to policy interventions at the macro-level. Encouraging changes to neighborhoods and structural inequalities would likely be more effective. The most sustainable solution to lack of access to food would be improving the quantity and quality of options within walking distance. However, given current circumstances in which grocery store operators are reluctant to open locations in economically depressed areas with declining populations, specific public transportation services that cater to the needs and destinations of grocery shoppers are needed. These needs include adequate space and cooling for groceries and destinations such as Eastern Market (the city's largest farmer's and retailer's market). Providing better public transportation is key to expanding access to both food and physical activities in the current neighborhood contexts.

Decades of "cheap food" policies in the United States have subsidized the production of unhealthy foods (Guthman 2007). These longstanding policies have made corn and foods related to corn, such as corn-fed beef and products laden with corn syrup, far more prevalent and affordable than fruits or vegetables. As Monsivais and Drewnowski (2007) have pointed out, these high-density foods are more affordable and more resistant to inflation than low-energy-density (low-calorie). Inverting the relationship between the healthfulness and affordability of foods could be achieved by redirecting subsidizes to healthier, low-energy-density foods.

Health code violations are higher in Detroit grocery stores than suburban counterparts (Guest and Turk 2006). The sanitation of local stores could be improved by imposing greater penalties for violations (and repeat violations). Participation in community garden programs, such as the nationally renowned Garden Resource Collaborative Program, should be subsidized to increase access to fresh produce. Discussion of bringing large-scale farming operations to Detroit has been in the news recently (Gallagher 2010), but smaller-scale gardens might provide more economic opportunities for residents. Grocery stores partnering with these gardens would improve the quality of food and also provide an engine for neighborhood gardening opportunities to expand.

In 2013, Whole Foods and Meijer's built stores in Detroit—the first major grocery chains in several decades to open within the city limits. However, Whole Foods located in the relatively affluent Midtown area, while Meijer's opened on 8 Mile Road, the northern edge of the city. The stores are not accessible to most of Detroit's areas of concentrated poverty, including the neighborhoods in this study.

Despite these significant challenges, an examination of the food procurement of low-income Detroit residents shows that resident efforts to obtain acceptable foods are meaningful, elaborate, and widespread. Nutritional knowledge plays an important role in these strategies, as residents use it avoid the pitfalls of their local food system.

Notes

1. Popular culture and media are replete with examples of an individualistic focus on obesity. *The Biggest Loser*, a weight-loss, reality television program, places fat people squarely in competition with one another. A recent AFP headline read, "Obesity Now a 'Lifestyle' Choice for Americans, Expert Says." In the article, a health economist at-

tempts to portray obesity as a rational choice in a society where unhealthy food is cheap (Zeitvogel 2008).

2. This idea was suggested by Renee Anspach (personal communication, November 4, 2008).

3. I specifically avoid making contacts at or near food sources such as grocery stores or restaurants. I found post offices in each community allowed more representative neighborhood samples. Most post office users had personal transportation, which often meant that they were among the roughly 60 percent of neighborhood residents with household incomes above the poverty line.

4. The consequences of highway construction, white flight, deindustrialization, and urban renewal in Detroit's African-American communities are discussed at length by Thomas Sugrue (2005).

Bibliography

Acheampong, Irene, and Lauren Haldeman. 2013. "Are Nutritional Knowledge, Attitudes, and Beliefs Associated with Obesity among Low-Income Hispanic and African American Women Caretakers?" *Journal of Obesity* 2013: 1-8.

Auchincloss, Amy H., Ana Diez Roux, V., Mahasin S. Mujahid, Mingwu Shen, Alain G. Bertoni, Mercedes R. Carnethon. 2009. "Neighborhood Resources for Physical Activity and Healthy Foods and Incidence of Type 2 Diabetes Mellitus: The Multiethnic Study of Atherosclerosis." *Archives of Internal Medicine* 169, no. 18: 1698-1704.

Barnes, Sandra L. 2005. *The Cost of Being Poor: A Comparative Study of Life in Poor Urban Neighborhoods in Gary, Indiana*. Albany, NY: SUNY Press.

Bazata, Debbra D., Jennifer G. Robinson, Kathleen M. Fox, and Susan Grandy. 2008. "Affecting Behavior Change in Individuals With Diabetes: Findings From the Study to Help Improve Early Evaluation and Management of Risk Factors Leading to Diabetes (SHIELD)." *The Diabetes Educator* 34, no. 6: 1025-1036.

Bourdieu, Pierre. 1977. *Outline of a Theory of Practice*. (R. Nice, translator). Cambridge, UK: Cambridge University Press.

Campos, Paul, Abigail C Saguy, Paul Ernsberger, Eric Oliver, and Glenn Gaesser. 2006. "The Epidemiology of Overweight and Obesity: Public Health Crisis or Moral Panic?" *International Journal of Epidemiology* 35, no. 1: 55-60.

Cheadle, Allen, Bruce M., Susan Curry, Edward Wagner, Paula Diehr, Thomas Koepsell, and Alan Kristal. 1991. "Community-level Comparisons Between the Grocery Store Environment and Individual Dietary Practices." *Preventive Medicine,* 20, no. 2: 50-61.

Cockerham, William C. 2005. "Health and Lifestyle Theory and the Convergence of Agency and Structure." *Journal of Health and Social Behavior* 46, no. 1: 51-67.

Corbin, Juliet, and Anselm Strauss. 1990. "Grounded Theory Research: Procedures, Cannons, and Evaluative Criteria." *Qualitative Sociology* 13, no. 1: 3-21.

Correa, Nancy Post, Nancy G. Murray, Christine A. Mei, William B. Baun, Beverly Jean Gor, Nicole B. Hare, Deborah Banerjee, Toral F. Sindha, and Lovell Allan Jones. 2010. "CAN DO Houston: A Community-Based Approach to Preventing Childhood Obesity." *Preventing Chronic Disease* 7, no. 4: 1-11.

DeVault, Marjorie L. 1991. *Feeding the Family: The Social Organization of Caring as Gendered Work.* Chicago: University of Chicago Press.

Drewnowski, Adam, and Nicole Darmon. 2005. "The Economics of Obesity: Dietary Energy Density and Energy Cost." *American Society for Clinical Nutrition* 82, no. 1: 265S-273S.

Emerson, Robert M. 2004. "Working with 'Key Incidents.'" In *Qualitative Research Practice,* edited by Clive Seale, Giampietro Gobo, Jaber F. Gubrium, and David Silverman, 457-472. London: Sage.

Emirbayer, Mustafa, and Ann Mische. 1998. "What is Agency?" *American Journal of Sociology* 103, no. 4: 962-1023.

Gallagher, John, 2010. "Is Urban Farming Detroit's Cash Cow?" *Detroit Free Press,* March 21, 2010, 25(A).

Giddens, Anthony. 1977. *Central Problems in Social Theory: Action, Structure and Contradiction in Social Analysis.* London, UK: Macmillan.

Glaser, Barney G., and Anselm Strauss. 1967. *The Discovery of Grounded Theory.* Chicago: Aldine.

Guest, Greta, and Victoria Turk. 2006. "Food Violations Higher in Detroit," *Detroit Free Press,* October 24, 2006, 1(F).

Guthman, Julie. 2007. "Can't Stomach It: How Michael Pollan et al. Made Me Want to Eat Cheetos." *Gastronomica* 7, no. 3: 75-79.

Gwantley, John Langston. 1980. *Drylongso: A Self-Portrait of Black America.* New York: Random House.

Hasson, Rebecca E., Tanja C. Adam, Jaimie S. Davis, Louise A. Kelly, Emily E. Ventura, Courtney E. Byrd-Williams, Claudia M. Toledo-Corral, Christian K. Roberts, Christianne J. Lane, Stanley P. Azen, Chih-Ping Chou, Donna Spruijt, Mark J. Weigensberg, Kiros Berhane, and Michael I. Goran. 2010. "Randomized Controlled Trial to Improve Adiposity, Inflammation, and Insulin Resistance in Obese African-American and Latino Youth." *Obesity* 20, no. 4: 811-818.

Hoisington, Anne, Jill Armstrong Shultz, and Sue Butkus. 2002. "Coping Strategies and Nutrition Education Needs Among Food Pantry Users." *Journal of Nutrition Education and Behavior* 34, no. 6: 326-333.

Katz, Jack. 1983. "A Theory of Qualitative Methodology: The Social System of Fieldwork." In *Contemporary Field Research,* edited by Robert M. Emerson, 127-148. Prospect Heights, IL: Waveland.

Kelley, Robin D.G. 1998. *Yo' Mama's Disfunktional!: Fighting the Culture Wars in Urban America.* Boston: Beacon Press.

Kieffer, Edith C., Brandy R. Sinco, Ann Rafferty, Michael S. Spencer, Gloria Palmisano, Earl E. Watt, and Michele Heisler. 2006. "Chronic Disease-Related Behaviors and Health among African Americans and Hispanics in the REACH Detroit 2010 Communities, Michigan, and the United States." *Health Promotion Practice* 7, no. 3: 256s-264s.

Kirkup, Malcolm, Ronan De Kervenoael, Alan Hallsworth, Ian Clarke, Peter Jackson, and Rossana Perez De Aguila. 2004. "Inequalities in Retail Choice: Exploring Consumers Experiences in Suburban Neighbourhoods." *International Journal of Retail & Distribution Management* 32, no. 11: 511-522.

Labonte, Ron, and Ann Robertson. 1996. "Delivering the Goods, Showing Our Stuff: The Case for a Constructivist Paradigm for Health Promotion Research and Practice." *Health Education & Behavior* 23, no. 4: 431-447.

Mancino, Lisa, and Jean Kinsey. 2008. "Is Dietary Knowledge Enough? Hunger, Stress, and Other Roadblocks to Healthy Eating." www.ers.usda.gov (accessed January 13, 2009).

Mari Gallagher Research and Consulting Group. 2007. "Examining the Impact of Food Deserts on Public Health in Detroit." www.marigallagher.com /site_media/dynamic/project_files/1_DetroitFoodDesertReport_Full.pdf (accessed January 5, 2009).

McEntree, Jesse C. 2009. "Highlighting Food Inadequacies: Does the Food Desert Metaphor Help this Cause?" *British Food Journal* 111, no. 4: 349-363.

Monsivais, Pablo, and Adam Drewnowski. 2007. "The Rising Cost of Low-Energy-Density Foods." *Journal of the American Dietetic Association* 107, no. 12: 2071-2076.

National Institutes of Health (NIH). 2011. "Diabetes and Pre-Diabetes Statistics and Facts." ndep.nih.gov/diabetes-facts/index.aspx (accessed July 13, 2013).

Nestle, Marion and Michael S. Jacobson. 2000. "Halting the Obesity Epidemic: A Public Health Policy Approach." *Public Health Reports* 115, no. 1: 12-24.

Olshansky, S. Jay, Douglas J. Passaro, Ronald C. Hershow, Jennifer Layden, Bruce A. Carnes, Jacob Brody, Leonard Hayflick, Robert N. Butler, David B. Allison, and David S. Ludwig. 2005. "A Potential Decline in Life Expectancy in the United States in the 21st century." *New England Journal of Medicine* 352, no. 11: 1138-1145.

Parker, Edith A., Amy J. Schulz, Barbara A. Israel, and Rose Hollis. 1998. "Detroit's East Side Village Health Worker Partnership: Community-Based Lay Health Advisor Intervention in an Urban Area." *Health Education & Behavior* 25, no. 1: 24-45.

Raphael, Dennis, and Toba Bryant. 2006. "The State's Role in Promoting Population Health: Public Health Concerns in Canada, USA, UK, and Sweden." *Health Policy* 78, no. 1: 39-55.

Rose, Daniel J. 2011. "Captive Audience? Strategies for Acquiring Food in Two Detroit Neighborhoods." *Qualitative Health Research* 21, no. 5: 642-651.

Saguy, Abigail C., and Kevin W. Riley. 2005. "Weighing Both Sides: Morality, Mortality, and Framing Contests Over Obesity." *Journal of Health Politics, Policy and Law* 30, no. 5: 869-921.

Schulz, Amy J., and Lora Bex Lempert. 2004. "Being Part of the World: Detroit Women's Perceptions of Health and the Social Environment." *Journal of Contemporary Ethnography* 33, no. 4: 437-465.

———. David R. Williams, Barbara A. Israel, and Lora Bex Lempert. 2002. "Racial and Spatial Relations as Fundamental Determinants of Health in Detroit." *The Millbank Quarterly* 80, no. 4: 677-707.

Stolley, Melinda R. and Mariam L. Fitzgibbon, 1997. "Effects of an Obesity Prevention Program on the Eating Behavior of African American Mothers and Daughters." *Health Education and Behavior* 24, no. 2: 152-164.

Sugrue, Thomas. 2005. *The Origins of the Urban Crisis: Race and Inequality in Postwar Detroit.* Princeton, NJ: Princeton University Press.

Tellez, Marisol, Sohn Woosung, Brian A. Burt, and Amid I. Ismail. 2006. "Assessment of the Relationship between Neighborhood Characteristics and Dental Caries Severity among Low-Income African-Americans: A Multilevel Approach." *Journal of Public Dentistry* 66, no. 1: 30-36.

Tepper, Beverly J., Young-Suk Choi, and Rodolpho M. Nayga, Jr. 1997. "Understanding Food Choice in Adult Men: Influence of Nutrition Knowledge, Food Beliefs and Dietary Restraint." *Food Quality and Preference* 8, no. 4: 307–317.

Travers, Kim D. 1996. "The Social Organization of Nutritional Inequalities." *Social Science & Medicine* 43, no. 4: 543-553.

United States Census Bureau. 2011. "American Community Survey, 2010." factfinder2.census.gov (accessed January 7, 2013).

United States Department of Agriculture. n.d. "Food Deserts." apps.ams.usda.gov/fooddeserts/foodDeserts.aspx (accessed July 13, 2013).

Widick, B.J., and Horace Sheffield. 1989. *Detroit: City of Race and Class Violence.* Detroit: Wayne State University Press.

Wyatt, Sharon B., Winters, Karen P., and Patricia M. Dubbert. 2006. "Overweight and Obesity: Prevalence, Consequences, and Causes of a Growing Public Health Problem." *The American Journal of the Medical Sciences* 331, no. 4: 166-174.

Zeitvogel, Karen. 2008. "Obesity Now a Lifestyle Choice for Americans, Expert Says," *Agence France-Presse*, January 10, 2008.

Zenk, Shannon N., Laurie L. Lachance, Amy J. Schulz, Graciela Mentz, Srimathi Kannan, and William Ridella. 2009. "Neighborhood Retail Food Environment and Fruit and Vegetable Intake in a Multiethnic Urban Population." *American Journal of Health Promotion* 23, no. 4: 255-264.

———. Schulz, Amy J., Barbara A. Israel, Sherman A. James, Shuming Bao, and Mark L. Wilson. 2005. "Neighborhood Racial Composition, Neighborhood Poverty, and the Spatial Accessibility of Supermarkets in Metropolitan Detroit." *American Journal of Public Health* 95, no. 4: 660-667.

CHAPTER 7

Is the Cup Half Empty or Half Full? Economic Transition and Changing Ideas About Food Insecurity in Rural Costa Rica

David Himmelgreen
Nancy Romer-Daza
Allison Cantor
Sara Arias-Steele

Introduction

Costa Rica is known for its luxuriant foliage, exotic fauna, and spectacular landscapes. This, along with a stable democratic government, relatively low crime, and a high quality of life, has made "The Green Republic" (Evans 1999) a magnet for tourists and retirees alike. For example, in 2008, more than two million tourists from North America, Europe, and Central and South America, visited Costa Rica (ICT 2009). Moreover, according to the U.S. Department of State, there are over 20,000 U.S. retirees now living there. Costa Rica shares borders with Nicaragua and Panama and has coasts on the Pacific Ocean and the Caribbean Sea. The country has a land mass of 51,100 square kilometers (130th largest in the world), a population of almost 4.7 million people, high life expectancy (78.06 y) and literacy rate (96.3 percent), and universal health care coverage (CIA World Fact Book 2013; Evans 1999). The rise in tourism in Costa Rica and elsewhere in Latin America is reflected in a shift away from an agricultural-based economy towards a tourism economy that generates foreign capital to spur economic development (Leatherman and Goodman 2005). In Costa Rica in particular, there is a well-developed high technology sector that includes information technology (e.g., Sykes Industries employs 23,000 workers in the country), especially in the Central Valley where the capital city of San Jose is situat-situated and where the majority of the population resides. Despite the very prominent role that coffee and fruit exports have played in the Costa Rican economy in the past, food production was enough to meet the in-country demand. While Costa Rica still grows fresh produce (e.g., bananas, pineapples, coffee) for internal consumption and export, it is increasingly relying on the importation of food to feed its people. For instance, there was more than a 170 percent increase in food imports between 1992 and 2005 reflecting an increase from about 0.75 million metric tons in the early 1990s to nearly two million metric tons by the mid-2000s (Thow and Hawkes 2009). While the manufacture of electronics (e.g., microprocessors and medical components) makes up a growing proportion of Costa Rica's economic activity, most of these items are exported. As of 2012, Costa Rica had an estimated trade deficit of $5.35 billion (CIA World Fact Book 2013). In addition to tourism, the Central American Free Trade Agreement (CAFTA) has had an impact on the Costa Rican economy more recently. CAFTA was narrowly ratified (51 percent to 48 percent) in a public referen- dum in 2006 (AlterNet 2007), and while there has been modest economic growth since then, there have also been increasing economic inequality and a de cline in the funding of social programs (e.g., 6.3 percent reduction in education) {Tico- times.net 2012). There has also been a widening gap in wealth.. For example, in 2012, the wealthiest 20 percent of Costa Ricans earned over 18 times more than the poorest 20 percent, a 1.3 times increase since 2010. In that same year, 21.6 percent of Costa Rican households were living in poverty (Ticotimes.net 2012)

Tourism and the sharing of cultural ideas and values, free trade agreements and the flow of goods and services, improved transportation and communications systems, widespread labor migration and widening social networks, and the spread of multinational corporations are all part of the process of globalization in which the good, the bad, and the ugly of economic development emerge to impact the daily lives of Costa Ricans (*Ticos*) in both urban and rural areas. Albeit brief, the previous discussion highlights some of the positive and negative aspects of globalization in Costa Rica. On the one hand, Costa Rica is the most stable country in Central America with a robust market economy, well educated workforce, and good overall health indicators. On the other hand, there is growing economic inequality, a significant number of households living in poverty, and rising rates of non-communicable chronic diseases which are associated with changes in lifestyle, dietary patterns, and overall nutritional status (Martin

2005; Popkin 2002), food insecurity (Himmelgreen et al. 2006), and mental health issues (Weaver and Hadley 2009).

Within this context of rapid change, we have been conducting research in partnership with the Monteverde Institute (MVI), a non-governmental organization located in the Monteverde Zone (MVZ—a rural area in the Northwest of the country) since 2005. More recently, we completed a three-year longitudinal study to examine how the shift from agriculture to a mixed economy of tourism and agriculture (coffee, dairy, and hydroponic farming) is affecting the lifestyle, diet, nutritional status, and mental health among residents living in the uppermost region of the zone where tourism is most prominent. The main reason for focusing on this area is that most of the health research in Costa Rica is being conducted in the Central Valley where more than two thirds of the population resides (govisitCostaRica.com 2013) and where health and economic resources are concentrated (Sáenz et al. 2011; CIA World Fact Book 2013). Thus, this research seeks to describe the changing health situation in the MVZ and to compare it to other places in Costa Rica and elsewhere. In addition to conducting research in the area, two of the co-authors (Himmelgreen and Romero-Daza) have collaborated with MVI to offer the Globalization and Community Health Field School for more than ten years, an intensive program that trains students on methods, theory, and ethics to carry out community health assessments and to conduct community-driven research projects. Together, these initiatives have been the impetus behind several community programs to improve the food security situation in the MVZ.

Aims and Research Setting

Study Aims

The aim of this chapter is to examine how the transition from an agricultural economy to a mixed economy of tourism, and to a lesser extent agriculture, affects food-related decision making, in the context of rising economic inequality and food insecurity in four rural towns in the MVZ. Three of the towns are greatly impacted by tourism while the fourth is still mostly engaged in agriculture. However, even in the latter town some households have opened their farms to visitors for guided tours and for demonstrations of common agricultural activities such as the milking of cows, the processing of compost, etc. This chapter reports on data related to people's food experiences and perceptions in the context of economic and lifestyle changes in the MVZ. Data were collected from 215 participants, of which 187 (87 percent) were women. Household food security was measured and qualitative experiential data on food insecurity and the factors that influence food-related decision making were analyzed through a content analysis.

Below we present results in the following sequence: 1) description and comparison of household socio-demographics; 2) description of the prevalence and severity of food insecurity using the Household Food Insecurity Access Scale (HFIAS); and 3) presentation of interview and focus group data on the factors (identified in five themes) that influence food-related decision making in the context of economic change in the MVZ. As will be shown, the shift towards a mixed economy where tourism predominates has both positive and negative effects on the lives of the participants.

Study Setting

The MVZ is located in the Northwestern Tilarán Mountains in the province of Puntarenas. Situated along the Continental Divide at an altitude of 1200 to 1400 meters above sea level, the upper-most region of the zone is characterized by weather patterns where the sweeping upward warm, humid Caribbean air currents collide with dryer, cool winds from the Pacific. As a result, some areas of the zone receive in excess of 251 centimeters of rain annually, and experience temperatures that range from the mid-50s to the upper-70s (Fahrenheit) over the year, and very strong seasonal winds (Guswa and Rhodes 2007). The upper-most region of the zone is often shrouded in afternoon clouds and is home to the Monteverde Cloud Forest Preserve, one of the world's most threatened ecosystems (Vivanco 2006; Nardkarni and Wheelwright 2000). Given the diverse topography of the MVZ, the convergence of these climatic conditions gives rise to a large number of micro-ecological niches, each with diverse flora and fauna. This makes the zone an ideal place for bird watchers and other nature lovers (Vivanco 2006; Honey 1999).

There are over 20 towns of varying size and well-over 5000 residents spread throughout the MVZ ranging from the Pan American Highway to foothills, hamlets, and larger mountain communities such as Santa Elena, the principal tourism hub. Nestled in the upper-part of the zone is the town of Monteverde, which was founded by North American Quaker families in the late 1940s. The original settlers started dairy farming that eventually gave rise to a well-known milk cooperative and the Monteverde Cheese Factory. However, the MVZ was inhabited by native *Ticos* since the 1920s if not earlier (Vivanco 2006). Although not fully documented, artifacts (e.g., pottery and tools) discovered by local farmers suggest the residence of earlier indigenous cultures (Personal Communication, Noe Vargas, July 2011). *Ticos* and Quakers live year round in the MVZ while increasing numbers of tourists, students, and researchers visit seasonally to vacation, study, and conduct research (Himmelgreen et al. 2006). Moreover, as retirees settle in the MVZ and businesses open, the price of land is rising, making it difficult for locals to buy property and tempting farmers to sell their farmland in return for financial security. Historically, small family farms have been an important feature in the economy of the zone. They often organized into food cooperatives where member households and larger-scale farms proportionately shared in the financial and labor inputs in addition to the profits of their production (University of Georgia n.d.). While there are fewer today, these cooperatives provide mutual assistance during the agricultural cycle and play a prominent role in the marketing and distribution of products (Alvarado et al. 1998).

During the last three decades, there has been a steady increase in the number of tourists visiting the MVZ. In fact, the area is now the second most popular tourist destination in the country (ICT 2009). While most of the visitors participate in eco-tourism activities, the MVZ also receives a considerable number of longer-term visitors who engage in language learning or who participate in educational programs, including field schools and semester-long courses. The 40 km road, of which 26 km are unpaved, spanning from the Pan American Highway to the upper-most Monteverde Cloud Forest Preserve, passes through large and small towns along the way. About 250,000 tourists visit the MVZ annually; this number is likely to rise once the entire road is paved (Monahan 2004). This huge influx of people and associated economic, structural, and cultural changes are having an impact on the lifestyles, and health of residents (Romero-Daza et al. 2008; Friedus and Romero-Daza 2009; Romero-Daza 2013; Himmelgreen et al. 2006; and Himmelgreen et al. 2013; Ledezma and Mario 2010; Cantor et al. 2013). Public health concerns include rapidly changing diets associated with dietary delocalization and food insecurity, reduced physical activity (especially among youth), child and adult obesity, and a rise in cases of hypertension, type 2 diabetes, and asthma. The MVZ provides the perfect setting for examining the downstream effects of globalization on health and well-being.

Methods

The data presented here come from the first year (2008 into 2009) of a three-year longitudinal study funded by the National Science Foundation (BNS 0753017). The U.S.-based research team included the PI, one of the Co-PIs, and a University of South Florida graduate anthropology student who happened to be a Costa Rican national. The local team included four *Tico* nationals who worked as researchers for MVI. The development of the research instruments and protocols started during spring 2008, and the team members were trained and piloted the instruments later that summer before officially beginning data collection. Data were collected through surveys—including the administration of the HFIAS scale—with the entire sample (N=215), individual interviews (N=100), and focus groups (N=10 participants).

Measuring Household Food Security Status

In this study, food security, which exists "when all people at all times have access to sufficient, safe, nutritious food to maintain a healthy and active life" (WHO 2013), was measured annually with the Household Food Insecurity Access Scale (HFIAS). The HFIAS is designed to measure the experience of food insecurity, and is useful for identifying prevalence at the household level, as well as for monitoring changes over time (Coates et al. 2007). Cross-cultural research suggests that the experience of food insecurity involves universal domains, which include insufficient food intake and its physical consequences, inadequate food quality, and uncertainty and worry about food (Swindale and Bilinsky 2006; Coates 2006). The 18-question HFIAS is intended to measure the core domains of food insecurity experienced over the previous 30 days. The first nine questions measure the occurrence of food insecurity while the following nine measure the frequency of occurrence (Coates et al. 2007). The HFIAS classifies households into four levels of food insecurity: food secure, mild, moderate, and severe. Categorization is based on affirmative responses to experiencing severe conditions and/or more frequent experiences of conditions (Coates et al. 2007). The HFIAS protocol involves procedures to tailor the questions to be locally/culturally appropriate. This includes not only translating the questionnaire, but also working with key informants and other individuals representative of the study population to refine the translated questions so that core concepts are accurately conveyed. Although there are other food security scales that have been validated regionally (e.g., Latin American and Caribbean Food Security Scale [FAO 2012]), the protocol for making the HFIAS culturally appropriate was the reason it was chosen for this study.

Experiences and Perception of Economic Change and Factors Influencing Food-Related Decision Making

In addition to administration of the surveys and HFIAS scale, interviews (N= 100) and focus groups (N=10 participants) were conducted by the native Spanish speaking researchers to examine participants' experiences and perceptions of economic change in the MVZ and to discuss those factors that affect food-related decision making. As part of the interviews, participants were also asked to discuss whether household food access and availability had changed since they were children. A content analysis was done on the summaries of the interviews as well as on transcripts from interviews and focus groups. Five main themes emerged from the qualitative data: 1) food prices, 2) work patterns, 3) social support systems, 4) food access and availability, and 5) food preferences. In addition to reporting on the frequency in which words and phrases associated with these themes occurred, direct quotes are presented to provide more nuanced understanding of economic and dietary change in the zone, and of the ways in which participants cope with food insecurity. One of the authors, a native Spansh speaker, translated and transcribed the interviews and focus group transcripts. Another author, a non-native Spanish speaker, also reviewed the Spanish and English versions of these documents.

Data Management and Analysis

Qualitative data were compiled in a Word document and coded for recurring patterns. Coding involves "a word or short phrase that symbolically assigns a summative, salient, essence-capturing, and/or evocative attribute for a portion of language-based or visual data" (Saldaña 2009:3). Codes were collapsed into the five major themes, which were used to address the aims of this study. Using Microsoft Word, 2010, codes were searched and the frequency of codes and phrases associated with each theme was tallied and entered into Microsoft Excel, 2010; these data were further imported into SPSS (version 21) for additional statistical analysis (IBM 2012; Microsoft 2010). Themes were cross-tabulated with food insecurity in a Pearson's chi-square test of independence. The results of this analysis revealed that there were no statistically significant differences in the number of times that a theme was mentioned by food security status. Socio-economic and cultural variables for the larger study sample and subsample were assessed using descriptive statistics. These variables were also included in a bivariate analysis using Spearman's correlation coefficient to determine significant correlations among variables.

Results

Household Socio-demographics and Food Security Status for the Total Sample (N=215)

As shown in table 7.1, 215 households participated during the first year of the study. Most of the household respondents were women (87 percent), the biological mother or other female relative caregiver of study children (not discussed here). The mean age of the respondents was just over 40 years. Most of the households were located in the town of Monteverde (69.5 percent), which is located just 3km away from the main tourist town of Santa Elena. Both towns are dependent upon tourism but the former also includes households that are involved in dairy and pig farming and small-scale vegetable production. Nearly 25 percent of the households were located in Santa Elena, and nearly 7 percent in San Luis, a small town where most households are involved in agricultural production. More than 67 percent of all the study households reported having one or more members working in the tourism industry (e.g., hotels, restaurants, tour guides, and transportation). Most of the respondents reported being married or in common law marriages (84.9 percent) and over half of them attended/graduated from high school or university. The mean number of persons living in the household was almost four. The respondents reported an average $263 in household monthly food expenditures and $539 in total monthly expenditures. According to the respondents, households spend approximately 56 percent of their monthly income on food.

Table 7.1 Household Socio-demographics and Food Security Status Sample Demographics N=215		
	Frequency	Percent percent
Sex		
Female	187	87.0
Male	28	13.0
Civil Status (n=199)		
Married	128	64.3
Common law union	41	20.6
Single	30	15.0
Education		
University complete	13	6.6
University incomplete	14	7.1
High school complete	27	13.8
High school incomplete	142	72.4
Food Security Status		
Food secure	106	49.3
Mild insecure	58	27.0
Moderate insecure	43	20.0
Severe insecure	8	3.7
Work in Tourism (n=214)		
Yes	144	67.3
No	70	32.7
	Mean	Standard Deviation
Number of People Living in the House	3.86	1.50
Age (n=214)	40.2	11.7
Monthly Food Expenditures	132478.87 Colones (263 USD)	90889.09 (180.14)
Total Monthly Expenditures	271303.00 Colones (539 USD)	180579.05 (357.91)
Percent of Income Spent on Food	56	.38

Household food security status is also presented in table 7.1. On the one hand, nearly half of the study households reported being food secure during the previous 30 days. Based on the HFIAS questions, the respondents in these households did not report problems with access to or availability of food to meet their dietary needs. On the other hand, 27 percent of the households experienced mild food insecurity, 20 percent moderate food insecurity, and 4 percent reported severe food insecurity. The three levels of food insecurity (i.e., mild, moderate, and severe) measure several constructs associated with problems related to food access and food availability, namely a) uncertainty or anxiety over food access and lack of resources to get food; b) the perception that food is of insufficient quantity and quality; c) actual reported reductions of food intake; and d) the consequences of reduced food intake such as going to sleep at night hungry or going a whole day without eating due to the lack of food in the household (Coates et al. 2006). As Coates and colleagues report, as food insecurity worsens, affirmative responses to questions concerning anxiety and worry, compromised dietary quality and quantity, and reported consequences of hunger increase. The mean HFIAS score was 1.78 (SD=0.89), which indicates that on average households were experiencing mild food insecurity during the 30 days prior to administration of the HFIAS. Mild food insecure households do not experience the most severe conditions (running out of food, going to bed hungry, or going a whole day and night without eating) but may worry "about not having enough food sometimes or often, and/or [being] unable to eat preferred foods, and/or eat[ing] a more monotonous diet than desired and/or some foods considered undesirable, but only rarely" (Coates et al. 2007:19).

Table 7.2 Correlations between Household Demographics and Food Security Status

Bivariate Correlation: Spearman's Rho, Sample, N=215

	Food Secure	Mild Food Insecurity	Moderate Food Insecurity	Severe Food Insecurity
Age	-.004	-.098	.113	.001
Civil status	-.046**	.137**	-.127	.076
Educational level	.051	.009	-.100	.055
Number of people living in the house	-.039	-.023	-.004	.165*
Percentage household expenditures spent on food	.028	.006	-.012	-.064
Monthly expenses for food	.079	-.027	-.074	.011

Total monthly expenditures	.038	.016	-.067	.003

*Correlation is significant at the 0.05 level (2-tailed).
** Correlation is close to significance at the 0.01 level (2-tailed)

Sociodemographics and Food Security Status for Subsample (N=100)

One hundred households from the larger sample were recruited to be interviewed and/or to participate in two focus groups, each with five respondents. Selection of participants for the subsample was done through a convenience sampling strategy that included informational talks about the project in all the study sites and enrollment of the first 100 households that volunteered to participate. Comparisons were made between the total sample (N=215) and the subsample. For most sociodemographic variables there were no statistically significant differences between the total sample and subsample. However, it should be noted that the subsample included slightly younger respondents (38.77 y vs. 40.15). When compared to the total sample, the subsample households were less likely to be located in the town of Monteverde (48.4 percent vs. 69.5 percent), had a lower percentage of food secure households (43 percent vs. 49.3 percent), a higher percentage of households with mild food insecurity (37 percent vs. 27 percent), and a lower percentage of severe food insecurity households (15 percent vs. 20 percent).

Correlations between Socio-demographics and Food Security Status: Total Sample and Subsample.

As table 7.2 shows, bivariate analysis for the total sample (N=215) using Spearman's rank order correlation shows that there is a positive correlation between being food secure and being married (Spearman's r= .46) and between the number of people living in the household and severe food insecurity (Spearman's r=.165). For the latter, as the number of people in the household increased, so did the likelihood of experiencing severe food insecurity. Correlations between other socio-demographic variables and food insecurity status were not statistically significant. For the sub-sample, there was a marginally significant negative correlation between civil status and households being food secure (Spearman's   r = -.199; p= 0.057) and a positive correlation between civil status and mild food insecurity (Spearman's r= +.199; p= 0.058). Although the statistical significance is not as strong as seen in the total sample, being married is correlated with household food security while being single is correlated with mild food insecurity in the sub-sample. Finally, there was a marginally significant positive correlation between the number of people living in the household and severe food insecurity in the subsample (Spearman's r= +187; p= .062).

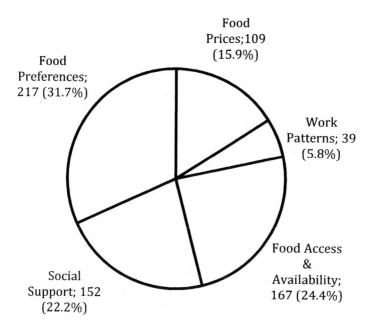

Food Prices;109 (15.9%)

Food Preferences; 217 (31.7%)

Work Patterns; 39 (5.8%)

Food Access & Availability; 167 (24.4%)

Social Support; 152 (22.2%)

Figure 7.1 Factors that Affect Food-Related Decision Making.

Quantitative Results from Interviews and Focus Groups (N= 100)

Based on the content analysis of the interview summaries, transcripts, and focus groups, five major themes emerged as being salient factors that influence food-related decision making among the participating households. These themes, mentioned 684 times by the respondents, were: 1) food prices, 2) work patterns, 3) food access and availability, 4) social support systems, and 5) food preferences). Figure 7.1 shows the number of times that each theme was mentioned by respondents. While work patterns (5.8 percent) and food prices (15.9 percent) were the least frequently mentioned, food preferences (31.7 percent) and food availability (24.4 percent) were more likely to be mentioned. Support systems for coping with food insecurity (22.2 percent) were also mentioned quite frequently by the respondents. What follows are the results from the content analysis of respondent interviews and focus groups for each of the themes.

Theme 1: Food Prices

The topic of food prices was a recurring theme discussed by respondents, and was conceptualized using codes that emerged from the data (e.g., high prices, price not considered a factor, additional costs, paying attention to price, vendor price, price and quality, financial status). Of the 684 respondent comments, nearly 16 percent focused on food prices. However, food prices alone did not necessarily determine what foods would be purchased. Among respondents who did discuss high food prices, many mentioned that the prices had gone up in the time that they have lived in the zone, on average 21 (SD= 15.4) years. Additionally, some attributed increases in the cost of food to tourism, indicating that overall prices for services and commodities, including food, are high because they are set for tourists. One participant noted that competition for jobs within the tourist industry lowered wages for local employment, which made the higher prices even more unaffordable for residents of the zone. *"If there has been a negative effect because of tourism, it's paying tourist prices; they charge high prices as if we were tourists"* (32 year-old woman). In fact, some of the respondents indicated that prices were so high that they had to leave the MVZ to do their grocery shopping. A small number of respondents stated that they purchased what they like, regardless of the price, suggesting that their food preferences inform their decisions on what to buy. However, most participants reported that, in addition to the actual cost of food, other economic factors also impact their food acquisition patterns.

Lack of transportation and the expensive cost of transportation (vehicles and fuel) influenced participants' decisions about where and when to shop. For example, many respondents stated that they did not go to the weekly farmer's market in Santa Elena because of the cost of transportation, especially when having to pay taxi fares which could exceed $20 each way for those living in more remote areas. Additionally, some respondents reported making other sacrifices in order to pay for the high prices of food. A 19-year-old woman stated that *"(e)ating is the priority, and then if there is extra (money), you can do something with it..... So, sacrifices are made in order to buy, to pay for expensive food, so....there is priority given to food and later you can go for the luxuries, if you can manage it."* In general, respondents paid attention to food prices when deciding where to shop or what to buy. Many participants used the word *fijarse* (to pay attention to) when discussing this theme. *"I buy the basics and always pay attention to the prices,"* said a 61-year-old woman.

Some participants stated that prices at the farmer's market were the same as the supermarket, but they preferred to shop at the farmer's market because the setting offered them the opportunity to socialize with friends or neighbors while supporting local farmers. Unlike the supermarket, with its narrow aisles and crowded quarters, the indoor stadium where the farmer markets takes place offers plenty of room for about 40 vendor stands arranged around the periphery of the building. There is also ample space for non-vendors providing educational information, as well as for artistic performances given by dance groups and choirs. The stadium also includes a kitchen area where different community groups prepare and sell breakfast for the general public, and this area, as well as the ample central space, is often used as a gathering place for people attending the market. In addition, participants often reported that they have more of an opportunity to select the produce, by touching it or even sometimes tasting it before making a purchase. A 41-year-old woman said "you can choose and touch the foods and also this fact of making the purchase directly from the producer, I love this, still I would buy like this to keep it going, even if the prices were the same as the supermarket. I don't care. I prefer to buy at the farmer's market." Although there was general consensus among other participants that the prices at the farmer's market were less expensive than at the supermarkets and other food markets, a few respondents indicated that prices were actually more expensive, and many discussed differences in vendor prices. One participant noted that price is dependent on who is buying the food and on the time of day, and suggested that the food prices at the farmers market need to be standardized.

> [It shouldn't be that] because I am Tica they give me a good price and because a tourist comes they give them another price. I would like it if the farmer's market had a standard price ..., as time passes then they have to raise prices because gas prices go up and everything. Last Saturday because a large amount of people came, things were sort of cheap and another day the prices go up in order to gain more profits (56 year old woman).

However, most respondents reported higher prices at the supermarket in comparison to vendors at the farmer's market or *pulperias* (local food stores). The issue of fluctuating prices was a common concern for respondents, and was identified with the code "price stability," referring to unstable food prices or needing/wanting to control food prices. Additionally, price and quality, as well as financial status were other factors that influenced respondents' decisions about where to shop. For some, food prices were more important than quality, although many discussed paying attention to both prices and quality. Most respondents shopped at various locations, which included the two large supermarkets in town, local smaller groceries, butcher shops, the farmer's market, and other locales outside of town.

Seasonality of various foods and tourism meant that both the quality and price of food varied throughout the year depending on demand, availability, and weather. Moreover, a household's financial status also plays a role on what could be purchased. Although quality was a priority, respondents sometimes bought less of a particular item because they did not have much money. One 46 year-old woman said *"It's traumatic every time you buy less because you don't have enough money."* Many respondents discussed awareness about needing to save money not only for food purchases, but also for transportation to and from a store. Macro-economic influences on prices were recognized as influencing local food prices. For example, participants noted that the price of food at the farmer's market was often dependent on market attendance and tourist demand. According to respondents, tourism and food costs are inextricably linked with the tourist industry.

Theme 2: Shifting Work Patterns

About 6 percent of the 684 respondent comments referred to employment patterns in the zone as being significantly influenced by tourism, and to the fact that the tourist economy is tied to food access and availability. On the positive side, the general consensus among these respondents is that tourism-related work has created more employment opportunities over time. For example, development of infrastructure (e.g., paved roads, internet connections), construction (e.g., hotels, restaurants, gift shops, second supermarket), and tourism work itself, were mentioned by respondents as the stimulus for job creation in the MVZ. Similarly, with more tourism-jobs in the zone, the buying power of locals is greater than in the past. However, this is tempered by the fact that food prices have dramatically increased over time. In essence, the respondents reported that while there are more jobs, remuneration for work has not kept up with the cost of living. Hence, it is very difficult to make ends meet.

On a related issue, respondents reported increased availability of food from outside the zone and from outside Costa Rica, most notably from North America. Increasing demand for these foods is seen as reflecting both demand by tourists and increasing consumerism among locals. One respondent, for example, pointed out that consumerism is changing people's relationship with food in the MVZ, resulting in an increase reliance on store-bought food instead of household food production. Several respondents mentioned that people have left their farms, creating a generation gap where younger people are less likely to be engaged in growing food. This phenomenon was less prevalent in towns like San Luis, where farm work is still a way of life for many, although some elders did express a concern about lost agricultural knowledge among younger people. Shifting livelihoods have altered food access and availability in the zone, as reliance on tourism-related jobs takes people away from food production activities. Although respondents indicated that there is increased work and an associated increases in family income, some expressed their concern about the low wages and others pointed out that the seasonal nature of tourism creates a situation where available jobs are limited during certain times of the year when tourism is low.

Conflicts between food security and work arose in two distinct ways. First, work schedules increase the consumption of unhealthy foods or fast foods because working adults lack time for food preparation. When discussing the types of foods people typically eat, a 52-year old woman said: *"fast foods I think because now mothers are working and the quickest foods to prepare for the kids are hamburgers or a hot dog."* One woman from a focus group added that *"(y)ou are not able to cook (referring to the work conflict), so the youth eat more junk foods."* Second, work schedules can affect when people go food shopping. Respondents, for instance, indicated that there is a conflict between their work schedule and the hours that the farmer's market is open which limits their opportunities to shop there.

Theme 3: Food Access and Availability

Food access and availability were mentioned 167 times (24.4 percent), the second most frequently cited theme by the respondents. In the past, food availability and variety were limited because most food was grown locally and availability depended on what local farmers could grow (mostly root vegetables and beans). Cropping or planting decisions were based on weather conditions in the zone, such as seasonal rainfall and gusty winds. However, according to respondents, since the 1950s, there was an expanded role of dairy farming in MVZ as the original settler families established the Monteverde Cheese Factory to provide employment for locals and increase revenues throughout the area. It should be noted that the cheese factory was recently sold to a Mexican multi-national corporation and that there was growing concern over it closing during the next few years. In the past, protein sources mostly consisted of eggs, dairy from cows, fat from pig lard, and starch from root vegetables or from homemade bread or tortillas. Money from selling produce and livestock was used to buy food commodities such as oil, flour, and rice, although rice was difficult to acquire because it was expensive and few markets sold it. Fruits (except for bananas) were not common in the upper MVZ in particular, due to the colder climate. The limited variety of fruits was a significant concern in the past. A 43-year-old woman said that *"(t)he only disadvantage (in our diet) was fruit and anything grown in warmer zones was not available or would arrive very spoiled."* Many respondents believe the reason why fruits are so uncommon in the local *Tico* diet today, despite being more readily available, is because people did not grow up eating them.

In addition to the foods produced and availability at the market, people reported that food access was also tied to limited income. *"People ate what was available...we didn't worry too much about quality but on what was available (quantity), what our parents were able to buy...in reality we were too many children and we couldn't have meat every day, so our meals were mostly made up of vegetables, milk and tortillas,"* said a 43-year-old man. An 85-year-old woman respondent corroborated that certain foods such as rice were luxury items. *"Meals were mostly beans ...two small spoonfuls of rice in each plate and a lot of beans. We would eat the beans first and save the rice for last,"* she stated. Only recently, with the rise of tourism, has food availability increased, including rice. With more markets (including supermarkets) in the MVZ catering to tourists and residents, there is a greater variety of food available. Yet, this has also hampered local food production. As a 56-year-old woman stated: *"progress made people stop planting. We used to grow our food but as the town progressed, people started working to earn money in different ways so they prefer to buy instead of plant."* A 43-year-old woman said: *"other changes that occurred [due to tourism] are that people have sold their land to hotels or foreigners because of the lack of time or money required to plant."*

While more foods are available in the MVZ today, the downside is that there are fewer people farming, the cost of food is going up as more tourists visit, and wages are not keeping up with the cost of living, thereby limiting access to food and resulting in increased consumption of lower cost foods that are often highly processed. Several focus group respondents addressed the latter issue and the fact that most restaurants cater to tourist food preferences. As one woman said *"people... eat what is economically convenient because of high prices and those who own restaurant businesses cook what tourists eat. Only now do I see places that have casado or what the locals eat."* With regard to this last point, it should be noted that there are now more restaurants in the MVZ that are selling typical Costa Rican dishes, thereby catering to local food preferences. A lot of the traditional food items, such as rice, beans, and vegetables are of high nutritional value, while others are high in calories and fat, including plantains and yucca, which are usually deep-fried. These restaurants also tap into tourist notions of health conscious eating by offering, for example, a wide variety of natural fruit juices (while many of these juices are made with sugar, they are sweetened with refined sugar and/or made with whole milk).

Theme 4: Social Support Systems

Respondents mentioned social support systems 152 times (22.2 percent and second most of all responses) during interviews and in focus groups. Their comments suggest that social support has changed over time, and especially since the rapid rise of tourism in the zone. Many respondents indicated that in the past there were closer-knit communities, where, during times of seasonal food shortages, food sharing and food exchanges among neighbors were the norm. For example, a 32-year old woman remarked that *"communities were often very*

*small and I would trade tamales with the neighbor around Christmas or buy on
credit from the only local supermarket since everyone knew each other.*" This
"trust system" of payment or sharing of food items stemmed from the familiarity
that existed within small agricultural communities where many households experienced alternating periods of food abundance and food shortage during the
planting and harvesting seasons.

In the 1980s, the situation began to change as more people moved into the
MVZ to work in the tourism industry and as expatriates bought up land and retired there. To some extent, familiarity and sense of community seem to be fading. This is exacerbated by the fact that younger residents are leaving to go to
school or to take advantage of work opportunities elsewhere in Costa Rica and
abroad. Nevertheless, in a hypothetical situation of not having enough food,
most respondents admitted that they would still seek help from family members,
including more distant kin, now that families are more likely to be dispersed.
Today, there are also more government assistance programs through school
meal programs for children. Charitable giving of donated food and clothing by
local churches was also identified as a significant resource. Private organizations, such as the Instituto Mixto de Ayuda Social (IMAS), provide aid in the
form of job training, stipends for household goods (e.g., food, clothing, and
medication), specialized assistance (e.g., elderly/ disability/child care), and assistance with payments of rent and bills for those who qualify as urgently in
need (IMAS webpage: http://www.imas.go.cr/).

While the majority of respondents knew of IMAS, they did not report using
its services. For many, relying on social services provided by either IMAS or by
churches and other organizations was something that was done as a last resort. A
54-year-old woman illustrated this when describing that she would "*go… to my
family first and see if they would lend me some help. There is much talk that the
government lends out help, sometimes pensions, but I wouldn't trust so much in
that.*" It could be argued that the reason that these services are under-utilized by
people in the zone is because there are plenty of jobs available (even if they do
not pay that well). Moreover, the cultural custom of the single male breadwinner
is slowly fading as a cultural norm because more women are entering the workforce. In addition, respondents also reported holding more than one job in order
to make ends meet. As a result, adults have less time available for household and
family activities, including food preparation. Thus, while self-reliance and hard
work are valued, they do not guarantee household food security. Stagnant wages, the rise in the cost of living, increased reliance on store-bought foods, and
diminished support systems are major challenges in the zone and will likely continue to be in the years to come.

Theme 5: Food Preferences

The most frequently mentioned theme by respondents was food preferences (217 times; 31.7 percent of total responses). The content analysis revealed that external (e.g., tourism, student homestays, child preferences, and advertising) and internal factors (e.g. taste preferences from childhood, health concerns, and importance of traditions), as well as food quality (e.g., chemical free, seasonal, and organic) and price influence food preferences.

Tourism has had a major impact on the food preferences of the respondents. While respondents reported that restaurants cater to the tastes of the tourists by introducing foods such as hamburgers and pizza, they also pointed to the positive influences that tourists have on local diets. For example, a 56-year-old woman stated *"(t)here are a lot of people who have learned from tourists what it is like to eat whole grain foods, use more fruits, vegetables and salads because before, it was only rice, beans and meat...and people see that it is healthier and so, from what I've seen, it [tourism] has affected a little or at least made people more conscious about their food choices."* A 73-year-old woman added *"I see the positive because people now eat more vegetables, eat more variety because some [tourists] eat more healthy and others do not, but one tries to copy the good parts and eat healthier and worry about exercising more."* Finally, a 67-year old woman commented *"in many households, one has adopted the custom of preparing and acquiring more balanced foods, increasing the different types of salads and other types of fruits."*

In addition to regular tourism, student homestays have become quite common given the number of people who come to the zone to learn Spanish or to participate in field schools and other educational or training programs. Some homestays are short (a week) while others may last an academic semester or longer. Costa Ricans in general, and especially those in rural areas, are known for their hospitality and openness to visitors. Thus, many homestay families are eager to provide foods that students desire in addition to feeding them typical *Tico* dishes. Inevitably, the entire family ends up eating the same thing or adopting certain preferences from the visiting students. This can result in higher consumption of healthier foods such as whole wheat bread and organic produce, but at the same time can also lead to increases in consumption of highly processed and less nutritious foods such as hotdogs, potato chips, and cookies. *"In 20 years, I didn't know what sausage was and now my children eat hamburgers and sausages...in this culture, fast foods, box lunches, smoothies, French fries, salsas, it has become a culture of eating these things,"* stated a 77-year-old woman. A 30-year-old woman added, *"the tourist is used to eating junk food and so, the Tico gets out of work (for lunch) and buys pizza or chicken."*

Many parents discussed how they now feel pressured by their children to purchase snack foods, sugary cereals, chocolate, and cookies. Participants believe that this dynamic is further influenced by television advertisements that affect the children's food preferences. While parents mentioned that they sometimes gave in to their children's requests, purchasing decisions are largely dependent on how expensive these desired items are, how much money is left after buying staple food items, and balancing snacks and sweets with a healthier meal.

With a greater variety of food available in the MVZ now, personal food preferences are slowly changing. Unlike their parents and grandparents, who grew up on traditional *Tico* foods such as *gallo pinto* (rice and beans) and *casados* (rice, plantain, black beans, salad, and meat or poultry), younger people have been exposed to both *Tico* foods and food popular in the U.S., in particular (e.g., hamburgers, hotdogs, pizza, fried chicken, and French fries). Despite the pressures that could lead to the adoption of less healthy diets, for example, the lack of time for food preparation and the omnipresence of food advertising some respondents indicated that, they do strive to maintain their *Tico* identity and to promote healthy eating, limit their children's exposure to junk food and prepare healthy meals. For example, a 54-year-old respondent commented on the success she has had teaching her children *"to eat vegetables and salads and not look for things they would like, such as junk food...it's working because now they eat healthier, they like eating healthy. They take care of themselves better than me or my husband."* Further, *"children receive more education in that sense (nutrition). In school, they give classes on health and nutrition,"* she added. The same sentiment was expressed by several respondents, indicating that people are conscious about the need for a healthy diet and strive to achieve a balance between the nutritional needs of their families and the day-to-day pressures faced by families (e.g., limited time to cook, changing conceptions about what foods are considered more desirable, etc.).

Finally, while the quality of food was extremely important regarding food preferences, a slight majority of the respondents commented that food prices (going back to a previous theme) are often an important factor in defining what is actually eaten. As the results presented in relation to food prices suggest, while jobs may be plentiful in the zone, they are seasonal, and salaries do not keep pace with the cost of living, thereby limiting residents' access to the increasing variety of food in the MVZ. At the end of the day, respondents have to stretch their food dollars, and in doing so, food preferences shift in relation to household resources. These limitations in economic resources lead to a situation in which some individuals are able to adopt a healthier diet while others must sacrifice quality for quantity, despite their knowledge and desire for more nutritionally rich food.

Discussion and Conclusion

Globalization has been defined as a process of increasing interconnections and linkages, within societies and across geography, due to improved communication and expanded world trade (Solomons 2001). One significant outcome of globalization has been the rapid expansion of tourism in countries such as Costa Rica. Tourists from around the world in search of spectacular beaches and lush forests, mountains and volcanoes, and a wide array of flora and fauna visit "The Green Republic" (Evans 1999) in the millions annually. In addition, visitors from all over the world come to Costa Rica for a variety of educational experiences including language learning and participation in other instructional programs such as field schools. While the overall economy of Costa Rica has benefited by the increase in tourism over the years, there is also a downside with increasing economic inequality, for example, occurring over time (Ticotimes.net 2012). Today, approximately 1.1 million Costa Ricans are living in poverty, the highest number since 1990. Further, tourism, as an outgrowth of globalization, has been shown to affect the food security status, diets, and health via the nutrition transition in Costa Rica and elsewhere. For example, food imports have risen more than 170 percent between 1992 and 2005 in Costa Rica (Thow and Hawkes 2009), while local food production has significantly declined in certain regions. This has implications regarding food access and availability. As demand for goods and services increases to meet the needs of items for export (e.g., medical equipment components) so does the cost of living and this is particularly reflected in food prices. This is a major concern in areas where there is food delocalization, where decreases in local food production lead to reliance on more expensive sources of food produced elsewhere. Similarly, since wages often do not keep pace with the cost of living, local residents are often at higher risk for food insecurity, and, as they attempt to stretch their food dollars, dietary quality and, ultimately, health are sacrificed.

The synergistic impact of globalization, tourism, and the nutrition transition on health in Costa Rica is evidenced by the data presented here. Combining qualitative and quantitative approaches, this paper examined how the economic transition from an agricultural economy to a mixed economy of tourism and to a lesser extent agriculture (coffee, dairy farming, and hydroponics) is affecting food-related decision making in the context of economic inequality and a high prevalence of food insecurity in several towns in the upper-part of the MVZ. Previous research shows high rates of food insecurity, adult overweight and obesity, and child obesity (Himmelgreen et al. 2006; Himmelgreen et al. 2013), and increasing rates of hypertension, type 2 diabetes, and asthma (Ledezma and Mario 2010) living in the upper part of the MVZ where most tourism activities take place. For instance, a study done in 2004-05 (Himmelgreen et al. 2006) showed that over 70 percent of households experienced some degree of food insecurity. In the data presented here from 2008-09, the number of food insecure households dropped to about 50 percent. While this is a significant improvement, caution must be taken in interpreting the findings since the food insecurity scales used for these two studies were different and one of the towns examined in the earlier study was located farther down in the MVZ where tourism does not predominate. Even if one could make a direct comparison between the two study periods, the fact is that food insecurity is still high and that nearly 25 percent of households in the more recent study experienced moderate or severe food insecurity, in which dietary quality and/or dietary quantity are compromised. The factors that affect food-related decision making in the context of the high rate of food insecurity are evident from the five themes that emerged from the content analysis. Further, these themes are directly tied to the positive and negative consequences of tourism in the MVZ.

Most respondents viewed tourism in a positive light at least in regard to job opportunities, increased food availability, and positive dietary health messages from tourists and homestay students. At the same time, they were also very concerned about making ends meet and being able to access the wider array of foods. The situation described here illustrates the results of neoliberal policies that aim at increasing the number of jobs and the net economic gain for the country's economy, while disregarding the factors that affect the day-to-day life of workers: fair wages, quality of employment, work stability, and income equality. Respondents expressed very clear concerns about the seasonality of employment in tourism, about the fact that wages could not keep pace with the increasing cost of living, and about diminished family and neighbor social support mechanisms (e.g., food sharing and buying on credit) as compared to earlier times (however, they did mention that there is more government and private foundation assistance now, although none of them reported using these services). Similarly, respondents expressed concern about younger people not working the land and the resulting loss of knowledge about farming, about the fact that food preferences are changing in good and bad ways in response to the increasing number of tourists and students visiting, and about the fact that they have to make hard choices when it comes to the quality versus the price of food. In the end, the findings presented here suggest that the shift towards a mixed economy, where tourism predominates in the MVZ, has both positive and negative effects on the lives of the respondents and their families. Additionally, these results underscore the fact that globalization processes are playing out in different ways in different settings (Nash 1994) and that policy makers and researchers alike must promote policies and implement program designs that take into account the positive and negative aspects of tourism, as well as the local social, cultural, and economic conditions that exist on the ground.

Bibliography

AlterNet.Org, *News Portal.* 2007. http://www.alternet.org/ (accessed August, 2013).

Alvarado, Alfredo, Frank J. Smith, and T. Jot Smith. 1998. "Baseline Study of Land Use Management and Decision Making Processes with a Focus on Non-Traditional Crops, Small Farmers, Agro-Industry, and Development Policy in Costa Rica." Collaborative Research Support Program, U.S. Agency for International Development. http://intdss.soil.ncsu.edu/download/documents/CRica_Baseline.pdf (accessed May, 2006).

Anderson-Fye, Eileen P. 2004. "A 'Coca-Cola' shape: Cultural Change, Body Image, and Eating Disorders in San Andres, Belize." *Culture, Medicine, and Psychiatry* 28, no. 4: 561-595.

Cantor, Allison, Jenny Peña and David Himmelgreen. 2013. "We never ate like that, not fast food, or junk foods." Accounts of Changing Maternal Diet in a Tourist Community in Rural Costa Rica." *Ecology of Food and Nutrition* 52, no. 6: 479-496.

Central Intelligence Agency (CIA). 2013. "The World Fact Book 2013–2014," Washington DC: Central Intelligence Agency. https://www.cia.gov/library/publications/the-world-factbook/geos/cs.html (accessed August, 2013).

Coates, Jennifer, Anne Swindale and Paula Bilinsky. 2006. *Household Food Insecurity Access Scale (HFIAS) for Measurement of Household Food Access: Indicator Guide* (v.2). Washington, DC: Food and Nutrition Technical Assistance Project, Academy for Educational Development.

Daltabuit, Magali. 1998. *Ecologia Humana en una Comunidad de Morelos.* Mexico DF: Universidad Nacional Autonoma de Mexico.

———, and Thomas L. Leatherman. 1998. "The Biocultural Impact of Tourism on Mayan Communities." In *Building a New Biocultural Synthesis: Political-economic Perspectives on Human Biology,* edited by A.H. Goodman and T.L. Leatherman, 317-338. Ann Arbor: University of Michigan Press.

Evans, Sterling. 1999. *The Green Republic: A Conservation History of Costa Rica.* Austin: University of Texas Press.

FAO. 2012. *Escala Latinoamericana y Caribeña de Seguridad Alimentaria (ELCSA): Manual de Uso y Aplicaciones.*

Food and Nutrition Technical Assistance. 2013. "Household Food Insecurity Access Scale (HFIAS)." http://www.fantaproject.org/publications/hfias.shtml (accessed August, 2013).

Friedus, A., and N. Romero-Daza. 2009. "The Space Between: Globalization, Liminal Spaces and Personal Relations in Rural Costa Rica." *Gender, Place and Culture* 16, no. 6: 683-702.

GoVisitCostaRica.com, *Delfina Travel Group Inc.* 2013, http://www.govisitcostarica.com/ (accessed August, 2013).

Gurri, Francisco D., Gilberto Balam Pereira, and Emilio F. Moran. 2001. "Well-Being Changes in Response to 30 Years of Regional Integration in Maya Populations from Yucatan, Mexico." *American Journal of Human Biology* 13, no. 5: 590-602.

Guswa, Andrew J., and Amy L. Rhodes. 2006. *Meteorology of Monteverde, Costa Rica.* Northampton, MA: Smith College.

———, and Amy L. Rhodes. 2007. *Meteorology of Monteverde, Costa Rica.* Northampton, MA: Smith College.

Himmelgreen, D.A., N. Romero-Daza, E. Amador and C. Pace. 2013. "Tourism, Economic Insecurity, and Nutritional Health in Rural Costa Rica: Using Syndemics Theory to Understand the Impact of the Globalizing Economy at the Local Level." *Annals of Anthropological Practice* (Peer Reviewed, In Press).

———, Nancy Romero-Daza, Maribel Vega, Humerto Brenes Cambronero and Edgar Amador 2006. "'The Tourist Season goes down but not the Prices.' Tourism and Food Insecurity in Rural Costa Rica." *Ecology of Food and Nutrition* 45, no. 4: 295-321.

Honey, Martha. 1999. *Ecotourism and Sustainable Development: Who Owns Paradise?* Washington DC: Island Press.

IBM, *SPSS Statistics for Windows, Version 21.0.* 2012. Armonk: IBM Corp.

ICT (Instituto Costarricense de Turismo). 2009. *Anuario Estadístico de Turismo* San José, Costa Rica.

Kabagambe, Edmond K., Ana Baylin, Damon A. Allan, Xinia Siles, Donna Spiegelman, and Hannia Campos. 2001. "Application of the Method of Triads to Evaluate the Performance of Food Frequency Questionnaires and Biomarkers as Indicators of Long-Term Dietary Intake." *American Journal of Epidemiology* 154, no. 12: 1126-1135).

Leatherman, Thomas L., and Alan H. Goodman. 2005. "Coca-Colonization of Diets in the Yucatan," *Social Science and Medicine* 61, no. 4: 833-846.

Ledezma, Acevedo, and Oscar Mario. 2010. "*Analisis de Situacion Integral en Salud. Caja Costarricense de Seguro Social.*" Unpublished report, Monteverde, Costa Rica.

Martine, J.A., J.H. Ledikwe and B.J. Rolls. 2005. "The Influence of Food Portion Size and Energy Density on Energy Intake: Implications for Weight Management." *The American Journal of Clinical Nutrition* 82, no. 1: 236S-241S.

Microsoft, 2010. "Excel," in *Microsoft Excel for Mac 2011 Version 14.3.6.* Santa Rosa: Microsoft.

———, 2010. "Word," in *Microsoft Word for Mac 2011 Version 14.3.6.* Santa Rosa: Microsoft.

Monahan, Jane. 2004. "Unique Costa Rica Rainforest at Risk," *BBC News World Edition.* http://news.bbc.co.uk/2/hi/americas/4061833.stm. 2004.

Monge, R., and O. Beita. 2000. "Prevalence of Coronary Heart Disease Risk Factors in Costa Rican Adolescents." *Journal of Adolescent Health* 27, no. 3: 210-217.

Nadkarni, Nalini M., and Nathaniel T. Wheelwright. 2000. *Monteverde: Ecology and Conservation of a Tropical Cloud Forest.* Athens: Oxford University Press.

Nash, June. 1994. "Global Integration and Subsistence Insecurity." *American Anthropologist* 96, no. 1: 7-30.

Nunez-Rivas, H.P., R. Monge-Rojas, H. Leon, and M. Rosello. 2003. "Prevalence of Overweight and Obesity among Costa Rican Elementary School Children." *Pan American Journal of Public Health* 13, no. 1: 24-32.

Popkin, B.M. 2002. "The Shift in Stages of the Nutrition Transition in the Developing World Differs from Past Experiences!" *Public health nutrition* 5, no. 1A: 205-214.

Romero-Daza, N., Tewell, D. Himmelgreen, O. Ramirez-Rubio and E. Batres-Boni. 2013. "Tourism and HIV Involving Women in the Design of Educational Materials in Rural Costa Rica," *Anthropology in Action* 20, no. 1: 18-30.

———, and A. Freidus. 2008. "Female Tourists, Casual Sex, and HIV Risk in Costa Rica," *Qualitative Sociology* 31, no. 2: 169-187.

Sáenz, R. Mdel, M. Acosta, J. Muiser and J.L. Bermúdez. 2011. "The Health System of Costa Rica." *Salud Publica Mex* 53, no. 2: s156-s167.

Saldaña, Johnny. 2009. *The Coding Manual for Qualitative Researchers.* London: Sage.

Solomons, NW. 2002. "Ethical Consequences for Professionals from the Globalization of Food, Nutrition and Health." *Asia Pacific Journal of Clinical Nutrition* 11: S653-S665.

Swindale, Anne, and Paula Bilinsky. 2006. "Development of a Universally Applicable Household Food Insecurity Measurement Tool: Process, Current Status, and Outstanding Issues." *The Journal of Nutrition* 136, no. 5: 1449S-1452S.

Thow, A.M. 2009. "Trade Liberalization and the Nutrition Transition: Mapping the Pathways for Public Health Nutritionists." *Public Health Nutrition* 12, no. 11: 2150-2158.

Thow, A.M. and C. Hawkes. 2009. "The Implications of Trade Liberalization for Diet and Health: A Case Study from Central America." *Globalization and Health* 5, no. 5: 1-11.

TicoTimes.Net. 2012. *San Jose, Costa Rica* 2012, http://www.ticotimes.net/ (accessed August, 2013).

Vivanco, Luis A. 2006. *Green Encounters: Shaping and Contesting Environmentalism in Rural Costa Rica.* Berghahn Books.

Weaver, Lesley Jo, and Craig Hadley. 2009. "Moving Beyond Hunger and Nutrition: A Systematic Review of the Evidence Linking Food Insecurity and Mental Health in Developing Countries." *Ecology of Food and Nutrition* 48, no. 4: 263-284.

WHO. 2013. "Trade, Foreign Policy, Diplomacy and Health," in *Food Security.*

PART IV

Women's Agency
and
Contested Practices

CHAPTER 8

Salvadoran Immigrant Women and the Culinary Making of Gendered Identities: "Food Grooming" as a Class and Meaning-Making Process

Sharon Stowers

Introduction

Let me begin this chapter with a narrative from my ethnographic field observations that I wrote one evening after visiting a Salvadoran immigrant household in Somerville, Massachusetts.

There was the usual amount of chaos that occurs at Cecilia's house at dinnertime. The TV was blaring, while the five kids, her three and her aunt's two, argued over which cartoon to watch. Cecilia would not let them play outside: the tenants upstairs were drunk and on the verge of a fistfight on their back porch. Marvin, Cecilia's younger brother, arrived from his job at the market with a bag full of rejected, unripe avocados and proceeded to pitch the "baseballs" to the kids who were now running in and out of the kitchen playing tag. Sandra, Cecilia's aunt, was talking on the telephone in the closet next to the kitchen, which for the household of eleven people, six adults and five children, offered the only privacy, besides the bathroom, in their small, dark apartment.

Tonight Cecilia was making carne guisada, a beef stew of vegetables infused with onion and tomato. It required a multi-step process, which took time and attention. She had three pans going on the stove at once, plus the comal for the tortillas. Amidst the flying avocados, the kids grabbing at her delantal, and my attempts to sweep the kitchen floor with her old broom, she skillfully or-

193

chestrated the sizzling pots of food while patting the fresh masa dough into thick tortillas.

"Why are you cooking so much, Cecilia?" I asked. It was a hot Wednesday night. Cecilia was obviously tired; she had only just returned from her long day at the foam factory. "My husband and brother-in-law expect a big meal when they get home," she remarked with contained resentment, and yet I knew she prided herself a good cook. She usually made her husband at least four hand-made tortillas every evening, but tonight, the carne guisada seemed over the top. Most American families would have ordered out for a pizza under such conditions. But by the time her husband and bother-in-law barreled into the kitchen, dirty and tired from their day jobs, the carne guisada was steaming with the sweet smell of onions and the tortillas were stacked warm on a plate.

"Cecilia is a good cook; doesn't the dinner look delicious?" I blurted out to her husband who had just ordered the kids to be quiet. "Well, maybe," he said gruffly, not happy to see me visiting his wife again, "but not as good as in El Salvador where the meat is fresh." I knew he hadn't eaten much fresh beef in El Salvador; he had left his poor pueblo during the war, escaping poverty and violence. After migrating North, he did not forget his impoverished family back home; he spent the last decade working six days a week and two jobs to support his extended family and Cecilia's parents in their small pueblos in El Salvador. They grew fully dependent on his monthly remittances. When he first migrated, he had just wanted to make money and return to his country to build a big house, but he could not return to his homeland; he would forfeit his temporary documentation status and work papers here. Now he just wanted to buy a house in his neighborhood—the $1,200 a month rent was too much for this small, dilapidated apartment. But purchasing a house in his community of Somerville, Massachusetts was hardly possible with his limited income and high expenses. This certainly wasn't the life he had imagined when he migrated north.

Cecilia set a large piece of meat on the plate and surrounded it with the aromatic vegetables and a mound of rice. She placed the dish on the kitchen table, in front of her weary husband, along with the warm stack of tortillas. Although he had to eat quickly, he savored his dinner eating it "Salvadoran style"—using a tortilla to scoop up each bite. With every mouthful of this ideal Salvadoran meal, he tasted mythical notions of his life in El Salvador and the hope of the life he wished to live here. In this chaotic kitchen in the middle of Somerville's poorest neighborhood, for a few moments, he consumed "the good life" in Salvadoran terms; he could feel like he "had made it" and was king of his castle before rushing off to his night job cleaning offices. (Stowers 2003)

After Cecilia's husband left for work that evening, she sat in the kitchen table and cried, spilling out the litany of problems she was dealing with: *"things are not good with my husband,"* she confessed to me; *"he works all the time and has no time for the children,"* and now the children *"are misbehaving."* Furthermore, household members argued over privacy and money. Her job was *"horrible,"* she continued, and she *"make[s] very little money with only two weeks vacation after seven years,*" and her "*aunt only gives her $20 a week for food.*" Thus I observed in Cecilia's household how some of the effects of modernization were manifested through strained economic and gender relations. The politics of documentation, the economics of immigrant labor, and racism placed Salvadoran immigrants' identity and well-being at risk in the public sphere, and these exigencies seeped into the household. Both adults and children suffered from these stresses.

Salvadoran immigrants, like Cecilia and her family, began fleeing their country in large numbers in the 1980s, when civil war, poverty, and ecological crises pushed many to seek shelter in the United States. The causes of these crises are overdetermined. But it is clear that post-World War II economic development in El Salvador did not benefit the majority of the population. Indeed, the expansion of a market economy in agriculture and the concentration of land ownership in the hands of the few further impoverished the rural peasant population. By the 1980s, food insecurity grew to epidemic proportions for the poor, while the few wealthy families not just consumed conspicuously, but also increasingly repressed the poor. In the early 1980s popular protest and its repression, led to civil war, which was fought largely in rural departments, further degrading the standard of living of peasants, not to mention the violation of their human rights. Those that could find a way to flee did, both internally and internationally, many to the United States.

Chain migration, family reunification, and economic opportunities also pulled many North. Machuca (2010) estimates that as many as 2.7 million Salvadorans immigrants may now live in the United States, half of whom do not have legal immigrant status. In Somerville, Massachusetts, Salvadoran immigrants came largely from La Unión, San Miguel, San Vicente, Morazán, and Chalatenango, rural departments that suffered severe food insecurity and violence during the civil conflict, which raged from the 1970s to the peace accords in 1992. Salvadorans were attracted to Somerville, a densely populated, small city in the Metropolitan Boston area, in part because in 1987 it became a designated "sanctuary city," a city that did not police Salvadorans documentation status. Undocumented immigrants thus could feel relatively safe in the city, and although Somerville repealed its sanctuary status after only five years, Salvadorans, both legal and undocumented, continued to flow into the city in the 1990s. In 2000, there were at least 2,200 Salvadoran immigrants living in the Somerville, but statistics for Salvadorans are not especially accurate, in part because so many immigrants in the community were undocumented (Somerville Population Trends FactSheet n.d.; Stowers 2003).

Due to shifting immigration laws and ambivalent American policy towards the Salvadoran conflict, Salvadoran immigration statuses in Somerville were varied and complex, creating households with family members with differing levels of access to resources and power. Salvadoran immigration statuses included several subcategories, but for the purpose of this discussion, three major categories of undocumented, temporarily documented, and documented status are most relevant.[1] Needless to say, a Salvadoran's documentation status affected how visible he/she could be in the public sphere, his/her employment opportunities and wages, and his/her access to safety net programs. Women in the household were especially vulnerable to these stressors because they were more likely to be undocumented than men, tended to earn lower wages, and were limited by traditional gender expectations that continue post migration (Abrego 2009).

The intense social and gender interactions in Cecilia's kitchen, fuelled by economic and documentation stresses, were not atypical of those in other Salvadoran immigrant households at mealtime. In some respects, Cecilia's household, where many of the adults had temporary documentation status and temporary work papers, was comparatively better off than the households of newly arrived undocumented Salvadorans, which experienced many of these same stresses only more so. Recent immigrants tend to have weaker social networks and less economic stability, and were at risk of immediate deportation. Given this context, it was understandable that Salvadoran immigrant men and women felt their sense of self and well-being undermined.

Outside of the household, Salvadoran immigrant men, especially, felt their authority, dignity, and middle-class aspirations assaulted. Employed in the service economy, they often work at jobs they associate with women's work—cleaning and food preparation, which threatened their male identity. They also experienced their male and ethnic identity undermined by harsh supervisors and racism. And, as unskilled labor, they could not earn enough money to realize their dreams of a middle-class life by purchasing a home. In response to the disintegration of their gender, ethnic and class identity, they attempted to re-create an idealized "traditional" Salvadoran household in order to hold to their fading dreams. Thus Salvadoran men demanded, inside the household, that their women rescue them from the reality of daily life; she must assume the ideal "traditional" gender role, in which she cooks "the good life" into the ideal meal. Through her culinary expertise and care, a Salvadoran immigrant woman "groomed" food to infuse it with Salvadoran immigrant ideals, which he (as well as she and their children) could not access easily outside the home. Moreover, her place at the stove nurtured her husband and assured him of his male authority and maintained the fantasy of a Salvadoran (lower) middle-class householder.

Salvadoran immigrant women from rural pueblos were invested in not only reproducing but also re-inventing their role in the United States as food experts and culinary nurturers; it was a cornerstone of a "traditional" and ideal Salvadoran female identity. Her culinary labor affirmed her connection with a female cultural history, contributed to the household economy, and earned her the respect of her family and community. Moreover, Salvadoran men and women were invested in this ideal culinary process as a way to re-invent Salvadoran culture, values and idealized gender roles for their children. This "traditional" arrangement of a woman laboring for her husband and children in the non-capitalist economy of the home, while her male partner predominately sold his labor in the market place, has been posited by some postmodern Marxist theorists as a "feudal domestic" class process.[2] But Salvadorans' effort to re-create an ideal middle-class household was in crisis. While a Salvadoran woman's production of Salvadoran cuisine re-created Salvadoran cultural ideas for her children and made "poverty, racism, and dispossessed statuses of all kinds" (McCracken 1988, 109) tolerable for men, her access to the good life remained ever more elusive. She could not as easily embrace the fantasy of a middle-class life in a household where she increasingly experienced her husband and other males in the household exploiting her domestic labor while giving her little time and emotional support in return.

This chapter, based on ethnographic research conducted between 1998 and 2000 in Somerville, with participants who gave informed consent, describes but one out of many possible narratives of how Salvadoran immigrant women within the household asserted their agency in re-creating Salvadoran cuisine to re-invent both their own and their male partners' notions of ideal domestic gender roles and their dreams of a middle-class lifestyle. To these ends, Salvadoran women, through their skill of food preparation, not only participated in important economic class processes in the household, but also produced culinary meanings for their families' consumption.

In the following pages, I analyze this complex economic and ideological activity by using the postmodern economic theories developed by Resnick and Wolff (1987) Fraad, Resnick, and Wolff (1994) and Gibson-Graham (1996). Specifically, I demonstrate how Salvadoran immigrant women produced meanings of ideal gender identity, class, and homeland through their role as food "groomer." I describe how Salvadoran women's food grooming was both a non-capitalist class and ideological process, and I contrast it to the capitalist class process of commercial food preparation. I then reveal how Salvadoran women, as food groomers, constructed "traditional" notions of male identity by attempting to satisfy the gastronomic nostalgia of both their male partners and the community. Finally, I show how culinary gendered relations within the Salvadoran household had begun to experience a crisis of modernization, and women suffered some of its worst effects.

Salvadoran Immigrant Women: A Culinary Identity

Daily, Salvadoran women in Somerville, in the privacy of their households, applied tremendous skill, effort, and time to produce Salvadoran-style meals for their husbands and children. Their effort to "groom" food to sustain their loved ones was remarkable in execution and persistence because, like many working-class and middle-class Americans, their efforts to produce home cooked meals were constrained by the forces of modern life. In modern America, especially within the last few decades, women increasingly left the kitchen to work outside the household, often handing over food preparation tasks to the prepared food industry. While structural forces thwarted women's cooking at home, the feminist movement railed on the role of women subjugated to their husbands as domestic servants and encouraged them to liberate themselves from the stove. The material and ideological pressures that undermined or devalued household food production, for example, contributed to making America a nation both that dines out, mostly on fast food, and where preparing at home a "substantial," but not elaborate, meal is considered a luxury.

For Salvadoran immigrant women, the structural pressures to forgo the time and energy investment of creating their traditional cuisine were tremendous: they lived in overcrowded apartments with little space to cook, often labored at home baby-sitting for the children of others or worked erratic hours outside the home as domestic help or chambermaids and received wages below the poverty line. Thus they were especially vulnerable to throwing in the (dish) towel and heating up a can of beans or microwaving a cheap box of frozen French fries and chicken nuggets. Yet Salvadoran women resisted. Their identity, their cultural ties to their homeland and history, their financial security, and their relationships to their husbands and children depended on their culinary labor.

For Salvadorans in Somerville, household food production was traditionally the domain of women. To be sure, Salvadoran women were not alone in this circumscribed role; cross-culturally women have performed food rituals for centuries. It was a role that has defined the female, as woman, partner and nurturer. In the last few decades, although not without criticism, a new feminist literature began to examine a woman's role as cook in its complexity, highlighting the more nurturing and even creative aspects of this sometimes mundane task (Avakian 1997). While some modern American women may celebrate the notion of a home cooked meal, they may find it difficult to comprehend how important food and cooking are for an agricultural people in the developing world, a daunting and often grueling task that sets the rhythm of the day and centers household life around the mother and the kitchen. In rural El Salvador, for example, women engage in labor-intensive domestic food production, a role ascribed at birth. And for many, their labor yielded only a subsistence diet, not a cuisine. Here is testimony of a Salvadoran woman's experience of food preparation during the early 1980s:

> *For a woman in the countryside the day starts very, very early. Even before the sun has risen she gets up from her rough bundle of a mattress and, trying not to wake her husband or step on her children, she goes outside her little shack and starts grinding up corn into flour for tortillas. Tortillas are the little pancakes that everyone eats for breakfast, lunch and dinner. You really get sick of tortillas, I can tell you! Grinding the corn is hard work, because it's still done by hand; it gives you muscles like a rock.* (Carter et al. 1989, 31)

Thus was the traditional role for rural women in El Salvador—still today; like women in many developing countries, they labored long hours to produce food for their families even when food was scarce. Rural Salvadoran women spent many hours *tortiando* [*making tortillas*]: cutting corn off cobs, soaking it with *cal*, grinding it and then spending the entire meal on their feet over a *comal*, patting and grilling *tortillas* so that they are fresh and hot for the family, a ritual I witnessed and enacted with several women in a *pueblo* in La Unión. Some rural Salvadoran women experienced their daily feudal domestic arrangement as oppressive and thus during the 1980s, they organized around their common experience of male dominance, poverty, and exploitation, which helped fuel a popular woman's movement in El Salvador during the civil war (Carter et al. 1989).

Both Salvadoran women and men, as subsistence agriculturists, engaged in intensive hard labor to produce and prepare food to fulfill basic nutritional needs, giving food great significance to them. When I asked Salvadorans in Somerville why food was so important in their lives, they consistently responded, *"We work hard for our food."* The labor Salvadoran men and women expended to provide for their families even the most basic human nutrition made food and eating a value in itself. Ricardo, a legal resident, recalled his hard labor for food in the fields of the wealthy land-holding oligarchy:

> *I used to pick coffee and cotton and everything on the farm not far from me. I would pick three sacks of coffee a day! Do you know—a sack? Yes, three sacks full. And cotton, I would pick with both hands. My fingers right here near my nails would get all cut up from the cotton plant. I cut the sugar cane too; it's not easy with a machete, slicing those plants down—three cuts like this. Now everything is different. The war came, for twelve years. The guerrillas—they fought in the fields and now everything is dirty. People are poor and now they have no farms to work on. Yes, they did give some of the land back, but the poor people never got that land.* (Stowers 2003)

For Salvadoran women and men, producing food during times of scarcity or for wealthy landholders was not the ideal role they aspired to reproduce. For rural Salvadoran women especially, their aspirations of a culinary identity were modeled after women with both more resources to grow and/or purchase food and the time to prepare it. In village households with access to land, cash income and/or remittances, women labored not only to make tortillas but also to produce home-made cheese, kill and pluck chickens, and cut fruit for *refrescos*. Culinary production was labor intensive, but it could also be an expression of female identity as food expert and culinary nurturer. This identity gave rural Salvadoran women status in the community, kept their male partners happy, and established them as the authority over their children's stomachs and the caretaker of their children's well-being.

The Culinary Construction of the Ideal Salvadoran Woman

Rural Salvadoran women who migrated to Somerville attempted to re-construct an ideal gender and culinary identity to preserve a sense of self in a strange and foreign land. When Salvadoran women crossed the Mexican border, they especially put their physical and psychological well-being at risk; testimonies of women "crossing over" the border have been horrific by many accounts (Menjívar 2000). Moreover, their at-risk status continued when they settled in Somerville; they had to negotiate a place of self in a modern urban environment and economy without many of the skills necessary to earn a middle-class living. With little or no formal education, some Salvadoran immigrant women could not read or write in their native language. Moreover, the majority of the women who participated in my study could not speak or read English, even those who had lived in the United States for many years. While considered "unskilled labor" for a modern economy, Salvadoran immigrant women had expertise in the art of running a household, and this was poignantly expressed through their culinary talents. Thus many Salvadoran immigrant women from rural areas were invested in re-inventing themselves in a "traditional" female role; it was familiar; they were skilled at it, and it was what they thought was best for their husbands and children. While a woman's culinary class position may have been exploitative, borrowing from Gibson-Graham's analysis (1996), her work in the kitchen was compensated with love from her family and respect from her community. Yet the barriers to her participation in the market economy inhibited women's ability to transform their exploited class position within the household (Gibson-Graham 1996).

Salvadoran Women and the Art of Food Grooming

Many Salvadoran immigrant women from rural areas hoped to establish a middle-class culinary and household ideal in Somerville. Doing so allowed them to claim their identity as food experts and culinary nurturers of their male partners and children. As culinary expert, the Salvadoran woman was the center of the household, orchestrating the symphony of tasks necessary to produce the food she felt would sustain her family in a brave new world. Her knowledge about food was living testimony of a female oral history and hands-on pedagogy. Salvadoran women cook out of this history and lived experience with an art and attentiveness of someone who knows food: how to grow it, how to tell when it is ripe, and how it should feel, smell and taste. A woman's ability to "groom" food was central to an ideal female identity. In this process she coaxed out of raw organic material a *plato típico*, and into it she infused meanings. Thus she "groomed" the food, as one would a child, not only making the object of her grooming her own, but also making it an extension of herself—her knowledge, her nurturing, her labor—creating meaningful material for others to consume.

How does grooming food create meaning? Grant McCracken (1988) theorized on how consumers groom material goods to capture their meaning. Consumer goods, he argues, derive their meaning from a "culturally constituted world" and sometimes consumers may need to groom those goods in order to transfer the object's meaning to themselves (1988, 71-89). For example, a middle-aged man may invest time and energy polishing or "grooming" a sports car, which is a grooming strategy to enhance and transfer the car's culturally constituted meaning of status and lifestyle to its owner. Grooming rituals are significant when the meanings they hold are elusive; in other words, according to McCracken, the object's meaning can never really take up residence in the consumer. This occurs when the owner of the sport car cannot become the freewheeling, wealthy young bachelor that the car represents to him. Thus the consumer must repeatedly "groom" the good to access the object's fleeting significance. Although McCracken did not elaborate on how grooming extracts meaning from goods, it is clear from his examples that time, energy, and attentiveness are inherent and necessary in grooming rituals (Stowers 2003).

Salvadoran women invested time and energy in extracting meaning from their food. Corn, was not just central to Salvadoran cuisine, but central to Salvadoran culture. As a signifier in Salvadorans' culturally constituted world, following from McCracken (1988), Salvadoran women extracted corn's meaning through labor-intensive rituals. I would like to build on his theory to explain how, through their labor, Salvadoran immigrant women invested or "supercharged" food with meaning (1988, 86). I posit that Salvadoran women through their attentiveness, time and labor infused food with meanings for others to extract through their consumption. Thus Salvadoran women in the household through their act of food "grooming," were, in essence, culinary meaning makers.

Food grooming is a meaning making process that requires expert knowledge, high quality fresh ingredients, energy and time. Importantly, food grooming requires a connection between the food groomer, the culinary product and the food consumer. Food grooming can be contrasted with modern forms of mass food preparation, where there is little if any personal connection between the food preparer, the product and the ultimate consumer, which I will explore in a moment. But first, let us return to Cecilia's kitchen on another day when she was instructing me on the art of preparing Salvadoran cuisine through what I call "grooming." This scene not only underscored her culinary expertise and her practice of infusing tortillas with meaning for her husband's consumption but also exposed the symbolically impoverished concept of the recipe and my naiveté about food, even as a "certified food and nutrition expert."

Cecilia, like most Salvadoran women I cooked with, had knowledgeable hands. Cooking was a tactile experience—feeling the food was an essential part of the process. Measuring ingredients was a foreign and useless concept. Early on in my fieldwork Cecilia agreed to teach me how to make tortillas. We mixed up a bowl of fresh masa harina with water.

"How much water?" I asked, my pen ready to inscribe the recipe.

"Enough" she replied.

"How much is enough?" I asked, "a cup, two cups?"

Mixing the dough with her hands she said emphatically, "Enough, feel it— you will know when it is right." She gestured to me to stick my hand in the bowl of mushy, sticky dough. How will I ever replicate this? I thought. She had already added the water to the corn flour so it was too late to measure it—and she didn't seem to have any measuring cups anyway.

Bastante agua, I wrote in my notebook under the heading: Tortilla Recipe. I then felt the dough, and she continued.

"Roll a ball like this—not too big." She grabbed a small handful of dough and gave it to me. "Cup your hand a little. Then turn it while you use your finger to form the edge. Pat it back and forth from one hand to the other, but turn it too so that it is just thick enough all around. That makes it good... see, it is easy."

"Easy?" I said sarcastically to Cecilia. "Look at this!" Trying to follow her instructions, I had flattened my dough ball into a misshapen mess.

"My tortilla looks strange," I said making a face. I held it up for the kids to see and joked, "It is a tortilla gringa!" Cecilia laughed while the kids raced around us shouting and chasing each other.

"You just need to practice... see." She quickly made another. Then Elisa, her charming but feisty four years old daughter, reached into the bowl, grabbed a handful of dough, rolled a ball and proceeded to teach me the technique.

"Sharon, like this...watch me, watch me!" Elisa shrieked, addressing me informally. She shaped and patted the dough while she hopped on one foot and danced around us delighted to be a part of the pedagogical process.

I tried several more times—the second attempt failed because I dropped the dough ball onto the floor; another I stretched so thin that I had to patch it with a piece of the sticky masa; a third was too small—slightly larger than a half dollar.

"That one is for a diet!" Cecilia exclaimed laughing so hard she was choking back tears. She had already placed her and Elisa's tortilla on the hot comal, which, after wiping her tearing eyes, she turned over each one with her bare hand.

"Cecilia, my tortillitas look horrible," I lamented as I laid my little, lumpy, barely round disks on the hot surface of the blackened flat pan. "Even Elisa's looks better," I admitted, "and she's only four!"

Cecilia looked down at my pathetic attempts browning next to hers. "Don't worry," she consoled me, "you already have a husband, and he probably does not like tortillas anyway." (Stowers 2003, 2012)

Cecilia's expert knowledge of the tactile *masa* dough and her skill at *tortiando* expressed not only her lived experience in El Salvador as a young girl performing this female ritual, which she taught to her daughter, but also her immigrant experience. Although she was unable to use fresh-hulled corn for her dough, she nonetheless prepared tortillas with the attentiveness necessary to produce a meaningful product for her husband. Cecilia confirmed her identity as a food expert and wife each time she performed *tortiando*. While her ability to make tortillas validated her identity to herself, she also established her husband's identity as authority figure and breadwinner; he provided the money to purchase the ingredients and she made tortillas for him and they had to be good. *Tortiando* is a powerful symbol for gender roles and power, which I will explore below. Here I would like to discuss further the distinction between food groomer and food preparer.

Food Preparer: A Class Process

A commercial food preparer is engaged in a capitalist class process, following a Marxist analysis further developed by post modernist scholars Stephen Resnick and Richard Wolff (1987). She/he produces both necessary labor (for her/himself) and surplus labor (above her/his needs). The capitalist appropriates the surplus labor in the form of use values (food products) for profit. In this process, the food "worker" uses standardized techniques and recipes to produce, perhaps, a "tasty" meal. More likely, however, the goal of his or her labor is to earn wages, create profit, and, secondarily, to provide calories for human consumption.

The food "worker," even the most proud and conscientious, rarely knows the food consumer for whom he "labors." Many are also alienated in the food production process. Moreover, the food worker is not necessarily engaged in the cultural economy of meaning making. That is to say, the food preparer is not personally conscious of infusing meaning into each Big Mac she/he assembles for a customer. It is safe to generalize, excepting the gourmet chef, that the average food service worker who engages in a capitalist mode of food preparation is not necessarily invested in his culinary output, the food's semiotics, or the public's palate. Rather, she/he is, in essence, a "hand" of capitalism for which a processed commodity food becomes a "value added" vehicle for profit.[3] Historically this Taylorization of food preparation sprang from the home economics movement of the late 1800s and was intimately tied to the development of nutrition knowledge production, techniques, and practices and the State's attempt to change the diets of immigrants (Aronson 1978). The capitalist class structure and the Taylorization of food production and preparation go unchallenged and are encouraged by the nutrition apparatus even today.[4]

The sterility of meaning in the mass production of standardized "cuisine" has proven problematic for the fast food and processed food industry. Customers want to feel there is a caring cook preparing for them nurturing, commercial "home cooked" meals. The food industry thus spends millions of advertising dollars each year inventing culinary meanings to assuage our fantasies: it constructs images of mother, home, and comfort for us to consume in our burger.[5] Corporate America understands the power in meaning making and increasingly considers this crucial to its profits and corporate brand.[6] But the food processing and fast food industries have not convinced us that they care about us and want to nurture us with pizza that tastes like cardboard and processed breakfast cereal products that practically glow-in-the-dark. Rather, it has been successful in convincing us that it is normal for food to be devoid of meaning in our lives. Thus many Americans seem willing to stand, not sit, at a Dunkin' Donuts and gulp down a breakfast they barely taste or remember. Fast, not meaningful, is often our criterion for our meals, not withstanding the culturally-elite culinary movements of slow food and farm-to-table of recent years. In fact, the elite have the time and money to invest in food grooming, purchasing gourmet kitchens and stocking them with organic produce. One wonders just how much food grooming is occurring in these kitchens on a regular basis. The well-heeled still frequent expensive restaurants where they pay trained chefs to groom food embedded with meanings of status, exclusivity, and sustainability.

Food Grooming: A Class and Meaning-Making Process

Food groomers create delicious, significant, and, often, memorable meals. Through their skill, they encode the grammar of the meal with messages of homeland, love, and values. To these ends, food groomers engage in both class and cultural processes. Like the capitalist class structure, the household is also the site of class processes. Some Marxist scholars have identified the "traditional" household, in which the female performs domestic labor and the male participates in the capitalist class process outside the household, as the site of a "feudal class" structure (Fraad, Resnick, and Wolff 1994; Gibson-Graham 1996). In this post-modern redefining of a feudal class process, the wife produces necessary labor (for herself) and surplus labor (for her husband and children) in the form of use-values (cooked food, cleaned rooms, etc.) which are appropriated by her husband and child for their consumption (Resnick and Wolff 1987; Fraad, Resnick, and Wolff 1994; Gibson-Graham 1996). In contrast to the capitalist class processes, in this non-capitalist class process, the wife is not paid wages in exchange for her surplus labor, but rather her husband as the "lord" of the manor appropriates her surplus labor directly through use values.

The above is a simplistic example of Resnick and Wolff's (1987) theory, which emphasizes that both women and men are engaged in multiple class positions and multiple economic, social, and cultural processes both within and outside the household. Furthermore, these postmodern Marxist theorists make the distinction that while in the traditional feudal structure a husband may exploit his wife (appropriate her surplus labor), he may not necessarily oppress her (directing and controlling her behavior). Gibson-Graham (1996), for example, found this to be occasionally true among Australian mineworker households, where women who performed surplus labor for their husbands did not necessarily feel unhappy or unfulfilled. Thus Gibson-Graham (1996, 224) "did not depict the feudal household as something that should necessarily be undermined or abandoned, despite the things we saw in it we didn't like, and despite our interest in promoting communal class processes." I am adopting a similar position in this narrative.

Important for our Salvadoran case, Fraad, Resnick and Wolff (1994) further asserted that the household is a site of cultural and political processes. However, while Resnick and Wolff (1987), Fraad et al. (1994) and Gibson-Graham (1996) acknowledge the household as the site of gendered processes, they do not analyze how meaning of gender, homeland, or a middle-class ideal as a class process is produced, appropriated and consumed for those within and outside the household. Following their analysis of the household as a non-capitalist site of non-commodity production and exchange, I assert that the food groomer participates in class, gender, and other meaning making processes within the household. Thus the food "groomer" is more than a food preparer engaged in an economic class process; she is a food expert engaged in meaning-making; she is invested in the food preparation process, its outcome, and its consumer. In food grooming, the authority on food and its preparation resides in the person of the food "groomer," not in the expertise of a recipe. The food groomer does not produce a standardized, sterile product, but rather she puts a distinct stamp of the self on it. Moreover, the food "groomer" has a conscious attentiveness to the food; she is invested in the grooming process and cares about the quality of her labors. She is not so much concerned with efficiency but rather produces food with the effort and time appropriate for meaningful consumption. Lastly, the food groomer holds the belief that through her labor she imparts values and attributes to her culinary masterpieces. Those who are responsible for cooking in the household, I posit, are at risk of becoming food workers, as opposed to food groomers, when cooking becomes just a burden and neither they nor their family care about the meanings of the dinner or how it turns out, just as long as the food is edible and can be prepared and consumed quickly. In this sense, the household cook is engaged in a class but not necessarily a meaning- making process.

International films have valorized food groomers and the food grooming process. The popular film, *Like Water for Chocolate* (1993), adapted from the book by Mexican author Laura Esquivel (1992), depicted luscious, memorable scenes of Mexican women chopping, slicing and boiling meanings of carnal pleasure, life, and death into food. Similarly, the Danish film, *Babette's Feast* (1987), directed by Gabriel Axel, told the story of a French cook who spent her lottery winnings to groom soul and carnal sensuality into a seven-course gourmet meal for two unsuspecting, God-fearing and pleasure-deprived old maids. In

Chocolat (2000), a mysterious female opened a shop in an uptight French village and infused passion into her Guatemalan chocolate, to the unexpected delight of her customers. Culinary meaning making is not gender specific; in *Eat Drink, Man Woman* (1994) an Asian restaurateur cooked his love and care for his three daughters into meals, which he produced at home during his time off. In all four films, the food groomer supercharged food with meaning, and the diner decoded the culinary message through the palate—if not through the soul.

Salvadoran Immigrant Women As Food Groomers

In my work with Salvadoran immigrants in the late 1990s and early 2000s, Salvadoran women were food groomers; they were culinary experts invested in the meaning and quality of food, its preparation, the outcome of their labor and ultimately the food consumer's pleasure.[7] Their attentiveness to food and whether it was suitable for consumption was critical to the food grooming process. Central to Salvadoran food grooming was the freshness and quality of the food; women rejected the idea that food should come from cans or the freezer. When grocery shopping with Salvadoran women, I spent an extensive amount of time in *mercaditos* and supermarkets squeezing tomatoes, *plátanos* and mangos, picking through beans, and examining cheese for freshness. Salvadoran women were not unique among Latinas in their search for quality fresh food; I have met and known many Latinas who have engaged in these processes. While waiting in a checkout line at a supermarket, for example, a Colombian woman approached a Salvadoran woman and myself and asked in Spanish, *"How are the mangos here, are they good?"* Recognizing the *Salvadoreña* as someone who cared about the quality of mangos, she emphatically continued, *"I do not want to waste my time in this store unless the mangos are good and ripe!"* My Salvadoran companion agreed, which led her into a long conversation about mangos, children and rents.

Although meeting Salvadoran standards for fresh food required much time and money, Salvadoran immigrant women readily spent both when they could. When I told Emilia that her *sopa de pollo* (chicken soup) tasted delicious, she remarked, *"I go to Cambridge once a week. There I can get fresh chicken, just killed. They are much better."* This trip to Cambridge was not easy for Emilia; it required coordinating a ride and finding someone to care for her three children. Moreover, the chickens cost almost twice as much as ones purchased in the discount food market near to her house. Cecilia, for example, could, at the very most, spend $200.00 per week to feed some ten people plus guests. Even so, she would buy fresh fruit for the children, which would always disappear quickly. It was important that they had this, she told me, even when purchasing it was a hardship. Salvadoran immigrants placed a high value on eating fresh food. The time and care women invested in obtaining quality, fresh ingredients embodies their food preparation efforts with meaning.

Salvadoran immigrant women did not want to substitute one ingredient for another when grooming food. Canned beans, for example, did easily substitute for fresh dried ones, especially for more expensive Salvadoran beans. Often, Salvadoran women would purchase food directly from *viajeros*: independent couriers who traffic food and other goods from and to El Salvador. Thus Salvadoran women in Somerville, in search for an authentic taste of home, could purchase from a *viajero* Salvadoran cheese, dried salted fish, herbs and spices from their particular town or region in El Salvador. *Viajeros* also provided Salvadorans with fresh cooked food and produce from El Salvador on a regular basis, even though United States customs law restricted some of these products.[8] When purchasing food from local commercial vendors, Salvadoran women often had to go to more than one market because they did not have the exact product or brand name they desired. According to a Salvadoran *mercadito* owner, the demand for Salvadoran food in the United States has even created a market for wholesale food providers who prefer to distribute to local *mercaditos*.

Indeed, Salvadorans I spoke with were particular about their ingredients. I learned that if we were making tortillas, I could only buy Maseca brand corn meal—any other brand would not do. In the case of Maseca, using Central American produced cornmeal was not merely a preference, but a necessity to produce the pliable texture of dough to make tortillas. Maseca, unlike most American brands, was processed with *cal* [lime], as was the corn used for *masa flojur* in El Salvador. Lime not only makes the dough sticky enough to form a tortilla, but increased the bioavailability of the vitamin niacin and the amino acid lysine (Katz, Hediger, and Valleroy 1975). Both nutrients are essential for health and are especially critical in a limited staple diet of tortillas and beans. Salvadoran women's refusal to substitute food items was the antithesis of a major tenet of capitalism: substitution. Capitalist food production and modern dietary practices are based on the principle that one food can be easily substituted for another, which encourages consumption variety and an ever-expanding market of consumption choices (Aronson 1978). While resisting substitution may not make Salvadoran immigrant women good capitalist food purchasers, it made them "food groomers" *par excellence*.

Salvadoran women's attentiveness to food carries through from the procurement to the preparation process. The care and skill Salvadoran immigrant women executed to turn food into a meal cannot be characterized as mere food preparation; it was much more than merely slapping a hamburger into a pan or even following a recipe in a cookbook. For Salvadoran immigrant women from rural areas, the idea of a recipe was foreign. As a savvy nutritionist from the WIC program (the federal Special Supplemental Nutrition Program for Women, Infants, and Children) observed about her participants: *"If I would offer a cookbook to someone [Salvadoran] they would say, 'why?' They don't use recipes."*

Salvadoran women found my attempts to record their food preparation procedures amusing. It even became the subject of jokes; during a meal with the Cardoza family, I commented to Liliana how much I enjoyed her cooking; her husband teased me about my research, *"It is delicious because my wife read a book that someone wrote about Salvadoran food and how to cook it!"* We all laughed hysterically at the absurdity of Liliana ever wanting or needing to do this. As Felipe revealed through his *chiste* (joke), the authority or know-how of Salvadoran cuisine did not live in nor could be captured by a recipe; this authority resided in the woman herself. A recipe could not convey this knowledge about food production any more than reading a menu can convey the experience of eating a meal.

Salvadoran women coached me on how to pay attention to the process of cooking in ways foreign to me as a "certified food and nutrition expert"—just being with food, touching it, getting to know it. That one could know food in this way diminished the recipe as the authority. When making *pan dulce*, I was told that I would recognize when the batter was ready: *"It looks ready and when you feel it with your finger, you know [it is done cooking]."* Moreover, I could feel when the *masa* was just *"right"* to make tortillas, or I would know when I made the *pasteles just the right size.* I should also be able to sense how long to cook *tamales*; in fact, in not one cooking encounter could a Salvadoran tell me how long it took to boil, bake or grill a food. This approach to food preparation entailed a conscious discipline that was different than precisely following a recipe; it was the discipline of paying attention to the food as though making a meal mattered. Thus when making *tamales*, for example, I could not just throw a few garbanzo beans into the filling. I had to pay attention and follow each woman's particular (and often well guarded) food grooming techniques that put her stamp of love and care on each dish. For example, I was directed by one woman to *"put five garbanzo beans in each tamal–no more, no less."* It also mattered how I wrapped the *tamale*, but each food groomer had her own, often contradictory, method: I must *"wrap the tamal with the shiny side of the tinfoil facing inward"* or else *"it was not good."* In other instances, with other cooks, I had to *"wrap the tamal with the shiny part on the outside"* because this makes *"it cook better."*

Salvadoran women have a unique culinary style that they cultivated and in which they took pride. Their cooking could earn them status or criticism. In fact, Salvadoran immigrant women engaged in *criticando* (critical gossip) about a Salvadoran woman's ability to cook, especially if she sold food from her home. In the community, women were judged by their cooking, and those who had a good reputation would be called upon to cook their specialty for parties and community events. They took pride in their culinary goods and their unique version of Salvadoran fare. During my cooking lessons, each woman would let me in on her special recipe, which branded her product with a stamp of herself. *"My secret,*" one young woman told me as she stirred the huge pot of *masa* on the stove, "*is to put [the secret ingredient] in the masa while it cooks so that it won't boil, that makes the tamales good!*" Each woman I cooked with had her unique style of cooking standard dishes, whether it be *pollo encebollado* (chicken stewed with onions), *arroz con leche* (Salvadoran style rice pudding), or *sopa de res* (beef soup). Like an artisan, each *mujer* (woman) crafted a unique object of consumption that not only reflected her skill but also produced a particular kind of taste—of home—in their cuisine. But this elusive taste of home—El Salvador—could never quite be captured (Stowers 2003, 2012).

Moreover, Salvadoran women conveyed their care and attentiveness to food to the intended food consumer. To Salvadoran women, the purpose of making a meal was not merely to provide unadorned sustenance, but also to let others know that they labored for him or her. The labor and time investment in food preparation was intrinsic to conveying this feeling. Salvadoran immigrant women spent hours cooking to embody food with this nurturing message. A good dinner, according to Ana, for example, took, "*about an hour and a half to prepare, but sometimes more.*" When cooking with Salvadoran women, I spent at least an hour of preparation time for most entrées, and for special meals, like *tamales*, several hours. Thus for Salvadoran women who worked an extended day outside the home, preparing Salvadoran fare for her family often meant staying up late or waking up early. Salvadoran women took great pains to transmit this message of care and attentiveness through food. As one young Salvadoran women informed me, "*You wouldn't put bones in a tamale. You must spend the time to take them out or else people will not think you cared enough to do that for them.*" In this case, *tamales con huesos* (tamales with bones) may be a sign to more middle-class Salvadorans that lower-class women do not care for their guests if they commit the class-based *faux pas* of putting bones in their tamales.

Salvadoran immigrant women especially identified as nurturers of children through their cooking. That their children accepted the food they gave them and ate well was critical as a reflection of their skill as a mother. "*The food I make for my children it is healthy for them, and I always make sure they eat!*" exclaimed a woman from Chalatenango. Salvadoran immigrant women were happy to tell me their children ate "*everything, everything*" and this was positive because it made them feel like a "*good mother,*" "*happy,*" and "*satisfied.*" These comments reflected many I heard from Salvadoran women who proudly took on the role of culinary nurturer and producer of surplus meaning for her children. Moreover, when Salvadoran children rejected the food mothers offered, Salvadoran mothers felt distraught. For example, an experienced mother articulated her concern: "*It worries me—my children do not want what I make for them.*" This intense reaction to a child's lack of appetite reflected not only the mother's feelings of rejection, but also her personal history of food scarcity that she experienced in El Salvador.

Women's food grooming demonstrates a complexity which may or may not be decoded by their American born children (Stowers 2003, 2012). When the consumer did not "get the message," it threatened the household economy of symbolic production, placing the food groomer at risk of becoming a food preparer. But more often friends and guests deciphered the code; they understood and appreciated Salvadoran women's efforts to create an ideal Salvadoran meal. In essence, the grooming process was not complete unless the consumer extracted from his/her meal its message, and nurturing was one of the most powerful messages it conveyed. In the household, the grooming rituals reinforced Salvadoran ideals of the woman as wife, mother, and nurturer and the man as husband, patriarch, and breadwinner, both embodying traditional values of hard work. Thus while participating in a feudal domestic class process, Salvadoran immigrant women, by their act of food grooming and encoding Salvadoran middle class values into each meal, created the illusion of being middle class for their families and themselves. Their labor of food grooming sent a message of nurturing and tradition; however, it also signified gender boundaries, female identity and, sometimes, female submission.

The Culinary Making of Men

A Salvadoran woman, in constructing her female identity, also constructed gender boundaries and produced a male identity for her husband. Thus through her surplus culinary labor, a Salvadoran immigrant woman "fed" her man not only messages of sexuality and nurturing, but concrete evidence of his male dominance and her submission. "*Food is the domain of women in the Salvadoran community*," a female Guatemalan academic who worked with the community informed me. I found her observation only ostensibly true. Both Salvadoran men and women were invested in culinary gender boundaries, but these boundaries were more permeable than her statement suggests. Salvadoran women asserted their culinary expertise as important aspects of their identity and Salvadoran men were invested in her assuming this role. His wife's exclusivity in food grooming established him not as the tortilla maker but as the breadwinner—an ideal, "traditional" male role in El Salvador. Food was the province of an immigrant Salvadoran woman in Somerville not only because she was a culinary expert, but also because her authority as food groomer created gender boundaries and an identity for Salvadoran men.

Salvadoran men in Somerville regarded Salvadoran women's ability to turn food into something that fed the senses and the soul as absolute, powerful, almost magical—a task only a woman could perform. As one male informant revealed to me, "*Men are afraid to cook. The food doesn't taste as good unless women cook it.*" Arnaldo's comment suggests that the gender boundaries between men and women were clearly defined through the exclusivity of women as culinary expert. It is she who made the food taste good. It was her food grooming that infused food with meaning—a mystical task that a man could not or should not do. *"Men do not know how to make tortillas,"* a Salvadoran male from San Miguel adamantly let me know. *Tortiando* was a female's expertise and Salvadoran immigrant men wanted no part of making them, only eating them. To them, a woman's place was in the kitchen cooking for them, an ideal also held in El Salvador among lower middle-class and peasant families. Middle-class urban families could and typically did purchase domestic labor to prepare food for the patriarch; however, this was not the same as having one's wife groom food. For example, a young Salvadoran woman in her thirties from San Salvador remembered, *"In El Salvador we had a servant to cook for us. But my father wanted my mother to cook for him. So she would cook for my father because he liked her cooking best."*

Her father's insistence that his wife, not the servant, groom his food was because she infused into the food her nurturing and sexuality. His wife's labor to create surplus use value and meaning for him further affirmed his identity as patriarch in the household and as breadwinner. In El Salvador, men held the ideal that a woman should stay at home and the male should be the breadwinner: *"In my country, we do not let women work, they [men] go to work and the women stay home and cook,"* a young Salvadoran male claimed. Men held these culinary boundaries as ideal for them and their women.

Culinary gender boundaries were manifested in spatial boundaries within the household: the kitchen was a woman's, not a man's place. During a focus group, a Salvadoran man from a small pueblo responded definitively when I asked if any males in the group knew how to make tamales: *"Men do not know how to make tamales—the kitchen is a woman's place!"* The other men in the room wholeheartedly agreed—men did not belong in the kitchen cooking! While this was a popular ideology among men and women, I found that men did assist in the kitchen. On principle, however, men feared crossing culinary boundaries not only because it placed their gender identity at risk, but also because food and food grooming were such potent symbols of women's power and sexuality.

Through food grooming, Salvadoran immigrant women also groom men's shared cultural code of desire: the Salvadoran Ideal Meal (Stowers 2003, 2012). This meal typically includes high-protein and fat-rich foods: large portions of meat or fish, beans, rice, Salvadoran cheese, *crema* and handmade tortillas. Most importantly, though, this archetypal meal is symbolically rich, a meal infused with the good life: an idealized El Salvador and the arrival into the middle class (Stowers 2003, 2012). In grooming this meal, a Salvadoran woman makes a man feel like a man. Men so closely associated women's food grooming with sexuality and nurturing that Salvadoran women symbolically became food. During my fieldwork, Salvadoran immigrant men (and sometimes women) often compared women's bodies to food. For example, I was told that a woman was round like a *"mango"*; her breasts were like *"melones"*; her legs were like those of "*pollos*" (chickens) or her "*healthy looking*" thighs were like "*rellenitas*" (small sandwiches stuffed with meat). Women and food and "women as food" were especially on the minds of young, single Salvadoran men. A young newly migrated, single male lamented to me, "*We really miss the women in this country—we really miss the pupusas.*" For him, *pupusas* were not just a savory dish that women produced. They were also a potent symbol for the female body and the emotional and sexual companionship that young, single Salvadoran males especially crave in response to their cultural and social alienation and marginal living conditions. Leaving female partners behind and arriving as single males, they took up residence in a community demographically dominated by males. Moreover, I found, as did Mahler (1995) and Menjívar (2000), they usually worked only with men, formed male resources networks, and lived with other men in crowded apartments, all of which limited their opportunity to meet single women. Deprived of home groomed food, they sought out culinary delights in restaurants and from *cocineras* (female cooks) as a bridge to their culture, community, and *anhelo* (longing) for female companionship and emotional support. The association of women's sexuality with food and food preparation was not unique to Salvadoran men living in Somerville; it was a common metaphor in Latino slang, music and literature.[9] But for Salvadoran immigrants, songs and discourse spiced with references to food as codes for women and sensual desire—in part, a reaction to traditional cultural mores that demanded sexual modesty—have heightened importance in the destabilizing immigrant environment of the United States.

Salvadoran men experienced women's food grooming not only as sexual, but also as motherly and nurturing. A man's female partner, as did his mother, groomed the meaning of care for him into her culinary goods. This culinary care and appreciation for it was expressed by one of my household case-study participants, Felipe, who commented about his wife, "*I can't believe how my wife takes care of me. She cooks me everything, everything—she feeds me anything I want. When I am sick, she brings me soup.*"

Felipe's wife's role, nurturing him through food, was not unlike that of Tejano Mexican-American women living in migrant farming communities, described by Brett Williams (1984). In Williams's study, women spent their meager financial and temporal resources to "groom" *tamales* for their men in the face of deplorable farm worker conditions. Williams (1984, 116) found in this community, "Only women make *tamales...Tamales* are thus labor-intensive food items, which symbolize and also exaggerate women's routine nurturance of men." Although Somerville was not at all close to a migrant camp, Salvadoran families analogously faced seemingly insurmountable stresses and impoverished conditions in which men felt a loss of dignity; they craved and demanded the nurturing of women. Like Tejano migrant males, they needed their woman to "groom" nurturance into their food to buffer them against their surroundings "which tacitly proclaim their worthlessness" (Williams 1984, 121). Felipe, who experienced the humiliation of low wages and racial slurs at his workplace in Somerville, felt his worth as a human being affirmed by his wife's culinary care.

Some women embraced their roles in domestic-feudal arrangements and as culinary nurturers of men, and they did not feel oppressed by it. For example, Williams (1984) asserted that Tejano migrant women did not feel oppressed by their culinary domesticity; they respected the authority of their men and embraced their role as cook through which they exercised control over food in the household. In the Cardoza household in Somerville, this was true—but only to a point. Liliana, Felipe's wife, exercised control over the household food resources; she decided what to cook, made the food budget and told her husband what foodstuffs to purchase. Like Tejano women, she was proud of her culinary skills, which earned her respect from her husband, her family and her community. In fact, Liliana was the model food groomer; she cooked with attentiveness and care and her family understood and appreciated her culinary messages. But their household was not the typical Salvadoran household in Somerville. Felipe and Liliana had worked hard to re-create this Salvadoran ideal household, and they had the resources to accomplish their goal. Because Felipe migrated in the 1980s and won his political asylum case early on, he became documented and was eventually trained as a semi-skilled laborer. He was even able to purchase a home before the real estate boom hit Somerville in the 1990s. Moreover, Liliana, although she knew no English, ran a small daycare business from her home and also sold homemade *pan dulce* and *tamales* to her church community. It was not surprising, therefore, that of all the Salvadoran immigrant families with whom I worked, Felipe and his wife were most able to reconstruct Salvadoran values for themselves and their children. They unequivocally claimed their Salvadoran identity, used their resources to help newly arrived Salvadorans, and were community role models. On occasion, Liliana complained that she worked hard in the kitchen and that her husband had free time to exercise and play soccer, but she did not express her role of food groomer as oppressive. Unlike Liliana and the Tejano women in William's study, however, many Salvadoran immigrant women in Somerville did not have as much control over their culinary activity as it might appear. Their husbands and other males in the household attempted to control both their culinary production and their lives.

Although many Salvadoran males and females want to re-create traditional ideals of male and female gender roles post migration, the political, economic and cultural climate in the United States challenged their efforts, setting their domestic economy of meaning making into crisis. Politically, for example, culinary gender roles were at-risk both inside and outside the household due to the political economy of migration and labor, which often forced men to enter the kitchen and cook. In Somerville, men found this somewhat unsettling, although they had many of the skills needed to perform culinary tasks. To my surprise, rural Salvadoran men migrated with substantial cultural capital about food and its preparation—more than they were willing to claim publicly. In my private conversations with Salvadoran men I was astounded at how much they actually knew about food and food preparation compared to Anglo men. As children in El Salvador, Salvadoran men recalled how they helped their mothers prepare food, and as agriculturalists, they articulated a detailed understanding of food production. Salvadoran men described for me how to make pineapple vinegar from fresh pineapples, how to slaughter a cow or pig and cook each part, how to kill a chicken and how to cook it, and how to make fresh cheese. Yet, in all cases, they were adamant that food preparation was the province of women and that they would not publicly lay claim to any knowledge about it. However, Salvadoran immigrant men often had to cross this gender boundary.

Upon migration, Salvadoran men reluctantly entered the kitchen out of necessity. Without a Salvadoran wife, for example, young, single men (often living together) had to cross the culinary gender boundary and cook for themselves. Such was the case for Joseph who embarrassingly told me: *"When I first came here it was very different. I didn't have my food; I didn't know how to cook. In El Salvador, men do not have to cook or clean the clothes. I had to do it here."* Moreover, some men found that they had to assist their wives in the kitchen because she would go out to work, but many were uncomfortable about this. They made reference to how this was not traditional or acceptable in their culture. *"Here we can cook, but back in El Salvador—they would laugh at us,"* a Salvadoran man in his early thirties informed me when I caught him stirring a pot of *sopa de pollo.* Many men were not happy helping out in the kitchen at home but accepted this role in the workplace.

Hispanics were disproportionably employed in commercial food service, and many of these were men (Mydans 1/8/95). Rarely were immigrant Salvadorans employed as waiters or chefs, but rather they held low-paid positions as busboys, fast food workers and cooks' assistants (Mahler 1995). In my study, men seemed less uncomfortable about crossing the culinary boundary at work because they were earning wages and grateful to be employed. In fact, some men with whom I spoke proudly told me they worked at a restaurant. *"I work at the Hillcrest; first I was a busboy, but now I am helping out in the kitchen,"* claimed a Salvadoran man from La Unión. Another newly migrated undocumented Salvadoran man in one of my case study households offered that, *"I was happy to get a job at McDonald's because I need the money."* Neither his gender or class identity seemed to be threatened, even though he had been a dentist in El Salvador. Some men who held jobs in food service even prepared restaurant foods in their house. *"Sometimes I make spaghetti at home,"* a Salvadoran man employed in an Italian restaurant proudly informed me. Another male in one of my case study households made a shrimp and pasta dinner for his family and me, a dish he had seen made at work. Typically, however, men who were employed in the food industry still insisted that at home the females in the household must cook for them.

Many Salvadoran immigrant men attempted to control their wives' culinary and symbolic production, usurping her power in the kitchen. Often it was the men, for example, who grocery shopped, selected the foods they desired, and then told their women what to cook. Both Salvadoran men and women claimed that men's domination over women's culinary activities was "traditional" in El Salvador, but the tensions around Salvadoran immigrant men's attempt to control the culinary production of women seemed to have intensified here. For example, a Salvadoran woman from Santa Ana claimed: "*In El Salvador the men shop for food because they have the money and they carry the bags if they are heavy. Here many men shop for food too—my husband does the shopping... The men tell the women what they want to eat also.*"

The Heavy Toll of Grooming Food

Salvadoran immigrant men typically made demands on what Salvadoran women created in their kitchens. For example, Salvadoran women knew they must "groom" *tortillas* for their husbands, a ritual they performed daily for years on end. "*I make tortillas because my husband insists that I make them,*" remarked Selina, an overburdened Salvadoran wife whose comments reflected many I heard about *tortilla* making and husbands. It was not that they did not like or want to make *tortillas* for their husbands or children; they felt that it was important. But it was their husbands' demands on them that felt oppressive, and for some women it became a symbol of their dissatisfaction with their husbands' control over their lives. Moreover, many Salvadoran men demanded they be fed a full meal, on time, after work: "*Salvadoran men expect their meal on the table when they get home. I know many women who for many years made sure their husbands' meal was there ready for him,*" commented Miriam, a young Salvadoran woman, further adding, "*Thank God my husband is not like this.*"

Miriam was not the typical Salvadoran immigrant, however. Her extended family was one of the first to migrate to Somerville in the 1970s. She herself had migrated very young, was now attending college part-time, had a good job and had purposefully sought out and married a nontraditional Salvadoran man. Her financial independence and non-traditional ideology contributed to her ability to engage in an egalitarian marriage. A few financially independent Salvadoran women I met in Somerville resisted marrying altogether. I found this surprising: there was cultural pressure for Salvadoran women to find husbands or male partners at a young age. These women did not claim to have husbands or boyfriends in El Salvador, which was another reason why some Salvadoran women did not seek out male partners in the United States. It was clear that at least one of these women, Dora, did not want to be domestically dominated by any Salvadoran man and had resisted marrying:

I am single. The Salvadoran men are very macho—not all of them, but most. In
El Salvador, the woman only stays in the house and the man goes out to work.
The man will buy the food or even tell the woman what to cook. She takes care
of the children. Here the women work; they are more independent, but the men,
they do not like this. (Stowers 2003)

Dora migrated from a lower middle-class family and held documentation
immigrant status in the U.S. Although she spoke no English, she was a successful proprietor of a Latino clothing shop in East Somerville. She did not have to
depend on a man to support her. But most undocumented Salvadoran women
had little choice but to find male partners who provided not only companionship
but also access to resources. Rural women usually migrated with little cultural
capital and were more likely than men to have only a grammar school education
(World Bank 1998). Many of Somerville's Salvadoran immigrant women who
had migrated from rural areas had only attended school for a few years prior to
arriving in the U.S. Since males typically migrated first, they were more likely
to have temporary documentation status, which entitled them to work papers.
Salvadoran females, who migrated later to join male partners, brothers or
friends, were less likely to have work papers. Undocumented Salvadoran wom-
en, however, found jobs more easily than undocumented men, often as domestic
workers; still, they typically worked part-time, had erratic hours, and earned
meager wages (Menjívar 2000). Few single Salvadoran women had significant
social networks in the U.S, and women could not benefit from male resource
networks because they felt that in exchange for male assistance—such as for car
transportation—men would demand sexual favors from them (Menjívar 2000).
When Salvadoran women worked for wages, they generally earned less money
than Salvadoran men (Menjívar 2000). Thus Salvadoran immigrant women were
financially and socially vulnerable and had to depend on male partners, brothers,
and other male extended family members, especially if they were undocumented. As such, they were hardly in a position to challenge male power in the
household, unlike their children, who, as naturalized citizens, could and often
did. This situation caused Leana to assert, *"Salvadoran women often do whatever their husbands say—they don't have their own opinions. If he says not to
work here, they don't."*

But most immigrant Salvadoran men could not afford to keep their women
at home; she needed to earn wages outside the household to help her man actual-
ize the Salvadoran middle-class economic ideal. When Salvadoran women
worked outside the household, however, it was the antithesis of the middle-class
cultural ideal that placed Salvadoran women at home, in the kitchen. Both Salvadoran immigrant men and women held the ideal that women should be in the
house, and thus even when women were present in the community they claimed
not to be (Menjívar 2000). In essence, some Salvadoran women in Somerville

were hidden both within the clandestine identity of their undocumented or temporarily undocumented status and through their role as women.

One way a Salvadoran woman responded to both the expectation that she must stay home to reproduce the ideal middle-class household and to earn a cash income was to groom food in her kitchen to sell to the community. In this capacity, Salvadoran women participated in additional symbolic and economic non-capitalist class processes of self-employment (Resnick and Wolff 1987). In the capitalist economy, however, Salvadoran women's food grooming labor was devalued in both the home and the community. Women were not financially compensated when they groomed food for their families, although women's exploitation supported their husbands' ability to produce surplus labor for capitalist enterprises and produced children as future workers and citizens of the state. Furthermore, as a food vendor for the community, she was rarely able to make enough money even to support herself. She participated in a profession that had traditionally been dominated by women and thus was undervalued and underpaid.

Moreover, Salvadoran women working out of the household simply did not make food to sell only for income. Rather, the Salvadoran who groomed food in her kitchen had a symbolic role as an important member of the local economy providing a tasty message of comfort, hard work, and a palatable transnational bridge to El Salvador. She fed the gastronomic nostalgics of the Salvadoran immigrant community; her food grooming held the promise of transporting her patrons back to their home village. This promise often remained illusive: it was not merely the taste of their cuisine to which Salvadoran immigrants longed, but rather access through its taste to an imagined perfect past and a hoped for middle-class ideal in the present, neither of which could be actualized (Stowers 2003, 2012).

In the following example, Emilia who made a living as a *minuta vendedora* in El Salvador, attempted to re-create her livelihood in Somerville as a way to claim her identity, serve the community, and make money for her financially strained household. She taught me how to groom the values of hard work, caretaking and culture into a *minuta*. There were many lessons in this story, however, including a lesson for this anthropologist about the disjuncture between theory and practice and how the devaluation of women's culinary labor can turn food grooming into food production with the consequence of undermining an important cultural tradition.

It was a hot day in July, muy caliente, close to 100 degrees; by the time I climbed to the Rodriguez's third floor apartment, I could barely breathe. As usual I knocked on the door several times before Laura, their 5-year-old, cautiously opened it and peeked her head through the small crack. "La maestra, la maestra" she called out and ushered me into the small, crowded kitchen. Emilia, her mother, greeted me smiling, wiping her hands on her faded, yellow delantal. She was cooking, as usual, what, I wasn't quite sure, but I didn't have time to ask. In the commotion of my buenos días to Arnaldo, Emilia's husband, and the various children and adults currently living in the household, we heard a quiet knock. Everyone shifted positions in the small, stifling space so that the puerta could be opened again. In slipped a young Salvadoran girl, about nine years old. "May I have a minuta?" she asked Emilia.

I knew Emilia made and sold "Salvadoran" snow cones. A few weeks previously, she described to me how she was a minuta vendor in her cantón at the fiestas patronales–the celebrations honoring the patron saint of the village in El Salvador. She had proudly showed me her hand held ice shaver, a raspador, which she had brought with her from El Salvador thirteen years ago; apparently, she still used it to make the icy confections. She had described how she flavored the ice with honeyed syrups that she purchased from the viajero. She kept the brightly colored syrup bottles on her crowded kitchen table. Today they stood haphazardly alongside large, plastic, food storage containers, enormous cooking pots, a 10-gallon bucket half full of home made curtido, and a pyramid built of several 15 lbs. bags of Maseca, which looked ready to topple at any moment. The table was a metaphor for the configuration of people crowded into this pequeña cocina on this hot July evening.

She wants a minuta, I thought, smiling at the niña. This is great, I thought, now I can see how Emilia prepares minuta and maybe test my theory on food grooming.

Responding to the young girl's request, Emilia maneuvered her short, round, Indio body through the tight space around the kids, the small customer, her husband and myself. She opened the freezer and removed, with some difficulty, a huge metal cooking pot. Turning it over onto a dish towel placed on the table, she lifted the pot to reveal an enormous ice cube about one foot across and one foot deep. Taking the ice shaver in her hand, she began to scrape the ice, sweating profusely.

"Can I help?" I asked innocently. She quickly put the heavy, bulky, metal scraper in my right hand and motioned for me to raspar, and I began to "groom" the ice block. The shaver was large for my hand and no matter how I tried to mimic her motion it glided across the glossy ice surface. I opened the compartment of the raspador and to my disappointment it contained but a bit of snow! Emilia laughed and her eyes danced. She put her large, brown, strong hand over mine on the scraper.

"Scrape hard," she instructed me as she pushed firmly on my hand sandwiched between hers and the shaver. She let go and I tried again. My arm ached. This is grooming food, I thought. Again, I opened the raspador and discovered that I had produced hardly a tablespoon of white crystals.

I feverishly started to scrape again but realized that I should not pass up this opportunity to ask her about the meaning of this labor-intensive activity. "Emilia is it important to scrape the ice like this? Does it make the minuta taste better?" I asked.

Puzzled she looked at me: "¿Cómo?"

Ok, I thought to myself, I need to ask this another way. By now, however, I had become so involved in trying to formulate a question about the concept of grooming food, that I had stopped scraping and the small customer was getting impatient.

"The ice is melting!" Emilia said forcefully but with a bright smile. She grabbed the scraper from me and with her knowledgeable hands powered by her strong arms, she scraped enough snow to fill the paper cup, which waited in the hands of the quiet brown-eyed niña.

"Emilia," my words blurting into the process, "what I mean is that there are machines that can do this." I had never actually seen an electric ice shaver for home use, but I knew of the commercial type used for snow cones and frozen alcoholic drinks. By now Emilia was topping the ice shavings with candy-colored flavoring.

Trying to clarify myself, I piped up, "Would a minuta taste the same if it were made by a machine or is it important to make it a mano?"

Still puzzled by my question, she remarked, "It would taste lo mismo."

"The same—are you sure? Not different or better?" I inquired insistently hoping she would say something more in line with my theoretical expectations.

"Lo mismo," she repeated emphatically.

Damn, I thought, maybe this theory about grooming is for the birds. The silent young customer who had waited so patiently while la gringa tried to re-create a frozen bit of El Salvador paid her dollar and left.

Meanwhile, Emilia, apparently reflecting on my questions, asked, "Where can I get one of these machines? ¿Es muy cara?" [Is it very expensive?]

"I don't know," I said disappointingly. "I will try to find out."

"Pero una máquina es muy cara y no tengo dinero" [But a machine is very expensive and I have no money], she lamented.

What does she mean, I thought feverishly. Does she want me to buy her one? This thought produced an ethical debate in my brain, which was already overheated, and on cultural overload. How should I respond? Should I pretend I didn't hear her? Should I offer to buy her an ice-shaving machine and under-mine her traditional methods of food production—the very thing I hoped my re-search would help Salvadorans conserve? But before I could say anything there was another knock at the door.

"It's Ana's brother," announced Emilia's twelve-year-old daughter, Rosa. In walked a handsome, teenage male; he asked for a minuta too, but he wanted a double! Emilia smiled and handed me the scraper. I swore under my breadth but apparently Arnaldo heard me and chuckled.

"You are doing a good job, maestra!" he exclaimed encouragingly. Ar-naldo, of course, didn't offer to help; this was woman's work. He seemed, how-ever, to relish the idea of supervising us.

I could hardly breathe from the heat, but I started to raspar rápido. The sweat poured from my brow. "A double?" I choked out in a high voice. "This is hard work! Emilia, you need to charge this muchacho $10 dollars for this." She laughed and her eyes danced with the knowledge that she was the minuta expert I could never be. I wanted to fill the large cup only to the rim, but she insisted that it must be heaping. Assured that I had learned a lesson about minuta making, Emilia spelled me to finish the ice shaving and then piled more snow into the large cup. Arnaldo discussed soccer with the tall teenager while Emi-

lia, at the customer's request, squeezed fresh lime juice and sprinkled salt on the cold Salvadoran "ice pop."

Ok, I thought, wiping the sweat from my forehead with my sleeve; let me give this another theoretical shot. I turned to the Salvadoran adolescent, who, no doubt, was wondering why a blanca was in Emilia's kitchen scraping ice, and matter of factly asked, "Do you like this minuta as much as those in El Salvador?"

"Sí," he said hesitantly, wondering what I was getting at. "Emilia makes good minuta," he added emphatically. But his face had the cautious look Salvadorans have—pleasant but guarded—when they do not want to be publicly critical. I tried to clarify myself so that he could see it was not Emilia's ability as a minuta maker that was under question.

"If Emilia made minuta by a machine—a machine that scrapes the ice—would it taste the same?"

"No," he answered, "it is not the same. This is good. I have tasted American ice [popsicles]; they are no good." (Stowers 2003)

It was not just that hand-made *minuta* tasted better than machine made popsicles, I would discover. It was that Salvadorans liked to see the *minuta* being made, just as they liked to hear the pat of *tortiando*. *"Salvadorans want to see the women make the minuta; if you do not see them do it, it is not the same,"* a young Salvadoran woman from a rural town in San Miguel informed me. Emilia's grooming efforts not only made the *minuta* taste good, but also infused them with goodness. The labor of women patting the *tortilla* or grooming the *minuta* affirmed the social connection between the laboring women and the consumer. It enhanced the gastronomic nostalgic's experience of realizing his or her ideal memories of *fiestas* in their village. Salvadorans felt a connection with the food "groomer" who they often observed making the food. It was not a necessity that they observed this to enjoy their meal, but they were profoundly aware of the labor grooming the food entails and they appreciated it. Emilia's labor made meaning for others and she was proud of a skill that affirmed her own identity, but her *minuta* grooming was also hard work, especially in a capitalist economy where food grooming was devalued. While she could only charge her poor neighbors a dollar or two for her icy confections, her income as a *minuta* maker was a pittance ($10 to $20 per week in the summer) compared to her rent and living expenses. Unlike in El Salvador, she could not afford to re-create her food grooming in a domestic feudal arrangement in the household and as a profession in Somerville.

In El Salvador women could make a living as an independent food *vendedora*, but in the United States Salvadoran *vendedoras* faced many obstacles to developing a viable business, which became clandestine operations (Chavez 1992; Carvajal 1994). Emilia needed to make more money: she and Arnaldo needed to move out of the small apartment that they shared with an undocumented Salvadoran family that has caused them and their children severe problems. Emilia considered using an ice-shaving machine to relieve her of this laborious task, but she did not have the capital to purchase one. I honestly didn't think she wanted or would have used an electric ice shaver; rather, I understood her remark as her way of letting me know that she was cash poor.

A few months after this evening, Emilia found a job in a commercial bakery that mass produced bagels. Although she only earned the minimum wage, it was still more money than she could make as a food vendor in her community. She was happy to be paid for her labor, and she hoped that some of the money she earned would help her and her husband eventually to buy a house. But Emilia had to work a "double shift"; she had to produce surplus labor (extracted as profit) in a capitalist class process where her wages were above that of *minuta* making, but below the poverty level. Moreover, her husband Arnaldo was not willing to cross the gender boundary at home: he insisted, along with her other gendered tasks, that she groom for him the Salvadoran Ideal Meal. Emilia's surplus labor was exploited in two class structures: the enterprise and the household. Moreover, in the commercial food enterprise Emilia was transformed into a food preparer and, it could be argued, Arnaldo's increasing control over her culinary labor and limited time placed Emilia at risk of essentially becoming a culinary serf.

The Making of Culinary Serfs

This was but one of many examples of how modernization introduced contradictions and tensions to a Salvadoran ideal traditional "feudal" domestic household, which among other effects, challenged gender processes, placing female and male identities at stake (Fraad, Resnick and Wolff 1994). As we have seen, these tensions were particularly exacerbated for Salvadorans, who were at the mercy of documentation liminality and immigrant labor exploitation. Modernization impacted gender relations and resulted in the abuse of power within the household, where males not only exploited their wives but also oppressed them by directing and controlling their behavior. Fraad et al. described this scenario:

> The male's responsibilities and obligation to support and protect his family may be exercised inside the household in ways that maximize the female burden of performing surplus labor. He may dictate that, as the 'master' of the house, his tastes and preference must prevail regardless of their impacts on "his" wife and children....
>
> The rights and obligations of partners in marriage—the political processes within the relationship between them—are pushed and pulled in all manner of contradictory directions by all other processes of the society in which the marriage exists. Marriage rights and obligations, and even the marriages themselves, become objects of conflicts and struggles. These struggles over power within the household are also complex causes and effects of struggles there over class and gender processes ....

Among the possible results of such interconnected struggles is violence by one spouse, usually male, against the other. (1994, 23-24)

This quote does not fully reflect the authors' postmodern class and cultural analysis of the crisis of the feudal domestic household; Fraad et al. emphasized that this crisis can produce positive and not just negative effects that transform household class structures, marriages, and even political processes outside the home. For undocumented and liminally documented Salvadoran immigrants, however, the political, economic and cultural forces that shape and determine their lived experience produce many negative outcomes, especially for women and children. The crisis of modernization on the Salvadoran immigrant household may result, for example, in the abuse of male power where Salvadoran women experience men trying to control their behavior. This effect has become evident to health care workers and WIC personnell in Somerville who informed me that Salvadoran men often monitored their female partners' visits to the WIC office and the health clinic. A WIC nutritionist related to me with sincere concern: "*A lot of the [Salvadoran] women have very strange relationships with their men. When they get here [the WIC office] they call them. They tell other people that their husbands lock them in their apartments all day. This is upsetting to me—why are they worried?*"

When I repeated this scenario to a few Salvadoran women, they did not balk. "*He is jealous,*" they agreed, adding that it was common for Salvadoran men to control their wives' behavior. Leana, who was married to a Salvadoran and worked at the WIC office in the community health clinic confirmed this analysis: "*Salvadoran men are very jealous, sometimes they go to the WIC appointment or the clinic with their wives; or, they [wives] have to call their husbands to let them know when they arrive and when they are finished.*"

Salvadoran men may be jealous of their wives but no doubt their insecure identity and feelings of disempowerment are also due to the myriad factors that produce Salvadoran immigrant men and women as liminal and nonexistent subjects of the state. In that Salvadoran women's food grooming and Salvadoran cuisine were such potent symbols for Salvadoran men's desires, no wonder it became a site of contestation of power in the household. Salvadoran men insisted that Salvadoran women re-create the culinary bridge to their taste memory and idealized gender roles through production of the Salvadoran Ideal Meal. The assertion of male control over Salvadoran immigrant women's culinary labor was one factor that threatened to transform women's food grooming into food preparation; Salvadoran women became little more than food workers under the oppressive supervision of a husband through the subjugation to his demands. Moreover, as some Salvadoran men became more assimilated and began to understand that the cultural code of the American middle class was to have a thin wife, they developed a double standard of expectations of culinary meaning.

They insisted that their wives go on a diet. This demand threatened not only a Salvadoran woman's identity but also her own enjoyment of the savory bridge to her ideal past life. Simultaneously, however, these Salvadoran men continued to insist that Salvadoran women labor to make culinary meaning for them. Cecilia, for example, while she felt tremendous pressure to produce the Salvadoran Ideal Meal for her husband began denying herself the pleasure she experienced through consuming this meal. She started to eat "*diet*" food because her husband said she was "*too fat.*" His demands that she lose weight caused her great distress, as did his demand that she continue to feed his insatiable gastronomic nostalgia. By way of coming full circle in this chapter, I would like to return to Cecilia's threatened role as a food groomer with this observation:

> *Cecilia finally got some time off for vacation. Her husband would not let her take the kids out of town to visit relatives, so she decided to explore the local Metropolitan area with her children. On a weekday, Cecilia, the kids, and I went to the Boston Children's Museum, and they had a wonderful time, happy to be furloughed from the dark, hot apartment. I realized it was getting late when I caught Cecilia looking nervously at the clock. She hesitantly informed me, "I am a little worried that I will not be home to make dinner for my husband."*
>
> *Elisa overheard her mother and immediately piped in: "You'll get fired mommy." Understanding that her mother's role as food groomer had increasingly become that of food preparer, Elisa informed her brothers that it was time to leave and promptly headed toward the door.* (Stowers 2003)

I have analyzed how Salvadoran immigrant women participated in a capitalist "feudal domestic" class process in the household, and although ostensibly exploitive, their food grooming activities also produced valuable meanings of gender identity, class status and access to a taste of El Salvador for her community. While the traditional role of a Salvadoran immigrant woman in the kitchen may look to an outsider as only a slave to her *comal* and husband, to the extent that this work is not appropriated by the dynamics of the market economy, her work as a cultural laborer nourished the stomach and souls of a community in the shadows, creating access to an idealized El Salvador and the dreams of a hoped for middle-class life, Salvadoran style.

Acknowledgments

Research for this chapter was originally funded by a Wenner-Gren Foundation grant for pre-doctoral research.

Notes

1. Salvadorans in the 1980s through the early 2000s fell into many different immigration categories, and the documentation one had, or did not have, determined one's access to employment, private and public resources. Permanently documented immigrants, legal residents, held green cards or became naturalized citizens, with full political rights. But most Salvadorans who were not undocumented held only temporary documentation status, such as temporary protective status (TPS/DED), political asylum re-applicant (ABC), or suspension of deportation (NACARA). Some immigrants were on time-limited visas. A significant percentage of the participants in this study had no legal immigration status; they were undocumented, more derisively termed "illegal." The U.S. born children of an immigrant, regardless of immigration status, are American citizens.

2. I am indebted to the theoretical work of Stephen Resnick and Richard Wolff, Harriet Fraad, Katherine Gibson and Julie Graham (J.K. Gibson-Graham) for my analysis of the Salvadoran household. These theorists have struggled with the term feudal to describe the particular type of economic arrangement I have described here. However, after much consideration, Gibson-Graham decided that no other term, including "traditional domestic," accurately described the type of economic relationship characteristic of this arrangement and thus opted to use "feudal domestic." See Gibson-Graham (1996), especially pages 212-214, for their rationale.

3. In the food processing industry, the term "value-added" is used to describe processed foods whose "value" as a raw whole food has been enhanced through processing, typically adding sugar, salt or fat, which increases the profit margin of the product far above its market worth as a food staple. The industry's "value-added" term does not refer to the surplus labor used to create the product, which remains invisible.

4. Kate Kane (1989, 141) describes how the fast food meal and the labor which produces it exemplifies the fulfillment of the home economics movement's goal, which sought to rationalize domestic labor through the emphasis of "nutritional value, predictable results, economy, and appearance of food." The issue of class in commercial and domestic labor is absent from the standard nutrition curricula accredited by the American Dietetic Association used to train nutrition professionals. It is also absent from popular and even progressive nutrition education materials. In these contexts, food discourse is about nutrients such as calories, saturated fats and vitamins, a phenomenon I label nutrithink (Stowers, 2003).

5. See Kane (1989) for an analysis of how McDonald's commercials use images of women and motherhood to promote their products.

6. Ernest Sternberg (1999, 5) in The Economy of Icons: How Business Manufactures Meaning asserts that "The driving force in this newer economy is not information but image. Now the decisive material is meaning, production occurs through the insertion of commodities into stories and events, efficiency consists in the timely conveyance of meaning, celebrity underlies wealth, and economic influence emanates from the controllers of content."

7. Over the years my palate benefited from the diligence of other Latina food groomers, especially from my Puerto Rican mother-in-law, who is a wonderful food groomer. Her job as an academic required her to live in Arizona, but whenever she traveled to New York City, she loaded up her suitcase with fresh plátanos in order to make the family tasty Puerto Rican fare.

8. Menjívar (2000) reported that *viajeros* in San Francisco supplied regular customers with fresh produce. On visiting Salvadorans in Somerville, I had the occasion to eat fresh contraband produce that contained seeds, such as *nance* and *pitos*, which were restricted from entry.

9. Salvadoran music, like much Central American music, often includes lyrics in which food is used as sexual innuendo. See, for example, "Hits *Centroamericanos*," Hemisphono Records, 1996, which is a collection of many such popular songs, including *La Pastilla del Amor, Atol de Elote, Sopa de Frijoles.*

Bibliography

Abrego, Leisy. 2009. "Economic Well Being in Salvadoran Transnational Families: How Gender Affects Remittances Practices." *Journal of Marriage and Family* 7 (November): 1070-1085.

Aronson, Naomi. 1978. Fuel for the Human Machine: The Industrialization of Eating in America. PhD Dissertation, Brandeis University.

Avakian, Arlene Voski. ed. 1997. *Through the Kitchen Window: Women Explore the Intimate Meanings of Food and Cooking.* Boston: Beacon Press.

Carter, Brenda, Kevan Insko, David Loeb, and Marlene Tobias, editors. 1989. *A Dream Compels Us: Voices of Salvadoran Women.* Boston: South End Press.

Carvajal, Deborah. 1994. "Making Ends Meet in a Nether World: Salvadorans Have Built a Secret Economic Network to Survive." *New York Times,* December 13.

Chavez, Leo R. 1992. *Shadowed Lives: Undocumented Immigrants in American Society.* Irvine, CA: Harcourt Brace College Publishers.

Fraad, Harriet, Stephen Resnick, and Richard Wolff. 1994. *Bringing It All Back Home: Class, Gender and Power in the Modern Household.* London: Pluto Press.

Gibson-Graham, J.K. 1996. *The End of Capitalism (as we knew it): A Feminist Critique of Political Economy.* Cambridge, MA: Blackwell Publishers.

Kane, Kate. 1989. "Who Deserves A Break Today? Fast Food, Cultural Rituals and Woman's Place." In *Cook By the Book: Food in Literature and Culture,* edited by Mary Anne Schofield, 138-146. Bowling Green, OH: Bowling Green State University Popular Press.

Katz, S.H., M.L. Hediger, and L. Valleroy. 1975. "The Anthropological and Nutritional Significance of Traditional Maize Processing Techniques in the New World." In *Biosocial Interrelations in Population Adaptation,* edited by E.S. Watts, F.E. Johnson and G.W. Lasker, 195-234. The Hague: Mouton.

Machuca, M.R. 2010. "In Search of Salvadorans in the U.S.: Contextualizing the Ethnographic Record." *Urban Anthropology: Studies of Cultural Systems and World Economic Development* 39 (Spring, Summer): 1-46.

Mahler, Sarah J. 1995. *American Dreaming.* Princeton: Princeton University Press.

McCracken, Grant. 1986. "Culture and Consumption: A Theoretical Account of the Structure and Movement of Cultural Meaning of Consumer Goods." *Journal of Consumer Research* 13 (June): 71-84.

———. 1988. *Culture and Consumption: New Approaches to the Symbolic Character of Consumer Goods and Activities.* Bloomington and Indianapolis: Indiana University Press.

Menjívar, Cecilia. 2000. *Fragmented Ties: Salvadoran Immigrant Networks in America.* Berkeley and Los Angeles: University of California Press.

Mydans, Seth. 1995. "Mexican Cooking Without Any Salsa." In *New York Times*, January 8.

Resnick, Stephen A., and Richard D. Wolff. 1987. *Knowledge and Class: A Marxian Critique of Political Economy.* Chicago: University of Chicago Press.

Somerville Population Trends FactSheet. http://www.somervillema.gov/sites/default/files/CompPLan/Pop%20Trends%20Factsheet%20FinalWebsite.pdf (accessed March 21, 2012).

Sternberg, Ernest. 1999. *The Economy of Icons: How Business Manufactures Meaning.* Westport, CT: Praeger.

Stowers, Sharon, L. 2003. "Hungry for the Taste of El Salvador: Gastronomic Nostalgia, Identity, and Resistance to Nutrithink in an Immigrant Community." PhD Dissertation, University of Massachusetts, Amherst.

———. 2012. "Gastronomic Nostalgia: Salvadoran Immigrants' Craving for Their Ideal Meal." *Ecology of Food and Nutrition* 51 (August): 374-393.

Williams, Brett. 1984. "Why Migrant Women Feed Their Husbands Tamales." In *Ethnic and Regional Foodways in the United States,* edited by L.K. Brown and K. Mussell, 113-126. Knoxville: University of Tennessee Press.

World Bank. 1998. *El Salvador: Rural Development Study.* Washington, DC: The World Bank.

CHAPTER 9

The Social Life of Coca-Cola in Southern Veracruz, Mexico: How Women Navigate Public Health Messages and Social Support through Drink

Mary Alice Scott

Introduction

I have lost count of the number of Cokes I have consumed today. At each household visit, meeting, and brief encounter, it seems, I have been offered and have accepted a Coke. I feel slightly nauseous and light-headed, certain it is the Coke and not the intense heat and humidity of the semi-tropical climate of southern Veracruz, Mexico. I rarely drink such sugary drinks. In fact, I even water down my juice at home. I grew up drinking mostly water and skim milk due to living with parents who had the resources to implement what they understood to be healthy food choices for the family. But I am trying to be a good anthropologist, respecting people and developing relationships by gratefully accepting what is offered. And the truth is, I *am* grateful for the cold drinks, the welcoming conversation, and the few minutes to sit by an electric fan. I'm struggling both with the climate and the shock of actually starting fieldwork.

In these first few weeks in the field, I struggle with my choices to drink or not drink a Coke, plagued by the feeling that I am harming my body irrevocably and by the fear that I will lose my tenuous relationships with people if I refuse the sweating glass of dark, sugary liquid. I am certain that I can feel the ill effects of Coke immediately on my teeth and in my stomach. At the same time, I nearly always hope that the woman I am interviewing will send one of her children or grandchildren to the corner store to buy a cold two-liter bottle of some soft drink. Without refrigeration in most houses, the purified water from the large jugs sitting in the kitchen is often warm and less than refreshing—a fundamental characteristic of Coca-Cola if one takes heed of the advertising. In some houses, even that jug is missing because it costs 20 pesos and delivery generally only happens once every few days. Coke quickly becomes a symbol of tension and frustration, as well as relief, for me.

This reflection on Coca-Cola as a medium of interaction and mechanism of relief, while also being a particularly insidious point of tension during my fieldwork, serves as an entry point to a much broader and intricate connection among public health, corporations, and community. But it is also not static. As I stayed longer in the field, my relationship to Coca-Cola began to change. Although I still disliked the sticky sweetness that lingered on my teeth after drinking a Coke, my stomach adjusted, and I began to crave it after a long, hot day of wandering around town seeking interviews and dropping in at people's homes. The oppressive heat and humidity sapped my energy, and my body seemed to now be telling me that the sugar and caffeine-filled beverage that I knew would be awaiting me at the next interview was, in fact, just what I needed.

I found myself trying to rationalize my choice to accept another Coke rather than ask for water, but I was also learning that the rules of being a respectful guest were more flexible than I first believed. I told myself that it would be impolite to decline the Coke (not true, as I had done it before with no negative repercussions and had seen other people do it as well). I also rationalized the amount I was drinking: I don't drink it very much, so one won't hurt (also no longer true, as I was now regularly drinking at least one a day). As I continued to reflect on my changing relationship to soft drinks after returning from the field, I realized that I had internalized the public health message that Coke is bad for you. It rots your teeth and gives you diabetes. It is full of empty calories, and a *good* person (read: intelligent, responsible, health-conscious person) would always choose the (usually) readily available purified water instead.

In this chapter, I take my own experience with navigating the complexities of consuming Coca-Cola and other soft drinks as a starting point to examine the conflicting roles that such drinks played in the lives of women in Los Cañales, Veracruz, Mexico—where I conducted my anthropological fieldwork during 15 non-consecutive months from 2007-2009. I argue that in order to understand the seeming conflict between women's recognition of the health consequences of drinking soft drinks and continued extensive use of them, one must move beyond simple notions of non-compliance, fatalism, and lack of proper education. Instead, a broader understanding of health and well-being that includes conceptions of respect, enjoyment, safety, and sociality in the context of a lack of resources to maintain healthy diets is necessary.

Coca-Cola in the Field: A Selected Review of Literature

I am certainly not the first social scientist to be concerned with understanding and analyzing the conflicting roles of Coca-Cola and other soft drinks in local communities. Anthropologists and sociologists in particular have examined Coca-Cola as a symbol of globalization, a metaphor for life practices, experiences, and values, and as the product of a transnational company that at the very least turns a blind eye to violent and destructive practices in countries outside the United States. While I will reference these works and a few others written by journalists briefly in the discussion that follows, I am here looking at Coca-Cola more in the sense that anthropologist Daniel Miller (2002: 246) has examined it as a "meta-commodity"—"the term Coca-Cola comes to stand, not just for a particular soft drink," he says, "but also for the problematic nature of commodities in general."[1] I most directly draw on this positioning of Coca-Cola as a "meta-commodity" that has meaning far beyond its specificity as a soft drink in order to argue that Coca-Cola and other soft drinks are multi-valent and contradictory experiences in the daily lives of women in Los Cañales.

Therefore, I am not specifically looking at Coca-Cola in this chapter as a symbol of globalization or an example of global commodity chains as many others have done (although I also do not completely ignore this aspect). It certainly could be examined in that way in Los Cañales and other rural Mexican communities, but others have done this work articulately. Nor do I directly engage with the passionate research and activism focused on the Coca-Cola company's violations of human rights in places such as India (Aiyer 2007; Ghosh 2010; Raman 2007; Vedwan 2007), Colombia (Gill 2005, 2007, 2009), Guatemala (Frundt 1987), Mexico (Nash 2007) and other countries (see Rogers 2005). However, there is a link between these writings and actions and my own work in its focus on public health. I look at Coca-Cola as a public health symbol of bad choices and poor health. In the analysis below, I draw on the work above where it connects most directly to the arguments I make here.

The public health literature, parallel with the anthropological research, notes devastating impacts of the global reach of soft drinks like Coca-Cola. A selective review of recent research literature demonstrates links across a wide range of countries and social groups between soft drink consumption and type 2 diabetes (Basu, et al. 2013; Hu and Malik 2010; Malik et al. 2010; McNaughton et al. 2008; Vartanian, et al. 2007), obesity (Basu, et al. 2013; Hu and Malik 2010; Vartanian, et al. 2007; Zienczuk, et al. 2012), cardiovascular disease (Brown, et al. 2008), chronic kidney disease (Bomback, et al. 2010), toothache (Yuen, et al. 2011), and adolescent mental health problems (Lien, et al. 2006) among other issues.[2]

Obviously this immense amount of data leads public health professionals to develop programs to reduce soft drink consumption as part of a range of intervention strategies to promote healthier practices, reduce disease burden, and alleviate health disparities. What is often missing from these education, intervention, and prevention strategies is attention to the complex context within which soft drinks are consumed. In Los Cañales, as in many other Mexican communities, nurses from the public health center and the larger Mexican Social Security Institute (IMSS, by its initials in Spanish) clinic distribute brochures with sample daily menus to their patients who are trying to lose weight. While I was in the field, the nurses were actively pursuing a public health project called "*Vamos Por Un Millión de Kilos*" (Let's Go for a Million Kilos) sponsored by the Federal Ministry of Health. The program, as it played out on the ground in Los Cañales, involved participants reporting to the IMSS clinic weekly for a "weigh-in" and short discussion about dietary changes and exercise increases over the past week. The nurses recorded weight loss and added it to the total for the community (and presumably for the state as well once the records reached the higher levels of the IMSS administration.) At nearly every visit during which I was present, one of the first questions the nurses asked was how much the participant had reduced soft drink consumption during the week. Often the response indicated some reduction, but still generally high consumption. Also included were questions about the amount of fried food, pork, and desserts eaten during the past week, with little guidance about how to locate and prepare alternative, healthier foods.

In addition to sometimes narrowly conceived public health interventions, public health is increasingly a commodity bought and sold on a global market.[3] International health organizations sell public health as a solution to national and global problems. Locally-based organizations must show that they follow a particular model of public health in order to receive funding to provide health services even when they understand that local contexts do not support standard models of intervention. For example, in Mexico, families who live below the poverty line and who have not in the past qualified for health insurance are currently eligible for at least two poverty alleviation programs modeled after international guidelines for poverty reduction—*Oportunidades*[4] and *Seguro Popular*.[5] Together, these programs provide financial assistance and health insurance coverage to improve children's educational levels, maintain safe homes, and establish health protection. The programs are built on a model of *co-responsibility* in which families who receive the resources are required to engage in certain practices. In Los Cañales, these include agreeing to monthly reviews of household cleanliness by Ministry of Health staff, participation in neighborhood clean-up days, attendance at well-child check-ups, maintenance of vaccination cards for all family members, and participation in semi-regular public health meetings about such issues as rabies vaccinations for animals, household energy conservation techniques, personal hygiene, and preparation of healthy meals. While women in Los Cañales did express appreciation for what they learned and were able to access through these required activities, they also struggled to maintain their end of the bargain due to their multiple other responsibilities including paid work, household-related errands, and responsibilities with their children's schools.[6]

Los Cañales: Where My Struggle with Coke Began

In addition to these national programs, women in Los Cañales dealt with issues specific to their community. Los Cañales[7], Veracruz, Mexico is a mestizo sugar cane producing community with a population of approximately 5,000. Most community members are involved in some way with sugar cane production—growing it, harvesting it, or trucking it – although cattle ranching is a growing industry in the region. Much of the sugar that is eventually refined from their sugar cane is sold to soft drink companies. An increasingly polluted river runs through the center of the community, and women often use the river for washing clothes. As mentioned above, the climate is semi-tropical, meaning that temperatures during the summer were regularly over 90° F with very high humidity. Air conditioning was virtually non-existent given the high costs of electricity that few could afford. Electric fans, cold showers, and ice-cold soft drinks from small home-based corner stores were generally the only relief from the heat.

Two public health clinics, mentioned above, operate in the community—a clinic run by the IMSS and a clinic run by the Ministry of Health. In addition, many families in the community receive bi-monthly payments through the *Oportunidades* program as well as health insurance through the *Seguro Popular*. Both clinics and *Oportunidades* support public health campaigns at various times of the year. These campaigns include direct interventions, such as vaccinations, and education about the importance of a healthy diet.

While in the past, sugar cane growers were able to maintain relative financial stability through the combination of the sale of their crops to the regional processing plant and the resources provided through *Oportunidades*, in recent years payments from the plant have been reduced and less reliable. Transnational migration and increased economic instability have contributed to the fracturing of social networks as family members and friends can no longer provide to each other the assistance they once could. The data I analyze here comes from interviews with women in 75 separate households who experienced these conditions and participant observation in homes, community meetings and events, and health clinics.

In what follows, I primarily discuss Coca-Cola (or "Coke") specifically because this was generally the preferred drink when it was available. Because of its popularity, however, sometimes people had to settle for "lesser" soft drinks like Manzanita Sol (an apple-flavored soft drink also produced by The Coca-Cola Company), Sprite, and other soft drinks when Coca-Cola supplies ran out in local stores. As I will discuss further below, many women perceived these lighter-colored soft drinks to be less health damaging, but the dark-colored soda in the red and white bottle was more sought after. I also use the term "Coke" as it was used in my own community growing up. Asking someone if he or she would like a "Coke" did not necessarily mean specifically a Coca-Cola. Instead, it was a gloss for any soft drink. This use of the term draws attention to Coca-Cola's status as a global, invasive, but also dramatically successful commodity (Falk 1991; Foster 2008; Pendergrast 2000).

Coca-Cola as Facilitator of Social Networking

Visiting is a common practice in Los Cañales. Men and women alike spend a significant amount of time in other people's houses, particularly in the heat of the afternoon. Patricia's house is a good example of the activity of visiting. I worked closely with her throughout the course of fieldwork, interviewing her several times and spending entire days with her to understand the rhythms of her daily life. Her afternoon visitors frequently included her sister, her daughter and son-in-law with their two children,[8] and two friends of the family who regularly traveled through the town. If she had cash on hand, she would send one of her grandchildren[9] to the store to buy a two-liter, ice-cold Coke and serve it to the guests.

Although she did not directly express a strategic use of soft drinks to facilitate these social relationships, it could certainly be interpreted to function in that way. Guests lingered over their cold drinks as they caught up with Patricia. They offered her much needed emotional support given her particularly difficult situation. In addition to caring for her older daughter's two children, she was also concerned about her younger daughter's advancing kidney disease and need for dialysis. She feared that her husband was having an affair because he found her unattractive in her older age due to her struggles with obesity and diabetes. She was frustrated and concerned with her own health status. She had a constant pain in one knee that she thought was a result of sporadically treated diabetes, and she often alluded to the fact that her own mother had to have her leg amputated due to complications from the disease.

Perhaps Coke was part of the reason for Patricia's struggles, as she and other women well understood. However, in her current life context, Coke served as a tool to facilitate communication, friendship, and emotional support. Like Patricia, many women I interviewed in Los Cañales strategically worked to smooth disrupted social connections, maintain supportive relationships, and develop new friendships—sometimes consciously, sometimes unconsciously. This visiting practice, facilitated by the refreshing presence of Coke, was essential to many women's sense of well-being, although it was also at odds with public health messages and women's recognition of community-wide chronic health issues.

Coca-Cola as a "Safer" Choice

Diabetes is prevalent in Los Cañales, and women are quite concerned about their own health status, particularly as they see older members of their families suffering from diabetes-related complications. They are also concerned for the health of their children, among whom obesity is on the rise. On the other hand, soda bought from the store may be more reliably "clean" than the water women buy in large jugs. A commonly understood public health message was that the only safe drinking water in the community was that bought from purifying plants in large jugs or that which had been boiled for at least 15 minutes prior to use.

Boiling water was either too expensive or too labor intensive for many women. Boiling water on the gas stove that most women had in their homes required a significant amount of gas that was often carefully rationed for use in cooking food. Gas is distributed in tanks that households trade in for new tanks when they are empty. At the time of my research, a small tank of gas cost approximately US$20, equivalent to a monthly salary for some families. For most families, one of these tanks lasted two weeks to one month. Once the gas ran out, people had to cook over open fires, for which they had to gather firewood often located at some distance from the household in the outskirts of town. Women often chose to cook certain items—like beans—over an open fire even when gas was available in order to save the gas for foods that took less time to cook. In an already strained system, boiling water for 15 minutes was not an option for many – leaving them with the option to buy purified water.

During the course of my fieldwork, many women also reported that one must make careful choices of water distributors, only buying from those who are trustworthy. Stories circulated about distributors who refilled jugs not with purified water, but instead with tap or well water that is considered unhealthy to drink. They resealed the lids and sold the water as "purified." Men and women explained to me how to detect a resealed jug by carefully inspecting the plastic cap for evidence of tampering before removing it. Even after determining the safety of water bought from a particular distributor, jugs were sometimes hard to come by. One either waited for the (usually) young boy to arrive at the house carting full jugs of water on a tricycle outfitted with a small trailer for the purpose or went to the distributor's home or place of business to pick up new jugs of water. In either case, one could not depend on either distributor or water being available, particularly during the rainy season when roads could be washed out and tricycles could not always function. Buying soda instead of water was at least sometimes safer and more readily available, although more expensive, which complicates a simplistic notion that soda is categorically bad for your physical health.

Coca-Cola as Enjoyment

The issue is not just about physical health however. The World Health Organization, in the 1978 Alma Ata Declaration, asserts the need for a broader definition of health to encompass mental and social well-being as well as physical health. Looking at health from this perspective, Coca-Cola—if considered as a small bit of pleasure in what is often an economically, physically, and emotionally difficult life—can contribute to, rather than diminish overall health.[10] When I asked women why they continued to buy and drink soda even though they were aware of the potential negative health effects, they often argued that in the context of a life where enjoyment is sometimes difficult to find, it just feels good to sit out on the porch on a hot day and drink a cold soda. Why not cold water? Many women I interviewed did not have refrigerators, so if they wanted cold drinks, they had to buy them from stores that had refrigeration capacity. Most of those stores did not keep water in the refrigerated areas, saving space for the more desirable and profitable cold Coke. As my own experience illustrates, a cold drink is particularly enjoyable when the weather is hot and humid—the norm for Los Cañales.

Coca-Cola as Respect

Women also used Coca-Cola as a way of honoring guests either at parties or home visits. Sharing a Coke with a guest instead of water (or even "lesser" soft drinks like Fanta) establishes or maintains social relationships that may be essential in any number of situations, including a future health crisis. Coke is more difficult to find in the local stores than Fanta, sharing Coke with a guest requires that someone make a trip to locate and buy the Coke rather than just filling up a glass with water from the jug in the kitchen (if water is available), and buying Coke involves a visible financial investment in the visit. Therefore, sharing Coke maintains the social status of the host and ties (or re-ties) the guest into a social relationship through a socially meaningful gift.[11]

During the course of fieldwork, I attended countless graduation and birthday parties at which food and drink were always served. In some houses, only soft drinks were offered due to Protestant religious affiliation that banned the use of alcoholic drinks. In others, there was a choice between beer and soft drinks. Although a few women accepted a single beer at these functions, most opted for soft drinks which they also served to their children. I never attended a party that lacked the two-liter bottles of soft drinks quickly passed around the tables and drained. When I planned my own party at the end of fieldwork to thank the women who participated in my research and report some preliminary results and next steps to them, I felt the impulse to serve what I considered to be more healthy drink choices. The two women helping me plan the party insisted that women in the community would think I was being disrespectful and "cheap" rather than looking out for their health if I did not serve Coca-Cola.

Coca-Cola as Disease-Inducing Substance

Although Coca-Cola flowed through daily life in Los Cañales, women who participated in my research had clearly heard the public health messages about the dangers of drinking high-sugar beverages like Coca-Cola. Many had also experienced health consequences that they directly linked to soft drink consumption. Women's knowledge and understanding of best practices for improved health outcomes was extensive and generally accurately reflected the messages they received from nurses and other health professionals in the community. They clearly articulated the connections between "poor" eating habits and health consequences, particularly diabetes and kidney disease. Both of these diseases are prevalent in the community according to the biomedical practitioners I interviewed during fieldwork. In most of my interviews women had either experienced these diseases themselves or had a close family member who had been diagnosed with one of them. The major public health message about Coke that I heard during participant observation in local health clinics was to replace soft drinks with healthier choices such as water or lightly-sweetened *"agua de sabor"* (a drink made from mixing water and sugar with freshly squeezed or blended fruit). When I asked women what they did to prevent disease, this particular message was often the first one they discussed. For example, Brigida responded that she drank water or *"agua de sabor"* instead of soft drinks because there are high rates of diabetes in the community, which sugary drinks can cause (Brigida, Interview 2). Nanci also recognized that drinking too many soft drinks could result in kidney problems for both children and adults (Nanci, Interview 2). She suggested that one of the reasons that adults needed to drink fewer soft drinks was to encourage children to also change their habits. She planned to lower the amount of soft drinks her family consumed until she had completely eliminated them from the family's diet (Nanci, Interview 2). (And in fact, Ursula and Vetsaida had to stop giving their sons soft drinks because they had developed kidney disease and were often sick [Ursula, Interview 1; Vetsaida Interview Notes].)

Often, the message of replacing soft drinks with healthier drinks was embedded in a broader understanding of healthy consumption. Zenia said in response to my question about why there are high rates of diabetes in the community,

> *because we drink a lot of Coke, a lot of high-calorie things, sweets. [The doctor] says: "in place of ... drinking soft drinks, better an orange juice, hibiscus tea (actually an "agua de sabor"), plain water, that is better for you. Don't eat much red meat, better fish, chicken, eggs, cheese, and milk. And fruit, all kinds of fruit. And vegetables, chard, spinach, beets, lettuce, broccoli—things that have a lot of iron"* (Zenia, Interview 1).

These understandings were echoed by many women in different ways, including in terms of their discussions of controlling existing disease (Sonia, Interview 1; Yolanda, Interview 1; and see below).

Some women had also been prescribed special diets by doctors in order to control different diseases, not limited to diabetes. Jomi, for example explained the diet recommended by her doctor for the hepatitis and rheumatism with which she had recently been diagnosed. Her list of banned foods included high-fat meats, whole milk, chocolate, coffee, soft drinks, and canned food. Eating these foods, she said, would cause inflammation of her liver and joints and worsen her disease (Jomi, Interview 2). Although Jomi did not specify which soft drinks she should stop consuming, other women highlighted the greater health consequences of "dark" soft drinks like Coca-Cola and Pepsi compared with the "light" soft drinks like Sprite.[12] "Dark" soft drinks were understood to be more likely to cause kidney damage, a perception shared by at least one nurse in the community who conveyed that message regularly to her patients.

The messages women received about the negative effects of soft drinks were often reinforced by illness experiences. For example, Epifania told me that she suffered from colitis (inflammation of the colon and/or large intestine that sometimes also includes ulcers in the large intestine lining), and she said that when she drank soft drinks she felt that her stomach was boiling inside because of the carbonation in the drink in combination with her disease (Epifania, Interview 2). She informed me that I would not find a single healthy person in the community because everyone had kidney problems at the very least from drinking too many soft drinks, sometimes drinking *only* soft drinks (Epifania, Interview 2). While fear of developing these diseases may contribute to such overreporting, health statistics for the state of Veracruz confirm high rates. In 2000, the national rate of diabetes was 10.7 percent, but in Veracruz, it was 16.1 percent (PAHO 2010). There is no national registry for chronic kidney disease in Mexico. However, research suggests links between diabetes, obesity, and poverty and risk for chronic kidney disease. As diabetes and obesity rates rise in Mexico, it is likely that chronic kidney disease will also increase (Paniagua et al. 2007).

Although women had these kinds of negative experiences, they often communicated an inability or unwillingness to completely cut soft drinks out of their diets, often because of the more positive experiences with soft drinks that I described above. Nanci, discussing her experiences with gastritis, said that nothing she ate would stay down. She vomited everything. Pepsi, in particular, felt hot in her stomach, and she was convinced the soft drink was actually burning her inside. She felt progressively worse until her husband took her to the doctor. The doctor informed her that her gastritis was advanced and recommended that she stop consuming spicy foods, soft drinks, tomato, lime, and anything acidic. She has now recovered and eats and drinks everything including soft drinks (Nanci, Interview 2). Noemi similarly connected her heavy soft drink consumption to her frequent illnesses that included kidney pain. She said that she couldn't stop drinking soft drinks because she had been doing so for so many years (Noemi, Interview 1). Patricia also struggled with restricting her diet. She had diabetes and felt that there was no remedy for her disease. She understood that she could control it through maintaining a strict diet and taking the medication prescribed by the doctor. But, she said, *"sometimes I don't watch [my diet], that's the prob-*

lem that makes my sugar rise. Why? Because sometimes I take my little soft drink, and I can't drink soft drinks" (Patricia, Interview 2). Katia spoke of her husband's "*addiction*" to Coke in a similar way. At the time of my research, he was bed-ridden and in the last stages of kidney disease. Katia blamed his illness on Pepsi. Prior to falling ill, Katia reported that he would work all day in the fields without taking water to drink. Then he, like many other farmers, would return to the house tired and want a Pepsi—not water. The heat and exhaustion called for the coolness and caffeine in the soft drink rather than the warm, tasteless water that had been sitting in a jug on the porch all day (Katia, Interview 1). Patricia, Noemi, Katia, and other women talked about drinking Coke as an impossible-to-break habit. However this habit is constantly reinforced by the social usefulness of the drink in terms of developing relationships and the more general sense of well-being that a cold, carbonated drink can invoke on a very hot day.

Non-Compliance or Expanded Enactment of Well-Being?

Women are not "non-compliant" patients willfully ignoring sound health care advice, nor are they lacking in knowledge and understanding of the connections between diet and disease. Instead, they are agents who work strategically, emotionally, and perceptually to construct the best lives they can for themselves—lives that encompass a broad notion of well-being rather than a narrow biomedical one. Rather than viewing the women I worked with as "non-compliant" with public health messages or uneducated about their bodies, I argue that their actions are better understood as complex negotiations that require navigation of sometimes contradictory messages of health care staff, family and community, and their pocketbooks in order to sustain particular values about life, friendship and social status. They embody what one might consider a "contradictory consciousness" (Gramsci 1990) that must hold together their concerns about their current and future health and their concerns about their social networks and sense of well-being. By expanding the analysis of women's complex relationships to food in this particular case of Coca-Cola and other soft drinks, I also argue that this case contributes to operationalizing what has long been a standard definition of health outlined by the World Health Organization in the Alma Ata Declaration of 1978: health is "a state of complete physical, mental and social well-being, and not merely the absence of disease or infirmity." By doing so, this analysis shows the contributions that anthropological work on the social meanings of food can make to reconceptualizing how we might "do" public health.

The public health message equates certain choices deemed healthy with overall *better* choices and assumes that they are easy and desirable choices. It follows that those who opt for Coke are making bad choices and are therefore *bad* people – lacking in self-control, lazy, uncaring, apathetic, self-serving, etc. And these bad people will have to pay for their bad choices by dealing with rotting teeth, obesity, and diabetes. It's hard for me to break out of this kind of thinking myself, having grown up surrounded by it and having for the most part made the "better" choice throughout my life. However, there are other ways of thinking about the choices women in Los Cañales make. They *are* choices, as the women discussed here would readily agree, but they are choices that draw on a holistic vision of a life well lived rather than on a restricted vision of biological intervention.

The lens through which I view women's actions in relation to Coca-Cola consumption focuses explicitly on the complexity of the strategic and sensual choices people make to consume Coke and other sugary beverages in an attempt to challenge the "healthy choice equals good person" and its opposite rhetoric. This perspective is rooted in a critical public health and medical anthropology framework that argues that narrow understandings of health often lead to less-than-effective interventions to improve health outcomes. So, in this case, telling women that they should stop drinking and serving Coca-Cola in their homes in order to reduce instances of obesity, diabetes, and chronic kidney disease as well as to prevent their children from developing these health issues will not work because it assumes that women's choices are deliberately about poor health practices rather than about a different kind of health—social, communal, emotional.

Obesity, diabetes, and chronic kidney disease are serious health concerns in Los Cañales, and I do not mean to minimize them here. I also do not mean to demonize the public health nurses who work diligently in the community to address these and other health issues that at times seem to overwhelm the clinics and medical staff. For the most part, I observed a high level of care and concern for patients, albeit sometimes expressed as frustration. What I am arguing instead, following many critical medical anthropologists, is that food-related health planning and intervention will be more effective if it takes into account the multiple meanings of health as it relates to consumption rather than focusing narrowly on physical/biological health. Intervention should attend to women's agency and care for themselves and their families to co-develop with local communities more appropriate and achievable goals for well-being.

Acknowledgments

Research reported in this chapter was supported by a National Science Foundation Doctoral Dissertation Improvement Grant under Award Number 0752896 and a Fulbright program IIE grant. The content of this article is solely the responsibility of the author and does not necessarily represent the official views of the National Science Foundation.

Notes

1. Miller's argument focuses on meta-symbols as both part of material culture and as standing "for a debate about the materiality of culture." In that sense, his

argument goes beyond what I present in this chapter because I am here more interested in the materiality of experience and the consequences of engaging that experience than I am in developing theories of material culture.

2. Not all research supports significant relationships, however. See Janssen et al. (2005), who found links between lowered physical activity and obesity, but not soft drink consumption and obesity among adolescents and Pereira (2006), who found lack of rigor in many studies showing associations between increased soft drink consumption and higher rates of obesity.

3. This commoditization of public health underscores a similar expansionary process in the market for Coca-Cola, which actively seeks new markets as well as sources of ingredients like water, often at the expense of local populations (Aiyer 2010; Foster 2008; Pendergrast 2000).

4. The *Programa de Desarrollo Humano Oportunidades* (Program for Human Development "Opportunities," commonly known as *Oportunidades*) is a federal poverty alleviation program that focuses on education, health, nutrition, and income. It is an inter-institutional program that includes the Ministry of Public Education, the Ministry of Health, the Mexican Social Security Institute, the Ministry of Social Development, and the state and municipal governments. To be enrolled in the program, household income must fall below the official poverty line.

5. *Seguro Popular* is a sliding-scale federal health insurance program administered through Mexico's Ministry of Health. Families falling within the bottom two deciles in terms of income and who do not have access to other health insurance are eligible to enroll free of charge. Enrollment includes access to approximately 250 health interventions for the most commonly occurring health issues.

6. These programs and women's struggles with them are discussed in more detail in Scott 2010.

7. The name of the town as well as all research participant names are pseudonyms.

8. This daughter and her two children later moved in with Patricia due to the daughter's need for assistance with home dialysis.

9. These grandchildren were another daughter's children. They lived with Patricia because the daughter and her husband were working in Ciudad Juarez and did not feel comfortable with the child care facilities available in the city.

10. I should point out here that I recognize, as noted in the literature review, that soft drinks like Coca-Cola contribute to devastating health issues for women and that soft drink companies have been at the very least complicit in violations of human rights. The argument here is not meant to counter these important and valid critiques of an invasive and damaging industry, but rather to challenge the effectiveness of simplistic public health messages that do not take into account these alternative experiences with "unhealthy" foods.

11. This use of Coca-Cola in social rituals is also reflected in anthropological work on the substitution of alcohol with Coca-Cola in religious rituals in indigenous communities in Mexico (see Nash 2007).

12. Miller notes a similar distinction based on soft drink color among Trinidadians, although the meanings of the color are somewhat different. In Trinidad, the "red" sweet drinks symbolize a more traditional (but also East Indian) drink. This drink is considered to have higher sugar content. "The Indian population is also generally supposed to be particularly fond of sugar and sweet products and this in

turn is supposed to relate to their entry into Trinidad largely as indentured labourers in the sugar cane fields. They are also supposed to have a high rate of diabetics which folk wisdom claims to be a result of their overindulgence of these preferences" (254). The "black" sweet drink is most commonly associated with the mixed drink rum and Coke. But it is also consumed by itself (254-255).

Bibliography

Aiyer, Ananthakrishnan. 2007. "The Allure of the Transnational: Notes on Some Aspects of the Political Economy of Water in India." *Cultural Anthropology* 22, no. 4: 640-658.

Basu, Sanjay, Martin McKee, Gauden Galea, and David Stuckler. 2013. "Relationship of Soft Drink Consumption to Global Overweight, Obesity, and Diabetes: A Cross-National Analysis of 75 Countries." *American Journal of Public Health* 103, no. 11: 2071-2077.

Bomback, Andrew S., Vimal K. Derebail, David A. Shoham, Cheryl A. Anderson, Lyn M. Steffen, Wayne D. Rosamond, and Abhijit V. Kshirsagar. 2009. "Sugar-Sweetened Soda Consumption, Hyperuricemia, and Kidney Disease." *Kidney International* 77: 609-616.

Brown, C.M., A.G. Dulloo, and J-P Montani. 2008. "Sugary Drinks in the Pathogenesis of Obesity and Cardiovascular Diseases." *International Journal of Obesity* 32: S28-S34.

Falk, Pasi. 1991. "Coke is it!" *Cambridge Anthropology* 15, no. 1: 46-55.

Foster, Robert J. 2008. *Coca-Globalization: Following Soft Drinks from New York to New Guinea.* New York: Palgrave Macmillan.

Frundt, Henry J. 1987. *Refreshing Pauses: Coca-Cola and Human Rights in Guatemala.* New York: Praeger.

Ghosh, Bishnupriya. 2010. "Looking through Coca-Cola: Global Icons and the Popular." *Public Culture* 22, no. 2: 332-368.

Gill, Lesley. 2005. "Labor and Human Rights: 'The Real Thing' in Colombia." *Transforming Anthropology* 13, no. 2: 110-115.

————. 2007. "'Right There With You': Coca-Cola, Labor Restructuring and Political Violence in Colombia." *Critique of Anthropology* 27, no. 3: 235-260.

————. 2009. "The Limits of Solidarity: Labor and Transnational Organizing against Coca-Cola." *American Ethnologist* 36, no. 4: 667-680.

Gramsci, Antonio. 1990. "Culture and Ideological Hegemony." In *Culture and Society: Contemporary Debates,* edited by Jeffrey C. Alexander and Steven Seidman, 47-54. Cambridge: Cambridge University Press.

Hu, Frank B., and Vasanti S. Malik. 2010. "Sugar-sweetened Beverages and Risk of Obesity and Type 2 Diabetes: Epidemiologic Evidence." *Physiology & Behavior* 100: 47-74.

Janssen, I., P.T. Katzmarzyk, W.F. Boyce, C. Vereecken, C. Mulvihill, C. Roberts, C. Currie, W. Pickett, and The Health Behaviour in School-Aged Children Obesity Working Group. 2005. "Comparison of Overweight and Obesity Prevalence in School-Aged Youth from 34 Countries and their Relationships with Physical Activity and Dietary Patterns." *Obesity Reviews* 6: 123-132.

Lien, Lars, Nanna Lien, Sonja Heyerdahl, Magne Thoresen, and Espen Bjertness. 2006. "Consumption of Soft Drinks and Hyperactivity, Mental Distress, and Conduct

Problems Among Adolescents in Oslo, Norway." *American Journal of Public Health* 96, no. 10: 1815-1820.

Malik, Vasanti S., Barry M. Popkin, George A. Bray, Jean-Pierre Després, Walter C. Willett, and Frank B. Hu. 2010. "Sugar-sweetened Beverages and Risk of Metabolic Syndrome and Type 2 Diabetes." *Diabetes Care* 33, no. 11: 2477-2483.

McNaughton, Sarah A., Gita D. Mishra, and Eric J. Brunner. 2008. "Dietary Patterns, Insulin Resistance, and Incidence of Type 2 Diabetes in the Whitehall II Study." *Diabetes Care* 31, no. 7: 1343-1348.

Miller, Daniel. 2002. "Coca-Cola: A Black Sweet Drink from Trinidad." In *The Material Culture Reader*, edited by Victor Buchli, 245-263. Oxford: Berg.

Nash, June. 2007. "Consuming Interests: Water, Rum, and Coca-Cola from Ritual Propitiation to Corporate Expropriation in Highland Chiapas." *Cultural Anthropology* 22, no. 4: 621-639.

Pan American Health Organization. 2010. *Veracruz Initiative for Diabetes Awareness (VIDA) Final Report*. Washington DC: Pan American Health Organization.

Paniagua, Ramón, Alfonso Ramos, Rosaura Fabian, Jesús Lagunas, and Dante Amato. 2007. "Chronic Kidney Disease and Dialysis in Mexico." *Peritoneal Dialysis International* 27: 405-409.

Pendergrast, Mark. 2000. *For God, Country, and Coca-Cola: The Definitive History of the Great American Soft Drink and the Company that Makes It*. New York: Basic Books.

Pereira, M.A. 2006. "The Possible Role of Sugar-Sweetened Beverages in Obesity Etiology: A Review of the Evidence." *International Journal of Obesity* 30: S28-S36.

Raman, K. Ravi. 2007. "Community-Coca-Cola Interface: Political-Anthropological Concerns on Corporate Social Responsibility." *Social Analysis* 51, no. 3: 103-120.

Rogers, Ray. 2006. "Campaign to Stop Killer Coke." *North American Dialogue* 9, no. 2: 1-3.

Scott, Mary Alice. 2010. "Y La Mujer Se Va Pa'bajo: Women's Health at the Intersections of Nationality, Class, and Gender." PhD Dissertation; University of Kentucky.

Secretaría de Desarrollo Social (Mexico). "¿Quienes Somos?" SEDESOL. http://www.oportunidades.gob.mx/Wn_Quienes_Somos/index.html (accessed January 5, 2010).

Vartanian, Lenny R., Marlene B. Schwartz, and Kelly D. Brownell. 2007. "Effects of Soft Drink Consumption on Nutrition and Health: A Systematic Review and Meta-Analysis." *American Journal of Public Health* 97, no. 4: 667-675.

Vedwan, Neeraj. 2007. "Pesticides in Coca-Cola and Pepsi: Consumerism, Brand Image, and Public Interest in Globalizing India." *Cultural Anthropology* 22, no. 4: 659-684.

World Health Organization. 1978. "Declaration of Alma Ata," *World Health Organization*, http://www.who.int/publications/almaata_declaration_en.pdf (accessed December 18, 2013).

Yuen, Hon K., Ryan E. Wiegand, Elizabeth G. Hill, Kathryn M. Magruder, Elizabeth H. Slate, Carlos F. Salinas, and Steven D. London. 2011. "Factors Associated with Toothache among African American Adolescents Living in Rural South Carolina." *Social Work in Public Health* 26: 695-707.

Zienczuk, Natalia, T. Kue Young, Zhirong R. Cao, and Grace M. Egeland. 2012. "Dietary Correlates of an At-risk BMI among Inuit Adults in the Canadian High Arctic: Cross-Sectional International Polar Year Inuit Health Survey, 2007-2008." *Nutrition Journal* 11, no. 1: 73-81.

CHAPTER 10

"Women not like they used to be": Food and Modernity in Rural Newfoundland

Lynne Phillips

Introduction

Change in the way people measure themselves reflects a kind of cultural reform. I am interested in how new identities come into being and the power through which they emerge—thinking of power as something more diffuse than just the power of governments or corporations to enforce change. There are myriad ways in which identities can be made and unmade, including through institutions, expertise, and their tools of calculation. I am particularly interested in what impact changing identities can have on how we think about our food system. What is considered appropriate/modern or backward/ignorant ways to produce and consume food? What is thought of as enough food, or good food or bad food to consume? These questions refer to ideas that tend to be closely tied to our identities—to who we think we are—and to our habits and general conduct.

While modern ways of measuring who we think we and others are (or are not) have been around for some time, the mid-twentieth century is a particularly apt time for observing late modern changes in gender identity and their connections with food. The hopeful post-WWII period, ripe with ideas about progress and a better future, included notions not just of how much and what kind of food we should be eating but of what kind of women and men ought to be producing, buying, cooking and eating it.

The late modern period mobilized women as bound to the responsibilities of family care and good consumption and housekeeping. David Goodman and Michael Redclift's book, *Refashioning Nature* (1991), was one of the few to note this shift in women's work and identity as part of the emerging agro-industrial complex in North America, a complex that relied on a very different system of food production and diet than the classic family farm. The authors usefully identified the connections between, for example, the purchase of white goods (microwave ovens, freezers) and the emergence of frozen and "fast" foods that accommodated both new working conditions and new markets for agro-industry. Discursively, it was also a model that aimed to eliminate food insecurity in the world, though critics now point to its role in *increasing* food insecurity by jettisoning customary food production and promoting unhealthy eating patterns. Yet little analytical room has been given to understanding women's agency in this transformation. Indeed a convenient functional fit is assumed between the needs of late modern agriculture and the emergence of the modern woman as good housewife and caregiver.

Keeping in mind contemporary food security issues, in this chapter I unravel changing food and gender identities by focusing on mid-twentieth century rural Newfoundland.[1] Newfoundland's history challenges the idea of a modernizing agricultural system determining new notions of womanhood at the same time that it hints at rural women's participation in effecting an identity that enabled new forms of food calculation. This case helps us to understand the "modern" as a multi-faceted concept, its promotion producing contradictions and unintended consequences for women and for food security.[2]

Gendering Supplementary Agriculture

Newfoundland reluctantly became Canada's most easterly province in 1949. Before joining Canada, the island of Newfoundland was a country, though a colonial state and then a British Dominion until 1949. Throughout colonial and post-colonial rule, Newfoundland's economy has largely been dependent upon fish. For hundreds of years, poor and indebted fishing families gave the fish they caught to merchants in exchange for goods such as flour, tea, sugar, spices, condensed milk and molasses. Unlike most other parts of the world, then, when Newfoundlanders employ the term "rural" they mean fishing communities, not agricultural communities. But agriculture was not unimportant to their lives; most of the rural population was located in isolated coves, far from transportation routes or markets, and they were dependent on the land and the sea to make ends meet. Work on the land was primarily women's work: while the men fished, the women kept their eye on the fish drying on "flakes" on land and they gardened and raised animals—horses for farm work and transport, goats for milk and sheep for wool. They stored vegetables over the winter—potatoes, carrots, turnips, beets, cabbage, onions—in distinctive root cellars that can still be found throughout the Island.

For anyone interested in agriculture in fish-dominated Newfoundland, a good starting point is what in Newfoundland termed "supplementary agriculture." Supplementary agriculture (also known as home gardening, kitchen gardening, vegetable gardening, subsistence horticulture and small-scale agriculture) may be the most debated food-related concept in twentieth century New-Newfoundland, if we leave fish aside. Reviewing the available literature on Newfoundland during the 1940s-1960s period, one is never sure what to make of supplementary agriculture: is it a protector or saboteur of rural households? Has it disappeared or is it still "the most extensive and important type of agriculture in Newfoundland" (DMR-A1953 p. 28)?

Many would argue that supplementary agriculture has been a savior for fishing families. For example, Hilda Chaulk Murray titled her book on women's lives in outport Newfoundland *More Than 50%* because women worked long days undertaking supplementary but essential tasks for the household, not only taking on the land-based work related to the fishery (and occasionally fishing themselves) but keeping gardens, canning, baking, berry picking, knitting and tending animals to support the family. Both women and men viewed this work as essential for rural household survival (Chaulk Murray 2010; see also Porter 1995; Cadigan 2002).

But, at other times, supplementary agriculture in Newfoundland is viewed as detrimental to agricultural progress, as an inhibitor of more profitable forms of food production. The 1955 *Newfoundland Royal Commission on Agriculture* devotes an entire chapter to "Supplementary versus Commercial Agriculture," concluding that supporting the former is too expensive (extension to outport communities would cost too much), too risky (it could reduce the time spent on fishing) and "would really be an attempt to place a brake in the path of economic progress" (Province of Newfoundland 1956, 71). From this perspective, combining fishing and agriculture, as did fishing-farming households, is impractical, unappealing and inefficient. One should be a commercial fisher *or* a commercial farmer.

Still others think that supplementary agriculture does not exist, as in the case when observers (including states) refuse to "see" it despite its presence (Scott 1998). This view applies to people who think only of fish when they recall Newfoundland's past. But perhaps more importantly, supplementary agriculture is also the elephant in the room when governments or government consultants talk about the importance of commercial food and animal production as though no other forms of agriculture exist in the province. Silence about the ubiquitous presence of supplementary agriculture signals a kind of (androcentric) governance at work: it marks supplementary agriculture as an invalid form of food production and women's work in it as immaterial.

Supplementary agriculture is similar, then, to a more familiar term in the literature: subsistence production. Subsistence agriculture is a marginalized food system in the context of modern capitalism that has enabled poor folks all over the world to survive (Nash 2009). Indeed it was this image of supplementary agriculture that I had in mind when I read Whitaker's assessment of small-scale agriculture in 11 communities in post-Confederation Newfoundland (Whitaker 1963). This report was the product of an ARDA (Agricultural Rehabilitation and Development Administration, a Federal-Provincial collaboration) request for "factual data on the decline of small-scale gardening in Newfoundland" (Whitaker 1963, no page). It is worth noting the lack of clarity around terms. The report is also referred to as a "survey of *agricultural* decline" and it is stated that: "the actual distinction between kitchen gardens and vegetable production in general was not clear. This was not fully realized until after the survey" (Whitaker 1963, 77-8, my emphasis). Despite this limitation, the findings of the research are intriguing.

Whitaker's interviewers asked comparative questions about food production, using 1949 (Confederation) as the temporal marker. Summarizing the results in the 11 selected communities, the study confirms a decrease in small-scale agricultural production since 1949 (a perception of a decline had instigated the study in the first place); agricultural practices in most communities had changed very little, despite attempts to modernize agriculture on the Island throughout the first half of the twentieth century;[3] and rural women were withdrawing from vegetable gardening. What is surprising are the explanations offered for women's departure from this work: modern women, it seems, did not garden.

By 1963 in Deadman's Bay, for example, it was harder to make ends meet through fishing, and many of the men were looking to either lumber work or unemployment insurance (UI)—not agriculture—as a source of financial support. There was no evidence of the commercialization of agriculture. Of the 18 women interviewed in this community, all but one said that women were gardening "less than they used to" before Confederation. Why? Here is a selection of their explanations (Whitaker 1963, 118):[4]

> *"Times have changed, [there is] a more modern outlook."*
> *"Didn't know better years ago..."*
> *"Don't have to today"*
> *"Women not like they used to be."*
> *"[Women are] stylish and proud."*
> *"[Women] Just won't do it."*

There is clear reference here to new ideas about what woman should and should not be doing. That the women "didn't know better" in the past indicates that the "modern outlook" has taught them a lesson—that there is another life one could be living. Yet little change was occurring in agriculture here—as evidenced by the lack of modern equipment such as tractors, commercial inputs such as seeds and fertilizer, or a market-based orientation to crop production. This community had to have explained to them that it was possible to use commercial fertilizer instead of the traditional kelp or capelin as fertilizer. But for the women in the community, times had changed, and they did not sound at all like Chaulk Murray's "more than 50 percent" women.

Flat Bay, on the west coast of Newfoundland, is another case in point. According to this study (Whitaker 1963, 141-42), women were doing less garden work there because:

"There is no longer any need for the work"
"Modernization has affected the women's outlook to this work"
"Don't know why"
"[women are] too lazy"
"[women are] too independent"
"[women are] not interested"
"women are concerned more with their appearance today"
"women do not have the same energy"

Fascinating responses! Yet, the explanations for women's withdrawal from supplementary agriculture are not given the analytical attention they are due. While it is admirable that the interviewers in this 1963 report spent time learning about women's work (a rare occurrence in the agricultural literature), there is no attempt to explore further how women may have been the source of the decline in supplementary agriculture. Consternation regarding Newfoundland's stagnant agriculture continued. Meanwhile rural women were apparently in the process of embracing a new identity—one that distanced them from the image of the hardworking food producer.

The rest of this chapter focuses on this juxtaposition of "modern" rural women and what was considered "backward" agriculture by the provincial and federal governments in 1963. To explain this apparent paradox I identify some specific features of the Newfoundland landscape, keeping in mind how the economic and cultural reforms envisioned by others have shaped rural women's engagement with the "modern outlook."

Explaining the Paradox

Economic and Infrastructural Changes

There are some important political-economic circumstances that have undoubtedly played a role in the gender-food relationships I describe above. For example, by 1963 the fishing industry had changed. The development of the frozen fish industry decreased the demand for land-based activities undertaken by wives and children. Some women moved into the limited positions in the fish plants, paid work being an unusual opportunity for rural women (though generally they were paid at a lower wage than men). Clearly this kind of work meant these women would not be working in their gardens. But, interestingly, in general, families did not use the changes in the fishing industry—this severing of family labor from fishing with a more commercial approach to fishing—as an opportunity to expand gardens.

A partial explanation for the above point is a second important infrastructural feature: a commercial food distribution system was practically non-existent in Newfoundland. This was a long-standing problem. The *Newfoundland Journal of Commerce* said it best in 1947 (p. 8):

> Newfoundland is fully capable of producing all its needs in the common vegetable and the hardier fruits, [but] individualist attitude remains strong...This individualism is very marked in the area around St. John's where... country farmers each come to town, each in his own little horse cart or ford wagon, each selling to regular customers and each losing...time that could be spent farming.

Curiously, public markets did not develop in colonial Newfoundland, and a theme that persists well into the 1970s is the Island's poor food distribution system (Province of Newfoundland 1964; Crabb 1975a). It is one of the biggest concerns voiced by agricultural extension workers (known as Fieldmen, see below) who saw the potential of farming in the province consistently being thwarted by the lack of systematic marketing arrangements. It is unclear why this individualist orientation to marketing existed. Some blame it on Newfoundland's geography, a "land of broken topography and stony soils of low fertility" (DMR-A 1953, 28) that did little to inspire cooperative or centralized models. Others see it as a legacy of powerful segments of society preventing agriculture from becoming successful so that it did not compete with the fishing industry. But in either case, the inconsistent policies of Newfoundland's governments did not help to build trust in a food marketing system and individualist approaches prevailed.[5]

Finally, the expansion of a national road system, an important infrastructural symbol of modernity in Newfoundland, facilitated the distribution of imported food and undermined the prospects of local food producers. Throughout the twentieth century road building was seen to be important for Newfoundland's development, an island dominated by isolated communities more accessible by boat than by land. But Joey Smallwood, who pushed for Confederation and was the new province's first Premier in 1949, perhaps more than any other government leader understood that roads would help to govern autonomous communities and turn a fishing-based nation into the modern province he envisioned. While only $12 million was spent on roads between 1934-1949, Smallwood spent $467 million on roads between 1950 and 1965, excluding federal contributions (Rowe 1985). But becoming part of Canada in 1949 also meant that freight and customs tariffs were reduced or eliminated for Canadian products, and this loss of price protection, combined with transport development, meant more competition for local producers. In fact, the importation of food from the mainland became such a threat to local food production that "Buy Local" campaigns were launched in the 1950s.[6]

The sudden influx of imported food during the 1950s may explain the view, found in Whitaker's survey, that women "don't have to" work in gardening any more (Whitaker 1963, 118) or that "there is no longer any need" (Whitaker 1963, 141). Still, in most cases this is not the most significant reason given for women's decreased interest in gardening in the 1960s. For example, in Bell-burns of Whitaker's study, where a road came in the previous year, it was said that fewer women were gardening, not because of the availability of vegetables to purchase, but because of "the vanity that came with modern living" (Whitaker 1963, 18).

Becoming Modern: Cultural Reforms

While the above economic and infrastructural features are important for under-standing the changing Newfoundland landscape during this period, they cannot fully explain the gender-food relationships we are aiming to understand here. For that, we need to look at the kinds of cultural reforms to which food, people and work were subject in "modernizing" Newfoundland. As noted in the intro-duction to this chapter, the term cultural reform refers here to the subtle ways in which people come to render the self—reconfiguring their habits and conduct—as new measures for calculating life are deployed. I identify in this section three key cultural reforms that mobilized food, women, and agriculture in post-Confederation Newfoundland. These are: food as an aesthetic product; women as discerning mothers and housewives; and agriculture as a business and profes-sion, subject to scientific expertise.

The clearest evidence perhaps of the cultural reform of food in this time pe-riod is the challenge to the physical appearance of Newfoundland vegetable pro-duction: local vegetables were found to be less "presentable" than food arriving from away. A study by W. C. Shipley titled *The Market for Farm Products in Newfoundland, 1948-1950*, usefully compares vegetable production pre- and post-Confederation and finds healthy production levels in Newfoundland, with good to excellent quality before and immediately after Confederation (Shipley 1954; see also Singh 1964). What Shipley identifies as the main concern is that the Newfoundland farmer "should do a better job of presenting his product. This would include better cleaning and trimming of vegetables..." Shipley argues that products from the mainland are "preferred because of continuous supply, uniform quality, and standard packaging" (Shipley 1954, 43-44). Unlike their Canadian counterparts, then, Newfoundland producers were not preparing and packaging their food in ways that modern consumers were demanding. In 1956, this theme continues in the Annual Reports from the province's Department of Mines and Resources: "Our farmers have, however, been slow to follow the modern trend of pre-packaging vegetables for the self service grocery trade" (DMR-A 1956, 14). And, in 1959, a quote is repeated from a speech given two years earlier by the Minister of Mines and Resources at an Agricultural Exhibit: "Our farmers are going to have to meet the demands of modern merchandizing methods and go in more and more for putting up their produce in attractive packages" (DMR-A 1959, 37). This disciplining takes place despite the fact that vegetables were by then subject to the Vegetable Grading Act and had to be tagged Newfoundland Government Inspected (DMR-A 1953).

What is most interesting about this point is that, while Newfoundland farmers were being reprimanded for not making their food more presentable (though the quality was fine), Newfoundland women were said to be enamored not only with the new supermarket chains—the "self service" stores quickly establishing themselves throughout the province—but with the invention of cellophane. Why? "Because they can see at a glance through the cellophane wrapping what the article looks like and what the cost is" (Cooke 1950, 24-27). In 1952 this theme continues, as the Cellophane Division of Canadian Industries Limited credits housewives for their success: "Today's housewife shops with her eyes and buys what looks good but she is also extremely conscious of packaging for sanitation and cleanliness" (*Newfoundland Journal* 1952, 34). Such statements indicate that women were no doubt the food shoppers ("the 'kingpin' shoppers of the family"). But they also indicate two other significant changes: women no longer needed to rely on the advice of the man behind the counter (and could decide for themselves what "good food" to buy for their families), and they were encouraged to associate food presentation with food *sanitation*. Apparently excelling at food presentation, food "from away" became the obvious choice for the conscientious shopper.

There is no doubt that pressure was placed on Newfoundland women to buy new foods during this time period. The 1952 *Annual Report of Food* states that "Never before have there been so much come on [sic] in advertising to lure homemakers and housewives into buying this, that or the other" (1952, 22). Very rapid changes in diet took place in the province at this time. The post-Confederation period is associated with "an undue dependence upon food from cans, packets, cereals and other commercial preparations" (Eisener 2002). Within just a few years, grocery stores switched from selling "rough food" (Omohundro 1994), the products associated with the traditional Newfoundland diet, to food produced through multinational corporations. By 1954 L. Healey Grocers, for example, were selling Kraft dinner, Corn Flakes, Jello, pie crusts, and Coke.[7]

One cannot help but think of this dietary shift as a significant turning point for Newfoundland consumer identity, akin to that which took place throughout North America. This shift implicated not only a redefinition of good food, but a distancing of consumers from the realities—the messiness—of food production, i.e., that animals are butchered and vegetables actually come out of the ground. Being modern suggests having the means to keep nature and dirt at bay. This idea has implications for working in "rough food" gardens. Such work, tied to nature and dirt, destabilized the disassociation required of modern women; it complicated engagement with a "modern outlook." Gardening, in this new context, also culturally communicated poverty—since it signaled that one was not in a position to *buy* "good" food. Whitaker's survey of communities in 1963 provides a hint of this: "It seems that many feel farming is work that lacks prestige and is really for the uneducated" (Whitaker 1963, 89).

Newfoundland scholars have focused on the sudden appearance, with Confederation in 1949, of the welfare state in Newfoundland, with UI, family allowances, and pensions coming from the Canadian government. These sources of social support tended to buffer families from the extreme poverty that had plagued rural communities before Confederation. Fewer analysts have considered how gender was mobilized by these systems, however. It is not insignificant that within three weeks of joining Canada "baby bonuses" (family allowances) were delivered to Newfoundland mothers. Within the first year of Confederation, 50,051 mothers received almost $10 million (Blake 2004). The promise of baby bonuses was a powerful means to sell Confederation to Newfoundlanders—and Joey Smallwood had made sure that everyone in Newfoundland heard the message. Baby bonuses remained a recognized source of cash for rural households in the early 1960s, a point made clear in the eleven communities surveyed by Whitaker's team in 1963.[8] But the baby bonus to mothers also indicated an opportunity for rural women to measure themselves differently: it signaled new ideas about rural women's place in society, and that place was *not* in supplementary agriculture. Ironically, baby bonuses—a policy that implies dependence on the state—may have facilitated women's greater *independence* from food production.

This latter point requires us to consider the options available for rural women. Modern consumption presupposes a particular kind of woman, one who takes pride in her abilities to run an efficient household and reproduce a healthy and happy family. One of the key devices to promote and enable this identity was advertising. In the 1950s local newspaper ads were very much directed at women, not only to encourage them to buy particular kinds of food but to encourage them to be a particular kind of person. Similarly, craft exhibits and baking contests initiate seemingly harmless competition about who is a good housewife or cook but they also promote the desire to be in this role at all. For example, in a 1952 local newspaper Robin Hood flour advertised a baking contest featuring a woman in her kitchen pondering recipes. The ad asks: "Who is the Queen of all Newfoundland's wonderful cooks? It may be you!" (*Evening Telegram* 1952). It was also during this time that ads shifted from the basic goods approach (e.g., oranges for 29 cents a dozen) to ads that promoted a life style. One striking example of lifestyle advertising in 1952 is a man in a suit walking down a winding staircase in the morning, smelling Chase and Sanborn coffee in the air. Titled "Let him come down to a great cup of coffee," neither the price nor who made the coffee to lure him down to breakfast requires a statement (*Evening Telegram* 1952; see also Wright 1995).

At the same time that women were being mobilized as discerning shoppers and cooks in Newfoundland, babies were being promoted as astute adult-like consumers. Extensive newspaper advertising in the early 1950s directed mothers to their needs. Two examples will suffice, both in the same edition of the *Evening Telegram* (1952). One ad features a baby saying: "Guess I need an Interpreter...to make you, Mother, understand that Heinz Baby Foods are the best—how pure and naturally delicious they are...I don't know how I'd get along without them." The other ad assigns babies adult dietary needs by claiming that a new Heinz baby food product is a "complete meat-and-vegetable dinner," "a real banquet-style dinner in a single tin." Consumers were often offered coupons to receive the product free as part of a promotional trial.

There is, I suggest, much to appeal to the rural woman in these ads. Wise food shoppers, cooks and caregivers are accorded visibility and respect. In stark contrast to the status accorded supplementary agricultural work (as I elaborate below), activities associated with this emerging identity offered a not unreasonable future for women to embrace.

To fully explain this last point requires a look at a third cultural reform, one that is encapsulated in the figure of the Agricultural Fieldman. Fieldmen were the agricultural extension workers sent out by the Division of Agriculture of Newfoundland's Department of Mines and Resources to "implement agricultural policies in the field [and] assist farmers with day-to-day practical and technical advice on many and various problems" (DMR-A 1957, 22). Fieldmen had the unique opportunity to observe farmers' work and discuss farming issues firsthand. Their unpublished reports, I thought, would finally tell me something about supplementary agriculture. But this was not to be the case, or at least not quite in the way I had imagined.

Unlike the published Annual Reports of the Agricultural Division, the fieldnotes submitted by the fieldmen are more personal, and include the fieldmen's challenges and frustrations.[9] They voice concerns about not making any progress with the farmers, not having enough time to do all their work, and not having a government that pays sufficient attention to marketing and storage issues. They find "producer disorganization and backwardness" (Fieldmen Reports 1960, 109), and farmers working without proper knowledge about animal care and crop production. Farms are too small, marketing chaotic, and there are no "reliable facts" to do agricultural planning.[10] The fieldmen also express being uncomfortable with their conflicting tasks as educator, reporter and judge—the former requires getting to know farmers as people, the latter "good, stiff, consistent inspection" (Fieldmen Reports 1960, 131). But there is not one word in these reports about supplementary agriculture, at least not in the reports written by the fieldmen permanently stationed in the regional districts of the Island.

These fieldmen focused on promoting their views of proper agriculture: full-time farming, large commercial enterprises, and a personal orientation to "absorb" agricultural expertise. From the federal and provincial government's perspective, Newfoundland agriculture had to become more efficient if products were to compete with the mainland. To become more efficient, farms had to be larger and farmers had to attend to their agricultural investments year round. While Division staff and consultants spent much of their time devising plans for the most efficient production of every kind of crop and animal imaginable, fieldmen instructed farmers about "knowledge and information on *modern* farming practices and techniques" (DMR-A 1959, 26, my emphasis). They did this through farmer organizations, exhibitions, field days, and radio programs.

One way to analyze the place of agricultural exhibitions, experimental farms and model farms in this kind of context is to understand how they serve as "technologies of invisibility" (Biehl 2005). Seeing like a Fieldman, informed by science-based expertise and a business logic (see Ayre 1960), means that only certain forms of agriculture *can* be observed. The cultural work of promoting commercial agriculture ensures, then, that supplementary agriculture and women's work in it simply do not exist. Through this lens, women who might well have been interested in supplementary or other forms of agriculture are rendered invisible, though in plain sight. Not seen or heard, there is no agricultural future for them to embrace. While field days were "praised by farmers as an excellent means of education" (DMR-A 1959, 26), a photo taken during the field trip to survey an experimental farm in 1958 attended "by some 60 farmers from all over the province," indicates that all the farmers are male.

Interestingly, women and supplementary agriculture are mentioned in one, and only one, of the fieldmen's reports, and it was written by the only fieldman not permanently stationed in the region for which he was responsible: the Northern Peninsula and Labrador. And, unlike the others, not only are women visible in his reports, but he takes the gardens they tend seriously:

> We have visited every kitchen garden...and given advice. Distributed kitchen garden literature. Had soil samples taken...The people in these areas have very good gardens, growing cabbage, turnips, potatoes, some carrots, some beets and lettuce...Most all gardens in the area are looked after by the women folk (Fieldmen Reports 1960, 198-199).

This fieldman challenges convention by recognizing gardening, but he explains his decision paternalistically: "After all, their living depends on this, so in my opinion, the *most we can hope* is to help in the way we have already been doing. Promote supplementary farming only" (Fieldmen Reports 1960, 200, my emphasis). Supplementary agriculture is thus rendered visible in the only region deemed unable to undertake commercial agriculture. In the 1950s it appears that Labrador was the only region permitted government support for supplementary gardening and the raising of home use livestock (DMR-A 1956, 17). This is interesting because Labrador, and the region's significant aboriginal populations, have long played the role of the "Other" within the Newfoundland context; indeed it took until 2001 for Labrador to be recognized explicitly as part of the province.

This fieldman's entry inevitably leads us to more questions to explore. One cannot help but wonder...by withdrawing from supplementary agriculture, did Whitaker's "modern" rural women from whom we heard in 1963 help to reinforce the "non-modern" stigma attached to supplementary agriculture elsewhere and to other populations? What is "kitchen garden literature," what was its purpose, and how did it differ from other distributed agriculture literature? And, if we leap into the present, what should we make of the very "modern" call to grow our own vegetables? What does this call signal about gender and contemporary forms of supplementary agriculture, and our changing relationships to dirt, work, education and concepts of self-worth? These questions are not answerable here, but their exploration in the future may help us to interrogate further both the historical alignments of the past and the possible technologies of calculation at work in the present.

Back to the Future: Final remarks

The inclination of rural women in Newfoundland to engage as consumers, housewives and mothers in the modern food system indicates that they were not just docile bodies for corporations or governments. Their agency is evident in their development of an identity that removed them from the hard life and work of being female in rural communities. Baking contests, baby bonuses, and self-serve shopping may sound trivial to contemporary readers, but these devices offered new means by which women could measure themselves as valued, as worthy.

The demise of supplementary agriculture in mid-twentieth century Newfoundland in part reflects the success of rural women in Newfoundland to effect a new identity, one based on novel ideas about working, eating, and living in a modern economy. When rural women were disconnected as subsistence workers from the commercializing fishing economy, they sought outlets where they might gain (or regain) respect in a period of rapid transformation. A reasonable outlet might well have been supplementary agriculture, had it been promoted by the government and its extension workers during a key period of rapid change in diet and lifestyle. Instead, supplementary agriculture remained invisible as a legitimate form of agriculture—unless one lived in the peripheral north.

While there may not be firm evidence that a gardening identity had become akin to being the Other, a pertinent point remains as to the paradoxical outcomes of women's "agency." For in this case women's engagement with a new identity—framed by concerns about food presentation, packaging, and sanitation—aided the emergence of a modern food system that has not been kind to our health or to the environment. Today, despite pockets of alternative/local food initiatives in Newfoundland and Labrador, most food is imported through chain stores, there is a poor record of eating vegetables and fruit, and the province has high rates of obesity and diabetes. It may be said that rural women's "success," then, has come at a cost.

In 1966 the province's Department of Mines and Resources proclaimed that the supermarket would soon replace the root cellar as the source of vegetables for Newfoundland consumers (DMR-A 1966); they predicted well. But this dramatic transformation did not take place effortlessly or without consequences; the development of certain ways of thinking, of behaving, and of *being* was required. It stands to reason, then, if we are to achieve food security—if we are to develop a healthier, accessible, more inclusive food system in the future—we will need to take into account these deep-seated and widespread cultural effects.

Acknowledgments

I would like to acknowledge and thank Valerie Green for her creative, persistent and timely research assistance for this project. Thank you also to Jane and Kevin Aucoin and Jo Shawyer for their support and to Sally Cole and Janet Page-Reeves for their comments on this chapter. Many thanks to the patient people working in the QEII Library, especially in the Centre for Newfoundland Studies, at Memorial University, St. John's, Newfoundland and Labrador.

Notes

1. In 2001 the province's official name changed from "Newfoundland" to "Newfoundland and Labrador." Newfoundland is an island and Labrador is the province's northern connection to the mainland. I deal primarily with the mid-twentieth century in this chapter and therefore refer to the province of Newfoundland, as it was called during this time period.

2. The research for this paper is based on the following sources: Annual Reports from the Newfoundland Department of Mines and Resources, Division of Agriculture (here referenced as DMR-A) from 1952-1966, Fieldmen Reports, Government Commissions, the *Newfoundland Journal of Commerce*, local newspapers and the extant literature on rural communities in 1950-60s Newfoundland.

3. For evidence of the many attempts to modernize Newfoundland agriculture in the first half of the twentieth century, see James B. Sclater (1910); A. H. Seymour (1910); W. W. Baird (1934); A. B. Banks 1937; J.A. Hanley (1940); D. J. Gillis (1947).

4. It should be noted that the interviewers do not always clarify who is supplying these answers.

5. Agricultural policy flipped-flopped with remarkable consistency. For example, although there was no change in government, only two years before the 1955 *Newfoundland Royal Commission on Agriculture* declared its position against supporting supplementary agriculture, the 1953 *Annual Report* of the Department of Mining and Resources, referring to supplementary agriculture, stated that "It is very important that for the present some effort should be made to retain and encourage this type of agricultural production. During the past year much of the work of the Agricultural Division has been devoted to [its] maintenance...Every member of the Agricultural Staff has worked to

keep alive an interest in supplementary agriculture and to encourage it whenever and wherever possible" (DMR-A 1953 p. 28-29).

6. See Department of Mines and Resources, Division of Agriculture, *Annual Reports* (1953 and 1958); see also the advertisement "Always Insist on Newfoundland Grown Farm Fresh Vegetables" in *The Daily News*, August 3, 1959. It was no secret that Smallwood, who remained Premier until 1972, did not see a bright future for vegetable production in Newfoundland. He is quoted as saying "I have never, since the coming of Confederation, had abundant enthusiasm for Newfoundland's farming possibilities, as far as root crops and grains are concerned" (quoted in Crabb 1975b).

7. This information comes from a Special Collections Box for James Ireland made available through the Centre for Newfoundland Studies. James Ireland was a full time farmer from the Goulds who donated his financial records, including sales and purchase receipts between 1940-1970. He bought the noted items from L. Healey Grocers in 1954. He bought a refrigerator from William Clouston Ltd. the same year for $50.00.

8. Women were likely to convert their baby bonuses into groceries or other items for the family. Some of the women in Cecilia Benoit's study in Stephenville confirm this practice (Benoit 1995).

9. The only year to which I had access to the (unpublished) Fieldmen reports was 1959. The reports were written in 1960 on the 1959 situation.

10. The lack of reliable data may have been due to the fact that many farmers had declined to provide information to agricultural surveys (see DMR-A 1959, p. 8).

Bibliography

Ayre, A. G. 1960. "The Farmer has to be Businessman," *Newfoundland Journal of Commerce* 27, no. 10: 14-17.

Baird, W. W. 1934. *Report on Agricultural Conditions and possibilities of development thereof in Newfoundland.* St. John's, NF: Department of Natural Resources, Agricultural Section, Bulletin No. 1.

Banks, A. B. 1937. *Progress Report of the Agricultural Division in Newfoundland 1934-1937.* St. John's, NF: Newfoundland Government.

Benoit, Cecile. 1995. "Urbanizing Women Military Fashion: The Case of Stephenville Women." In *Their Lives and Times: Women in Newfoundland and Labrador, a Collage,* edited by Carmelita McGrath, Barbara Neis and Marilyn Porter, 113-127. St. John's, NF: Killick Press.

Biehl, João. 2005. "Technologies of Invisibility: Politics of Life and Social Inequality." In *Anthropologies of Modernity: Foucault, Governmentality, and Life Politics,* edited by Jonathan Xavier Inda, 248-271. Oxford: Blackwell.

Blake, Raymond. 2004. *Canadians at Last.* Toronto: University of Toronto Press, 2004.

Cadigan, Sean. 2002. "The Role of Agriculture in Outport Self-sufficiency." In *The Resilient Outport: Ecology, Economy, and Society in Rural Newfoundland,* edited by Rosemary Ommer, 241-262. St. John's, NL: ISER, Memorial University.

Chaulk Murray, Hilda. 2010. *More Than 50%: Woman's Life in a Newfoundland Outport: 1900-1950.* St. John's, NL: Flankers Press.

Cooke, Ronald J. 1950. "Food Picture for 1950," *Newfoundland Journal of Commerce* 17, no.5 (May 1950): 24-27.

Crabb, Peter. 1975a. "The Marketing of Farm Products in Newfoundland." Paper presented at the IBG Rural Geography Study Group Conference. University of Birmingham, September, 1975.

——————. 1975b. "Agriculture in Newfoundland: A Study in Development." Thesis (PhD), University of Hull.

Department of Mines and Resources, Division of Agriculture. 1952-1966. *Annual Reports*. St. John's, NF: Government of Newfoundland.

Eisener, Amanda C. 2002. "Feeding Babies, Making Mothers: Infant Feeding Practices in St. John's, Newfoundland." Thesis (M.A.), Memorial University of Newfoundland.

Evening Telegram (advertisements). 1950-1954. St. John's, Newfoundland.

Fieldmen Reports, 1959 (unpublished), Department of Mines and Resources, Division of Agriculture, Special Collections, QEII library, Memorial University of Newfoundland, 1960.

Free Farms for Thousands in Newfoundland: Midway Between Europe and America, Britain's Oldest Colony. 1910. No author. St. John's, NF: Chronicle Job Print.

Gillis, D. J. 1947. *Agriculture in Newfoundland.* Department of Natural Resources, St. John's, Newfoundland: Government of Newfoundland.

Goodman, David, and Michael Redclift. 1991. *Refashioning Nature.* New York: Routledge.

Hanley, J. A. 1940. *Second Report (1939) on the Development of Agriculture and Land Settlements in Newfoundland.* Department of Agriculture and Rural Reconstruction, St. John's: Newfoundland Government.

Nash, June. 2009. "Global Integration and Subsistence Insecurity." *American Anthropologist,* 96, no. 1: 7-30.

Newfoundland Journal of Commerce. 1947. "Agriculture Progress Unspectacular but Steady" (no author) 14, no. 11: 8

——. 1952. "It Pays to Let the Women Have the Last Word." (no author) 19, no. 12: 34.

——. May 1952. "Annual Report on Food for 1952," (no author) 19, no 5: 16-22.

Omohundro, John, T. 1994. *Rough Food.* St. John's, NF: ISER, Memorial University.

Porter, Marilyn. 1995. "'She was the Skipper of the Shore Crew': Notes on the History of the Sexual Division of Labour in Newfoundland." In *Their Lives and Times: Women in Newfoundland and Labrador, a Collage,* edited by Carmelita McGrath, Barbara Neis and Marilyn Porter, 33-47. St. John's, NF: Killick Press.

Province of Newfoundland. 1956. *Report of the Newfoundland Royal Commission on Agriculture 1955.* St. John's: Queen's Printer.

——. 1964. *Demand for Agricultural Products—Imported and Domestic—in Newfoundland.* ARDA Project No. 7.

Rowe, Frederick. 1985. *The Smallwood Era.* Toronto: McGraw-Hill Ryerson.

Sclater, James B. 1903. *Newfoundland Agriculture.* St. John's, NF: Standard Office Print.

Scott, James C. 1998. *Seeing like a State: How Certain Schemes to Improve the Human Condition have Failed.* New Haven, CT: Yale University Press.

Seymour, A. H. 1910. *Report of A.H. Seymour on the Possibilities of Agricultural Development in Newfoundland, 1909.* Newfoundland Agricultural Board. St John's, NF: The Board.

Shipley, W. C. 1954. *The Market for Farm Products in Newfoundland, 1948-1950*, Ottawa: Queen's Printer Department of Agriculture, Economics Divisions. Ottawa: Queen's Printer.

Singh, B. 1964. *Demand for Agricultural Products—Imported and Domestic—in Newfoundland*. ARDA Project No. 7, Department of Mines, Agriculture and Resource. St. John's Newfoundland.

Whitaker, I. 1963. *Small-Scale Agriculture in Selected Newfoundland Communities*. A survey prepared for the ARDA administration, ARDA project: no. 14024, rev. no. 1013 St. John's, NF: Institute of Social and Economic Research, Memorial University of Newfoundland.

Wright, Miriam 1995. "Women, Men, and the Modern Fishery: Images of Gender in Government Plans for the Canadian Atlantic Fisheries." In *Their Lives and Times: Women in Newfoundland and Labrador, a Collage*, edited by Carmelita McGrath, Barbara Neis and Marilyn Porter, 129-143. St. John's, NF: Killick Press.

PART V

Empowerment
and
Challenging the System

CHAPTER 11

Labor and Leadership: Women in U.S. Community Food Organizing

Christine Porter
LaDonna Redmond

Introduction

The United States has a food system largely built on the backs of women, en-slaved Africans, Native Americans and—most recently—migrant laborers from countries to our South. In other words, the US has never had a healthy and just food system nor a food secure society. Fortunately, tens of thousands of Americans are working to create one that is healthy and just, including building food security for all families and communities. That work, loosely forming the U.S. community food movement,[1] has increasingly—if not sufficiently—tackled un-doing racism and classism as inherent to creating a just food system. However, rhetoric and action aimed at undoing sexism in the work, including attending to gross gender disparities in food security, has largely been missing.

In this chapter, we aim to add gender to race and class as an anchor for achieving equity and food security through food system change. This anchor is partly for ethical reasons. In a deep democracy, those most affected by an issue should be most involved in deciding what to do about it, and women are dispro-portionately affected by food insecurity and are most involved in the movement to create food security. A gender anchor is also important for strategic reasons, as both feminine and feminist leadership show promise for building food securi-ty and effective alternatives to our dominant, industrial food system. Gender equity in the food movement means not only crediting the labor and leadership

261

that women provide in the U.S. community food movement for food security, particularly women of color and women in communities facing disproportionate food insecurity, but amplifying their voices in guiding the work to ensure every person in this and future generations is well nourished.

We tackle this topic drawing from three sources. One, we turn to the limited (but growing) literature and social media on gender in U.S. food system work and loosely build our analysis within feminist, postcolonial and critical race theory frameworks. Two, we analyze input of 181 people who responded to a survey we sent over food-system-related email lists in the U.S.[2] We asked people to name national and local leaders in the community food movement. We also asked for gender of the listed leaders and of the respondents and also if the leader or respondent identified as person of color. Respondents were also invited to comment if they wished; 94 did so. Three, we draw on our personal perspectives and experiences with community food work. LaDonna became a food justice activist when the country's broken food system got personal. In 1998, she was living on the west side of Chicago, raising two children, when her youngest son developed food allergies. She started wondering why it was easier in her neighborhood to buy liquor, cigarettes, and even guns than it was to find an organic tomato. In 2012 she organized the Food + Justice = Democracy working conference while leading the food justice program at the Institute for Agriculture and Trade Policy. Currently she works as founder and leader of the Campaign for Food Justice Now (CFJN). LaDonna is an African-American, middle-class woman. Christine is a white, middle-class female academic. Drawing from her "apprentice activism" and her PhD studies in social theory and nutrition, Christine now directs a five-year, $5-million action research project called Food Dignity. Food Dignity supports and studies community food system work with five community organizations.[3]

Gender and Food

U.S. society has so many ways of creating and perpetuating inequity, though the trifecta of racism, classism, and sexism arguably form the American axis of social injustice evil. In the U.S. food movement, race and class have been garnering some action and analysis. Gender largely has not. For example, Growing Food and Justice for All Initiative (GFJI) "is an initiative aimed at dismantling racism and empowering low-income and communities of color through sustainable and local agriculture" (GFJI). The Detroit Black Community Food Security Network (DBCFSN) has been a key driver in the Undoing Racism in the Detroit Food System effort. A content search of the largest discussion list in the U.S. food movement finds over 100 emails mentioning "racism" over the past two years; two emails used the word "sexism" (COMFOOD 2013). (Though, as this is out of over 6,000 emails, racism is not receiving great focus either.) An equally unscientific but indicative comparison of web searches using Google shows about 3 million results for the following word combination: sexism food system. Swapping in the word "racism" instead of "sexism" yields over 20 times that number of results.

Academic literature about the US food movement overall is still limited, but it has in some cases tackled racism and classism (e.g., Slocum 2006, Guthman 2008), including in an edited book devoted to the topic (Alkon and Agyeman 2011). Gender garners little attention and feminism almost none. As one paper that does tackle this topic asks: "how do we explain the perplexing absence of a feminist agenda in women's actions in food-system work?" (Allen and Sachs 2007, 5). This *is* perplexing since, as a review of women's food blogs notes, "food is an inherently feminist topic. Women are inundated on a daily basis regarding food—whether being told how to properly (and perfectly) prepare it, or how to control our intake of it for 'ideal' weight purposes" (Nathman 2013).

Talking about gender but not sexism (or, more powerfully, patriarchy) is a weak strategy for ending gender oppression. However, a gender lens forms a necessary part of the foundation for undoing sexism and, thus, is better than silence on gender. Therefore recent scholarship that raises the visibility of women's work in the U.S. movement is valuable, even if not done with a particular focus on gender oppression (Costa 2010, White 2011, Harper 2009). The global literature on gender and food security provides a model for this work, with a stronger focus on gender equity. The report "Women's Rights and the Right to Food," by Olivier de Schutter, U.N. Special Rapporteur on the Right to Food, exemplifies this work. The report notes that if women had the same access to resources that men have, global malnutrition could be reduced by up to 17 percent (de Schutter 2012).

Inequity through Food

Food is extremely gendered in most cultures, including ours. For example, in the U.S., compared to men, women still spend over twice as much time on food preparation and clean-up (Bureau of Labor Statistics 2012a) and do about two-thirds of the grocery shopping (Hale 2011). Food insecurity among adults also falls largely to women, as many chapters here painfully illustrate. Over 11 percent of mothers who are parenting alone experience not just food insecurity, but "very low food security"–a state that the U.S. Department of Agriculture (USDA) used to call hunger.[4] Add in race, and the picture worsens. African-American households suffer food insecurity at three times the rate of white households (Coleman-Jensen et al. 2012). Also, for generations in the South-eastern U.S., the answer to "who is in the kitchen" in middle-class white homes was African-American women (Sharpless 2013).

The pay gap by gender and, especially, the combination of race and gender is even worse in the food system than in the paid economy more generally. In food work, white women earn 63 cents to a white man's dollar; black and Latina women earn about half what white men earn (Liu and Apollon 2011). For example, while food preparation is largely "women's work," once that work reaches the pay and status level of chef/head cook professions, that role is largely filled by men (78.5 percent) (Bureau of Labor Statistics 2012b).

Fortunately, the U.S. is enjoying a movement for food justice and sovereignty that include goals of creating food security for all people. Initiatives such as urban farms, community and home gardens, farmers markets, and small food business incubation all create opportunities to improve household and community food security. For example, among farm workers who started home food gardens as part of an action research study, household food insecurity dropped tenfold (Carney et al. 2012). More anecdotally, in the Food Dignity project for which Christine is principal investigator, dozens of families who have received support from one of the five community partners in the project report increasing their household food production and generating income through gardens, small livestock production, and farmers markets or other direct sales. This work raises a labor and leadership question: since women are most affected by food insecurity and most involved in household food work, what is their role in this movement, and what should it be?

Food Movement Labor & Leadership

Women appear to do their share, or more, in work to create a more just food system. With no official movement "membership," it is impossible to count, but experience and anecdote indicate that women predominate in U.S. community food movement action. For example, the (white and male) founder and director of Kitchen Garden's International (KGI) noted:

> My unscientific theory is that men aren't pulling their share of the weight in the food garden movement. It is based on two things: KGI's demographics (both our mailing list and Facebook page) which are 75-80 percent women and my personal experience as a parent volunteer helping with school gardens in my town where I'm surrounded exclusively by committed, hard-working women. (Doiron 2011)

A paper examining gender in a Michigan community-supported-agriculture (CSA) initiative found that 85 percent of working members and 77 percent of the board were women (DeLind and Ferguson 1999). Similarly, over 85 percent of respondents to our survey (which was publicized over food movement lists) identified as female. If women are doing their half or more of this food movement, then men are getting much more than their share of the credit for and voice in that work. While representation in leadership is only one measure of gender equity in the movement, it is an important one. One respondent in our survey wrote, *"I get really tired of seeing a few males trotted out over and over as the spokespeople for community food systems... I think women are doing and have done the lion's share of this work, usually quietly and in ways that don't blow their horns.*" This mirrors an observation by food movement journalist Tom Philpott: "We have our sage (Michael Pollan), our eminence gris (Wendell Berry), our star small farmer (Joel Salatin), our genius urban farmer (Will Allen), and our local-food chef (Dan Barber)." These *"anointed ones,"* he notes, are all male (Philpott 2010).

We asked survey participants to list up to six national leaders. Overall, of the 55 people who were mentioned by at least two respondents as national leaders, half are women, over a third are persons of color, and a quarter are both. However, males cluster more tightly at the top. Will Allen received the most mentions, with nearly half mentioning him. Over a third listed food journalist Michael Pollan. First Lady Michelle Obama came a distant third, with 17 percent of people listing her as an influential leader. Table 1 below lists the 15 people named most often by survey respondents. Of these top 15 leaders, 60 percent are male, 40 percent are people of color, and 20 percent (i.e., 3) are women of color. In the full list of over 150 different people mentioned as leaders, 56 percent are male.

Table 11.1: Survey Results of the Top 15 Most-Mentioned National Food Movement Leaders

Leader Name		Number of Mentions	percent Respondents (n=181) Mentioning the Name
1.	Will Allen	85	47 percent
2.	Michael Pollan	66	36 percent
3.	Michelle Obama	30	17 percent
4.	Alice Waters	27	15 percent
5.	Malik Yakini	24	13 percent
6.	Joel Salatin	23	13 percent
7.	Mark Winne	18	10 percent
8.	LaDonna Redmond	14	8 percent
9.	Marion Nestle	13	7 percent
10.	Kathleen Merrigan	11	6 percent
11.	Raj Patel	11	6 percent
12.	Winona LaDuke	11	6 percent
13.	Wendell Berry	11	6 percent
14.	Andy Fisher	10	6 percent
15.	Mark Bittman	10	6 percent

Women fared better in the local leadership question. Again, survey participants could list up to six names of people they saw as influential locally in their
community's food work. Who was listed depended, of course, on where respondents lived; this likely was not nationally representative. However, out of
the seven names listed at least five times, five are women.[5] Overall, 60 percent
of the people named as local leaders were identified as female. That is nearly the
inverse of the national leader list. About 22 percent of the local leaders were
identified as being people of color and 13 percent as women of color.

Feminine and feminism in full color

The authors of the Michigan CSA paper mentioned above suggest that women
were involved in the farm "within a feminine as opposed to a feminist" framework (DeLind and Ferguson 1999, 191). While not inherently precluding feminism, a feminine lens emphasizes the merits of traits such as caring and social
connectivity traditionally associated with women, without necessarily tackling
inequity (and while possibly sometimes reinforcing it). Vandana Shiva outlines
such merits in one of her classic works (Shiva 1988); a recent piece in *The Atlantic* on how empathy of women farmers would make food safer and improve
animal welfare exemplifies a feminine lens (Faruqi 2013).

Feminism, on the other hand, aims to end gender oppression. While women
may be more likely to be feminine and/or feminist, men can be either or both as
well; and certainly the gender equity struggle requires both sexes to succeed.
Similarly, ending racism requires white allies, and racism remains a perennial
struggle in U.S. feminism work. Histories of a white-women-led feminist
movement and a men-of-color-led civil rights movement leave feminist women
of color with little space to call home. This feminist erasure of women of color
is relived, for example, in a recent column in *Ms. Magazine*, which notes that
"today's proponents of a 'natural food revolution' sometimes forget history—
and return us to patriarchal fantasies of happy housewives at their hot stoves"
(McGrath 2013, 42). This review forgets the history of black women in fields
and kitchens, drawing on mainstream white feminist history and discussing
white women in the kitchen, and then closing with a nod to ending racism by
quoting a male leader of color (Yakini, see table 1) in the movement.

From this place of double marginalization, women of color have built a radical and practical body of work on how to undo racism and sexism (most
notably, Moraga and Anzaldúa 1981, Anzaldúa and Keating 2002). This work
underpins a more inclusive and radical vision of feminist leadership which, we
argue, the food movement needs to generate food security and, to some extent,
seems to be demanding.

Feminist leadership

Our survey asked for names of influential people. These questions fit conventional and largely white and male notions of individualist leadership (Batliwala 2010). Dozens of respondents challenged this by naming groups or leaving the names blank, and through comments such as:

The way your survey is structured, you will likely will get mostly talkers and not the ones who are truly influencing others.

While leadership is important; the power of community and building community and recognizing community is the key... we really need to resist the deification of leaders and by listing organizations, groups, or nothing at all in the slots for names.

I'm not completely comfortable with the idea of community food system leadership; to the extent that a community food system becomes identified with a single person, it becomes less a product and project of the community involved.

More important than getting involved with name-dropping it is best to think of anyone working in the movement as a community food systems leader.

Social change action, moral motivation, and collaboration constituted the dominant themes in participant comments about leadership. These themes fit a post-colonial feminist vision of leadership, which works as "a *means*, not an end. We build leadership capacity and skills *for* something, *to do something* or *change* something, and not because leadership is a product or service for consumption. This is especially true in social justice contexts" (Batliwala 2010, 5). Respondent comments also fit with feminist leadership as defined by a Dutch organization working to end violence:

Feminist leadership should be oriented to a different arrangement of the human order: re-distribution of power and re-distribution of responsibilities. Fighting societal inequalities. Changing economic and social structures, beginning with transformation of psychic structures. Bridging personal freedom with collective freedom. Aiming at cooperation instead of competition. (Admira 2004)

Within the food movement, LaDonna envisions such re-distribution in what she calls Food Justice 2.0. In Food Justice 2.0, the movement is informed and led by the narratives of people most affected by food insecurity; in other words, women and of people of color. To collectively better understand the inequities in the food system, the work to change it must include people who have faced these inequities in finding solutions. The public health issue of violence is connected to the public health issue of chronic, diet-related diseases. In LaDonna's community, it is about living or dying. You can die by the gun or from the lack of proper food. The stories that we tell ourselves in the food movement are as important as the stories that we've left out, such as those missing from the Ms. column cited above. We must include in this the narrative of modern slavery; our food system today is still based on the exploitation of the labor of immigrants in this country. While we are talking about access to free-range chickens and grass-fed beef, we need to also be talking about immigration reform and fair wages for those farm workers. The people who serve us, who fix our food, should be paid fairly. This requires incorporating the truth about our food system and facilitating a deep engagement with the communities that feel most exploited. The food movement, to be effective, must aim to end oppression, including by crediting, building, and following leadership in and from these communities, including, and especially, women of all races.

Fostering an Anti-Racist and Feminist Food Movement

Oppression is intertwined and so must be the work to end it. Ending sexism hinges on ending racism. Ending racism hinges on ending sexism. Pushing women, and especially women of color, *"off the edge of the table"* is one of the ways oppression manifests. However, food also provides a powerful opening for ending oppression. Producing food produces power. Sharing food builds relationships. Preparing our peoples' foods cultivates culture and spirit. We all must eat and communities controlling their food systems offers a route to freedom: "food sovereignty implies new social relations free of oppression and inequality between men and women, peoples, racial groups, social and economic classes and generations" (Forum for Food Sovereignty 2007). The food movement can realize this vision by developing anti-racist and feminist leadership around four "ps": power, politics and purpose, principles and values, and practices (Batliwala 2010). Below, we outline strategies for each, including drawing from examples from work we have helped to organize, including Food Dignity and CFJN.

Power

"Power produces; it produces reality" wrote Foucault (1975/1995, 194). Making equitable and oppression-free (including hunger-free) social relations a reality requires feminist and anti-racist leadership in articulating, transforming, building, and sharing power. Such leadership means:

- Facilitating ongoing power analysis, aiming to making "the practice of power visible, democratic, legitimate and accountable, at all levels, and in both private and public realms" (Batliwala 2010, 18). For example, in the Food Dignity project that Christine directs, community partners conducted a power analysis of their own organizations in the 2013 annual meeting, and have asked for a project-wide one by the next meeting.

- Collaborating and coalescing, with less individualistic notions of leadership. As one survey respondent questioned, *"We do need to coalesce to have more 'power' as a movement. Is influential leadership the answer? Will these influential leaders create unity, be mutually supportive, and share their power?"* Another argued, *"Organizations are the leaders, not the individuals who happen to be directing or managing the organizations. Leaders are about 'we' not I."*

- Defining the principles and purposes of the work, in which the movement invests its productive power, and holding movement actors accountable to these principles and purposes. A survey participant said, *"Those who cherish dignity and the right to safe, affordable food should help ensure that on the issue of community food systems, there is no unaccountable change."*

Principles and Purposes

Conventional, individualistic guides to leadership are cast as amoral, e.g., one might just as easily employ all "7 Habits of Highly Effective People" to destroy a community as to build it (Covey and Nathan 2011). In stark contrast, feminist leadership demands articulation of values and goals, including an "affirmative vision of change... rather than focusing only on oppression." (Batliwala 2010, 25). The U.S. food movement has articulated much that it is, perhaps nearly unanimously, *against* (e.g., genetically modified organisms, concentrated animal feeding operations and commodification of food). Perhaps more importantly, it also envisions and is working to build and to own an alternative food system that feeds us all without exploiting one another or the land.

For example, CJFN supports the right to food and aims to end all forms of exploitation in the food and agriculture system via constituent engaged advocacy and participatory democracy. Food Dignity envisions a society where each community exercises significant control over its food system; this control should be achieved with dignity as the path and the destination, via radically democratic negotiation, action and learning in ways that nurture all of our people and sustain our land for current and future generations.

The People's Movement Assemblies of the Food + Justice = Democracy conference that LaDonna organized defined "food justice" as "the right of communities everywhere to produce, process, distribute, access, and eat good food regardless of race, class, gender, ethnicity, citizenship, ability, religion, or community." This vision includes freedom from exploitation, workers' rights to fair labor practices, racial justice, and gender equity. The path is explicitly "values-based: respect, empathy, pluralism, valuing knowledge." (Food + Justice = Democracy PMAs 2012) Theses transformative agendas for both process and outcomes would be well served by more explicitly feminist labor and leadership practice.

Practice

Promising practices for engendering more feminist labor and leadership in the work of the US community food movement include the below.

- Talk not just about gender, but explicitly about sexism and patriarchy (Similarly, talk not just about race, but about racism and white supremacy).
- Use Historical Trauma to frame the narrative of food and agriculture system of exploitation that addresses the issues of colonialism and capitalism and acknowledges the impact on communities of color and tribal nations.
- Connect gender-specific issues to food justice. An example of this in the food movement is international, when four years ago the *Via Campesina* peasant movement for food sovereignty made ending violence against women a top priority. Their slogan for one recent conference was "Sowing the seeds of action and hope, for feminism and food sovereignty!" (La Via Campesina 2013).
- Articulate ways that gender oppression intersects with other forms of systematic oppression (Yet also do not compare them; the work of social change is not an oppression Olympics). This, with historical trauma, means acknowledging the tensions woman of color face in false but often forced choices between work for gender vs. racial equity, including by racism in the feminist movement and sexism in civil rights movements. The U.S. work on labor (in)justice in the food system provides a leading model for this (Jayaraman 2013, Liu and Apollon 2011).
- Pass on the credit. Consider and reconsider who is asked to represent the work. Hand the microphone to "grassroots" feminist and anti-racist leaders (Cutting and Themba-Nixon 2006). For example, Christine recently declined to be interviewed for a radio program about the work of one of the Food Dignity community partners until and unless people from that organization were interviewed first, or instead.
- Lead by building leadership. For example, Food Dignity is supplying $150,000 in mini-grant funding to the five community partner organizations which are, in turn, using this to support citizen solutions to food insecurity. Early experience shows that more and longer-term mentorship of emerging leaders is needed; this is a gap CFJN aims to help fill.
- Create and protect spaces for feminist leadership development. GFJI hinted at this with a recent Women of Color in Leadership conference call. A "RAD women in the food movement" email list formed recently, initially through personal networks of its two founders. Several other gender-specific spaces for women of color are forming; for Example, the Women of Color in Food and Agriculture retreat held in St. Simone's Island and WHY Hunger efforts to create online materials that acknowledge the role of women in the food movement. In Food Dignity, community partners had a

meeting of their own preceding the most recent full team workshop; both were facilitated by Detroit's civil rights leader and DBCFSN member Lila Cabbil.

- Self-educate. Gender and racial equity is as much the work of men as of women, of whites as of people of color. Audre Lorde's wisdom shared 35 years ago still holds today: "women of today are still being called upon to stretch across the gap of male ignorance... this is an old and primary tool of all oppressors to keep the oppressed occupied with the master's concerns" (1979/1981, 100). For example, Malik Yakini (listed 5th in table 1 and a co-founder of DBCFSN) is doing that work, calling himself a "recovering chauvinist" while facilitating an anti-racism workshop with the Food Dignity team and inviting insights from participants on this front.

East New York Farms! (ENYF!) of United Community Centers in Brooklyn, New York is one of the community partners in Food Dignity. African-American food blogger Erika Nicole Kendall cites their work in a recent column she entitled "America's food debates are just white men talking: the Big Food-versus-Michael Pollan rhetoric ignores what low-income communities are already doing to get healthy." She shows how communities like East New York are "making their *own* solutions" (Kendall 2013).

The work of ENYF!, CJFN, and Food Dignity form just small parts of a larger food movement to build "Food Justice 2.0" that includes food security for all communities. The social justice leader Winona LaDuke (who appears in the 11th spot in table 1) is widely quoted as saying, "*if you're not at the table you're on the menu.*" To succeed, the U.S. food movement needs feminist and anti-racist leaders from communities most affected by food insecurity, not off the edge of nor on the table, but at the head.

Acknowledgments

Food Dignity is supported by Agriculture and Food Research Initiative Competitive Grant no. 2011-68004-30074 from the USDA National Institute of Food and Agriculture (www.fooddignity.org). Christine would also like to credit Food Dignity partners and feminist food movement leaders E. Jemila Sequeira and Gayle M. Woodsum in influencing her part of this work.

Notes

1. By this "movement" we mean those working to create local and regional alternatives to the dominant industrial food system and/or to resist that food system. This includes most of those using the phrases community food security, food justice, food democracy, and/or food sovereignty to describe their work. The movement also includes locovore groups; though these do not always work with the social justice goals of the others, they are literally growing alternatives to "big ag." It excludes most conventional

anti-hunger work via food banking and federal food programs, which help feed people but do not aim to change the food system.

2. We sent the survey link to comfood@elist.tufts.edu, growing_foodandjustice@lists.riseup.net, and local-foods@lists.extension.org. It was almost certainly forwarded to other food-related email lists as well. The two leadership-identification questions were: "Identify 3 to 6 people who come to your mind first when asked: who are the most influential leaders in the community food movement in the United States? And "Identify 2 to 6 of the most influential local community food movement leaders in your community (however you define that)".

3. See www.cfjn.org and www.fooddignity.org.

4. The word "hunger" formed part of the official definition of food insecurity until it was discursively eradicated in 2006, when the USDA renamed "food insecurity with hunger" as "very low food security." According to the panel tasked with reviewing USDA's "food insecurity" definitions and assessment, the word hunger "refers to the *consequence* of food insecurity that, because of a prolonged, involuntary lack of food due to lack of economic resources, results in discomfort, illness, weakness, or pain that goes beyond the usual uneasy sensation." (Committee on National Statistics 2006: 47) Their report noted that hunger was an "individual-level concept" while the food security measures that USDA used were household level.

5. The women listed are Karen Washington, Miriam Grunes, Nancy Romer, Karen Early, and Nikki Henderson. The men are Robert Pierce and Will Allen. With the exception of Washington (based in New York) and Henderson (based in the West-Coast Bay area), these leaders are all in or near Wisconsin. Respondents were disproportionately (17 percent of them) from that state, likely because the Growing Food and Justice email list (one of several used to distribute the survey), while national, was fostered by Will Allen's Wisconsin-based Growing Power.

Bibliography

Admira. 2004. *Organizational Development Toolkit: Feminist Leadership*. Accessed June 27 2013. Available from www.zenska-mreza.hr/prirucnik/en/en_read_management_leadership_8.htm.

Alkon, Alison Hope, and Julian Agyeman. 2011. *Cultivating Food Justice: Race, Class, and Sustainability*. Cambridge, MA: MIT Press.

Allen, Patricia, and Carolyn Sachs. 2007. "Women and Food Chains: The Gendered Politics of Food." *International Journal of Sociology of Food and Agriculture* 15, no. 1:1-23.

Anzaldúa, Gloria, and Analouise Keating, eds. 2002. *This Bridge We Call Home: Radical Visions for Transformation*. New York: Routledge.

Batliwala, Srilatha. 2010. "Feminist Leadership for Social Transformation: Clearing the Conceptual Cloud." New York: CREA. Accessed June 27, 2013. Available from www.justassociates.org/sites/justassociates.org/files/feminist-leadership-clearing-conceptual-cloud-srilatha-batliwala.pdf.

Bureau of Labor Statistics. 2012a. American Time Use Survey-2011 Results. Washington, DC: US Department of Labor.

———. 2012b. Employed Persons by Detailed Occupation, Sex, Race, and Hispanic or Latino Ethnicity. Washington, DC: US Department of Labor.

Carney, Patricia A, Janet L Hamada, Rebecca Rdesinski, Lorena Sprager, Katelyn R Nichols, Betty Y Liu, Joel Pelayo, Maria Antonia Sanchez, and Jacklien Shannon. 2012. "Impact of a Community Gardening Project on Vegetable Intake, Food Security and Family Relationships: A Community-Based Participatory Research Study." *Journal of Community Health* 37 no. 4:874-881.

Coleman-Jensen, Alisha , Mark Nord, Margaret Andrews, and Steven Carlson. 2012. "Household Food Security in the United States in 2011." USDA Economic Research Service. www.ers.usda.gov/publications/err-economic-research report/err141.aspx#.UZmK15yjmWY.

COMFOOD. 2013. *COMFOOD: A Listserve Focusing on Community Food Security.* Tufts elists. Accessed June 24 2013. Available from https://elist.tufts.edu/wws/info/comfood.

Committee on National Statistics. 2006. Food Insecurity and Hunger in the United States: An Assessment of the Measure. Washington, DC: National Research Council of the National Academies.

Costa, Temra. 2010. *Farmer Jane: Women Changing the Way We Eat.* Layton, UT: Gibbs Smith.

Covey, Stephen R, and John Nathan. 2011. *The 7 Habits of Highly Effective People*: Enterprise Media.

Cutting, Hunter, and Makani Themba-Nixon, editors. 2006. *Talking the Walk: A Communications Guide for Racial Justice.* Oakland, CA: AK Press.

de Schutter, Olivier 2012. *Women's Rights and the Right to Food.* United Nations General Assembly.

DeLind, Laura B, and Anne E Ferguson. 1999. "Is this a Women's Movement? The Relationship of Gender to Community-Supported Agriculture in Michigan." *Human Organization* 58, no. 2: 190-200.

Doiron, Roger. 2011. *COMFOOD mailing list*, Aug 30.

Faruqi, Sonia. 2013. "Agriculture Needs More Women: A Psychological Case for Safer Food and More Humane Farming." *The Atlantic*, September 25.

Food + Justice = Democracy PMAs. 2012. *Principles of Food Justice.* Institute for Agriculture and Trade Policy Accessed July 2 2013. Available from http://www.iatp.org/documents/draft-principles-of-food-justice.

Forum for Food Sovereignty. 2007. *Nyéléni 2007- Final declaration* Accessed July 2 2013. Available from http://www.nyeleni.org/spip.php?article280.

Foucault, Michel. 1975/1995. *Discipline and Punish: the Birth of the Prison.* Translated by A Sheridan. New York: Vintage Books.

GFJI. *Growing Food and Justice for All Initiative, About Us.* Accessed June 24 2013. Available from http://www.growingfoodandjustice.org/About_Us.html.

Guthman, Julie. 2008. "'If they only knew': Color Blindness and Universalism in California Alternative Food Institutions." *The Professional Geographer* 60, no. 3: 387-397.

Hale, Todd. 2011. *In U.S. Men are Shopping More than Ever while Women Are Watching More TV.* Neilsen, March 11. Accessed June 25 2013. Available from http://www.nielsen.com/us/en/newswire/2011/in-u-s-men-are-shopping-more-than-ever-while-women-are-watching-more-tv.html.

Harper, A. Breeze, ed. 2009. *Sistah Vegan! Decolonizing Our Diets, Healing Our Bodies, Liberating Our Souls.* New York: Lantern Books.

Jayaraman, Saru. 2013. *Behind the Kitchen Door*. Ithaca, NY: Cornell University Press.

Kendall, Erika Nicole 2013. "America's Food Debates are Just White Men Talking: The Big Food-Versus-Michael Pollan Rhetoric Ignores what Low-Income Communities are Already Doing to Get Healthy." *Salon*, July 27. Available from http://www.salon.com/2013/07/27/americas_food_debates_are_just_white_men_talking/singleton/.

La Via Campesina. 2013. *Indonesia : Women Farmers of the World head to their IV International Assembly [Press Release June 4]*. Accessed July 8 2013. Available from http://viacampesina.org/en/index.php/main-issues-mainmenu-27/women-mainmenu-39/1413-indonesia-women-farmers-of-the-world-head-to-their-iv-international-assembly.

Liu, Yvonne Yen, and Dominique Apollon. 2011. "The Color of Food." Race Forward (formerly the Applied Research Center). Accessed December 27, 2013. Available at: http://urbanhabitat.org/files/food_justiceARC.pdf

Lorde, Audre. 1979/1981. "The Master's Tools Will Never Dismantle the Master's House." In *This Bridge Called My Back: Writings by Radical Women of Color*, edited by Cherrie Moraga and Gloria Anzaldúa. Watertown, MA: Persephone Press.

McGrath, Maria. 2013. "Back to the Kitchen." *Ms.*, Winter, 42-45.

Moraga, Cherrie, and Gloria Anzaldúa, eds. 1981. *This Bridge Called My Back: Writings by radical women of color*. Watertown, MA: Persephone Press.

Nathman, Avital Norman. 2013. "The Femisphere: Foodies and Food Politics." *Ms. Magazine Blog*, http://msmagazine.com/blog/2013/03/12/the-femisphere-foodies-and-food-politics/.

Philpott, Tom. 2010. "Acknowledging Women's Role in the Sustainable Food Movement." *Grist*, October 22. Accessed January 30 2012. Available from http://grist.org/article/food-2010-10-22-acknowledging-womens-role-in-the-sustainable-food-movement/.

Sharpless, Rebecca. 2013. *Cooking in Other Women's Kitchens: Domestic Workers in the South, 1865-1960*. Chapel Hill, NC: University of North Carolina Press.

Shiva, Vandana. 1988. *Staying Alive: Women, Ecology, and Survival in India*: Kali for Women New Delhi.

Slocum, Rachel 2006. "Anti-Racist Practice and the Work of Community Food Organizations." *Antipode* 38, no. 2: 327-349.

White, Monica M. 2011. "Sisters of the Soil: Urban Gardening as Resistance in Detroit." *Race/Ethnicity: Multidisciplinary Global Contexts* 5, no. 1:13-28.

CHAPTER 12

"I would have never…":
A Critical Examination of
Women's Agency for Food Security
through Participatory Action Research

Patricia L. Williams

Introduction

Food insecurity is not only a serious public health concern and social problem globally (Commission on Sustainable Agriculture and Climate Change 2012; Powledge 2010, 260-265; Darnton-Hill and Coyne 1998, 23-31), some would argue that it is also a violation of basic human rights (De Schutter 2012; Riches et al. 2004, 1-56; Riches 1999, 203-211; Rideout et al. 2007, 556-573). At an individual and household level, food insecurity is understood as lacking physical and economic access to sufficient, safe and nutritious food to meet dietary needs and food preferences for an active and healthy life (Food and Agriculture Organization 1996), an issue embedded within the larger contexts of community and global food systems (Winne 2008; Anderson, M., Cook, J. 1999, 141-150). In relatively wealthy countries such as Canada and the United States, food insecurity has affected growing numbers of people in the last decade (Health Canada 2012; Health Canada 2011; Coleman-Jensen et al. September 2012; Nord et al. 2000, 41; Nord, Andrews, and Carlson S. November 2007; Tarasuk, Mitchell and Dachner 2013). In Canada, 1.7 million households, slightly more than 12.5 percent reported some level of food insecurity in 2012, up by about 300,000 households compared with 2008 (Tarasuk, Mitchell and Dachner 2013). In Atlantic Canada's province of Nova Scotia (NS), rates of household food insecurity have consistently been significantly higher than the national average (Health Canada 2012; Health Canada 2011; Tarasuk, Mitchell and Dachner 2014), with 17.5 percent of households reporting food insecurity and 23 percent of children living in food insecure households in 2011 (Tarasuk, Mitchell and Dachner 2014). Furthermore, there is evidence to suggest that the extent and depth of food insecurity may be increasing for some (Brinkman et al. 2010, 153S-161S; Williams et al. 2012a, 183-188).

Food insecurity is understood to be a result of social organization (Travers 1996, 543-553). The current neoliberal context of policy and social relations has resulted in social inequalities related to marginalization through race, class and gender (Agarwal 1997, 1-1; Laraia, Borja, and Bentley 2009, 1042-1047). In Canada, there is abundant evidence that women experience disproportionate levels of food insecurity (Health Canada 2011; Marcoux 1997; Fukuda-Parr 1999; Tarasuk, Mitchell and Dachner 2013). While acknowledging the existence of hegemonic gendered, economic and racialized structures of domination surrounding the role of women in food preparation, Sukovic, Sharf, Sharkey & John (2011) point to the power of food, particularly its preparation, as a means to empower otherwise oppressed and marginalized women. Similarly, Friedman (1999) and others (Barndt 2008; Desmarais 2007) examine the powerful role that food can play in the development of personal (Sukovic et al. 2011, 228-247; Winter 2004, 2) and communal agency (Skinner, Hanning, and Tsuji 2006, 148-161). Friedman (1999) challenges us to consider how, when and why our patterns of work, trade and family life came to be and how this has impacted key practices and structures that facilitate acquiring and sharing food. Consistent with this approach, Cox (1995) contends that a political economy approach allows us to stand "back from the apparent fixity of the present to ask how… existing structures came into being and how they may be changing, or how they may be induced to change" (32). The interaction among economic relations and material capabilities (e.g., resources to buy and sell certain foods and who benefits or is harmed in these market relationships), socially constructed knowledge or ideas (e.g., ideologies, discourse) and organizational forms of power (e.g., ways in which people organize themselves into groups within society through institutions and networks) all shape food systems and related policies (Andrée 2007), enacting in favour of hegemonic structures of domination and consequently contributing to food insecurity.

Analysis of the three sets of relations of force described by Gramsci (1971, 181-184) and others (Andrée 2011)—the material, institutional and discursive— and their interplay across three levels of mutually constitutive political activity—civil society, the state and global order—can help in understanding the conditions that contribute to power relations in food systems (Andrée 2011) and thus having an impact on household food security. However, analysis of agency to have influence on these forces may also be an important lens for understanding social change (Fullan 1999; Policy Working Group of Acting Change Together for Community Food Security (ACT for CFS 2013). Communities are a critical locus for action to impact policy (Hancock 2009), however, working with communities to address food insecurity must be done in ways that foster democratic participation, shared power and knowledge, value for different ways of knowing, and agency for social change, approaches that together have the potential to expose power relations and social inequalities contributing to food insecurity. Fundamental challenges to addressing these power relations are the discursive tensions in how food security is understood and approached either as an individual or as a collective responsibility (Dorfman, Wallack, and Woodruff 2005, 320-336) and the interrelated, yet conflicting understanding of how the issue of food insecurity is addressed (i.e., sustainable food systems versus antipoverty approaches) (Power 1999, 30-37). These challenges serve to constrain the development of an equitable and coherent approach to building food security for all, and highlight the importance of Gramsci's notion of 'convergence' "the moment when seemingly separate spheres, actions, actors, or ideas are drawn together to create a fundamental *connection* between them" (Policy Working Group of Acting Change Together for Community Food Security (ACT for CFS) 2013; Jones 2006). While not acknowledged explicitly, the goal of convergence has been central to efforts to build capacity to affect policy change that contributes to "food security for all in Nova Scotia and beyond" (www.foodarc.ca/about/).

Our work in NS over the past decade with family resource centers (FRC)[1] has been an insightful and fulfilling journey, one where women with first-hand experience with food insecurity have demonstrated how they themselves have become agents of change, building awareness of and challenging their situations through unique and participatory approaches to food costing. In general, food costing entails collecting information on the cost of foods that make up a basic nutritious diet.[2] Unlike traditional practice, where professionals undertake all steps of the food costing research, Participatory Food Costing (PFC) uses participatory action research (PAR) methodology (Minkler and Wallerstein 2008; Minkler M 2000, 191), the "systematic inquiry, with the collaboration of those affected by the issue being studied, for the purposes of education and taking action or effecting social change" (Green et al. 1994, 194). In PAR it is posited that involving people with first-hand experience of food insecurity in data collection, knowledge sharing, and project decision making provides a "sense of ownership" over the information and increases the likelihood of taking action to affect social change (Israel, Schulz, Parker and Becker 1998, 173-202).

A participatory approach, when applied to food costing, means that women experiencing food insecurity and those with a stake in the issue (e.g., staff at FRCs, women's centers and other community-based organizations, as well as other key state and civil society actors including academics, representatives from key government departments,[3] and civil society organizations and coalitions), work together to undertake the research. This may include involvement with decision-making around data collection and analysis, as well as the communication and dissemination of research results. Specifically, individuals who take on the role of food costers are trained and supported[4] to work with others in their communities to collect and use research on the accessibility of a healthy diet. Food costers participate in analyzing and interpreting the data as part of a team, which includes the project principal investigator and coordinator, a steering committee and working group, research assistant and students, and play a critical role in disseminating the research results at local, provincial, national and sometimes international levels. Overall, this capacity building process aims to enable project partners and others to work together to influence policy and to create the conditions to strengthen food security in communities across the province.

Six cycles of PFC have been undertaken by the project partners; following each cycle a report entitled *Can Nova Scotians Afford to Eat Healthy?* (e.g., Nova Scotia Food Security Network and Food Action Research Centre (FoodARC) 2013; Mount Saint Vincent University and Nova Scotia Food Security Network 2011) is developed through iterative processes including consultations with government[5] and community partners. The report essentially "paints a picture" of the cost and affordability of a basic nutritious diet for families of various sizes and income sources in NS, including families who rely on minimum wage earnings, income assistance and public pensions. Findings from the report are formally released and communicated through a number of channels (academic, community and government) with the support of project partners. In addition to this primary report, the knowledge produced through PFC has been shared by a variety of communication strategies such as briefing notes, academic and community publications and presentations, workshops, social networking, media coverage and partner websites at local, provincial, national, and international levels.

The research presented here explores the role that PAR plays in creating the conditions for the development of personal and collective agency for addressing three sets of relations of power—the material, institutional and discursive—that impact food insecurity. The purpose of this chapter is to present an account of the sense of agency that was experienced by low-income women in NS, Canada through their involvement in a PAR project on food security and how it has contributed to collective agency of project partners and a growing movement to address food insecurity in NS.

We have contributed to improved conditions for addressing food insecurity in NS, as highlighted in this chapter, and reflexive practice (Brookfield, 1998) and developmental evaluation (Patton, 2004), both approaches that support learning and evaluation in complex and constantly changing situations, have been used to inform and guide PFC. However, there are also limitations to our approach that are important to acknowledge. These include: the need to expand multi-sector partnerships and relationships with those who are less "like-minded"; more inquiry into the differences in power and privilege and vulnerability that exists among different partners and stakeholders; the need to align with current governments' mandates, academic tenure and promotion processes and ethics review board expectations; and 'blind spots' such as the pervasiveness of negative public perceptions and judgments of those living in poverty and related assumptions that putting a *'face'* on food insecurity combined with PFC data would lead to a sympathetic ear. Another limitation is the researcher fatigue that comes with the reality that "this is people's lives we are fooling with, and when we are working with them, we can't leave people high and dry as we have asked them to change their lives and staying involved is the moral imperative", while for some, their work priorities may shift from food security, so it no longer 'fits' their role. There is also the misalignment of the pace of research with and the need for rapid-response mechanisms to anticipate and respond to needs of partners and stakeholders—which our research and experience has helped to expose early on.

Methodology and Methods

This chapter was developed from data gathered as part of a larger PAR project funded through the NS Department of Health and Wellness (project overview and methodology described above). Qualitative data collected in several phases from 2002-2012 are used to frame the findings presented here. Critical discourse analysis (CDA), a theoretical positioning and methodological approach that examines how power structures are socially reinforced and contested through discourse (Wodak and Meyer 2009) informed our qualitative approach to examine the data sources listed in table 12.1. However, we were more concerned with what PFC participants described, and less with how they discussed their experiences (a necessary component of discourse analysis). As a result, we performed a more grounded qualitative analysis, while relying on the critical premises of CDA approaches to guide our work. These premises include recognition of neoliberal social structures, interlinking of politics and economics, and the hegemonic ways in which the neoliberal power manifests itself in the way people perform ideology, speak of their place in society and relate to the institutions of power. The qualitative data were primarily drawn from three reports representing data sets totaling 32 interviews, 17 focus groups and a document review.

The analysis focused on identifying the development of agency as expressed by participants drawing upon a political economy perspective (Andrée 2007; Policy Working Group of Acting Change Together for Community Food Security (ACT for CFS 2013) to identify conceptual categories and patterns relating to this process. Text from the secondary data sources was read consecutive times and themes were identified and coded. Coded data were analyzed for coherence and interpreted for patterns within each theme. Interconnections between theme categories were explored through constant comparison (Parry

2003) in order to provide holistic interpretation of the data. Interpretations were shared with select project community and academic partners; their input informed the development of this chapter.

For these studies, ethical approval was obtained from Research Ethics Boards at one or more of the following NS institutions: Mount Saint Vincent University, Dalhousie University, and Acadia University. The "Findings" section that follows presents a systematic analysis of these data, and it also emphasizes first-person accounts as a way to minimally mediate in their voice with minimal modification. The section makes up the centerpiece of the paper, and includes an extensive and rich set of direct quotes in an attempt to include the participants' voices in as direct a manner as possible.

Table 12.1: Data Sources

Secondary data examined	Description of data included in reports	Data collection methods	Participants (n)	Time frame
Photovoice Report: Pictures that Represent Voices...Examining Impacts of Participatory Food Costing on Communities and Organizations. (Mount Saint Vincent University and Nova Scotia Food Security Network, 2013).	Photographs taken by research participants/co-researchers; transcribed conversation of the structured dialogue where participants discussed their photos. Participants were asked to answer the question: How has your involvement in PFC impacted or contributed to changes within your community and/or organization?	Structured dialogue (PHOTO method)	FRC staff involved in PFC for five or more years (n=5)	2012
The Nova Scotia Participatory Food Costing Projects (2001-2011): Evaluative Learning from Ten Years of Participatory Research. (Williams, Anderson, Hunter, Watt, 2013)	Synthesis report that aimed to provide a retrospective roadmap and analysis of PFC activities encompasses several study reports, evaluative theses and reports and project newsletters, publications, meeting minutes, and other relevant documents from 2001-2011.	In-depth interviews	Food costers involved for at least one year (n=12)	2003
		In-depth interviews	Food costers and support people (n=3)	2003
		Focus Groups	Five focus groups with food costers and support people	2003
		In-depth interviews	Principal Investigator and Coordi-	2004

			nator x 2 (n=4)	
		Focus group	Project steering committee (n=5)	2004
		Focus group	Community champions (n=10)	2004
		Focus Group and Questionnaire	National advisory committee (n=7)	2004
		In-depth Interviews	Food costers involved for 4-8 years (n=7)	2010
		Interviews	Food costers involved for 1-8 years (n=6)	2010
I would have never thought that I would be in such a predicament: Voices from Women Experiencing Food Insecurity in Nova Scotia. *J Hunger Environ Nutr.* 7(2-3): 253-270. (Williams et al., 2012).	Transcripts from Story Sharing Workshops where participants discussed their own experiences with food insecurity and what being involved with the PFC project has meant to them	Structured dialogue	Eight sessions with women with experience of food insecurity (n=56)	2003

Findings

Participants in the study represented a diverse group of partners who participated in the PFC project for various periods of time between 2001 and 2012. The data were predominantly derived from women with experience of food insecurity who participated as food costers,[6] some of whom were receiving governmental income assistance, some of whom were working for minimum wage or slightly more, some with children and some without, and some without formal higher education, whereas others had a university degree or were pursuing postsecondary education. In addition to women experiencing food insecurity, partners who played a supportive role working to address food insecurity (such as staff of FRCs); decision makers within community, government and academic institutions;[7] students; and community members participated in aspects of the

PFC data collection that were included in this analysis.

Five distinct but interrelated themes emerged that were considered central to the development of agency for influencing hegemonic structures: (1) Raised awareness of personal experience with food insecurity; (2) Acquired knowledge and awareness about food insecurity; (3) Increased ability to influence and take action; (4) Acquired feeling of belonging to community/group; (5) Increased interest and capacity to network. Across these themes was a general sense that PAR processes, including both individual and collective supports, contributed to creating the supportive environments that fostered the development of agency across all three realms of power within the political economy: the ideas, organizational forces and economic relations (figure 12.1).

Capacity Building for Social and Policy Change

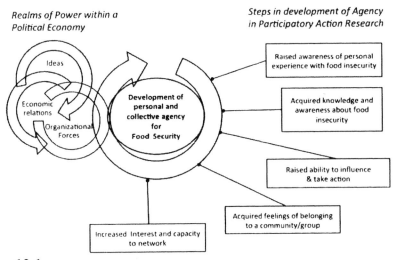

Figure 12.1

Ideas: Creating New Discourse on Food Insecurity

Raised Awareness of Personal Experience with Food Insecurity

At the foundation of PFC is the belief that the engagement of individuals affected by food insecurity, primarily low-income women, in all stages of the research is necessary to build capacity for policy change at multiple levels to address food insecurity. The findings show that PFC supported women experiencing food insecurity to develop ways to challenge overwhelming disempowerment and powerlessness related to structures of power. For many food costers, being involved with PFC has had a positive impact on their emotional and mental health, and their self-perceptions of being (or not being) "worthy" and taking a broader perspective on food insecurity has provided some relief from guilt and self-blame at a personal level. As one food coster explained:

> *I've suffered food insecurity myself um and years ago I used to think that it was me, that it was my bad budgeting, that I wasn't a good parent um because I couldn't stretch my food dollars and, and with all the information that I've learned over the past ten years [from PFC], it's not me at all...you know, it's the fact that, you know, is, is I'm paid pretty good um but being the only income for four or five people family um you know um we don't do it right um...so it's not me, it's, it's you know, society, it's food.* (Food Coster, Williams, Anderson, Hunter, Watt, 2013, 33).

As a result of participating in PFC, others discovered they were able to find their own voice in their communities and were better able to help others struggling with food insecurity to be able to move forward in their lives. For some, both reduced self-blame and feelings of shame have allowed them to recognize and utilize the power that comes from their experience in educating and supporting others dealing with food insecurity. As the following food coster explains, "*...yup, and we were on the (income assistance) system and lived on the system and, you know, I was ashamed of that years ago and now I'm not. I tell people and I tell moms that I work with that, you know, there is a light at the end of tunnel*" (Food Coster, Williams, Anderson, Hunter, Watt, 2013, 33). Similarly, the following food coster explains how through a story sharing component of the PFC qualitative research, she was able to share her experience and comfort and motivate other participants dealing with food insecurity:

> *But, umm, I am just a very social and outgoing person, and like I said straightforward so I don't mind saying like well, you know, this is what happened to me and this is how I dealt with it, or... to be involved in something like this and say this really needs some attention and this is why and here's the proof of why. So, sometimes I hope that I can maybe motivate other people to say okay well you know what, I've been there too. And since you were comfortable with sharing that. I don't feel uncomfortable sharing* (Food coster, Williams, Anderson, Hunter, Watt, 2013, 34).

Participants built their confidence as a result of feeling valued and included in the project. As one food coster shared: "*So what has my involvement meant for me? This gives me the ability to do something for myself, my family, and my province... just by doing that it's built up my self-esteem*" (Food coster, Williams, Anderson, Hunter, Watt, 2013, 17). Another woman talked about PFC as contributing to positive self-esteem:

To some degree even though I know it's the hardest job in the world being a stay-at-home mom, you feel kind of unproductive and under-valued and that kind of stuff. And to be involved in a project like this that it's so important to so many people and providing it does effect some change. Umm... It could benefit a lot of people and to know that I took part in that... That I guess... I don't know... Call it an ego booster or, you know, a self-esteem improvement, whatever... But, it's been interesting and I've enjoyed and it makes me feel like I'm actually doing something that matters (Food coster, Williams, Anderson, Hunter, Watt, 2013, 17).

Qualitative PFC research has also served to educate and challenge stereotypes associated with living on income assistance. "*I've used it [the food costing report] to challenge stereotypes... But still seriously $244*[8] *a month and that includes everything including your cleaning supplies. ... I do use it to challenge stereotypes and I use it to educate people who are going to be going into the field. I am often asked to go into community colleges or university classes and talk about poverty and I always talk about the food costing data*" (FRC staff person E, MSVU and NSFSN, 2013, 15). Another FRC staff person shared: "*Again it's around assumptions for me. And people making assumptions that people who are food insecure don't know what to do with food. And I hear that from folks all the time. 'Don't tell me what to eat. I know what I'm supposed to eat—I feel bad enough as it is.' It's not that people don't know, it's not that people don't—it's that they are unable to.*" (FRC staff person E, MSVU and NSFSN, 2013, 17).

It has also raised awareness that people, especially women, often experience stress and isolation when living with food insecurity:

You realize that you're not alone and that there are people out there that are really working to try and fix this problem and uh just to know that there's people there on your side and that they get it...you know they aren't pointing fingers at you because you're struggling with this kind of stuff and also like when I say this to the families I'm working with now and I'm saying you know you're not the only ones that are going through this and this is why, and I guess it just, it takes a little bit of guilt away...that may be attached to the food insecurity issue (Food coster, Williams, Anderson, Hunter, Watt, 2013, 18).

This awareness and understanding has lead to an integration of questions and discussions into FRC's regular programming to help parents tell their stories and contextualize their experience within the larger social issues that precipitate food insecurity. Shifts in the way that people think and talk about this issue are being encouraged: "*It's up to the moms if they want to have a discussion about this or not—it's really up to them—but often during programming when they are finishing off the cooking, we have really great discussions about the affordability of food and the stress that people are under in trying to access food.*" (FRC staff person D, MSVU and NSFSN, 2013, 8).

Women experiencing food insecurity developed personal agency and empowerment through the development of emotional recognition of the agency that they posed individually through their stories and through feeling valued to work collectively with other PFC partners to address food insecurity: "*A lot of the people that we (FRCs) have had as food costers have moved on to other things. They still keep in touch, but they are doing things that they never thought they would do in their lives as a result of being part of this project and being valued in a meaningful way. And by being valued by other people, they started to—I think anyway—started to value themselves a little bit more*" (FRC staff person E, MSVU and NSFSN, 2013, 13).

Acquired Knowledge and Awareness about Food Insecurity and Food Security

Using a participatory and collaborative model to engage with many different stakeholders allows ideas to be generated by a larger number of participants. Women with personal experience with food insecurity and partners who have a stake in the issue collectively create knowledge through multiple research methods and mobilize this knowledge through project reports, key messages and tools for dialogue and advocacy. The theme of "voice" continues in these observations as well, linked to the sense of having valuable knowledge. As one partner said: "*The whole main thing to me with this project is giving people the power and voice. It's not just professors or students. It's people who are actually living in this type of circumstance.*" (Food coster, Williams, Anderson, Hunter, Watt, 2013, 25). Being involved in PFC increased FRC credibility related to food insecurity: "*Other agencies and other players in this whole thing are turning to us as FRC as the go-to-guys now, because we know what we are doing. They are looking to us now for answers.*" (FRC staff person B, MSVU and NSFSN, 2013, 11). Another community partner remarked: "*I think within a FRC these tools and the data that they've collected, it makes us all like the experts in the whole subject in the community, so that when the papers hear [about issues like food security], they're calling the FRC and asking 'what can you tell us about that?' So now we're the experts in our communities to deal with food insecurity.*" (FRC staff person, Williams, Anderson, Hunter, Watt, 2013, 24).

Partners have been able to use the food costing findings to increase awareness of the costs of a nutritious diet and lack of affordability and access to food: "*Well, it's been very interesting and eye opening type of thing...it opened my eyes to like how much it really does cost to eat healthy and stuff like that.*" and "*I was amazed by the price that it cost for a family of four to eat healthy.*" (Food coster, Williams, Anderson, Hunter, Watt, 2013, 30). One participant described a greater knowledge of healthy eating and ways to cope with an inadequate food budget as a result of being involved with PFC:

It helps me kind of just make better choices since I've done the food costing because I can look at the food and say oh yeah well nutritionally really I don't need these cookies and you put them back you know or do you know what I mean and I do make more of a point now to make sure that most of the groceries I get are the yellow store brand or whatever because I know, because of the food costing, that they are adequate nutritionally which is something I always wondered about before. (Food coster, Williams, Anderson, Hunter, Watt, 2013, 38).

Awareness about the root causes of food insecurity (i.e., systems and policies that contribute to income inequalities and unjust food systems) increased among food costers as a result of their involvement in PFC. For example, participants indicated an increased understanding of the importance of policy as part of the action on food insecurity. As one participant noted with exasperation: *"Like uh they may say oh it's our policy well that policy didn't come down from god almighty. Man made the policy so if man made the policy then man can break his policy and simply make another one you know..."* (Food coster, Williams, Anderson, Hunter, Watt, 2013, 30). In addition, FRC partners have shared how PFC has broadened the way that they think and talk about food:

And we have talked about food in terms of those broader issues that might be kind of new for people. They might not have always thought about food in that sort of way, so why does local food cost more than something that's travelled across the world? You know that sort of thing. So I think that's the piece that the - that being involved in the food costing project has brought to our food programs. For the staff it's sort of broadened how we think about, you know, offering that to families. And sometimes it has resulted in some great discussion around those other [policy related] pieces. (FRC staff person D, MSVU and NSFSN, 2013, 15).

And I just can't get over the bureaucracy that stops blueberries that are right there from being accessed in our schools. When it's as simple as driving down the road. So for me it's about challenging policies and getting at that level. Like I know the food costing – that's part of what we are doing. The policy lens [Thought about food? Understanding the relationship between food security and well-being in Nova Scotia: A background paper and policy lens (2006) that was created in terms of looking at what is it that we need to think about whenever we are making decisions around whatever it is. (FRC staff person E, MSVU and NSFSN, 2013, 24).

With growing awareness about the influence of policy, came a broader understanding among participants of the impacts of food insecurity on emotional, physical, and psychological health, including its connection to chronic disease, and population health. Through their work with the PFC project, many individuals came to recognize the benefits that reducing health and social inequities could have on their own health and well-being and on society as a whole. As one food coster described: "*Like, food is a necessity. It's not... It's not a gift or it's not...You have to have it. It's a right. ...And I think if that if family eats better they will be less sick.*" (Food coster, Williams, Anderson, Hunter, Watt, 2013, 31).

Through their involvement in PFC, and particularly the local food component that was added to the PFC survey tool and training starting in 2005, FRCs, food costers and the communities they work with became more aware of the current issues that threaten to compromise the local food system. For example, in follow-up research with food costers and support people, some commented on their surprise to learn that so little local food was available in grocery stores in NS. One FRC partner shared: "*I grew up in [fishing community] right next to XXX plant and when we had to look up the price for fish and find out where it was from [as part of PFC]—China—I was blown away. So I think stuff like that is important for people to be aware of and know 'cause I don't think a lot of people do, especially the participants that we work with.*" (FRC staff person, Williams, Anderson, Hunter, Watt, 2013, 38).

Consideration of both sustainable food systems and poverty reduction approaches were recognized by PFC food costers as important and equally necessary steps in ensuring food security for all:

> *Our local stores and stuff you know to make those policies that ah you know they have to carry more local stuff you know um you know that our healthy foods aren't the most expensive foods in the store and uh you know just that it's available to everybody...you know, whether it's a matter of a making sure, you know, people have guaranteed incomes...but I think right now the thing is to get people to really buy into it and listen to it* [messages from food costing] (Food coster, Williams, Anderson, Hunter, Watt, 2013, 31).

Alongside the intention to help participants tell their stories, programming changes made by some FRC partners have incorporated ideas and approaches to help build awareness of the underlying causes of food insecurity. For example, one FRC partner described how they now introduce "bigger picture" questions into their food programs to help participants think about and express some of their food-system related issues, concerns or experiences (FRC staff person, MSVU and NSFSN, 2013, 8). The knowledge sharing and advocacy that has resulted from PFC has started to shift the idea of food insecurity from an individual to a societal issue and the recognition that policy change along with grassroots engagement is necessary to address it. Family Resource Centre partners described how their involvement with the PFC project has enhanced their understanding of food insecurity as a complex issue lacking simple solutions:

> *Through the food costing I realized that—you know because when I first went into it thinking ok I just wanna know what it's going [to] cost to feed a family—what does the government think it's costing, and what*

the reality of it is. And just realizing there was so much more in-
volved—so many more things to look at and you know just gaining
knowledge about food banks and I've learned so much through the pro-
ject that we share with families. (FRC staff person, MSVU and
NSFSN, 2013, 21).

Increased Ability to Influence and Take Action

Participants also reported that having evidence, viewed by FRC partners as *"the*
language of government" (Shaw, forthcoming), about the cost and availability
of a healthy diet helps to equip people and communities with valuable and credible information supporting their advocacy efforts and enabling them to challenge the assumptions and stereotypes associated with food insecurity: *"And I*
have [heard] people say, well people on social assistance don't know how to get
groceries....they are not buying the right food. Or they are not healthy...I said,
well, listen they have a cheque of $700 or $800, and really no money... They
should spend $500 just for the basic food." [referring to cost of basic nutritious
food basket in 2002 of $572/month for a reference family of four] (Food coster,
Williams, Anderson, Hunter, Watt, 2013, 34).

For many food costers and other FRC partners involvement in PFC has
been a springboard to them taking an active role in addressing food insecurity in
their local community: *"I'm always sharing that info [PFC findings] with peo-*
ple and trying to get them to see that that uh this isn't just one person's issue."
(Food coster, Williams, Anderson, Hunter, Watt, 2013, 30). One participant also
described feeling more empowered to make a difference in her community as a
result of being involved with PFC: *"It's always very exciting when um we get*
together in those groups and um I feel so you know you're gonna be able to go
there and you're going to be able to make a difference when you come back to
your home." (Food coster, Williams, Anderson, Hunter, Watt, 2013, 36).

Many food costers and support people have also been directly involved in
public education and advocacy activities to promote food security by engaging
with the media, politicians and their communities on behalf of the PFC project:

> *The advocacy piece is a piece that is very important to us as a center. I*
> *think that the food costing project has allowed the opportunity for*
> *moms, but also for us as an organization to have another way to advo-*
> *cate for changes to policies around food and that sort of thing and*
> *bring a lot of awareness about the circumstances that people are actu-*
> *ally trying to survive in really on a small amount of money* (FRC staff
> person, MSVU and NSFSN, 2013, 17).

Partners also share the report widely with students who work with them: *"We*
have shared [the food costing report] with students that we have doing place-

ments at our center. Particularly social work students, we always suggest they read it." (FRC staff person, MSVU and NSFSN, 2013, 16). The report and PFC processes are also incorporated into health and social science related undergraduate and graduate level curricula across several universities by project partners and others inside as well as outside of the province.

Taking action through sharing PFC knowledge has resulted in recognized policy change. This has included the recognition of food security as an integral piece of population health promotion through its incorporation in provincial strategies aimed at improving the health status of all Nova Scotians. For example, the issue of food security has been incorporated into the provincial strategy for prevention of chronic disease. However, partners are aware that food insecurity, and especially its most important determinant, poverty, are not priority items on the agenda of governments, in part because the general public is rarely voicing it as a concern.

Acquired Feeling of Belonging to a Community/Group

Participatory Food Costing has provided a venue for women experiencing food insecurity to have a say in the processes used, express their views, and be listened to. For women in disempowering situations, this meant they were able to become engaged in the PAR process to find their voice and were supported to question and, to a limited degree, have more control over the structures that impact their daily life. As one partner noted: *"You are giving a voice to the people who are living it. Yep. And it's not that they haven't been saying it for a long time, it's just nobody has really been listening."* (Food coster, Williams, Anderson, Hunter, Watt, 2013, 32). Similarly, one PFC partner who, over time, transitioned from her role as a food coster to an FRC family resource staff person explained: *"It [the project] kept me, I wanted to come back because I really felt like I had a voice and that I was being listened to. It is about giving people a voice and recognizing those wonderful things that they are so capable of doing."* (FRC staff person C, MSVU and NSFSN, 2013, 13).

Some food costers have described how PFC was a gateway to seeing themselves as not only being able to participate in the discourse of food insecurity but to shape that discourse: *"That's the one thing about this whole project right from the beginning is they've always been known to take our ideas and our input and revise it and put it in exactly the way we want to see it."* (FRC staff person, Williams, Anderson, Hunter, Watt, 2013, 25). Building on this, for some food costers, helping to shape the research and later sharing it with others holds particular meaning: *"Being involved later on, not just part of the food costing but doing the other parts too and being invited to that [e.g., story sharing project, dissemination workshop] um really made me feel a part of it...not that I was just collecting data but I was also actually being involved in the process afterwards too."* (Food coster, Williams, Anderson, Hunter, Watt, 2013, 17).

As a result of the participatory nature of the work, there has been a shift in the views of some decision makers within government and academic institutions about the power of collective action, and partner organizations now see working with those who have experience with food insecurity as being critical to informing policy change.

> *What I liked best is using parents as participants. That's definitely what I liked best. Using people, you know, who understand where you're coming from. If, and like I don't mean to offend anybody by saying this, but if it was all university professors or you know what I mean..., but... If they've never experienced food insecurity then they don't understand. Like they don't understand. So using parents who, you know, know all about it, it just gives it the whole different perspective. It's people who really want to make a change... I think by using participants and building on their capacity that you are going to get more passionate people who want to see this go places.* (Food coster, Williams, Anderson, Hunter, Watt, 2013, 27).

> *I think that often families that are, that experience poverty are just not listened to or considered that they don't have really anything important to add to the discussion. And I think that that's far from the truth. So I think it's a good reminder that we need to be listening to people that live in those circumstances when we're trying to figure out how to make changes in society to make it better...I think that's one of the good things about PFC is that it is participatory.* (FRC staff person, MSVU and NSFSN, 2013, 12).

Many food costers expressed a feeling of belonging to something bigger, evidence of their sense of collective agency. One participant who has been involved in PFC for over four years described how she has been supported and why she stayed involved with PFC: "*It's been easy to stay involved because I, I live what they are trying to change.*" (Food coster, Williams, Anderson, Hunter, Watt, 2013, 28). Another participant shared that: "*Staying involved has helped me see that there is a constant within the project of wanting to make, to make the difference...wanting to make it so that people see that there needs to be changes made.*" (Food coster, Williams, Anderson, Hunter, Watt, 2013, 28).

Increased Interest and Capacity to Network

In addition to supporting a much more locally based body of evidence, made more credible by the authenticity of voices it represents, involving stakeholders from different sectors and across different levels of the policy-making scale in PFC has broadened understandings of the issues of food insecurity and food security. Although the reach across different sectors and levels of policy making may at times be limited, the participatory process supported partners to develop an increased interest in and capacity to network across a variety of sectors and levels. Respondents described strengthening existing personal relationships, meeting new people, working with different organizations and sharing different perspectives. Not only did respondents feel that greater links were formed within the FRCs across the province, but they also felt that links were established between FRCs and those within other external systems, such as nutrition professionals, government partners and universities. In addition, PFC provided opportunities for women with experience of food insecurity to meet and collaborate with other people across the province allowing them to share what they have learned with others in their community. Partners recognized that these groups were all working towards the same goal and had many things to contribute to each other's efforts. One partner describes this as: "*I think the linkages and relationships...I think thats come through the project...that is a key benefit that people receive from being involved...more linkages and giving people the opportunity to talk about the issue with others...I think it has been really valuable to people that way.*" (Provincial Steering Committee Member, Williams, Anderson, Hunter, Watt, 2013, 25).

PFC has also provided an entry point for broad-based civic engagement in the policy change process, catalyzing community mobilization around food security and building capacity for change at multiple levels. Having stakeholders from different levels of influence across the policy-making scale has also allowed partners to generate tools to affect knowledge and attitudes about food security, that supports people to see the value in policy change both within their community and their institutions, and consider the ripple effects those changes can have. Increased interest and capacity to network has deepened and broadened conversations about food in Nova Scotian communities. One FRC partner described the impact for her: "*I approached the community health board... and was able to talk to them about food security and now I'm on the board of the community health board.*" (FRC staff person, Williams, Anderson, Hunter, Watt, 2013, 36). Another FRC partner described this "*ripple effect*":

I do like all the connections—the interconnectedness that goes beyond—it's almost like a ripple effect. Here's the center, food, here's all the people and all the organizations that have come together around food and here's the ripple and those connections are being made farther than we can see. We don't know what they all are; we just know that they are happening. Because I see food and all of those issues in the media more and more all the time. Or people are talking about them more and more all the time. It's like we are reaching this tipping point (FRC staff person, MSVU and NSFSN, 2013, 21).

Organizational Forces: Building Alliances and the Role of the Government in Addressing Food Security

Raised Awareness of Personal Experience with Food Insecurity

There was also evidence of the engagement of women experiencing food insecurity playing a role in the collective ownership of the process and a desire to build alliances through creating awareness and understanding of the issues. Following PFC training in May 2010, and recognizing their important and unique role in advocacy, 73.2 percent of food costers said they wanted to explore ways to use food costing results within their communities, 58.5 percent wanted to acquire skills related to facilitation, and 43.9 percent were interested in media training (Regional Training Workshop Evaluation Report, 2010, lines 312-316). Even as early as 2002 a steering committee member observed: "*I think there's been skills built and [community participants, i.e., food costers, are] feeling more confident ...more willing to take the lead in some areas.*" (Provincial Steering Committee Member, Williams, Anderson, Hunter, Watt, 2013, 36).

The alliances that were created through PFC with food costers, other FRC partners and other champions who had leadership capacity and experience with food insecurity strengthened the ability to work within and across hierarchical systems that contribute to food insecurity. Family Resource Centre partners also noted that the knowledge of inequalities gained through the PFC has had an impact with the families they work with, by: "*maybe creating a little anger and lighting a little fire under their bums. Because they are starting to want to speak out.*" (FRC staff person, MSVU and NSFSN, 2013, 21).

Acquired Knowledge and Awareness about Food Insecurity and Food Security

The diversity of the alliances that were created early in the project through PFC contributed to the feeling among partners that: "*We've also raised a fair bit of public awareness around the issue that wasn't there before we started doing this.*" (Provincial Steering Committee Member, Williams, Anderson, Hunter, Watt, 2013, 44).

Increased Ability to Influence and Take Action

The role within the PFC has changed for a number of the longer-term participants. Family Resource Centre partners described how, in many cases, participating as a food coster has served as a "*stepping stone*" to participants becoming more involved with their local FRC. Some participants who started as food costers have become trainers and supporters in FPC, while others have become involved in the project in other ways. For example, some have become members of the Food Costing Working Group or collaborators with the Social Sciences and Humanities Research Council funded community-university research alliance (CURA) (2010-2015), Activating Change Together for Community Food Security (ACT for CFS; see http://foodarc.ca/actforcfs/). One food coster described how she has become involved in ACT for CFS: "*I'm hoping that within everything that, because I'm also involved with the CURA [ACT for CFS]...I'm hoping that there will be a difference made.*" (Food coster, Williams, Anderson, Hunter, Watt, 2013, 37). Another food coster shared: "*You know I was asked to help make presentations, I was very involved in almost everything going...and even today if there is something going on, you know, [principal investigator] or somebody sends out a note just to find out who is interested in doing what and it makes me feel that I'm valued.*" (Williams, Anderson, Hunter, Watt, 2013, 36).

Food costers and other partners see themselves as part of a growing alliance; there was an increased desire to participate in change and to share stories or information about food insecurity, many became more involved with changing policy, and taking action and expressed an overall feeling that they can make a difference in their communities. Consistently, food costers conveyed excitement about continuing their involvement in PFC and participating in other food security initiatives. Among many partners this has sparked a renewed motivation to engage in advocacy for policy change. As one community partner commented: "*When I approach my Member of Legislative Assembly (MLA) or my Member of Parliament (MP) now, I know how to approach them, I am better prepared.*" (Food coster, Williams, Anderson, Hunter, Watt, 2013, 40). Another food coster shared: "*I know being involved in this [PFC] wants to get me involved in other things like... I want to get involved in other things too.*" (Food coster, Williams, Anderson, Hunter, Watt, 2013, 35), and: "*It's been a very powerful feeling to be involved in this project. I'm actually doing something that uh something to make lives better that affects me too*" (Food coster, Williams, Anderson, Hunter, Watt, 2013, 35).

FRC partners across the province have been actively engaged in presentations on PFC in academic settings, including at an International Union for Health Promotion and Education conference in Geneva, Switzerland and Canadian Association of Food Studies conferences. Other FRC partners have been part of regional and national conferences (e.g., CIHR Institute of Gender and Health conference) as well as invited addresses on building food security in NS, (e.g., appearing before the Standing Committee on Community Services of the NS government to present evidence and insights from PFC). One FRC partner acknowledged: "*FRC are being recognized as major players in the food costing arena by our communities and other organizations because stuff that we've been saying before is now backed up by data. We've been saying it all along but now we've got data behind us.*" (FRC staff person, MSVU and NSFSN, 2013, 11).

This active engagement in PFC by FRC partners has been amidst increasing demand for services and no funding increase for these community-based programs[9] since they were first established by the federal government about 20 years ago (Williams, Langille, and Stokvis 2005). It seems ironic that this core partner is severely underfunded despite documented success in working with individuals and families most vulnerable to food insecurity in Canada (Williams, Langille, and Stokvis 2005). Thus, a gap that PFC partners have identified in the past which still requires attention is continued advocacy and partnership building at a Federal level to ensure adequate resourcing of community-based initiatives so they can do much needed front-line work to support individuals and families most vulnerable to food insecurity in Canada. As well, they are important players in sharing their experiences and perspectives as they have done through PFC to affect changes in their communities and beyond, which is necessary to improve population health (Williams, Langille, and Stokvis 2005).

Acquired Feeling of Belonging to Community/Group

At the organizational level, discussions provided evidence that linking occurred between different FRCs across the province. Links between Centers were beneficial as they encouraged the formation of new connections, building stronger existing connections, and sharing resources:

> Well actually I strengthened a lot of relationships. I've always talked to people on the phone, like the different resource centers and I actually got to meet and put names to faces. Different times you know we would call up on what each others center is doing and I've got different programs from like [FRC] that I met through here [PFC]. Down in [community where FRC is located] I can call them up and say ok you mentioned this program at the last meeting we were at, tell me about it. Right so I've got some new stuff for the [family resource] center because of that. And I just because I've actually met them and done something with them I'm just more likely to call them and say you know what's this, what's that. (FRC staff person, Williams, Anderson, Hunter, Watt, 2013, 19).

Likewise, many food costers have commented that meeting and making connections with new people has been a benefit of involvement: "*What did you like best about the project? ...yeah it was going out and doing the food costing, I think and um you know and teaming up with another participant.*" (Food coster, Williams, Anderson, Hunter, Watt, 2013, 19).

While some FRC partners used a mentoring approach prior to becoming involved with PFC, others have adapted or developed a similar "train the trainer" and mentoring model to that used in PFC. Through collective learning a mentoring model has been widely implemented in FRCs, and has in turn impacted many levels of FRC programming and contributed to increased community sharing, learning of knowledge and skills and engagement with other groups such as seniors. One FRC partner shared,

We are training participants and then they're training other people, which is what a great skill to be able to give them right? They're becoming like the teachers themselves. We take more of a mentoring approach now. Now we are working with our seniors too, we are starting to access that population. And they are going to be coming in and do some of this preserving for us because they do have that knowledge that's getting lost. (FRC staff person, MSVU and NSFSN, 2013, 10).

PFC is supported by diverse interest groups and the evidence suggests that strong partnerships have been formed between community, university and government partners with some indication of collective agency: *"If you have everybody working together and you have everybody doing the same all across the province then your voice is gonna be heard."* (Food coster, Williams, Anderson, Hunter, Watt, 2013, 32).

Increased Interest and Capacity to Network

Participatory Food Costing has helped create networks within and across hierarchical systems that contribute to food insecurity and thus, that have the potential to contribute to food security. It has helped build broad-based support, both monetary and moral, to start to create the conditions for policy changes necessary to support food security. In terms of moral support a FRC partner described how early involvement in PFC increased their awareness of food insecurity in Canada, and an understanding that organizations were working to make a difference: *"I didn't even know there was organizations working to address food security. When you think of food security, you think of Third World countries. You don't think of countries like Canada as in trouble. But after this you realize there are."* (Food coster, Williams, Anderson, Hunter, Watt, 2013, 34).

Moral support has also occurred through the broad-based civic engagement in the policy change process that has resulted from PFC. In turn, the research has gained credibility within communities, government and academic settings and by funding agencies and peer review panels through community participation. Partners are seen as having expertise in processes for engaging those who are marginalized and who have experience with food insecurity to have their voices heard. Their expertise in processes for building capacity at multiple levels for addressing food insecurity has also been widely recognized. In a PFC evaluation from 2004, one community partner noted that *"our name is getting out there as a contact"* for the media about the issue of food security (Williams, Anderson, Hunter, Watt, 2013, 44).

The participatory processes involved in PFC have accommodated the complexity of the issue of food insecurity by allowing and encouraging people from various backgrounds and perspectives to come together to work on improving food security and food systems in NS. It provides a platform for mutual learning, contribution and moving the work forward because it brings people from diverse perspectives and backgrounds together. For example, as a result of PFC the first ever provincial food security network in NS (the Nova Scotia Food Security Network) was established in 2005 with leadership across community, government, and academic partner organizations.

There has also been moral support for the work beyond NS. For example, using the "train-the-trainer" online resource, two municipalities in New Brunswick, Canada (Moncton and Saint John), have implemented PFC projects, and dieticians in several other provinces have expressed interest in adapting this approach (Williams et al. 2012c, 181-188). Additionally, PFC has links with food security networks in most provinces, and elected officials across the political spectrum, nationally and provincially, have contacted the project for information and advice. University and community partners have also provided material and organizational support to PFC through student training and mentorship. Students have been involved with PFC through dietetic internships, thesis work, directed studies courses, community service learning and co-op/practicum placements. Ongoing partnerships with former students involved with PFC and/or other food security related initiatives (who now work in universities, communities, or government) suggests that students' involvement in PFC has not only increased their awareness of food insecurity, but in several cases their agency, to significantly proliferate food security work in NS. For example, Christine Johnson who is currently a faculty member at St. Francis Xavier University and Rita MacAulay, who is currently a Public Health Nutritionist with Capital District Health Authority, and was past founding Chair of the NS Food Security Network, were both involved with PFC as students and are currently Co-Directors on a Social Sciences and Humanities Research Council funded Community University Research Alliance (CURA).

Relationships and collaboration with government departments have contributed to mutual understanding that has allowed people with different understandings of food insecurity to work towards a solution together. The initial PFC initiative led to over thirty other research and knowledge mobilization projects being funded in NS with provincial and federal level government departments working in partnership with communities and universities. Public health, FRC and academic partners have been able to bring a food security lens to the development of the provincial healthy eating strategy in 2005, food and nutrition policy for public schools in 2006, and *Thrive! A Plan for a Healthier Nova Scotia* (Nova Scotia Department of Health and Wellness 2012), a comprehensive government strategy for childhood obesity prevention in 2012.

Monetary support from the Provincial Government for ongoing PFC occurred in 2005 as a result of food security being identified as a priority action in the provincial healthy eating strategy. Subsequently, food security (and specifically PFC) was incorporated in the then Office of Health Promotion's business plan, financial resources were dedicated to complete ongoing surveillance and monitoring of food costing for four cycles between 2007 and 2012. In addition, a knowledge mobilization project was funded from 2013 to 2015, and a Health Disparities position with the provincial government with an initial focus on food security was established in 2006. In 2007, FoodARC, was funded in conjunction with the author's Tier 2 Canada Research Chair at Mount Saint Vincent University and in 2010 a CURA, ACT for CFS project was funded. The current lead organizations, FoodARC and the Nova Scotia Food Security Network—both of which, in large part, grew out of PFC—were successfully nominated for the Canadian Institutes of Health Research (CIHR) Partnership Award in 2011. This award recognizes "…partnerships between organizations that exemplify excellence by bringing health research communities together to create innovative approaches to research, develop research agendas that are responsive to the health needs of Canadians and/or accelerate the translation of knowledge for the benefit of Canadians." The award also came with a $25,000 grant to support the work of the partnership and contributed in large part to bringing partners within the food movement together in May 2013 for a NS Food Gathering.

Economic Relations: Questioning Current Systems, Material Capabilities and Voice in Policy Processes

Findings suggest that PFC's focus on advocacy for policy change has helped to shift ideas and organizational forces but it is important to acknowledge that this success is occurring among limited groups; for example, women who are even further marginalized by race/Aboriginal status or those who are homeless are not represented. Moreover, with increasing numbers of Nova Scotian and Canadian households reporting food insecurity (Tarasuk, Mitchell and Dachner 2014), our research has clearly had limited impact on significantly reshaping economic relations that influence food security at the household level except in several notable ways: questioning current systems; changes to programming at FRCs; personal, household, and collective food practices and strategies (e.g., growing food, supporting local and fair trade food systems); changes to research funding allocation by government agencies and universities; and changes to employment prospects of food costers.

Raised Awareness of Personal Experience with Food Insecurity

FRC partners spoke about a failure to acknowledge the reality that they deal with "*on the ground*" to better the situations of those they serve and their observation that politicians and other decision-makers do not listen to those experiencing food insecurity: "*... I think it's going to be a long struggle to get people in places to recognize this um you know it just feels like we are taking baby steps all the time which is better than nothing but um I just I don't know, I don't know that we've got the right people to listen yet.*" (Food coster, Williams, Anderson, Hunter, Watt, 2013, 32).

Acquired Knowledge and Awareness about Food Insecurity and Food Security

PAR processes have empowered partners to question current systems. Partners felt that the continuity of the project for over ten years has led to an increased ability to do advocacy work with politicians:

> The fact that it is not something that has sat on the shelf um so often um FRCs get approached by groups, organizations, universities. We wanna do a study on this, we wanna do a study on that and they do the study and we never hear anything more about it or you find out that yes they did the study, here's the data so what. This has been an ongoing project for the past ten years for sure and I've been able to take the information that we have discovered, you know, and we have been able to talk to the politicians about, you know... raising um minimum wage and raising social service rates, so it's, it's real (Food coster, Williams, Anderson, Hunter, Watt, 2013, 23).

Instructional changes to programming at many FRCs, such as no-cost cooking, gardening and meal programs for families have also been offered as a result of being involved with PFC and recognition that many families cannot afford healthy food. As a result, many FRC attendees have learned new skills related to growing and harvesting food, and through cooking programs, gained experience with taking vegetables from the garden, and turning them into nutritious meals. These represent material structural changes, albeit even only if at a micro scale. As one FRC partner shared:

> We've started a community garden...we go and we've planted everything, and we were able to take that food back to our center. Sometimes we are eating it fresh, but of course this time of year we couldn't do that so have preserved a lot of it in freezing. And now we are going to do a lot of cooking throughout the winter, showing families what can be done with these simple fruits and vegetables. So it is all about what we can grow here, so we have the squash and the tomatoes and pumpkin. So we provide cooking programs for them. We use very basic tools, back to basics approach, where you try to make sure it's things that are available to families. And often times the families will have a meal together. Sometimes they take the food home too...And they can try different things. It's that same thing of letting them try something maybe they haven't tried before. (FRC staff person B, MSVU and NSFSN, 2013, 10).

Increased Ability to Influence and Take Action

There is some evidence that the purchasing practices of individuals and partners have shifted to support more locally based and fair trade food systems; practices that represent material change. One FRC partner shared:

I took a picture of the [sticker/barcode] because it's from my area. So it's local. ...So the reason I took this picture was because since we have been involved with the food costing, one of the things that we have done, and it's not official written down and it needs to be, but we've really taken a hard look at what we practice. We've really looked at what we do in terms of our food purchasing and in terms of our menus, in terms of all of the things that we do around food. So we have apples when they are in season, we have apples that are from our community. We go to the market and get them or we go to the local farmers markets that are open year round. (FRC staff person E, MSVU and NSFSN, 2013, 23).

Acquired Feeling of Belonging to a Community/Group

Family Resource Centre partners describe how, for some, being listened to and engaged through PFC was a gateway to the development of new confidence and skills which, though the courage of the women themselves, began to transform their lives and their material capabilities. One partner describes the transformation that occurred with one woman:

I know we had somebody involved with the food costing a number of years ago. And ohh my, I remember the very first time I met her she wouldn't even come out of her house. She just called and she said I heard about you and I heard that you work with families and I just need to talk. So I went over and I talked and I had to go over a number of times before she actually come out to group. But then she did and she started making connections and then she got involved in the food costing, and then she got involved at—she went to a national [dialogue on food security] conference and she spoke out. And she stood up and she said "I've been involved with this for a couple of years and when I first started I wouldn't even come out of my house" and she said "now I'm standing in front of you telling you this is me, this is my life. I can't afford to eat." Not only that but now in her life she's left an abusive relationship...She's out of that, she's looking after herself, she looks better than I've ever seen her. Her kids are doing great, she's got a job—that was not where she was headed. That's one person. (FRC staff person, MSVU and NSFSN, 2013, 13).

For some, the added confidence and involvement they gained through participation in PFC has also helped them transition into employment and leadership roles in their communities:

We (FRC) just trained one of our food costers to actually be a food mentor. So she'll be starting some programs in a couple of weeks. What we found with food costers, a lot of them have moved into maybe some staff positions, which is what I did. I began as a volunteer years ago, as a food coster, now I am a food mentor and I work at the resource center part-time. [Woman pictured] actually was a food coster too. She started as a food coster years ago when we started the project. (FRC staff person, MSVU and NSFSN, 2013, 14).

Partners valued the role of PAR in providing low-income women, who tend to be overlooked in policy processes, with ways to find and share their voices to influence these processes. As described above, together with civil society partners, they have been able to influence policy processes. One partner shared how she had observed that: *"I learned much from this project, particularly about the development of personal and community capacity and the role that this can potentially play in changing policy—also about how those who are actively experiencing food insecurity can participate in research and planning for change."* (National Advisory Committee member, Williams, Anderson, Hunter, and Watt, 2013, 25).

Increased Interest and Capacity to Network

The shifting of ideas and organizational relations, in particular through an ongoing relationship with decision makers within key government departments, has had a concrete influence on departmental policy. For example, data provided by the work of PFC was an impetus for the Department of Community Services to initiate modest increases in the personal allowance portion of income assistance benefits (Kay, C. Department of Community Services, Personal Communication, August 26, 2005 and Rathbun, J. Department of Community Services, June 14, 2007) totalling 42 percent[10] (i.e., $180 to $238/month/adult in the household) over the last decade thus impacting the material capabilities of participants. As well, while it cannot be attributed to PFC, there has been a 79 percent increase to the minimum wage in NS between 2002 and 2014. Our work examining the affordability of a nutritious diet for households earning minimum wage in NS from 2002-2012 shows that increases to the minimum wage in NS has resulted in a decrease in the potential deficit faced by each household scenario in meeting their basis needs including food, but that the minimum wage in 2012 remained inadequate to meet basic needs. For example, a family of four with two adults and two children, a lone mother with three children dependent on minimum wage earnings would still face a significant monthly deficit if they were to purchase a nutritiously sufficient diet (Newell, Williams, and Watt, In Press). Moreover, our analyses show that in spite of increases in income assistance individuals and families relying on assistance would be hundreds of dollars in debt at the end of the month if they actually purchased a basic nutritious diet (Williams et al. 2012a).

Discussion

Gramsci's theory of change purports that successful change processes depend on strategic and unified actions across all three realms of power (Policy Working Group of Activating Change Together for Community Food Security (ACT for CFS 2013). Participatory action research processes in NS, Canada have been successful in bringing about personal and collective agency in two of the three realms of social and policy change necessary for addressing broader structural forces underlying household food insecurity, ideas and organizational forces. They have not, however, had a significant impact on personal or collective agency to influence the third realm of power that is necessary for social and policy change, namely economic forces and material capabilities. Participatory processes have allowed people to engage in all three realms, but the economic realm (aside from increased employment prospects for food costers and minor changes to some practices and policies among individuals and organizations who are more directly involved) is the least developed and needs more active attention (without only adopting solutions commensurate with neoliberalism such as instituting children's feeding programs in schools exclusive of ensuring parents a livable income to care for their children) (McIntyre, Travers, and Dayle 1999; Williams et al. 2003).

These findings show that PAR processes help to undo the internalized hegemonic values (e.g., food as a mere commodity versus a human right, the undeserving poor, the importance of self-discipline, rugged individualism, etc.) thus challenging embedded and historically constructed ideology. The findings from the six cycles of PFC and related research projects have effectively put an end to any claim that people living in poverty would be able to enjoy the right to food if they simply made better expenditure choices. The findings also demonstrate the impact that engagement in PAR processes can have on the individual agency of women affected by food insecurity. This was evidenced by their willingness to share their stories and their conviction to begin to question the structures that shape their lives. Sharing their stories helped them realize they were not alone and that broader collective factors (Jacobson and Rugeley 2007, 21-39) were contributing to their food insecurity. This allowed them to begin to question the oppressive discourses that place blame on the individual thus helping to lift the shame, guilt, deprivation and social isolation that are common among low-income, food insecure women (Hamelin, Habicht and Beaudry 1999, 525S-528S; McIntyre, Officer, and Robinson 2003, 316-331; Williams et al. 2012b, 253-270).

The development of personal agency among the women with experience of food insecurity serves to build collective agency by revealing the institutional and systemic forces that constrain women and their families and keep them food insecure. This is accomplished by giving meaning to and strengthening the quantitative data on the affordability of a nutritious diet in NS among low-income individuals and families. This process highlights what Laverack (2006,

113-120) describes as the dynamic interplay of individual and community empowerment, outcomes that arise from "the redistribution of resources and decision making authority (power-over) or as the achievement of an increased sense of self-determination and self-esteem (power-from-within)" (113). Empowerment leading to increased agency requires a commitment to, and understanding of inclusion as a continuous process. Ponic and Frisby (2010, 1519-1531) critically examined the complexities of facilitating inclusion within health promotion in their attempt to address common assumptions that inclusion is a desirable and achievable health promoting practice. Among the multidimensional processes identified, a psychosocial dimension of inclusion was described. The authors suggest that within inclusionary programming "attention should be paid to the internalized effects of marginalization and exclusion" (1524). In Ponic and Frisby's study, addressing internal feelings of acceptance, safety/trust and belonging were experienced by their participants and were felt to be foundational aspects to the inclusionary process over the long term. This is consistent with participatory processes that value inclusion and meaningful engagement.

Participatory action research, moreover, allows participants to question the "natural order of things," thereby challenging structures/institutions. Through PFC, partners were trained as food costers and went into grocery stores to collect data about the cost of a basic nutritious food basket. This presented an opportunity to challenge the everyday act of grocery shopping and offered a grocery store as a site from which to gain knowledge, build resistance, and contest current systems. In her paper examining the multidimensional impact of community gardens, Ore (2011) describes a community garden as representing a similar "everyday space" that acts as a site of resistance by enhancing an understanding of how everyday actions can become political practices. Her suggestion that the potential within these spaces to enact social change allows marginalized communities an opportunity to "create something from nothing through their daily actions" (691). As a material symbol of both being able to provide basic needs and to nurture one's children, Devault (1991) has shown that food and the mundane activities of its provisioning and feeding others holds power for developing a sense of personal agency. Yet socio-economic constraints limit capacity for many women and others who are marginalized in our modern society to realize this power.

While participatory research processes focused on capacity building for policy change have served to encourage individuals to challenge some of the discourse and institutional and systemic forces that maintain women and their families in food insecure situations, our findings and our decade of experience with PFC show that participatory processes have done little to effectively impact the economic power relations underlying food insecurity. While PFC has helped to create the conditions where the economic structures and food systems that favor growth, while threatening social justice and sustainability are beginning to be questioned by people experiencing food insecurity and others, these structures and systems are not really vulnerable. For example, the most recent PFC results from 2012 (Nova Scotia Food Security Network and Food Action Research Centre (FoodARC 2013) and our analysis of the inadequacy of income assistance (Williams et al. 2012a, 183-188) and minimum wage (Newell, Williams, and Watt, In Press) between 2002 and 2012 in NS help to illustrate this. Our findings suggest that with concurrent increases in the cost of living, the 48 percent and 79 percent increases to the personal allowance component of income assistance rates and the minimum wage, respectively in NS is still insufficient, significantly in some cases, to compensate for the deterioration of the social safety net in NS and Canada, recurrent over the last 20 years (Torjman 2013).

Similar to our findings, Salmon, Browne, and Pederson (2010, 336-345) found that despite recognized gains in terms of demonstrated positive and empowering impacts in the lives of participating marginalized women drug users with respect to primary health care, the feminist participatory action research (FPAR) approach they used failed to improve the material conditions of women's lives. The authors attribute this finding to the nature of funding for such social justice work by Canada's neoliberal political framework. Knowledge gained through their study informed change at an organizational level but when their funding stopped, economic gains achieved by this group diminished. Salmon, Browne, and Pederson (2010) suggest, "FPAR can provide a mechanism for organizing against oppressive social, economic, and political structures, but it is unable to transform those structures that achieve and sustain improvements in the material conditions of women's lives." (342). Although PFC has occurred over a longer 12 year period, a challenge has been that the funding has been grant dependent with the maximum duration of funding being 2.5 years. There has, however, been a commitment by the provincial government in NS to fund PFC; this began in 2004 with funding to develop a model for ongoing food costing in the province and since 2006 has been funded as part of the provincial healthy eating strategy. It is unclear if this represents a shift in the previous reluctance to properly fund or resource organizations and initiatives that support marginalized populations, such as low-income women. While provincial departments have been more receptive and supportive and there may be indication of some change at local and provincial levels in Canada, not only in Nova Scotia (Williams et al. 2012c; Office of Health Promotion and Protection 2005; Nova Scotia Department of Health and Wellness 2012) but elsewhere (Koc et al. 2008; MacRae and Abergel 2012; Williams et al. 2012d; Carlsson and Williams 2008), obtaining the attention of federal government structures has been more difficult. Similarly, federal policies have resulted in some of the greatest setbacks to food security efforts, and there is growing reason for concern. Despite Canada's commitment to food as a basic human right in numerous international declarations (Raphael, Bryant and Curry-Stevens 2004, 269-273; Office of the High Commissioner for Human Rights 1966; World Food Conference General Assembly 1974), political will, particularly at a federal level to actually address the underlying structural barriers to food security, is significantly lacking. For example, the 2012 Mission on the Right to Food in Canada was a poignant exposé of Canadian society's failure to ensure that all Canadians are food secure. Moreover, leaders in the federal government, in response to Olivier de Schutter's (United Nations' Special Rapporteur on the Right to Food) visit, chose to publicly discredit the efforts made to expose the reality of food insecurity in Canada, and attempted to discredit de Schutter personally (Roberts, 2012). Moreover, there have been major cuts to federal government programs and departments that help to monitor and address issues like food insecurity among vulnerable populations such as low-income women (e.g., National Council of Welfare dismantled in 2012, Status of Women Canada). In addition, as mentioned previously more than 800 federally funded community-based programs[11] such as the FRCs that participate as partners in PFC have not received a funding increase since they were first established almost 20 years ago by the federal government despite their documented success (Williams, Langille and Stokvis 2005). Community-based programs, which are at risk because of funding policies, provide local supportive environments for many of the individuals and families most vulnerable to food insecurity in Canada, including women, children, and Aboriginal Peoples, as well as those in more hard-to-reach rural and remote areas. This is especially significant given the increasing demand that they have seen over the last decade (Williams, Langille and Stokvis 2005).

The complexity of systems change may help to explain why so little has actually changed systemically with respect to material capabilities and economic relations as a result of PFC. Long-term systems change involving marginalized groups such as low-income, food insecure women requires building relationships and trust-providing opportunities for meaningful collaboration before the process of the development of personal and collective capacity is possible. Our findings and that of others show that participatory research has the potential to influence processes and outcomes, but are time-consuming and require flexibility to respond to identified community needs, and to accommodate contributions from partners with diverse backgrounds, capacities, and needs (Williams et al. 2012c, 181-188; Salmon, Browne and Pederson 2010, 336-345; Masuda et al. 2011, 290-292; Barnidge et al. 2010, 55-63; Blair and Minkler 2009, 5-651). A discourse of "overwhelming odds" identified by Reid and Tom (2006, 402-421) in their community-based feminist action research with a group of low-income women also speaks to the complexity of systems change. The "overwhelming odds" discourse captured the struggle felt by those living in poverty whereby legitimacy resided in accepting and adhering to dominant discourses due to an overwhelming sense of how daunting the challenge is to bring about true societal change. Although this discourse was not evident in our data, I would argue that it is a discourse that is shared by many involved in advocating for food security. While it highlights an obstacle perceived to be so complex and so entrenched that it almost feels impossible to remove, it raises the question for us of the role of PAR in challenging and changing this discourse among low-income, food insecure women and others trying to support systems change.

As with any project with long-term goals and objectives, it is a challenge to evaluate the systems-level impacts of PFC because contextual changes are continually happening—changes to government policies, macro level ideologies, and economic forces and demographics. These processes make it difficult to attribute causal relationships between project outcomes and food security. While it has not been possible to follow-up with food costers and others no longer engaged with PFC, there is a general sense among PFC partners that PAR processes have contributed to the creation of supportive environments that fostered the development of both individual and collective agency.

There are also limitations related to the primary expectation among partners for the PFC project to quickly and efficiently lead to policy change to impact food insecurity. The realities of policy change, however, are embedded in personal, organizational and public policy decisions and ideologies that can be difficult (or take time) to shift. The ideas and values underlying PFC, related to the belief that everyone should have dignified access to food, is sometimes met with opposition from others with the underlying philosophy that if someone is food insecure, it must be a result of poor personal choices. While the latter assumption does not match many people's situational and economic realities, as PFC has clearly demonstrated, and PFC has contributed to shifting this discourse in NS, the pervasive stigmatization faced by people living in poverty (Reutter et al. 2006) is a significant challenge. These differing ideologies pose challenges to the work, as does the inability to conclusively define the parameters of a viable long-term solution to food insecurity. While working toward an "unknown" solution leaves room for creativity and innovation, the uncertainty it creates and the questions it raises (e.g., economic viability) can also be a limitation.

More inquiry is needed, especially in terms of how the actions highlighted by this research has affected how the media portrays these issues, how the language has been picked up by governments (ideational) and implemented in policies or new programs (organizational). However, it is possible to make some general conclusions. Drawing upon a political economy perspective, the impact of PFC was noted for agency in two realms of power relations—the ideas and organizational forces. The impact on agency to influence economic relations, however, was significantly limited. After over ten years of PFC, progress has been made, but an ongoing challenge remains in finding ways to shift all levels of power for improved food security in NS, specifically in terms of economic relations. It appears that especially in the economic realm, *not* a lot has changed to this point, but again this needs further examination.

Conclusion

This study aimed to examine the role that PAR plays in creating the conditions for the development of personal and collective agency for addressing food insecurity. While PAR processes are valuable in shifting the thinking among participants and partners, and creating and strengthening relationships at many levels, more remains to be done. The finding that PFC has done little to shift economic forces and material capabilities impacting the lives of women living with food insecurity in NS helps to illuminate where further inquiry needs to be directed. Given the major role economic relations plays in policy outcomes, there is a need to create a new economic order if only even on a small scale. The continuing commitment of many of the women who participated in PFC activities in addressing food insecurity in their communities speaks to their conviction that change is both necessary and possible (Williams et al. 2012b), and that participatory processes have potential for engaging civil society—most importantly, for marginalized groups, and in relation to policy processes. Findings from this work suggest that agency at local community levels may be valuable in effecting change. All of the core partners involved in PFC continue to be actively involved in research and advocacy efforts to inform food security–related policies and programs.

The personal and collective agency that has contributed to shifting power related to ideas and organizational relations in NS also holds potential for shifting economic relations, by helping to create a movement that contributes to a new economic order, for example, by bridging the disconnect between consumers and producers to challenge conventional food systems in support of more locally based food systems. An example of citizen-led sustainable change is the "Rural Action" initiative in Ohio, developed as a form of resistance to the devastating consequences of the coal mining industry in Rural Appalachia during the 1980s. Rural Action has successfully championed more sustainable, resilient and "locally owned" economic development through local food production systems, sustainable forestry, watershed restoration, environmental education, recycling and waste management, and education and advocacy on local energy issues (Rural Action 2013). Similarly, "The Deep South Wealth Creation Network," in partnership with the Ford Foundation's Wealth Creation and Rural Livelihoods Initiative, works to develop vegetable and livestock value chains for the purpose of sustaining the natural resources and improving the livelihoods of rural families in Alabama and Mississippi (Wealth Creation in Rural Communities 2013). Additional examples of how shifting ideas and organizations have in turn shifted economic relations include the success of microcredit, organic food and fair trade movements.

The belief that PAR has an important role to play in shifting economic relations is consistent with Gramsci's notion of "convergence" where "seemingly separate spheres, actions, actors, or ideas are drawn together to create a fundamental *connection* between them" (Policy Working Group of Acting Change Together for Community Food Security ([ACT for CFS 2013]; Jones 2006). While we are far from realizing convergence to truly address food insecurity, the personal and collective agency being realized by women and their families in NS and elsewhere is helping to redefine the limits of both our current economic and food systems, a condition necessary for unified action across all three realms of power.

Acknowledgment

The author gratefully acknowledges the Nova Scotia (NS) Department of Health and Wellness, Health Canada and the NS Health Research Foundation for funding support that enabled the Partners to undertake Participatory Food Costing in NS. Thanks to Erin Kelly for her support with data analysis, to Barbara Anderson, Peter Andree, Doris Gillis, Erin Kelly, Irena Knezevic, Debbie Reimer, Sarah Shaw, and Beatrice White for reviewing and providing their input on this chapter, and to Felicia Newell, Kendra Read, and Chris Stothert for technical support. A special thanks to the many partners who have contributed to Participatory Food Costing for their commitment to building food security for all, and in particular the women who so bravely shared their stories.

Notes

1. Family and parent resource centers were those in the Province of Nova Scotia funded by the Canada Prenatal Nutrition Program (CPNP) and the Community Action Program for Children (CAPC) throughout the province. CPNP and CAPC are federal programs in Canada that provide funding to community-based organizations to deliver prevention and early intervention programs to promote the health and social development of pregnant women and infants (CPNP), children aged zero to six years (CAPC), and their families facing conditions of risk. The populations reached by CPNP and CAPC share many similarities with the households most at-risk for food insecurity in Canada.

2. To conduct food costing, Canada's National Nutritious Food Basket (NNFB) is used (Health Canada 2009). The NNFB describes the quantity (and purchase units) of 67 foods that represent a basic nutritious diet for individuals in various age and gender groups. Stakeholders use this information to collect the price of the items and determine the cost of the basket for each age and gender group.

3. Primarily the NS Departments of Health and Wellness and Community Services but has also included Agriculture and Policy and Priority at Provincial level and Health Canada, Public Health Agency of Canada, First National and Inuit Health and Rural Secretariat at Federal level.

4. Supports include but are not limited to reimbursement of travel and childcare expenses and provision of honoraria to recognize the time contributed.

5. Primarily the NS Departments of Health and Wellness and Community Services.

6. Since 2001, over 200 food costers have participated with PFC. While there have been a few male food costers, and men have never been excluded from this role, the vast majority of food costers from 2001-2011 have been women. This may speak to the par-

ticular relevance and impact of food insecurity on women, and the role they play in relation to food for their families; their participation in PFC may indicate that women are interested and looking for ways to be part of the solution to food insecurity.

7. Includes Executive Directors of FRC and Women's Resource Centers, Chairs and Directors of University Programs and Centers, Managers within Public Health Agency of Canada, Chairs of Food Secure Canada, NS Food Security Network, NS Nutrition Council, etc.

8. Canadian dollars.

9. Specifically the Canada Prenatal Nutrition Program and the Community Action Program for Children.

10. Not adjusted for inflation

11. Specifically the Canada Prenatal Nutrition Program, the Community Action Program for Children.

Bibliography

Agarwal, Bina. 1997. "'Bargaining' and Gender Relations: Within and Beyond the Household." *Feminist Economics* 3, no. 1: 1-51.

Anderson, Molly D., and John T. Cook. 1999. "Community Food Security: Practice in Need of Theory?" *Agriculture and Human Values* 16, no. 2: 141-50.

Andrée, Peter. 2007. *Genetically-Modified Diplomacy: The Global Politics of Agricultural Biotechnology and the Environment.* Vancouver, British Columbia: University of British Columbia Press.

_____. 2011. "Civil Society and the Political Economy of GMO Failures in Canada: A Neo-Gramscian Analysis." *Environmental Politics*, 20, no. 2: 173-191.

Barndt, Deborah. 2008. *Tangled Routes: Women, Work, and Globalization on the Tomato Trail*, 2d edition. Lanham, Maryland: Rowman & Littlefield Pub Incorporated.

Barnidge, Ellen, Elizabeth A Baker, Freda Motton, Frank Rose and Teresa Fitzgerald. 2010. "A Participatory Method to Identify Root Determinants of Health: The Heart of the Matter." *Progress in Community Health Partnerships* 4, no. 1: 55-63.

Blair, Thomas, and Meredith Minkler. 2009. "Participatory Action Research with Older Adults: Key Principles in Practice." *The Gerontologist* 49, no.5: 651-662.

Brinkman, Henk-Jen, Saskia de Pee, Issa Sanogo, Ludovic Subran and Martin W. Bloem. 2010. "High Food Prices and the Global Financial Crisis have Reduced Access to Nutritious Food and Worsened Nutritional Status and Health." *The Journal of Nutrition* 140, no. 1: 153S-61S.

Brookfield, Stephen. 1998. "Critically Reflective Practice." *Journal of Continuing Education in the Health Profession* 18, no. 4: 197–205.

Carlsson, Liesel, and Patricia L. Williams. 2008. "New Approaches to the Health Promoting School: Participation in Sustainable Food Systems." *Journal of Hunger & Environmental Nutrition* 3, no. 4: 1-18.

Coleman-Jensen, Alisha, Mark Nord, Margaret Andrews, and Steven Carlson. 2012. *Household Food Security in the United States in 2011*, Economic Research Services, United States Department of Agriculture, Economic Research Report No. (ERR-141).

Commission on Sustainable Agriculture and Climate Change. 2012. *Achieving Food Security in the Face of Climate Change*, Copenhagen: CGIAR Research Program on Climate Change, Agriculture and Food Security (CCAFS).

Cox, Robert W. 1995. "Critical Political Economy." In *International Political Economy: Understanding Global Disorder*, edited by Bjorn Hettne, 31-45. London: Zed Books.

Darnton-Hill, Ian, and Eleanor T. Coyne. 1998. "Feast and Famine: Socioeconomic Disparities in Global Nutrition and Health." *Public Health Nutrition* 1, no. 1: 23-31.

Desmarais, Annette A. 2007. *La Via Campesina: Globalization and the Power of Peasants*. London: Pluto Press.

Devault, Marjorie L. 1994. *Feeding the Family: The Social Organization of Caring as Gendered Work*. Chicago: The University of Chicago Press.

Dorfman, Lori, Lawrence Wallack and Katie Woodruff. 2005. "More than a Message: Framing Public Health Advocacy to Change Corporate Practices." *Health Education & Behaviour* 32, no. 3: 320-36.

Food and Agriculture Organization. 1996. *Rome Declaration on World Food Security and World Food Summit Plan of Action*, Rome, Italy: Author, W3613/E.

Friedman, Harriet. 1999. "Remaking 'Traditions': How We Eat, What We Eat and the Changing Political Economy of Food." In *Women Working the NAFTA Food Chain: Women, Food and Globalization*, edited by D. Barndt, 36-60. Toronto: Second Story Press.

Fukuda-Parr, Sakiko. 1999. "What Does Feminization of Poverty Mean? It Isn't Just Lack of Income." *Feminist Economics* 5, no. 2: 99-103.

Fullan, Michael. 1999. *Change Forces: The Sequel*. New York: Routledge.

Gramsci, Antonio. 1971. *Selections from the Prison Notebooks*. New York: International Publishers.

Green, Lawrence W., M. Anne George, Mark Daniel, C. James Frankish, Carol P. Herbert, William R. Bowie, and M. O'Neill. 1994. *Study of Participatory Research in Health Promotion*, Ottawa, Ontario: The Royal Society of Canada.

Hamelin, Anne-Marie, Jean-Pierre Habicht, and Micheline Beaudry. 1999. "Food Insecurity: Consequences for the Household and Broader Social Implications." *The Journal of Nutrition* 129, no. 2: 525S-528S.

Hancock, Trevor. 2009. "Act Locally: Community-Based Population Health Promotion." In *A Healthy, Productive Canada: A Determinant of Health Approach: The Standing Senate Committee on Social Affairs, Science and Technology—Final Report of Senate Subcommittee on Population Health*, edited by W. J. (Chair) Keon, L. (Deputy Chair) Pépin, Ottawa, Ontario: Senate Canada.

Health Canada. 2009. "National Nutritious Food Basket," Heath Canada [database online], http://www.hc-sc.gc.ca/fn-an/surveill/basket-panier/index-eng.php (Accessed December 5, 2010).

Israel, Barbara A., Amy J. Schulz, Edith A. Parker, and A. Becker. 1998. "Review of Community-Based Research: Assessing Partnership Approaches to Improve Public Health." *Annual Review of Public Health* 19: 173-202.

Jacobson, Maxine, and Chris Rugeley. 2007. "Community-Based Participatory Research: Group Work for Social Justice and Community Change." *Social Work with Groups* 30, no. 4: 21-39.

Jones, Steve. 2006. *Antonio Gramsci*. Abingdon: Routledge.

Kindon, Sara, Rachel Pain, and Mike Kesby. 2008. "Participatory Action Research." In *International Encyclopedia of Human Geography*. Amsterdam; London: Elsevier, 2: 90-95.

Koc, Mustafa, Rod MacRae, Ellen Desjardins, and Wayne Roberts. 2008. "Getting Civil about Food: The Interactions Between Civil Society and the State to Advance Sustainable Food Systems in Canada." *Journal of Hunger & Environmental Nutrition* 3, no. 2: 122-144.

Lake, Sarah. Forthcoming. "Building Food Security in Nova Scotia from the Ground Up: A Case Study of the Kids Action Program Garden Project."

Laraia, Barbara A., Judith B. Borja and Margaret E. Bentley. 2009. "Grandmothers, Fathers, and Depressive Symptoms are Associated with Food Insecurity Among Low-Income First-Time African-American Mothers in North Carolina." *Journal of the American Dietetic Association* 109, no. 6: 1042-1047.

Laverack, Glenn. 2006. "Improving Health Outcomes Through Community Empowerment: A Review of the Literature." *Journal of Health, Population & Nutrition* 24, no. 1: 113-20.

MacRae, Rod, and Elisabeth Abergel, editors. 2012. *Health and Sustainability in the Canadian Food System: Advocacy and Opportunity for Civil Society.* Vancouver: University of British Columbia Press.

Marcoux, Alain. 1997. *The Feminisation of Poverty: Facts, Hypotheses and the Art of Advocacy.* Rome: Food and Agriculture Organisation, Population Programme Service, Women and Population Division.

Masuda, Jeffrey R., Genevieve Creighton, Sean Nixon, and James Frankish. 2011. "Building Capacity for Community-Based Participatory Research for Health Disparities in Canada." *Health Promotion Practice* 12, no. 2: 290-2.

McIntyre, Lynn, Kim D. Travers and Jutta B. Dayle. 1999. "Children's Feeding Programs in Atlantic Canada: Reducing or Reproducing Inequities?" *Canadian Journal of Public Health* 90: 196–200.

———, Suzanne Officer and Lynne Robinson. 2003. "Feeling Poor: The Felt Experience of Low-Income Lone Mothers." *Affilia* 18, no. 3: 316-331.

Minkler, Meredith, and Nina Wallerstein, editors. 2010. *Community-Based Participatory Research for Health*, 2d edition. San Francisco: Jossey-Bass.

———. 2000. "Using Participatory Action Research to Build Healthy Communities." *Public Health Reports* 115, no. 2/3: 191.

Mount Saint Vincent University and Nova Scotia Food Security Network, *Can Nova Scotians Afford to Eat Healthy? Report of 2010 participatory food costing.* Halifax, NS, 2011.

Newell, Felicia, Patricia Williams and Cynthia Watt. In Press. "The Affordability of a Nutritious Diet for Minimum Wage Earners in Nova Scotia (2002-2012)."

Nord, Mark, Margaret Andrews, and Steven Carlson. 2007. "Household Food Security in the United States, 2006." Economic Research Service, United States Department of Agriculture, Economic Research Report No (ERR-49).

———, Nader Kabbani, Laura Tiehen, Margaret Andrews, Gary Bickel and Steven Carlson. 2000. "Household Food Security in the United States, 2000," USA: Food and Rural Economics Division, Economic Research Service, U.S. Department of Agriculture, Food Assistance and Nutrition Research Report No. 21.

Nova Scotia Department of Health and Wellness. 2012. "Thrive! A Plan for a Healthier Nova Scotia. A Policy and Environmental Approach to Healthy Eating and Physical Activity," Halifax, NS.

Nova Scotia Food Security Network, and Food Action Research Centre (FoodARC). 2013. "Can Nova Scotians Afford to Eat Healthy? Report on 2012 Participatory Food Costing." Halifax, NS: Mount Saint Vincent University.

Office of Health Promotion and Protection. 2005. "Healthy Eating Nova Scotia," http://www.gov.ns.ca/ohp/healthyEating.html.

Office of the High Commissioner for Human Rights. 1966. "International Covenant on Economic, Social and Cultural Rights." Office of the High Commissioner for Human Rights [database online] http://www2.ohchr.org/english/law/cescr.htm.

Ore, Tracy E. 2011. "Something from Nothing: Women, Space, and Resistance." *Gender & Society* 25, no. 6: 689-95.

Parry, Ken W. 2003. "Constant Comparison." In *The SAGE Encyclopedia of Social Science Research Methods*, edited by Michael S. Lewis-Beck, Alan Bryman and Tim Futing Thousand Oaks, California: Sage Publications.

Patton, Michael Quinn. 2004. *Developmental Evaluation: Applying Complexity Concepts to Enhance Innovation and Use.* New York: Guilford Press.

Policy Working Group of Activating Change Together for Community Food Security (ACT for CFS). 2013. "The Political Economy of Food Policy Change: A Framework for Analysis."

Ponic, Pamela, and Wendy Frisby. 2010. "Unpacking Assumptions About Inclusion in Community-Based Health Promotion: Perspectives of Women Living in Poverty." *Qualitative Health Research* 20, no. 11: 1519-31.

Power, Elaine. 1999. "Combining Social Justice and Sustainability for Food Security," In *For Hunger-Proof Cities: Sustainable Urban Food Systems*, edited by Mustafa Koc, Rod MacRae, Luc Mougeot and Jennifer Welsh, 30-37. Ottawa: International Development Research Centre.

Powledge, Fred. 2010. "Food, Hunger, and Insecurity." *Bioscience* 60, no. 4: 260-265.

Raphael, Dennis, Toba Bryant and Ann Curry-Stevens. 2004. "Toronto Charter Outlines Future Health Policy Directions for Canada and Elsewhere." *Health Promotion International* 19, no. 2: 269-273.

Reid, Colleen, and Allison Tom. 2006. "Poor Women's Discourses of Legitimacy, Poverty, and Health." *Gender & Society* 20, no. 3: 402-421.

Reutter, Linda I., Miriam J. Stewart., Gerry Veenstra, Rhonda Love, Dennis Raphael and Edward Makwarimba. 2009. ""Who Do They Think We Are, Anyway?" Perceptions of and Responses to Poverty Stigma." *Qualitative Health Research* 19, no. 3: 297-311.

Riches, Graham, Don Buckingham, Ron MacRae and Aleck Ostry. 2004. "Right to Food Case Study: Canada." Rome: United Nations Food and Agriculture Organization, IGWG RTFG /INF 4/APP.2.

———. 1999. "Advancing the Human Rights to Food in Canada: Social Policy and the Politics of Hunger, Welfare, and Food Security." *Agriculture and Human Values* 16, no. 2: 203-211.

Rideout, Karen, Graham Riches, Aleck Ostry, Don Buckingham, and Ron MacRae. 2007. "Bringing Home the Right to Food in Canada: Challenges and Possibilities for Achieving Food Security." *Public Health Nutrition* 10: 556-573.

Roberts, Wayne. 2012. "Harpercons Play Hunger Games: Community Leaders Seek Apology from PM after his Ministers Tear into UN *Food* Rep." *Now* 13, no 42, June 14, 2012.

Rural Action. 2013. "Rural Action: Working Together to Revitalize Appalachian Ohio." http://ruralaction.org/.

Salmon, Amy, Annette J. Browne, and Ann Pederson. 2010. "'Now We call it Research': Participatory Health Research Involving Marginalized Women Who Use Drugs." *Nursing Inquiry* 17, no. 4: 336-345.

Schutter, Olivier De. 2012. *Olivier de Schutter, Special Rapporteur on the Right to Food: Visit to Canada from 6 to 16 May 2012.* Office of the United Nations High Commissioner for Human Rights, 2012.

Skinner, Kelly, Rhona M. Hanning and Leonard J.S. Tsuji. 2006. "Barriers and Supports for Healthy Eating and Physical Activity for First Nation Youths in Northern Canada." *International Journal of Circumpolar Health* 65, no. 2: 148-161.

Sukovic, Masha, Barbara F. Sharf, Joeseph R. Sharkey, and Julie S. John. 2011. "Seasoning for the Soul: Empowerment Through Food Preparation among Mexican Women in the Texas *Colonias.*" *Food and Foodways* 19, no. 3: 228-247.

Tarasuk, Valerie, Andy Mitchell, and Naomi Dachner. 2014. "Household Food Insecurity in Canada 2012," Toronto: Research to identify policy options to reduce food insecurity   (proof)   http://nutritionalsciences.lamp.utoronto.ca/wp-content/uploads/2013/07/Household-Food-Insecurity-in-Canada-2011.pdf.

Torjman, Sherri. 2013. "Ensuring the Welfare of 'Welfare Incomes'." Ottawa: The Caledon Institute of Social Policy.

Travers, Kim D. 1996. "The Social Organization of Nutritional Inequalities." *Social Science & Medicine* 43, no. 4: 543-553.

Wealth Creation in Rural Communities. 2013. "Wealth Creation in Rural Communities: Building Sustainable Livelihoods." http://www.creatingruralwealth.org/the-initiative/the-initiative/.

Williams, Patricia L., Barbara Anderson, Heather Hunter and Cynthia Watt. 2013. *Synthesis Report: The Nova Scotia Participatory Food Costing Projects (2001-2011): Evaluative Learning from Ten Years of Participatory Research.* Halifax, NS: Mount Saint Vincent University.

———, Cynthia Watt, Michelle Amero, Barbara Anderson, Ilya Blum, Rebecca Green-LaPierre, Christine P. Johnson and Debra E. Reimer. 2012a. "Affordability of a Nutritious Diet for Income Assistance Recipients in Nova Scotia (2002-2010)." *Canadian Journal of Public Health* 103, no. 3: 183-188.

———, Debra E. Reimer, Alan Warner, Liesel Carlsson, Satya Ramen, C. De Vreede, David Daughton, and Healther Hunter. 2012d. "Chapter 4: The Role of Social Economy Organizations in Building Community Food Security." In *Social Economy in Atlantic Canada,* edited by Sonja Novkovic and Leslie Brown. Sydney, Cape Breton: Cape Breton University Press.

———, Lynn Langille, and Nadia Stokvis. 2005. "CAPC and CPNP 10 years Later…What Have We Learned? What Can be Shared?"

———, Lynn McIntyre, Jutta B. Dayle, and Kim Raine. 2003. "The 'Wonderfulness' of Children's Feeding Program." *Health Promotion International* 18, no. 2: 163-170.

———, Michelle Amero, Barbara Anderson, Doris Gillis, Rebecca Green-LaPierre, Christine P. Johnson, and Debra E. Riemer. 2012c. "A Participatory Model for Food Costing in Nova Scotia: Sustainable Community Action for Food Security." *Canadian Journal of Dietetic Practice and Research* 73, no. 4: 181-8.

———, Rita MacAulay, Barbara Anderson, Kimberly Barro, Doris E. Gillis, Christine Johnson, Lynn L. Langille, Shelley Moran, and Debra E. Reimer. 2012b. "'I would have never thought that I would be in such a predicament'": Voices from Women Experiencing Food Insecurity in Nova Scotia, Canada." *Journal of Hunger & Environmental Nutrition,* no. 2-3: 253-70.

Winne, Mark. 2008. *Closing the Food Gap: Resetting the Table in the Land of Plenty.* Boston: Beacon Press.

Winter, Metta. 2004. "Cooking Up Fun!" *Human Ecology* 32, no. 2: 2.

Wodak, Ruth, and Michael Meyer. 2009. *Methods of Critical Discourse Analysis,* 2nd edition London: Sage Publications Ltd.

Index

About the Contributors

June Nash, Ph.D. is Distinguished Professor Emerita in the Department of Anthropology at the City College of the City University of New York and the Graduate School and University Center (CUNY). Her undergraduate degree was earned at Barnard College and her M.A. and Ph.D. in Anthropology are from the University of Chicago (1960). Her major publications include: *In the Eyes of the Ancestors: Belief and Behavior in a Maya Community* (1970); *We Eat the Mines and the Mines Eat Us: Dependency and Exploitation in Bolivian Tin Mining Communities* (1979); *From Tank Town to High-Tech: The Clash of Community and Industrial Cycles* (1989); and *Crafts in the World Market: The Impact of International Exchange on Middle American Artisans* (1993). She received the 1992 Conrad Arensberg Award from the Society for the Anthropology of Work. She has received grants from the National Science Foundation, the National Institute for Mental Health, the Social Science Research Council, the National Endowment for the Humanities, the Research Foundation of the City University of New York, and the MacArthur Foundation.

Teresa Mares, Ph.D. is Assistant Professor of Anthropology at the University of Vermont and is affiliated with the Transdisciplinary Research Initiative in Food Systems. She received her B.A. (Summa Cum Laude) in Anthropology and Foreign Languages and Literatures with a concentration in Spanish from Colorado State University (2002), and her M.A. (2005) and Ph.D. (2010) in Sociocultural Anthropology from the University of Washington. She also completed a graduate certificate in Women Studies at the University of Washington. Dr. Mares's research focuses on the intersection of food and migration studies, and she is particularly interested in the ways that the diets and foodways of Latino/a immigrants change as a result of migration. Analytically, Dr. Mares engages with theories and concepts of citizenship and transnationalism, identity and foodways, and contemporary social movements. She is committed to applied, community-based ethnographic methodologies and is currently developing a new study examining food security and food access among Latino/a dairy workers in Vermont.

Maggie Dickinson is a cultural anthropologist and a Doctoral Candidate at the City University of New York (CUNY) Graduate Center. Her current research, funded by the Wenner-Gren Foundation, looks at food insecurity and welfare policy in New York City. Her work is broadly concerned with race, gender, political economy, social policy and urban governance.

Janet Page-Reeves, Ph.D. is Research Assistant Professor with the Office for Community Health in the Department of Family and Community Medicine at the University of New Mexico (UNM) Health Sciences Center, and a Senior Fellow in the NM CARES Health Disparities Research Center at UNM. She received her Ph.D. in cultural anthropology at the City University of New York (CUNY) in 1999 with Dr. June Nash as her advisor. Her fieldwork in Bolivia explored the internal dynamics of an indigenous women's sweater-knitting cooperative, the operation of the international market for artisan products, and the politics of development funding. In New Mexico, Dr. Page-Reeves has extensive experience working collaboratively with a broad range of community, nonprofit, and university stakeholders. Her current research interests focus on food insecurity, diabetes, food allergy, youth farming/gardening, and the relationship between educational outcomes and health disparities.

Amy Anixter Scott, M.D., MPA. is a public health physician and administrator with experience working on local, state and national initiatives addressing childhood obesity, food insecurity, hunger, and health equity. Integral components of her projects have included quality-improvement training for healthcare providers and health sciences professional students. Her work often uses community engagement and service-learning initiatives for students.

Maurice L. Moffett, Ph.D. is a Research Assistant Professor in the Department of Family & Community Medicine at the University of New Mexico (UNM), and is affiliated Faculty in the Department of Economics, and Senior Fellow at the UNM Robert Wood Johnson Foundation Center for Health Policy. He is a Health Economist and Heath Services Researcher with an emphasis on the relationships between environment and health care on health outcomes. Dr. Moffett's research on food environment and food security has been supported by the W. K. Kellogg Foundation and the National Institutes for Health.

Veronica Apodaca, B.S, Executive Director of Santa Barbara/Martineztown Community Learning Center has more than ten years of experience working with underserved communities while utilizing her B.S in Health Education to create and implement programs that promote education and awareness. Her mission to continually serve her community and others inspires her to identify areas of need in order to create a flow of educational services that not only caters to K-12 youth but also provides adult educational opportunities to inspire lifelong learners and promote the development of capacity in the community for individuals to become agents of change.

Vanessa Apodaca, MA is a native New Mexican who received both her Bachelors and Masters degrees at the University of New Mexico. She has been involved in research, service and education on issues related to healthy communities in the Albuquerque area. Her interest in food, gardening and health have led her to work with people of all ages and walks of life.

Lois Stanford, Ph.D. is Associate Professor in the Department of Anthropology at New Mexico State University in Las Cruces, New Mexico. She has conducted fieldwork on agriculture, the avocado industry, and traditional food systems in central western Mexico, and is the author of the forthcoming book, *La Cocina Abierta: A History of Food in Mexico* (Reaktion Books). In New Mexico, her work focuses on food security, food sovereignty, and local foodsheds, and she is working on an edited volume on anthropological perspectives on food security. Her work also involves student engagement and training through service learning projects in minority communities and *colonias* along the U.S.-Mexico border, and she serves as president of the board of directors of La Semilla Food Center, a non-profit organization that focuses on youth education and garden projects, community education regarding food issues, and support for local foodsheds.

Megan Carney, Ph.D. is a cultural anthropologist with research specializations in critical medical anthropology, transnational migration, and women's health. She received a dissertation research grant from the University of California Institute for Mexico and the United States (UC MEXUS) to conduct fieldwork with Mexican and Central American migrant women in Southern California around food insecurity, nongovernmental food assistance, and state interventions to dietary health. Currently, she is researching the relationship of migrant mental health to state practices of immigration enforcement in the U.S., and migrant women's health behaviors and the consequences of austerity for healthcare in Italy. She is a Postdoctoral Research Associate at Arizona State University in Comparative Border Studies and affiliated faculty with the Department of Anthropology at the University of Washington. She received her B.A. in Anthropology from UCLA, and her M.A. and Ph.D. from UC Santa Barbara.

Daniel J. Rose, Ph.D. is Assistant Professor of Sociology at Chattanooga State

Community College in Tennessee. He earned his doctoral degree in Sociology from the University of Michigan-Ann Arbor in 2010. His dissertation research focused on the acquisition of food and levels of physical activity in two Detroit neighborhoods. Currently, he is researching nutritional knowledge in marginalized communities and efforts to increase access to food. He also leads a service-learning course focusing on food justice in Chattanooga, TN.

David A. Himmelgreen, Ph.D., is Professor of Anthropology at the University of South Florida. Himmelgreen specializes in human growth and development, dietary patterns, and the social determinants of health. He has conducted research in Lesotho, Costa Rica, India, and the United States. He recently completed a three-year study on the nutrition transition in Costa Rica and is currently conducting research on nutritional and mental health in food insecure households in Tampa, Florida. Himmelgreen co-directs the Globalization and Community Health Field School in Costa Rica which trains undergraduate students in anthropology, public health, and engineering to conduct community health research and program development. Himmelgreen serves as an editor for two academic journals, is a former Fulbright Scholar, and has received research funding from agencies including the National Science Foundation and the United States Department of Agriculture. He has published nearly 75 scholarly articles and edited volumes during the last 20 years.

Sara Arias-Steele is a second year doctoral student in the Department of Anthropology at the University of South Florida. She is in the biological anthropology track with a concentration in bio-cultural medicine conducting research on childhood obesity among Latinos in the Tampa Bay Area under the supervision of Dr. David Himmelgreen. She holds a Master's of Science in Forensic Anthropology from Boston School of Medicine and has previously published in the Journal of Diabetes, Science Translational Medicine and Diabetes, Obesity & Metabolism on the metabolic impact of gastric bypass surgery. She has been a student lecturer for Introduction to Biological Anthropology (ANT2511) at USF since 2013.

Allison Cantor has a master's degree in anthropology and is a third year doctoral student at the University of South Florida, working under Dr. David Himmelgreen. Allison is currently pursuing a degree in applied biological anthropology with a biocultural medical concentration and is obtaining a dual master's degree in public health. Her research focus is maternal health in a globalized world. In the U.S. she has conducted research on human maternal placentophagy, examining why women choose to engage in this practice in contemporary society. Allison conducted her master's research in Costa Rica focusing on the impacts of tourism on maternal diet, with implications for chronic disease in later life. In Peru, she worked as the project investigator to understand the local impacts of globalization and dietary delocalization on maternal health.

Nancy Romero-Daza, Ph.D. is Associate Professor in the Department of Anthropology at the University of South Florida. She is a medical anthropologist with specialization in HIV/AIDS research and intervention. Dr. Romero-Daza has conducted research on the impact of labor migration on the spread of HIV/AIDS in Lesotho, has studied HIV risk among injection drug users, crack users, and sex workers in the U.S., and has evaluated HIV/AIDS interventions such as Needle Exchange Programs and methadone maintenance programs. She has also examined the impact of tourism on the potential spread of HIV and other Sexually Transmitted Infections in Costa Rica, where she has involved rural women in the development of culturally appropriate HIV/AIDS materials. Along with David Himmelgreen (PI, USF), Romero-Daza conducted a three-year NSF-funded project on the impact of a changing economy on food security in Monteverde, Costa Rica and have offered the summer Globalization and Community Health Field School in Monteverde, Costa Rica since 2001.

Sharon L. Stowers, Ph.D., R.D. is Associate Professor of Anthropology at Harford Community College in Maryland, and a Registered Dietitian. She earned her Ph.D. in cultural and nutritional anthropology from the University of Massachusetts, Amherst in 2003. She also holds a Master of Applied Anthropology from the University of Maryland and a Master of Nutrition Education from Framingham State College. Prior to becoming an anthropologist, she worked several years as an urban public health nutritionist in Boston and owned Nutrition Education Services International in Washington, DC. She specializes in the areas of the political economy of food and nutrition, transnational migration, international development, and most recently, museum studies. Dr. Stowers has published in the fields of anthropology and nutrition and has created culturally relevant food guide models for Caribbean, Haitian and Salvadoran immigrant populations.

Mary Alice Scott, Ph.D. is Assistant Professor of Anthropology and cross-appointed Assistant Professor in Public Health Sciences at New Mexico State University. She received her B.A. in Women's Studies from Duke University and her M.A. and Ph.D. in anthropology from the University of Kentucky. Her areas of specialization are medical anthropology, gender theory, health disparities, political economy, and intersectionality. Her dissertation research focused on health issues faced by women living in a migrant-sending community in southern Veracruz, Mexico. Her current research examines the ways in which older people in marginalized social positions, such as being an undocumented immigrant and living with limited economic resources, navigate health care systems and public health messages. Her research has been funded by the National

Science Foundation, a Fulbright-García Robles grant, the University of Kentucky Graduate School, and the New Mexico State University College of Arts & Sciences.

Lynne Phillips, Ph.D. is Dean of Arts and Professor of Anthropology at Memorial University of Newfoundland, Canada. She received her MA and Ph.D. degrees from the University of Toronto. She has undertaken collaborative research on the United Nations, including the Food and Agriculture Organization, and in Latin America on issues related to public anthropology, feminist anthropology, food and agriculture, and health. Books include *Contesting Publics: Feminism, Activism, Ethnography* (2013*)*, with S. Cole, M. Carrier-Moisan and E. Lagalisse. Select journal articles on food are "Eating Cars: Food, Politics and Pedagogy, and Politics in a 'Community in Crisis,' *Environnement Urbain/Urban Environment* (2012); "Food and Globalization," *Annual Review of Anthropology* (2006); and, with S. Ilcan, "Responsible Expertise: Governing the Uncertain Subjects of Biotechnology," *Critique of Anthropology* (2007); "Making Food Count: Expert Knowledge and Global Technologies of Government," *Canadian Review of Sociology and Anthropology* (2003); and "'A World Free From Hunger': Global Imagination and Governance in the Age of Scientific Management," *Sociologia Ruralis* (2003).

Christine M. Porter, Ph.D. is Assistant Professor of Public Health, Division of Kinesiology & Health, at the University of Wyoming. She conducts action research in building social justice and radical democracy, largely though community food system work. Christine is principal investigator and project director for "Food Dignity" (www.fooddignity.org), which is a $5-million, five-year USDA-funded project that began in April 2011 with five community food organizing partners. Her most recent formal studies were in the Division of Nutritional Sciences at Cornell University. Her informal studies with community organizing and anti-racist mentors, including many of the people who are currently leaders and partners in the Food Dignity project, have equally informed her action research and her teaching.

LaDonna Redmond is a food-justice activist/writer/motivational speaker who has successfully worked to get Chicago Public Schools to evaluate junk food; launched urban agriculture projects; started community grocery stores; and worked on federal farm policy to expand access to healthy food access and production in communities of color. Very active in community journalism, she hosts a weekly radio show on KMOJ called "It's your Health" and writes a biweekly column for the *Minnesota Spokesman Reporter*. In her role as education and community outreach coordinator for Seward Community Cooperative, LaDonna is responsible for engaging community residents, local partners and organizations to participate in activities, programming, and special initiatives of the co-ops new Friendship store in Minneapolis. In 2009, LaDonna was one of 25 citizen and business leaders named a Responsibility Pioneer by *Time Magazine*. LaDonna was also a 2003–2005 IATP Food and Society Fellow. In 2007, she was awarded a Green for All Fellowship. LaDonna attended Antioch College in Yellow Springs, Ohio.

Patricia L. Williams, Ph.D. is Associate Professor and Tier 2 Canada Research Chair in Food Security and Policy Change in the Department of Applied Human Nutrition at Mount Saint Vincent University in Halifax, Nova Scotia. She is the founding director of the newly established FoodARC - Food Action Research Centre (www.foodarc.ca) which was awarded the prestigious Canadian Institutes of Health Research (CIHR) Partnership Award in 2011. She holds a Ph.D. in Interdisciplinary Studies from the University of British Columbia, and completed a CIHR-funded Postdoctoral Fellowship at the Atlantic Health Promotion Research Centre (AHPRC), Dalhousie University. Her research focuses on the use of participatory action research processes to engage multiple intersectoral partners, including those experiencing food insecurity, in understanding the determinants of, and solutions to food insecurity, and processes for building capacity for social and policy change. She has led several national studies on food security-related policy change and the use of plain language knowledge translation tools, including Thought about Food? (www.foodthoughtful.ca), in building capacity for policy change across Canada. She is a founding member of the Nova Scotia Food Security Network and Nova Scotia Food Policy Council, and a Research Associate at the Atlantic Health Promotion Research Centre at Mount Saint Vincent University.